KU-115-498

American Democracy in Peril
Seven Challenges to America's Future

THIRD EDITION

William E. Hudson
Providence College

CHATHAM HOUSE PUBLISHERS
SEVEN BRIDGES PRESS, LLC
NEW YORK · LONDON

Seven Bridges Press, LLC
135 Fifth Avenue, New York, NY 10010

Copyright © 2001 by Chatham House Publishers of
Seven Bridges Press, LLC

Photos in the Introduction are reproduced by permission
of the Prints and Photographs Division of the Library of
Congress.

All rights reserved. No part of this book may be reproduced,
stored in a retrieval system, or transmitted in any form or by
any means, electronic, mechanical, photocopying, recording,
or otherwise, without the prior permission of the publisher.

Publisher: Robert J. Gormley
Managing Editor: Katharine Miller
Production Supervisor: Melissa Martin
Cover Design: Judith Hudson
Frontispiece: Judith Hudson
Composition: ediType
Printing and Binding: Victor Graphics

Library of Congress Cataloging-in-Publication Data
Hudson, William E., 1948-
   American democracy in peril : seven challenges to America's
future / William E. Hudson. – 3rd ed.
      p. cm.
Includes bibliographical references and index.
   ISBN 1-889119-36-9
   1. United States – Politics and government. 2. Democracy –
United States. I. Title.
JK31 .H86 2000
320.473 – dc21
                                        00-008787

Manufactured in the United States of America
10 9 8 7 6 5 4 3 2 1

UNIVERSITY OF WALES SWANSEA
PRIFYSGOL CYMRU ABERTAWE
LIBRARY/LLYFRGELL

Classmark   JK31 HUD3

Location   Miners' Library

1005394139

A

SOUTH WALES MINERS' LIBRARY
LONG LOAN
Items must be returned by the last date
stamped below or immediately if recalled.
To renew telephone 01792 518603

'17 NOV 2000

14 FEB 2001

LLYFRGELL GLOWYR DE CYMRU
BENTHYCIAD HIR
Dylid dychwelyd eitemau cyn y dyddiad a
stampiwyd olaf isod, neu ar unwaith os
gofynnir amdanynt yn ôl.
I adnewyddu ffôn 01792 518603

Contents

Tables and Figures

Preface to the Third Edition

When I wrote the first edition of this book, the world had recent memories of thousands of Chinese students occupying Peking's Tiananmen Square (erecting there as a particularly eloquent symbol a copy of the Statue of Liberty) and of crowds in Eastern Europe demanding democracy in their countries. We Americans had every right to feel proud of our experience with democracy in the wake of these events of 1989, but I found the complacent reaction of some politicians, intellectuals, and ordinary citizens troubling. Their attitudes ignored the fact that, for all our progress toward democratic ideals in the United States, our political system fell far short of attaining them. Instead of assuming complacently that democracy is complete in the United States, I felt that Americans should draw from the efforts to establish new democracies around the world the resolve to join in this struggle by improving our own democracy.

I believe that attention to the need to struggle for more democracy in the United States is imperative because political developments in recent years have placed American democracy in peril. The challenges it faces, if uncorrected, may substantially reverse, in the next few decades, the degree of democracy we have attained. In order to initiate this important discussion, I identified and analyzed seven key challenges to the future of American democracy that seemed to have special relevance to the current era.

This book was written primarily for college students in their first course in American government. Its purpose is to stimulate them to think about how the facts they learn about American politics relate to democratic ideals. Like many Americans, students are frighteningly complacent about democracy; they assume that as long as periodic elections are held, democracy has been achieved. In this book I seek to remove this complacency by showing how current political practices not only fail to achieve democratic ideals but constitute challenges to democracy's very existence. Contemporary American democracy is in peril because too few Americans understand the challenges it faces. This book seeks to contribute to this understanding.

I have received many helpful comments and reactions to the book from students and faculty colleagues across the country. Most gratifying have been those comments that refer to the utility of the book for stimulating class discussion. As I wrote in the preface to the first edition, my primary aim in writing the book was to encourage student reaction to its arguments. I knew that I probably would not persuade all students by what I had to say, but I hoped to say it in a way that would engage their attention and involve them in democratic conversation. From what readers tell me, the book seems to accomplish this for most students.

As the new millennium begins, American democracy remains in peril. The challenges portrayed in this book continue to impede the ability of ordinary Americans to rule themselves. In preparing this new edition, I was able to revisit these challenges and document anew how each stands in the way of authentic political democracy. Although I considered revising the list of challenges, I concluded finally that these seven features of the American system remain the primary dangers to its democratic character in the twenty-first century. The factors that make these particular features of American political life — the separation of powers, radical individualism, citizen participation, trivialized elections, the "privileged position" of business, inequality, and the national security state — threatening to democracy seem as compelling to me today as they were in the early 1990s.

An author may not be the best judge of whether history moves in the direction his writings predict, but I have been impressed at how political events in the past few years have reinforced the arguments in this book. Three examples, all detailed more fully in the pages that follow:

1. Despite the early promise that the Clinton presidency might overcome the separation-of-powers challenge to democratic responsiveness, the system's institutional barriers soon proved insurmountable for many of Clinton's initiatives, most notably his universal health insurance plan. The contrast with British Prime Minister Tony Blair, in many respects Clinton's ideological and policy soul mate, who has had the advantage of British parliamentary institutions to put his electoral agenda promptly and decisively in place, underscores this book's argument for the superior responsiveness and accountability of parliamentary democracy.

2. The elections of the 1990s and the beginning of campaign 2000 showed a worsening of the pathologies of our trivialized elections. Most significant from the standpoint of democracy has been the collapse of any control over the influence of political money in elections. These elections demonstrated clearly the powerful and decisive role that the hidden election for campaign financing has in undermining the political power of ordinary voters and the democratic character of our elections. American elections have taken on as plutocratic a character as they have ever had in our history.

3. With each passing year of the post–Cold War world, events and continued massive military expenditures show that the national security state, with all its inherent dangers for democratic politics, is now a permanent feature of American society. Hopes for a peace dividend or conversion of the military-industrial complex to peaceful purposes have vanished as the Cold War habits of building ever more

expensive weapons systems go unchecked. That an obvious threat to justify their need cannot be found has not proved to be a major barrier to the high-tech dreams of military planners.

Before examining particular challenges, I offer in the introduction a review of the history of democratic theory in terms of four "models" of democracy, giving the reader a set of criteria against which to evaluate the challenges discussed later in the book. Then, throughout the book, I argue my own point of view regarding each challenge in as persuasive a manner as I can. I aim to stimulate and engage the reader in thinking critically about these challenges, rather than presenting the "neutral" and "objective" discussion common to most textbooks. The arguments in this book represent my personal conclusions about these challenges, based on many years of study and teaching. Students may often find my positions controversial, and they may discover that some other political scientists, perhaps including their own instructor, may disagree.

Besides accounting for recent trends related to each of the seven challenges, this new edition provides several new features. Updated anecdotes and data keep the arguments fresh for a new generation of students. I have sought to include examples from recent history that will be familiar to young students for whom even the Reagan years are a dim childhood memory — issues such as the unsuccessful effort to impeach President Clinton, the increasing role of "soft money" in the campaigns of 1998 and 2000, the sharp growth of economic disparities within American society, and the continued imbalance of the U.S. budget in favor of defense spending are reflected here. At the same time, I have not shied away from retaining historical references and facts. I find that my students are very curious about events of the past few decades, such as Watergate, the Vietnam War, and the civil rights movement, about which they know very little because they seem not to be remote enough for detailed treatment in high school history classes. That these events have much to do with the challenges to democracy discussed in this book make it a useful stimulus to teaching about them.

In this edition, I have added to each chapter a set of thought questions formulated to raise open-ended questions about key arguments in the chapters and further encourage critical thinking about the book. (An instructor's manual that expands upon this pedagogical effort and outlines this book's relevance to the basic American politics curriculum is available at the publisher's web site, www.chathamhouse.com.) Many books have been written in the past few years that relate to this book's themes, and I have added those that I consider most illuminating to the lists of suggested readings (including titles, marked with an asterisk, that argue views contrary to my own) at the ends of the chapters. Another new feature of this edition is a small list of web sites at the end of each chapter relating directly to chapter themes.

Again, I believe strongly that, at this time in history, Americans need to pay attention to the quality of our democracy. That this book may have contributed to promoting a conversation about the issue in political science classrooms is my greatest satisfaction as its author. Any reader of the present edition who would like to converse with me regarding any issue in these pages may contact me at bhudson@providence.edu.

NEARLY ALL THOSE acknowledged in the preface to the first edition contributed in some way to the improvements in this one. My Providence College colleagues continue to offer useful advice, particularly in regard to how the book "works" in their classrooms. Our former colleague, Tom Kriger (now at the University of Northern Colorado), made several suggestions based on his experience with the book, which made their way into the pages that follow. Bob Trudeau assisted enormously with this edition by asking his Honors American government students to comment on the book on his course web page. In addition to my nearby colleagues, I am grateful to the many political scientists from around the country, too numerous to list here, who have shared with me their and their students' reactions to the book.

The late Ed Artinian, founder of Chatham House, made this book possible, and his skill in promoting the book was the major factor in its success. I will be always grateful for Ed's support and encouragement over the years and happy to have had the opportunity to know and work with him. The Seven Bridges Press/ Chatham House staff are continuing the hands-on, author-friendly approach that was Ed's hallmark, as shown in their assistance in the preparation of this new edition. Finally, Loreto Gandara continues to inspire me in all things, including the desire to complete this new edition.

About the Author

WILLIAM E. HUDSON is professor of political science at Providence College, where he has taught since 1974. He earned his Ph.D. from Brown University after completing undergraduate work at Indiana University.

In addition to his course in American government and politics, he teaches courses on public policy, European politics, and community service. During 1993–94, he served as acting director of the Feinstein Institute for Public Service and has since been active in developing its curriculum in public and community service studies. He is currently a member of the Rhode Island Commission on National and Community Service.

Hudson is the author, with Richard Battistoni, of *Experiencing Citizenship: Concepts and Models for Service-learning in Political Science.* His publications on public policy have appeared in a variety of political science journals, including *Political Science Quarterly, Polity, Western Political Quarterly,* and *Policy Studies Journal.*

Models of Democracy

As I would not be a slave, *so I would not be a* master. *This expresses my idea of democracy. Whatever differs from this, to the extent there is a difference, is no democracy.*

—Abraham Lincoln

DEMOCRACY IS A complicated concept. The dictionary definition of "government (or rule) by the people" seems simple, but once we begin to think about the components of the definition, complexities arise. What does "government" or "rule" mean? Does government by the people mean that all the people are directly responsible for the day-to-day operation of government? Or is a scheme of representation acceptable? If so, what sort of scheme? How should it be organized? Elections? How often and for which offices? Does government have special meaning in a democracy? What is its proper scope? Who decides what is proper? The people, again? How is this decision made and expressed? And who are the people anyway? Everyone who lives in the governed territory or citizens only? What is a citizen? Can newly arriving people (immigrants) become citizens? Under what rules? Should the "people" include everyone or just those with a stake in the community, say, property holders? Should certain groups of people, such as criminals and traitors, be excluded from citizenship? This is just the beginning of a list of questions we could make about the meaning of "government by the people." Notice that in this short list of questions such additional complex concepts as *representation, citizen,* and *elections* are mentioned and suggest additional questions. The search for answers to all these questions is the concern of democratic theory, the branch of scholarship that specializes in elucidating, developing, and defining the meaning of democracy.

If we move beyond dictionary definitions and ask Americans what *they* think about democracy we find additional layers of complexity. Americans associate

---

Opposite: *Abraham Lincoln, 1863 (photo by Matthew Brady)*

diverse and often contradictory characteristics of their political system with democracy. Most Americans believe democracy requires majority rule, but at the same time they consider the protection of minority rights from the will of the majority to be a key component of democracy. In fact, most Americans place considerable emphasis on the importance of freedom from government interference in their lives as *the* crucial ingredient of democracy. The individualistic American values democracy because it helps her or him to lead a personal life freely, without government getting in the way. At the same time, patriotic Americans believe democracy imposes obligations — the duty to vote, for example, or to support the government in times of crisis such as war. Many Americans associate democracy with particular constitutional features, such as the separation of powers and the Bill of Rights. These same Americans would be surprised to see democracy performing quite well in political systems possessing neither of these features; Great Britain is one example. For some, American economic arrangements, usually described as the free enterprise system (capitalism), are a part of democracy. Others, as we later see, believe capitalism is a threat to political equality and, hence, democracy. Given these differing views, one can understand why the essay contest on "What Democracy Means to Me" remains a continuing tradition in American schools.

If we are to analyze various challenges to democracy intelligently, we need to clarify some of this confusion about what democracy means. We need some sophisticated standards to use in evaluating the degree and kind of threat each of the challenges we examine poses for democratic politics. For example, what democratic characteristics and values does increasing economic inequality or a growing military-industrial complex threaten? This chapter presents an overview of some of the basic concepts of democracy as found in democratic theory. It offers a base to be used in evaluating the challenges to contemporary democracy. Democratic theory is presented here in terms of four distinct "models" of democracy.[1] Each model provides a different understanding of democracy as it has been interpreted by different groups of political theorists. Four different models are needed because democratic theorists have not agreed on what procedures, practices, and values need to be emphasized for "government by the people" to be realized. The discussion of the models also provides a brief summary of the major issues and questions raised in modern democratic theory over the past two hundred years. Although some of the ideas in the models were first presented long ago, I believe each of the models offers viable alternative conceptions of democracy relevant to the United States today. The reader, however, should be warned that the discussion of democratic theory presented here is not meant to be a comprehensive review of the voluminous topic. Many important issues are not raised, and some important theorists are not discussed. Readers interested in a more thorough review of democratic theory should consult the works listed in the Suggestions for Further Reading at the end of this chapter.

The models discussed in this chapter are derived from writings on democracy since the eighteenth century. Only in the past two hundred years have humans had experience with democratic government in large nations. The theorists of what I call *modern* democracy agree that democratic politics is possible on such a scale, and they premise their discussions on this assumption. But before the emergence of modern democratic theory, certain historical experiences and political ideas prepared the way for these theorists, and these precursors are discussed in the next section.

PRECURSORS TO MODERN DEMOCRATIC THEORY

Democracy is an ancient concept. The idea of people participating equally in self-rule antedates recorded human history and may be as old as human society itself.[2] From recorded history, we know that the ancient Greeks had well-developed and successful democratic societies among their various forms of government. Several Greek city-states, most notably Athens, organized governments that involved the direct participation of their citizens in governing.[3] The Athenian Assembly (Ecclesia), composed of all male citizens, met more than forty times each year to debate and decide all public issues.[4] Officials responsible for implementing assembly decisions were either elected or chosen by lot; their terms of office lasted usually one year or less. From historical accounts and the analyses of classic Greek philosophers such as Plato and Aristotle, we know that Greek democracy involved many of the key concepts and practices associated with modern democracy. Political equality, citizen participation (and in Athens usually *lively* participation), the rule of law, and free and open discussion and debate were all part of Greek democratic practice.[5] Nevertheless, the Greek form of democracy had characteristics that limited it as a model for modern democracy.

The first and most obvious limitation was scale. The Greeks assumed the city-state, composed of a few thousand citizens, to be the appropriate size for the polity. Greek democracy was carried out within this small territory among several thousand citizens, a condition permitting face-to-face interaction in a single public assembly. Political interaction beyond the scale of the city-state involved either diplomacy or conquest — hardly a democratic procedure. During the fourth and fifth centuries B.C., when Athenian democracy was at its height, Athens ruled its conquered territories in a decidedly undemocratic manner. The idea that democracy could encompass more than a few thousand citizens in a single city-state would have been absurd to Greek democrats.

A second limitation of Greek democracy was its exclusivity.[6] Although all male citizens participated in governing themselves in Athens, this group constituted only a minority of the people who actually lived in Athens and were governed by the laws of the Ecclesia. The most obvious exclusion was the female half of the population (an exclusion that would prevail, until quite recently, in modern democracies). Likewise, the enormous slave population, larger than that of free citizens (about three slaves for each two citizens), had no right to political participation.[7] According to some scholars, one of the ironies of Greek democracy was that its existence depended to a great extent on the slave economy, which permitted citizens the leisure to perform public duties.[8] In addition to slaves and women, a large population of free individuals, immigrants from other Greek cities and other parts of the world, were denied citizenship rights even though they had lived in Athens for generations and its laws governed their lives. The Greek conception of democracy did not include the modern notion that democracy should provide opportunities for political participation to all (with only a few exceptions) who live within a polity and are subject to its laws.

Despite its limitations, Greek democracy remained the Western world's most complete expression of the ideal of "rule by the many" for two thousand years after its demise. Among the numerous empires, monarchies, oligarchies, and tyrannies that followed, the Greek experience remained an inspiration to those who sought to provide power to ordinary citizens to govern themselves. Until the eighteenth century, the few experiments with democratic government, like the Greek experience, involved political regimes encompassing a limited geographic area and a small population. During the Middle Ages and later in various locales, from Italian city-states to Swiss cantons, democratic experiments achieved some success, but scale and exclusivity continued to limit democracy. As in Greece, democracy meant all citizens gathering together in one assembly to make laws; size remained a practical limitation of the relevance of democracy to the governance of large nation-states.

Not surprisingly, given this experience, political theorists assumed that democracy was feasible only in small states where face-to-face interaction of the entire citizenry could occur. For example, the great eighteenth-century French political theorist Montesquieu argued that the ability of citizens to perceive the public good easily, which he considered a requisite of democratic government, was possible only in a small republic.[9] Even the influential democratic theorist of this same period, Jean-Jacques Rousseau, assumed a polity the size of his native Geneva to be the appropriate context for the application of his theories.[10] Only in a small state, where people could meet together in the relative intimacy of a single assembly and where a similarity of culture and interests united them, could individuals discuss and find the public good.

By the end of the eighteenth century, events began to overtake the small-state view of democracy and stimulate a more expansive and modern conception. Inspired by the Enlightenment values of liberty and equality, political activists agitated for more popular forms of government. These democratic aspirations stimulated two key historical events in the history of democracy: the American and French revolutions. Because these popular revolutions occurred in large nation-states, satisfying democratic aspirations required moving beyond the small-state limitation. Conceptions of democracy had to be developed to provide for popular government among millions living in large territories.

The idea of democratic *representation* offered the mechanism to solve the dilemma of organizing democratic government over a large territory.[11] The American and French revolutionaries intended to make democracy work through popularly elected assemblies: state legislatures in the United States and the National Assembly in France. Representative assemblies made democracy feasible in large nation-states, even if the direct participation of the entire people in a single democratic assembly was impossible; representatives would speak on behalf of their constituents. In his famous essay No. 10 from *The Federalist,* James Madison went so far as to

John Locke

turn the conventional wisdom of the political theorists on its head. He argued that representative democracy in a large territory would lead to a more stable popular government than was possible in a small democracy. The introduction of the concept of democratic representation in practice and theory opened the way for the modern conception of democracy.[12]

Along with the idea of representation, a set of political ideas found in the political philosophy called *liberalism* were influential in the emergence of modern conceptions of democracy. Liberal political philosophy was first articulated in the work of the sixteenth-century English philosopher Thomas Hobbes and later in the work of the seventeenth-century English theorist John Locke.[13] Although neither Hobbes nor Locke, as we soon see, would be considered democrats, their ideas about the nature of political life were influential in modern conceptions of democracy.

Liberal theorists begin with two basic assumptions about human nature: (1) humans are reasonable creatures who can use their reason to improve their social existence; and (2) humans are self-interested, that is, concerned with their individual well-being. Based on these two assumptions, theorists such as Locke and Hobbes argued that political society comes into being through a "social contract" among reasonable and self-interested individuals. These individuals understand the need for political order because they wish prosperity and security. For Hobbes, the social contract replaced a horrible "state of nature" in which selfish individuals spend their lives engaged in a "war of all against all," making human life "nasty, brutish, and short." In contrast, Locke had a more benign view of the state of nature, arguing that most reasonable humans could understand the laws of nature and the need to restrain their selfishness for the good of the community. But because some individuals might sometimes be unreasonable and likely to violate the natural rights of others, prudent people should see the advantage of forming a political society with their fellow citizens to protect themselves. Furthermore, this social contract would place "natural" rights on a more secure and stable basis than they had in the state of nature. According to Locke, government, not the goodwill of humans, would become the guardian of natural law. Despite their differing conceptions of the actual "state" of the state of nature, both Hobbes and Locke agreed that reasonable individuals would prefer the security of a social contract to the state of nature.

The purpose of the social contract, and of the government that follows from it, was to maximize the opportunity for individual self-fulfillment. Liberalism was distinguished from medieval and ancient political theories because it identified the individual, his or her rights, and the need for self-fulfillment as the goals of the political order. Individual goals, rather than the glory of God or some universal notion of "the Good," the sorts of goals assumed in earlier political theory, were the proper end of government.[14] For liberals, government existed to allow individuals to pursue whatever individual "goods" they desired. Individualism meant that each person, informed by reason, was the best judge of what was to be valued in life. The function of government was limited to protecting each individual's natural rights to "life, liberty, and property."

Among these individual rights, liberals counted the right to property among the most important. For Locke, the natural — that is, God-given — right to property was central to human existence. The main reason individuals would leave the state of nature and form a political commonwealth was the protection of that right: "The great and chief end of Men's uniting into Commonwealth's, and putting themselves under government, is the preservation of their Property."[15] Since protection of property and other rights is the reason people placed themselves under the authority of a government, it follows logically that government itself should not be allowed to interfere in the exercise of those rights. This liberal commitment to limited government means that individuals have broad leeway in acquiring and disposing of property, free of government control.

Obviously, such a view of government and individual rights of property was very compatible with the emergence of capitalist economic relations. Capitalist entrepreneurs in the late eighteenth and early nineteenth centuries sought to be free of the dictates of government. They found liberal political theory especially supportive of their efforts to accumulate wealth and make investments based on their individual estimates of profitability, rather than the dictates of government. Adam Smith, for example, argued in his *Wealth of Nations,* published in 1776, that economic prosperity, not chaos, would be the result if markets were allowed to function free of government interference, a view quite consistent with Locke's notions of property rights and limited government.

Liberal political ideas clearly imply a capitalist or free enterprise economic order. To what extent does liberalism also imply democratic politics? Liberalism emphasizes that individuals in a society are equally entitled to the protection of their rights and that all humans are equal in forming a social contract. Most Americans associate these liberal political values with democracy. The association is understandable because our American *liberal* democracy has been greatly influenced by our liberal political culture. Nevertheless, liberal thought, although not necessarily incompatible with democratic politics, does not lead necessarily to popular control of government.

Neither Hobbes nor Locke favored democratic government. Hobbes, in fact, felt that a liberal society could be best protected if, as part of the original social contract, people turned over all power to a single absolute sovereign (the *Leviathan*), who would provide law and order, protecting citizens in return for their absolute obedience. He so distrusted selfish human nature that he could see no way to control it except with an authoritarian government. But keep in mind that Hobbes advocated authoritarian government for *liberal* ends: to protect individuals' freedom to benefit from their labors.[16] In this respect, Hobbes's position is similar to the public statements of some modern military dictators, like Chile's former President Augusto Pinochet, who claim they must hold absolute power to protect law-abiding citizens and "free enterprise" from "communists and subversives."[17]

Locke favored some citizen participation in government, but he assumed that participation would be restricted to citizens who had a full stake in the commonwealth, namely, property holders. Although all citizens were obligated to obey government, having consented to the social contract that created it, Locke believed that only citizens with "estate" possessed the capacity for rationality that governing required.[18] Liberals required of government only that it protect individual liberty and not meddle beyond this limited sphere. For this purpose, a nondemocratic government, as long as its powers were limited, might be more trustworthy than a democratic one.

So, liberalism does not lead inevitably to democracy. Nevertheless, there are elements in the liberal vision that do suggest democratic politics. For example, both Hobbes and Locke believed that free individuals participated *equally* in the formation of the initial compact that establishes the state. Therefore, they saw no artificial distinctions between people that could justify different political rights for different individuals. So even though differences between citizens may arise in the actual control of government, the foundation of the state rests on the initial consent of all citizens, irrespective of differences in wealth or social status. Furthermore, the initial social contract means that government itself has a democratic obligation to understand that its powers derive from the initial consent of citizens, and to enforce laws and protect political rights equally. Failure to do so constitutes justification for revolution. These potential democratic sentiments find sublime expression in the American Declaration of Independence, which both embodies liberal doctrine and provides a call for democratic revolution:

> We hold these truths to be self evident, that all men are created equal, that they are endowed by their creator with certain inalienable Rights, that among these are Life, Liberty, and the pursuit of Happiness. That to secure these rights, Governments are instituted among Men, deriving their just powers from the consent of the governed.... That whenever any Form of Government becomes destructive of these ends it is the Right of the People to alter or to abolish it, and to institute new Government, laying its foundation on such principles and organizing its powers in such form, as to them shall seem most likely to effect their Safety and Happiness.

Certainly these liberal ideas provided fruitful stimulus to inspire Americans to democratic revolution.

The significance of liberal ideas for modern conceptions of democracy is clearly evident in the first of the four models described in this chapter, the Protective Democracy model. Like all the models to follow, this set of ideas shows three things: (1) how one group of "democrats" value citizen participation; (2) what they think the purposes of government are, or should be; and (3) what political arrangements they find most consistent with their thoughts on the first two items. In the pages that follow, I describe each of the four models: Protective Democracy, Developmental Democracy, Pluralist Democracy, and Participatory Democracy.[19] Toward the end of the chapter, a table summarizes and compares all four models.

PROTECTIVE DEMOCRACY

Protective Democracy is a model of democracy that advocates popular control of government as a means of protecting individual liberty. Its most explicit formulation is found in the work of two nineteenth-century British political philosophers, Jeremy Bentham and James Mill, who favored democratic government as the best means for securing a liberal society. Bentham, founder of the philosophy of *Utilitarianism,* believed that a capitalist, market society, as described by Smith and implicit in liberal theory, was most likely to achieve the Utilitarian ideal of "the greatest good for the greatest number." He and his disciple Mill felt that for a capitalist society to flourish, it needed government officials who would pass laws nurturing market relations and who would be restrained from using their powers to enrich themselves at the expense of the rest of society.[20]

Bentham and Mill felt the democratic institutions of universal male suffrage, the secret ballot, a free press, and most of all, frequent elections, offered the best chance of keeping government under control. For them, democracy was a method for protecting *both* citizens and capitalism's market relationships: "A democracy, then, has for its characteristic object and effect, the securing its members against oppression and depredation at the hands of those functionaries which it employs for its defense."[21]

If the members of society were self-interested and competitive, as Bentham assumed, then voters would be vigilant against government officials bent on violating their liberties. Voters would be ready to punish (at the polls) government officials who raised taxes too severely or whose policies reduced voters' incomes. Bentham and Mill were willing to embrace universal suffrage, even though this meant including in the electorate the

James Madison

poor, people with no property, and the working class. They were confident that middle-class political leaders like themselves could lead the lower class to support liberal, pro-market governments. After all, in their Utilitarian philosophy, the long-run best interest of even the poor lay in the successful operation of the market society. (This belief is still widely held in the United States, as in the "trickle down" economics of many conservative Republicans.)

Bentham's and Mill's confidence in the support of the poor and propertyless for liberal values contrasted sharply with earlier liberal anxiety about the participation of the poor. Just a few years earlier, in 1787, the American founding fathers also held an essentially liberal view of the role of the government. In the famous *Federalist* No. 10, James Madison asserts that "the protection of [the diversity of the faculties of men from which the rights of property originate] is the first object of government."[22] To Madison, the chief danger to limited government (a liberal goal) was the emergence of factions that might gain control of governmental power and use it in their own interest and against that of the rest of society. Of particular concern was the potential faction of the majority of citizens without property, who might use government to inflate the currency, abolish debts, or appropriate property directly.

This concern with the dangers of popular participation, or the "excesses of democracy," as the Founders put it, was a major factor precipitating the American Constitutional Convention of 1787. Many of the institutional arrangements established in the Constitution were intended to reduce the potential for a democratic majority to threaten individual liberty. Among the most important was the system of separation of powers, which divides lawmaking power among different institutions: the presidency, Congress, and the judiciary. In addition, Congress is divided into two branches, whose members are elected under different electoral schemes. This division of power assured that even if a democratic citizenry succeeded in capturing control of one institution of government, the other, separate institutions would manage to check the potentially tyrannical institution. Several articles, especially the Bill of Rights, also contain specific limitations on governmental power in order to protect individual liberty. All these provisions were intended to create a government that anyone bent on tyranny, whether a faction of the majority or a minority, could not easily use.

Combining the institutional vision of the American founding fathers with the democratic theory of Bentham and Mill suggests our first distinctive model of democracy. Protective Democracy values democratic institutions and procedures to the extent that they protect and nurture a liberal, capitalist, market society. According to this model, democracy exists so that free competitive individuals may have and enjoy a maximum of freedom to pursue material wealth (see table I.1 on p. 18). Some individuals may choose other objectives for their lives, but the basic assumption is that most people are motivated primarily to seek wealth. These individuals are likely to be interested in politics and to participate in politics only to the extent necessary to protect their freedom in the marketplace.

Liberalism heavily influences the Protective Democracy model. In this model, the prime purpose of government is the protection of individual liberty and property. In fact, the limits government imposes are needed precisely because there are threats to property inherent in an acquisitive and competitive human nature. For its part, government should never threaten property rights and should always protect individual liberty. And since the natural human tendency toward material greed and political tyranny lives in government leaders as well, individual liberty can best be protected if there are also clear and strong limits on government. Political institutions such as the separation of powers, federalism, and bicameralism are intended to limit the power of the government so that it will not behave in a tyrannical manner.

Political participation within these institutions provides further protection because citizens will be vigilant in protecting their freedoms. Although Protective Democracy is very concerned with equality in political rights, such as voting, and in equal protection under the law, Protective democrats are less concerned about the existence or potential threat of material inequality in society, and in fact they assume that such inequality will exist.

DEVELOPMENTAL DEMOCRACY
As we have seen, the Protective model of democracy assumes a negative view of human nature. Democracy's first aim is to prevent the inherent selfishness,

acquisitiveness, and even evil of humankind from controlling the state to the detriment of individual liberty. In sharp contrast to this negative view, the Developmental model of democracy assumes a much more positive view of people, especially people in a democratic society. Writing in the nineteenth century, John Stuart Mill (James Mill's son), wrote that man is not simply a "consumer and appropriator" (as assumed in the Protective model) but also an "exerter, developer, and enjoyer of his capacities."[23] As a result, people in democratic societies can come to possess "civic virtue," which permits them to look beyond their self-interest to the well-being of all of society. Through participation in governmental institutions and the affairs of their communities, people develop a broad appreciation of the public good and what it requires. They become public-spirited *citizens.*

The concept of the good citizen is central to the model we call Developmental Democracy. This conception of democratic citizenship is widely embraced in American society, not only in civics textbooks but also by such "good government" groups as the League of Women Voters. "Good citizens" are knowledgeable about, interested in, and active in government and civic affairs. They vote regularly, inform themselves on public issues, write to their elected representatives, and sometimes serve in public office. Democracy is desirable because it provides these opportunities.

Through their active involvement, good citizens contribute to the well-being of their communities, but they also receive something in return. Since democracy requires that citizens involve themselves in the community, it is a means for educating people, enhancing their capacity to improve themselves as well as their government. Democratic citizenship is an intellectual exercise, requiring ordinary people to make constant decisions about political issues and candidates. In making these judgments, citizens talk to one another, learn from one another, and develop their own intelligence.[24] Their active involvement in democratic institutions develops their characters in a more fully human direction.[25] In being responsible for public affairs, people learn to be more responsible human beings. The virtue of democracy is that it develops these positive aspects of human character. In sum, the Developmental model sees democracy as having a moral value and purpose: It requires good citizens and thus develops good people. Like the Protective model, the Developmental model accepts the need for representative democracy, but only because of the impracticality of a more direct form of democracy. According to John Stuart Mill:

> the only government which can fully satisfy all the exigencies of the social state is one in which the whole people participate; that any participation, even in the smallest public function is useful.... But since all cannot, in a community exceeding a single small town, participate personally in any but some very minor portion of the public business, it follows that the ideal type of a perfect government must be representative.[26]

Even though the Developmental model accepts the need for representation, as indicated in the last lines of the quotation above, the emphasis rests on the people's active control of their "deputies." In such a relationship, citizens must be full and active participants in both electing their representatives and monitoring their activities. This view of representation is quite different from that of the proponents of the Protective Democracy model. The Protective democrats, like Madison, thought representation improved on direct democracy because an elite, potentially more civic-minded than ordinary citizens, would control day-to-day policymaking. The Developmental democrats, expecting and encouraging *all* citizens to be civic-minded, accepted representation only as a practical necessity.

For most of American history, this Developmental model of democracy dominated Americans' interpretation of their political life. This view became ascendant during the Jacksonian era, when suffrage was extended to nearly all white males and the spirit of the common man dominated the frontier. This democratic spirit led the French observer Alexis de Tocqueville to conclude in the 1830s that "the people reign over the American political world as God rules over the universe."[27] From Abraham Lincoln to Woodrow Wilson, American political leaders articulated this vision of Developmental Democracy, as their views were reiterated in schoolroom texts and in the writings of political philosophers.

Toward the middle of the twentieth century, however, some intellectuals began to question the Developmental model's accuracy as a description of actual political practice in the United States. This questioning led them to develop our next interpretation of democracy, Pluralist Democracy.

PLURALIST DEMOCRACY

To a considerable extent, the Developmental model represents a democratic ideal: if political society were organized according to this model, popular control of government would be assured. But is it possible for such a political regime to exist? This key question troubled social scientists observing the emergent democratic regimes in such nations as the United States, Britain, and France at the turn of the century.

The question was especially troubling because social scientists saw a political reality that differed greatly from the ideals represented in the Developmental model. For example, instead of seeing average citizens actively engaged in political affairs, they observed that most ordinary people seemed to be apathetic and uninformed about politics. This left day-to-day governance in the hands of a political elite: party leaders, officeholders, "notables," and journalists. Moreover, average citizens were far from equal in their ability to influence public officials; some seemed to have more interest in politics and greater resources

for contact with political leaders. Democratic constitutions alone, they concluded, did not seem to create the sort of democratic politics described in the
Developmental model.

Among political theorists, these observations about the gap between the
democratic ideal and political reality led to two different responses. The first social scientists to describe this gap, in the early years of the twentieth century,
saw it as evidence that democracy was impossible. These "elitist" theorists —
Roberto Michels, Gaetano Mosca, and Vilfredo Pareto — argued that the experience with democratic institutions proved that democracy could never be
achieved.[28] For them, the ideas of democracy and democratic constitutions only
hid the reality of elite control of politics and government. For these theorists,
the actual practice of democracy differed little from politics in authoritarian
or oligarchical regimes because a small "political class" inevitably ruled all societies. A democratic constitution did not change this fundamental "iron law of
oligarchy."

By the middle of the twentieth century, another group of social and political scientists formulated an alternative response to the elitists' conclusion about
the impossibility of democracy. If the actual practice of politics in "democratic"
regimes did not measure up to the democratic ideal, then, instead of giving up
on democracy altogether, they suggested redefining democracy to fit actual political practice. Rather than let the standards of the Developmental model define
democracy, the "revisionists" sought to redefine democracy by careful observation of politics as it was actually practiced in "democratic" societies like the
United States.

In 1954 Bernard Berelson, Paul Lazarsfeld, and William McPhee made this
argument in their book *Voting*, which was based on a sophisticated survey of a
sample of citizens in Elmira, New York, at the time of the 1948 presidential election.[29] They found that the behavior of Elmira's citizens differed significantly
from the democratic ideal as presented in the Developmental model. Levels of
knowledge about the election were quite low for most citizens. More important,
there was great variation among citizens in the level of political interest and participation. Some people were highly interested and involved, others passive and
apathetic, while still others showed moderate interest. Overall, there were not
many "good citizens" among the population they studied.

But Berelson, Lazarsfeld, and McPhee did not conclude that these "facts"
meant a threat for democracy. Instead, they wrote that this mixture of involvement and apathy contributed positively to the stability of democratic politics:

> How could mass democracy work if all the people were deeply involved in politics?
> Lack of interest by some people is not without its benefits, too. . . . Extreme interest
> goes with extreme partisanship and might culminate in rigid fanaticism that
> could destroy democratic processes if generalized throughout the community. Low

affect toward the election . . . underlies the resolution of many political problems; votes can be resolved into a two party split instead of fragmented into many parties. . . . Low interest provides maneuvering room for political shifts necessary for a complex society. . . . Some people are and should be highly interested in politics, but not everyone is or needs to be.[30]

Thus, for these authors, apathy among some citizens, even among a large portion of a society, is considered a positive dimension of democracy. In fact, too many "good citizens," as described in the Developmental model, would constitute a danger to orderly democratic politics.

If, then, democracy is not to be defined by the activism of its citizens, how do "democratic" regimes differ from authoritarian ones? For the Pluralists, the answer to this question is *competitive elections.* This might seem paradoxical, given the quotation above concerning the dangers of electoral participation, but to the Pluralists, elections provide an opportunity for even apathetic and passive citizens to choose their political leaders. This choice distinguishes democratic regimes from authoritarian ones. Since Pluralists assume that the political elite will make actual policy decisions, the role of democratic citizens lies primarily and almost exclusively in their capacity to choose among alternative political leaders. As Joseph Schumpeter put it in a famous definition of democracy: "The democratic method is that institutional arrangement for arriving at political decisions in which individuals acquire the power to decide by means of a competitive struggle for the people's vote."[31] Elections are important, then, not because they provide *direct* citizen involvement in governance, but because they allow citizens to choose who their rulers will be. For the Pluralists, this assures that political leaders will remain responsive to the general preferences of the people and at the same time maintain the flexibility to make intelligent policy decisions without intrusive public meddling.

For the periods between elections, Pluralists assign to interest groups the important role of providing democratic responsiveness.[32] Most citizens, Pluralists observe, are not very aware of day-to-day governmental policymaking, but leaders of interest groups represent average citizens in those policy debates. Since some interest group represents almost everyone's interests, the activities of interest-group leaders are an effective democratic channel for the expression of the public's wants and needs. Moreover, interest-group leaders possess the knowledge and institutional skills to influence policymaking that ordinary people lack. They actively compete with leaders of other interest groups on a daily basis to convince elected officials to enact favorable policies.

For their part, elected officials seek to please as many groups as possible as a means of maximizing electoral support. To achieve this, they must fashion compromises satisfactory to a wide variety of groups. Government policies, then, represent democratic compromises reflecting the preferences of numerous interest groups and their members. Some Pluralists argue that even the concerns of those *not* represented by an interest group are taken into account in these compromises. Politicians need to worry about the preferences of "potential" interest groups that might form if some citizens become too dissatisfied with a policy compromise. For Pluralists, therefore, interest-group activity and regular competitive elections produce a democratic system responsive to the popular will, even though an elite is responsible for day-to-day governing and most citizens are relatively uninvolved in politics.

Finally, Pluralists emphasize that successful democratic politics rests on a base of social diversity. Society consists of many different and competing groups, interests, and associations, and government must be responsive to the legitimate aspirations of all these while it protects the right of various groups to exist. Pluralists feel that democracy can thrive only if the variety of associations inherent in society express themselves politically.[33] Consequently, the concentration of power in the state, a class, or any single part of society is the complete opposite of democracy. As long as power is widely dispersed among many groups, all provide a check against the accumulation of hegemonic power by any one of them. The competition among aspiring government leaders, the fairness of elections, the free interplay of interest groups, and the formulation of democratic compromises can work only if no single group is able to monopolize power and limit competition, undermine free elections, restrict interest groups, and bias policy compromises.

In conclusion, the Pluralist model emerged as social scientists observed apathetic, disinterested, and uninformed citizens in democratic societies. Based on their observations, they concluded that earlier democratic theorists, like those who created the Developmental model, had overestimated the capacity of most people to participate as active democratic citizens. If most people were apathetic toward political affairs, it seemed logical to look to the active political elite as guardians of democratic values and actual participants in policy formation. Most ordinary citizens could be assigned the more minor (although still important) role of voting in periodic elections to choose among alternative leaders. The basis of the Pluralist conception was the intermittent and indirect, even remote, participation of most people in political affairs.

PARTICIPATORY DEMOCRACY

But why are citizens apathetic? The Pluralists assume political apathy to be a natural inclination of most people. Unless political affairs directly affect people's immediate interests, most prefer to focus on their private concerns. In the 1960s, political activists and political theorists began to question this Pluralist assumption. They formulated a conception of Participatory Democracy, which sees apathy as a result of the lack of opportunities for significant participation, rather than a fact inherent in human nature. If most people preferred to concern themselves with their private affairs rather than public ones, this was because of the structure of social institutions, not human nature. For Participatory democrats, the solution to citizen apathy lay in restructuring political and social institutions so that citizens could learn, through participation, the value and joys of democratic citizenship.

The Participatory model, although it has antecedents in the earlier Developmental model, arose from the political turbulence of the 1960s. Its earliest formulations came from the manifestos of student political activists in such organizations as Students for a Democratic Society (SDS) and the Student Non-Violent Coordinating Committee (SNCC). In 1962 a small group of SDS members gathered in Port Huron, Michigan, to formulate a statement of principles, the Port Huron Statement, which included a call for "a democracy of individual participation."[34] Political, social, and economic institutions were to be reformed to make them more conducive to participation. In the South, the black and white student activists of SNCC attempted to put participatory ideals into practice in their efforts to register black voters. The battles for civil rights and later against the Vietnam War provided arenas to test the capacity of mass participation to influence public policy.

While students practiced Participatory Democracy in the streets, a number of political scientists challenged the then dominant Pluralist interpretation of American politics in scholarly journals.[35] They questioned whether the elite-dominated politics the Pluralists celebrated merited the label "democratic." They said that the Pluralists complacently praised the virtues of American politics while ignoring the structures that prevented the development of a more authentic democratic politics. Pluralists were criticized for claiming that interest groups offered wide representation to societal interests, even though many Americans did not belong to any voluntary associations and not all groups had equal access to policymakers. Most important, for discounting the ideals of democratic citizenship in the name of "realism," Pluralists were accused of ignoring and undermining analysis of how more effective structures of democratic participation might be constructed.

The Participatory model differs from previous models in its emphasis on the importance of democratic participation in nongovernmental as well as governmental institutions. The Developmental model (like the Protective and Pluralist models) views the democratic problem as subjecting governmental institutions and decisions to popular control. Participatory democrats agree with the need to control the government democratically, but they also point out that in modern industrialized societies it is not only government that makes authoritative decisions that individuals must obey or that has the capacity to apply sanctions to people who do not obey. Individuals are subject to the authoritative rules of their employers, unions, schools, churches, and other institutions. In fact, the decisions and rules of these institutions usually have a more immediate impact on people's lives than do government policies. The decisions an employer makes regarding salary, working conditions, or layoffs can have an immediate and, if adverse, devastating effect on an employee's life. In comparison to these decisions, the decision by the national government to emphasize a manned over an unmanned space program, or a local government's decision about which streets to pave, is remote or unimportant to most people.

In most cases, these nongovernmental decisions are made in hierarchical bureaucratic organizations, in an authoritarian manner, without any of the procedures and protection we associate with democracy. Participatory democrats feel that the absence of democracy in these nongovernmental settings undermines the capacity of citizens to function democratically and thus the overall quality of a society's democracy. The model presents three related arguments to support this idea. First, the lack of participatory opportunities in the workplace, the school, and the union deprives citizens of the chance to influence those decisions that are most meaningful to them. An opportunity to nurture those qualities of citizenship the Developmental theorists valued is lost when people are unable to influence decisions that directly affect their lives. Democratic participation would be much more meaningful to people if they could see such participation affecting decisions with direct impact on their day-to-day lives.

Second, people are apt to acquire nonparticipatory habits when subjected to an authoritarian environment on a daily basis. After spending the day following orders without question at the factory, a worker cannot be expected to return home in the evening to act like the civics textbook's inquiring, skeptical, self-actualizing citizen. Students who are taught primarily to obey authority in school are not likely to grow into effective democratic citizens. Third, Participatory democrats argue that a society can hardly be called democratic when so many socially and politically relevant decisions are in the hands of people who are not democratically accountable. For example, corporate officials sometimes make decisions, like deciding to close a factory, that affect the well-being of a whole community. The inability of the community's citizens to influence that decision is as indicative of a lack of democracy as their inability to influence the local property tax rate.

For Participatory democrats, the way to hold those who make decisions accountable is to expand participatory opportunities in society. Democracy is not just a concept relevant to government; it should be implemented in all instances where authoritative decisions affecting people's lives are made. Workers should be able to participate democratically in the running of their factories, students and faculty their schools and universities, and welfare recipients the welfare department. Through meaningful participation in these environments, people will

Table I.1 Models of Democracy Compared

	Protective Democracy	*Developmental Democracy*	*Pluralist Democracy*	*Participatory Democracy*
Goal or purpose	Protect liberty (market relations and private property)	Nurture citizenship	Protect and promote diversity	Foster participation
Role of citizens	Passive	Active	Passive	Active
Institutional mechanisms	Separation of powers and representation	Representations	Interest groups and elections	Neighborhood assemblies and workers' councils
Equality	Political	Political and social	Political	Economic, political, and social
Human nature	Selfish and acquisitive	Capable of civic virtue	Selfish and acquisitive	Capable of civic virtue

acquire the capacity to be more effective participants in influencing government. For Participatory democrats, creating effective democracy in our industrialized and bureaucratized society requires that there be a radical restructuring of institutions to increase people's control over the decisions that affect their lives.

THE MODELS COMPARED

Table I.1 compares and summarizes the characteristics of the four models of democracy described in this chapter. In the table, the purpose (goal, end) the model assigns to democracy uniquely defines that model. The Protective model values democracy because democratic institutions are thought to provide the best protection for individual liberties, particularly economic ones such as the right to individual control of property. Developmental democracy considers democratic politics the best method of developing the personal qualities associated with its idea of the "good citizen." Pluralists value the social diversity and system stability that democratic institutions encourage. And for the Participatory democrats, democracy is worthwhile because it permits people to participate in decisions that affect their lives. Each model's unique character seems to derive from the central purpose or goal it expects democracy to accomplish.

Other dimensions of the table direct our attention to values and characteristics the models share. For example, the Developmental and Participatory models obviously have a lot in common. Each assumes a positive view of human nature: people are thought to be capable of rising above their narrow self-interests. Through participation in democratic procedures and institutions, citizens acquire the quality of civic virtue, which enables them to evaluate public issues in terms of the public interest. Consequently, we should expect and encourage people to be active participants in political affairs in order to enrich both society and the individual. Both of these models also agree on the need for economic and social equality in democratic societies. When citizens come together to discuss the needs of the community, no artificial distinctions of political or social status should override the commonality of citizenship.

The differences between the Developmental and Participatory models center on their different evaluations of the impact of economic relationships on democratic politics. Developmental democrats do not view economic inequalities or class differences as significant barriers to equal citizenship. They emphasize the potential all citizens enjoy, no matter what their economic resources, to participate fully in governmental institutions. In contrast to this governmental focus, Participatory democrats focus on the importance of social relationships, particularly economic ones, outside government. For them, full and active participation in government alone cannot fulfill the requirements of democracy; democracy also means popular control of authoritative decisions in corporations, factories, unions, and schools. Moreover, social and economic inequality may impede the functioning of even political democracy. This broader view makes greater economic equality both a prerequisite for more meaningful participation and a likely consequence of popular power over economic decision making.

Like the Developmental and Participatory models, the Protective and Pluralist models share a common view of human nature. Both adopt the pessimistic position that humans are primarily selfish and acquisitive creatures, concerned primarily with increasing and maintaining their private wealth. From this assumption follows these models' shared expectation that most people will have only limited interest in public affairs. Moreover, especially for the Pluralists, the average person's limited interest and participation in politics is quite acceptable, for it contributes to the stability of the system and the liberty of all. If people are naturally rapacious and interested in their own welfare, their active involvement in government will only produce factional conflict and, if one faction wins, potential violations of liberty.

The Pluralist and Protective democrats also agree that equality in a democracy need only apply to political rights and opportunities. But they expect social and economic inequalities to affect the degree of actual participation, a natural reality that does not disturb them. Political leaders, whether elected representatives or interest-group leaders, will probably possess higher social status and be more affluent, but that does not interfere with their ability to speak and act for their constituents and followers, according to these two models. Universal suffrage and competitive elections are enough in themselves to assure equal representation for all economic interests. Furthermore, the "one person, one vote" idea assures that the voting power of the many will counterbalance the potential political advantages of the affluent few.

THE DISCUSSION SO FAR may have left some readers a bit confused. The preface said this chapter would offer a definition of democracy as a standard against which to judge alternative challenges to the well-being of democracy. Instead of a single such definition, I have presented four very different models, each claiming to provide a description of democratic politics. It appears that one of the challenges democracy faces is that no one can agree on what it means! What conclusions about the concept of democracy can be drawn from these various models? Can we identify some essential characteristics of democracy that will facilitate our identifying its challenges?

First, the models suggest that a part of the meaning of democracy is a continuing discussion of the meaning of democracy. You should note that these models have evolved historically in response to the practical efforts to establish and maintain democratic regimes during the past two hundred years. Democratic politics has been a new experience for humankind; it is understandable that conceptions of it remain in formation. There is obviously no single, authoritative blueprint for how democracy can be achieved. Instead, democratic politics involves a constant discussion among citizens about how best to organize their political life.

Despite the differences among the models, one can identify certain common elements that seem to have emerged during humankind's two-century discussion about democracy. First, all models assume that democracy means popular rule; that is, government based on popular sovereignty (as opposed, say, to the divine right of kings) and subject to popular control. The models differ on how popular control is to be expressed, but all merit the label "democratic" because they assume the need for control by the people. Second, all models assume political equality. None questions the fact that democracy requires all citizens to possess equal political rights, even though the models differ on the capacity of individuals to take equal advantage of those rights. What differentiates these models from authoritarian theories of government is the absence of any argument in favor of an aristocracy or the assignment of a privileged political role to any preordained class or group in society. Third, all assume the need for political liberty. Democratic discussion and popular control of governmental actions can occur only if all people feel free to express themselves and to try to influence government. In sum, these three values — popular rule, liberty, and equality — constitute the core of democracy's definition. All those who honestly call themselves democrats embrace these concepts.

The differences among these models do not mean that the models are mutually exclusive. Embracing one does not necessarily mean a total rejection of the others. Instead of containing mutually distinctive definitions of democracy, each highlights different values consistent with the other models and an implicit global definition of democracy. The Protective model, for example, emphasizes the importance of individual liberty and the need to protect liberty from government infringement. Participatory democrats would object to the Protective democrats' preoccupation with property rights, but would agree with the need to preserve the generic liberties required for free and open political participation. Pluralists emphasize the need for social diversity for effective democracy; the other models do not question this. The Developmental model calls attention to the value of good democratic citizenship, while the Participatory model emphasizes the value of searching for new ways for democratic citizens to make social decisions that control their lives. I do not mean to suggest that the disagreements among adherents of the various models are merely cosmetic, only that certain common values underlie them all.

What these models suggest and what this chapter shows is that democracy remains, even after much practical experience with democratic institutions throughout the world, an ideal to be continually sought after, rather than a settled system to be admired complacently. People in many countries, including the United States, strive to achieve democratic ideals. They aim to subject public decisions to popular control, protect individual civil rights and liberties, expand political equality, encourage participation in decisions that affect people's lives, foster social diversity, and promote good citizenship. Nevertheless, nowhere, not even in the United States, have these ideals been achieved. This is partly because our definitions of these ideals, like our definition of democracy, continually change. For example, in 1840 universal white male suffrage seemed to satisfy the aspirations of most American democrats; in today's United States the exclusion of women and nonwhites from voting is rightly considered a gross violation of democratic principles.

We can see, therefore, that the achievement of the democratic ideal is so difficult because the ideal itself is so demanding. The limitations of human nature and social organization are continual barriers in the way of successful democracy. Sometimes doing things nondemocratically is just simpler than wrestling with democratic procedures. This impatience with the demands of democracy often tempts some people in democracies to bypass democratic procedures.[36] Another way democracy is demanding is in the time and energy democratic citizenship requires — time many people would prefer to devote to their private affairs. Also, despite the almost universal lip service given to democratic ideals in the modern world, not everyone believes in democracy. The active opposition from individuals and groups opposed to democratic aspirations is surely a significant barrier to the achievement of democratic ideals. Whether it is a government such as Saudi Arabia's or Cuba's, a segment of society such as southern whites in the 1960s who opposed the civil rights movement, or the economic interests of corporate officials who resist public efforts to regulate their actions, the opponents of democracy remain powerful in every country and every segment of society. With such opposition, the world will never be absolutely "safe for democracy."

This recognition of the fragility of democratic political institutions brings us to the main point of this book. Observers of democratic politics are continually identifying threats to the future and well-being of democracy. When studying these challenges, several questions need to be asked: First, what is the implicit or explicit model of democracy each particular challenge seems to confront? Does the seriousness of the particular challenge diminish or increase depending on the model? Does the challenge threaten underlying values differently in the various models? Second, to what extent does the threat discussed undermine the democratic values of all the models, of democracy itself? Is the challenge so serious to democratic values that Protective, Pluralist, Developmental, and Participatory democrats should be equally concerned? Finally, what does the analysis of the various threats to democracy tell us about the models themselves? Which model of democracy seems to offer the best chance of overcoming the challenges American democracy faces in the modern world? In other words, how should our politics be structured if we are to thrive as a society?

Suggestions for Further Reading

Barber, Benjamin, and Patrick Watson. *The Struggle for Democracy.* Boston: Little, Brown, 1988. A history of democracy written to accompany a PBS documentary series on the topic. Videotapes of the television series are available from PBS.

Dahl, Robert. *On Democracy.* New Haven: Yale University Press, 1998. The most prominent American democratic theorist sums up his ideas on why democracy is the preferred system.

Macpherson, C.B. *The Life and Times of Liberal Democracy.* Oxford, England: Oxford University Press, 1977. A comprehensive review of the theoretical ideas underpinning the models of democracy presented in this chapter.

Margolis, Michael. *Viable Democracy.* London: Penguin Books, 1979. An analysis of why democratic practice has not lived up to democratic ideals, with a proposal to bring the two in line.

Miller, James E. *Democracy Is in the Streets.* New York: Simon and Schuster, 1987. A history of Students for a Democratic Society (SDS) that focuses on the political ideas of student activists in the 1960s.

Nino, Carlos Santiago. *The Constitution of Deliberative Democracy.* New Haven: Yale University Press, 1996. This book, by the late renowned Argentinian scholar and human rights activist, is an intricate reflection on the relation between constitutionalism and democracy. He proposes a theory of deliberative democracy to overcome the limitations of existing conceptions.

Pateman, Carole. *Participation and Democratic Theory.* Cambridge, England: Cambridge University Press, 1970. A prominent democratic theorist dissects the Participatory model.

Sandel, Michael J. *Democracy's Discontent: America in Search of a Public Philosophy.* Cambridge: Harvard University Press, 1996. An elegantly written and clear argument calling for a public philosophy that moves beyond the "procedural republic" of liberal rights and entitlements to a democracy grounded in the civic republican tradition and citizen self-government.

Cape C...

PRESIDENT IMPEACHED

ANALYSIS
Livingston
joins growing
casualty list

THE SUN...
...IN IRAQ, MISSION A...

IMPEACHED
Clinton faces Senate trial after divided House approves 2
President's
legacy forever
tarnished

Boston Sunday
Herald

...Clinton...
Senate to hold politic'...

Sunday Globe

...is impeached
House approves
2 of 4 charges,
paving the way
for Senate trial

The Provid...
Clinton im...
- Bitterly divided House passes...
- President, Democrats reject ca...
- Senate trial, 1st in 130 years, to...
Allies end
bombing
of Iraq,
declaring
success

Clinton vows to stay in...
President...
What's
next

UMASS WINS!
MINUTEMEN WIN DIVISION I-AA NATIONAL CHAMPIONSHIP/C1

TOY FOR JOY
Nearly $35,000 still needed
to reach fund drive goal/A12

Sunday Republican
CLINTON IMPEACHED
...won't resign as case heads to Senate
Democrats walk out
...speaker-elect to quit

CHAPTER 1

The First Challenge:
Separation of Powers

Nothing human can be perfect. Surrounded by difficulties, we did the best we could; leaving it with those who should come after us to take counsel from experience, and exercise prudently the power of amendment.
— GOUVERNEUR MORRIS

The evils we experience flow from the excess of democracy.
— ELBRIDGE GERRY

WE AMERICANS TEND to equate democracy with our particular constitutional structure. When I ask students to define democracy, several always respond by saying, "Democracy means a separation of powers — checks and balances between the branches of government." Like many Americans, these students identify government as it is practiced in the United States with democracy, and it is only a short leap then to define democracy in terms of the central feature of our constitutional structure: the separation of powers. This tendency is reinforced in the media, in schools, and in statements by government officials, all of whom treat the Constitution reverentially, including the ideas of separation of powers and checks and balances.[1] In fact, whenever there is a crisis in American government, the standard solution proposed is to seek a restoration of "proper governmental checks and balances."

The thesis of this chapter is that Americans are mistaken to equate the separation of governmental powers with democracy. In practice, especially in recent years, the constitutional separation between branches of government, particularly that between Congress and the presidency, has undermined the capacity of Americans to control their government. In their zeal to protect individual liberty, the

---

Opposite: *Banner headlines blare the news of only the second impeachment of a sitting president in America's history. (AP/Wide World Photos)*

central value of the Protective democracy model, the authors of the Constitution erected barriers to majority rule that have always impeded democracy and now, after more than two hundred years, have produced perpetually stalemated government. For most of our history, we managed to overcome the antimajoritarian bias of the Constitution through a combination of presidential leadership and political party organization. This system offered a temporary and partial solution to governmental deadlock, but over the past few decades even this partial system has no longer worked. Divided government, in which different political parties controlled Congress and the presidency, compounded the defects of the separation of powers in making the government inefficient, unresponsive, and unaccountable. Our eighteenth-century Constitution has become a major obstacle to achieving democratic government in the twenty-first century.

THE FOUNDERS' WORK

Both the signers of the Declaration of Independence and the drafters of the Constitution can be classified, in the terminology of the democracy models, as Protective democrats. They believed that the purpose of a democracy (or a *republic,* their term for representative democracy) was the protection of individual liberty. Their great fear was a tyrannical government that ignored individual rights and ruled without the consent of the governed. For the revolutionaries, however, the danger of tyranny emanated from a very different source than the tyranny the Constitution's authors feared. In 1776 a tyrannical executive, specifically King George III and his royal governors in the colonies, motivated the movement for independence. Only eleven years later, in 1787, the men who gathered to draft a new constitution worried mainly about the tyranny of popularly elected legislatures. What in the experience of the new American republic had caused this shift in concern?

During and after the Revolutionary War, most states enacted constitutions reflecting the popular spirit and republican enthusiasm that the revolution had produced. Because the revolutionaries distrusted political executives, the new state constitutions lodged most power in the legislatures. These institutions were structured to permit maximum responsiveness to popular majorities. State legislators were typically chosen in annual elections so that their constituents would have plenty of opportunity to hold them accountable. Accountability through annual elections was carried farthest in the radical Pennsylvania constitution, which required that before it could become law, legislation had to be passed twice, with an election between the two votes, permitting voters an opportunity to ratify directly the actions of their representatives. Although all states required voters to own some property, property qualifications were modest enough in most states so that suffrage was widespread (at least among white males). Voters also tended to elect representatives very much like themselves, producing state legislatures dominated by farmers and tradesmen, most with minimal education but with personal interests and concerns reflective of those who elected them.[2] Given the weakness of the national government under the Articles of Confederation, the democratic majorities in the state legislatures were the centers of power in the new American nation.

Fear and dissatisfaction with these state legislatures, particularly their democratic character, is what brought the founding fathers to Philadelphia for the purpose of revising the Articles during that hot summer in 1787.[3] As Governor Edmund Randolph of Virginia put it, "Our chief danger arises from the democratic parts of our [state] constitutions. . . . None of the constitutions have provided sufficient checks against democracy."[4] The Founders had two major complaints against the state legislatures. First, they considered state government to be too chaotic, with annual elections producing frequent turnover and legislators too prone to enacting the transitory passions of their constituents into law. Second, and more seriously, the Founders were dismayed at the sorts of laws being enacted in the states, particularly laws to inflate currency and abolish debts. For most of the convention delegates, these laws were a despotic attack on fundamental rights of property. They saw the laws as the consequence of debtor majorities in the states taking over state governments and promoting their interests at the expense of the propertied minority. Even where a propertyless majority did not control state government, such a majority might resort to violent acts to support their interest — acts that the inept and overly responsive legislatures were ill equipped to control. When, just a year before the convention, a revolt by debtors in western Massachusetts called Shays's Rebellion was put down with great difficulty by the state militia, the worst fears of the critics of state constitutions seemed confirmed.

Historians debate vociferously the motives and purposes of the men who wrote the Constitution. Was the Constitutional Convention an antidemocratic counterrevolution of wealthy and propertied Americans seeking to preserve their wealth and power from a democratic citizenry? Or was it simply an attempt by prudent statesmen, concerned that the new nation would dissolve into violence and chaos, to establish the structure of a stable representative democracy?[5] Whichever characterization of the Founders' motives is true, the record of the convention provides much evidence that controlling tyrannical majorities was the major agenda item. The result of the convention's work, the U.S. Constitution, reflects this concern, for it is a masterful creation with the central purpose of preventing the "tyranny" of a majority.

The new Constitution restricted majority tyranny in two principal ways. First, it established a strong national government capable of countering any tyrannical majority in a state. The central government gained new powers, such as the power to coin money and regulate commerce, and new instruments, such as a standing army, to enable it to overcome any state government under the control of a factional interest. Even though the convention did not go as far as James Madison wanted it to in giving the national government a veto over state legislation, it did replace the weak government under the Articles with a national government with muscle. But what prevented the national government from being subjected to a tyrannical majority? The answer was the second principal feature of the Constitution: the structure of governmental institutions we now call the "separation of powers."

The central insight of the separation of powers was to give the individuals controlling the different governmental branches partial control over the enactment of laws — control they could exercise independently of those controlling the other branches. The separate political base of each branch was the guarantee that the occupants of the different branches would be politically independent of one another and capable of acting autonomously. For example, the president was to be chosen by a special Electoral College completely independent of Congress. Likewise, the president had no role in the election of members of Congress. This logic was carried further in the separate election processes for the two congressional branches: members of the House of Representatives elected directly every two years in congressional districts and senators chosen by state legislatures, with only one-third of the Senate picked at any one time. And these politically independent individuals all had to agree before any policies were made.

Although the Electoral College never operated in the way intended in choosing the president and although we now elect senators directly, the separation-of-powers structure remains an excellent means of preventing a political majority from easily controlling government. A president elected to office with a massive popular majority in a national constituency cannot count on enacting the political platform he campaigned on into law. A majority of members of Congress, selected in a separate election process in their individual constituencies, may oppose the president's programs. Because of the separation of powers, voters are free (a freedom they exercise, as we later see, with increasing regularity) to vote simultaneously for a president who favors one set of policies and for a congressional representative who opposes those same policies. Even if, in a given election, a majority of voters choose both a president and a majority of members of Congress who agree on a set of policies, those policies can be blocked by the two-thirds of senators who are not chosen in that election. If in a "midterm" election (the congressional election that comes in the middle of a president's term) voters choose to send to Washington a decisive majority of representatives to enact a particular policy, that policy can be blocked by a presidential veto that needs the votes of only thirty-four senators to avoid being overridden. Add to this a judiciary made up of members with life tenure and the power to strike down what they consider unconstitutional legislation, and one has an excellent mechanism for frustrating majority rule.

The author of this system, James Madison, understood its political logic quite well. In *Federalist* No. 51, he argues that succeeding occupants of the various governmental branches will jealously protect the constitutional prerogatives of their particular branch and seek to prevent the other branches from accumulating too much power. For the separation of powers to work, "the interest of the man must be connected with the constitutional rights of the place."[6] In this way, "ambition" would "counteract ambition" as wary presidents would check the powers of Congress and congressmen would keep a watchful eye on power-hungry presidents. With their political independence from one another lodged in their independent electoral bases, the practical ability of the occupants of the different branches to check the power of the other branches was secured. In such a system, Madison and the other Founders believed, no tyrannical majority could simultaneously control all the relevant policymakers, and thus the rights of minorities were secure.

THE JEFFERSONIAN MODEL

The separation-of-powers structure erected formidable barriers in the way of forming a coherent governing majority in the United States, but it did not take long after the ratification of the Constitution for the ingenious politicians of the period to develop a way of uniting the branches of government behind a popular government. The key to uniting the branches was the political party, and the first practitioner of the method was the third U.S. president, Thomas Jefferson.

The Founders abhorred the idea of political parties; their prevention had been one of the goals of the Constitution. For James Madison, in 1787, parties were "factions," groups united by a common "passion" or "interest" adverse to the interests of other citizens. But in the first decade of the new republic, its leaders, including Madison, came to find the political party an indispensable institution for organizing voters and their representatives. By the end of the century, two vigorous political parties contested for power throughout the nation: the Federalists and the Democratic-Republicans. In a hard-fought election in 1800, the Democratic-Republican Party led by Thomas Jefferson decisively defeated the Federalists and captured the presidency and large majorities in both the Senate and the House of Representatives. As president, Jefferson, to a much greater extent than his Federalist predecessor, John Adams, used his position as national party leader to organize Congress on behalf of his political program and policies.[7] He devised a new model of government that could mobilize the country on behalf of an electoral majority in spite of the separation of powers. This model of government, which political scientist James MacGregor Burns labeled the "Jeffersonian model," has been the strategy for organizing coherent and responsible democratic government since Jefferson's presidency.

In the past two hundred years of American history, there have been frequent punctuations of creative democratic leadership producing policy innovation. During each of these creative periods, a dynamic president has used the Jeffersonian model to build an electoral majority and, then, with the support of party majorities in Congress, to bridge the separation of powers to enact new policies. These periods, with which we associate the names of our greatest presidents — Jackson, Lincoln, Theodore Roosevelt, Wilson, and Franklin Roosevelt — all had in common the Jeffersonian model. Periods of divided government, when different parties control Congress and the presidency, allow the separation-of-powers structure to impede developing coherent policies. These are periods of stalemate and deadlock, when no one seems to be in charge of government. Our history seems to show that, given the constitutional structure, the Jeffersonian model of leadership is a requisite for democratic change to occur.

Although the Jeffersonian model is the historical strategy for successful democratic politics in the United States, it does not overcome completely the antimajoritarian bias of the separation of powers. First, it permits only episodic periods of majority rule. Divided government remains a continuing possibility as long as the presidency and the two houses of Congress are elected independently. This is why we have come to associate democratic change in the United States with short periods of policy innovation followed by long periods of stasis. In addition, presidents are usually under tremendous pressure to enact their programs swiftly, in the first two years of office, for fear that the midterm congressional elections will bring a hostile majority into Congress. The result is incompletely enacted programs and a muddled record of presidential performance. Second, because of the separation-of-powers structure, the president has only limited control over the members of his own party in Congress. Members of Congress are dependent on electoral majorities in their individual constituencies, not on the national party organization or on the president's national majority. Sometimes the support of an individual constituency requires defying the president and the national majority, as President Clinton in his first term learned very quickly. Consequently, even when he has partisan majorities in Congress, a president cannot always employ the Jeffersonian model because of the recalcitrance of a minority within his own party.

While the Jeffersonian model has been a partial solution to the bias toward governmental stalemate inherent in the separation of powers, a critical requisite of its operation — one-party control of both the presidency and Congress — has been a rarity in recent years. Since 1952, in seven of eleven presidential elections voters have returned to office a president of one party and a Congress controlled by the other.[8] Because this situation is now so common, most Americans do not realize that divided government produced as a result of a presidential election was once extremely rare. Between 1832 and 1952, this situation occurred only three times. As table 1.1 shows, prior to 1952, divided government was almost exclusively a product of midterm congressional elections when voters sometimes voted in a congressional majority opposed to the sitting president. The midterm election of 1994 seemed to follow this older pattern, as Republican majorities captured both houses of Congress, in response to the first two years of Clinton's term.

Table 1.1 Divided Government by Type of Election, 1832–1998

	Presidential	Midterm
1832–1898	3	11
1900–1952	0	4
1954–1998	7	9

Source: Adapted from Morris P. Fiorina, "An Era of Divided Government," *Political Science Quarterly* 107 (Fall 1992): 390. Data updated to reflect elections after 1992.

The 1996 election, however, showed a renewal of the post-1952 era, as voters retained divided government in the face of a decisive Clinton reelection victory. Had the 1996 race followed the pre-1952 pattern, one would have expected the voters to return Democratic majorities to Congress as they reelected a Democratic president. The ratification of divided government in 1996, and again in 1998, emphasizes how recent years have differed from most of American history. For about 60 percent of our history, unified government, providing the possibility for the Jeffersonian model of governance, has prevailed. For most of the past three decades, however, political party has ceased to provide the bridge across the constitutional separation of powers that it once did.

Only recently have political scientists begun to explore the reasons for divided government in the contemporary era. A variety of explanations have been offered, including the decline of partisanship among voters, greater reelection resources of congressional incumbents, gerrymandered congressional districts, and the conscious choice of the electorate.[9] Although no clear agreement on an explanation of divided government has been reached, all those who have studied the phenomenon see a few characteristics of recent American politics related to it. First is the decline of political partisanship. Political parties have grown weaker organizationally in the past few decades, as have voter attachments to them. More voters, particularly among the highly educated and more affluent — a crucial "swing" voter group in close elections — are ticket splitters, voting for different political parties for different offices in a single election.[10] With an electorate indifferent to party, those holding elective office are more apt to ignore party discipline and vote independently, behavior that only reinforces the electorate's perception that party labels do not matter.

Second, in the 1980s, many commentators noted the particular partisan pattern of party control of the different branches starting in the 1950s. Democratic Party dominance of Congress meant that divided governments involved Republican presidents facing Democratic Congresses. Some political observers began to argue that each party had a "lock" on one branch of government. Political scientist James L. Sundquist saw this situation as merely a historical accident. Members of Congress had learned how to exploit the advantages of incumbency to achieve their reelection in the mid-1960s at a time when Republican presidential candidates were advantaged in amassing electoral votes in presidential races.[11] Other commentators believed voters were making a conscious choice in placing control of the presidency in Republican hands and Congress in Democratic ones. Voters supposedly wanted Republican presidents to manage foreign policy, provide for national defense, and restrain overall levels of government spending, but they were depending on congressional Democrats to protect social programs.[12] The partisan reversal of divided government to a Republican Congress and Democratic president in the 1990s has undermined this conscious-voter-choice theory. Unless one can explain why voters would suddenly choose to rely on Congress to cut spending and the president to guard social programs, recent divided government seems to be an accidental result of how voters make their decisions. Rather than considering the possible impact on the partisan control of either branch, voters cast independent votes for president and Congress based on candidates' individual characteristics and campaign promises, not on grounds of partisanship or calculations about dividing the branches between the parties. In an electorate in which party no longer counts for much, divided government happens.

Whatever the precise reason for the recent prevalence of divided government, it has brought concern for the consequences of the separation-of-powers system onto the political agenda. Partisan division between the branches prevents coping with our constitutional system in the traditional manner — the Jeffersonian model. Instead, Americans have had to observe the full effects of negotiating policy between two politically independent branches, each with separate policy agendas and political interests. The result has been a continuing spectacle of contentious and stalemated government, leaving many important policy problems — inadequate health care, future shortfalls in Medicare and Social Security funding, continuing economic inequality, deteriorating cities, and campaign finance reform — unaddressed. No wonder citizens have little confidence in American political institutions.

THE SEPARATION OF POWERS AND DEMOCRATIC VALUES

The Founders' preoccupation with the democratic value liberty (the central concern of the Protective model) caused them to construct an institutional structure that interfered with achieving two other key democratic values. First, in their zeal to prevent majority tyranny, they created a structure insufficiently *responsive* to political majorities. Responsiveness to citizens is an underlying concern of all the models discussed in the introduction, but of special concern to proponents of the Participatory and Developmental models. Second, the separation-of-powers design has so fragmented and divided responsibility for governmental policy that it has become impossible to hold elected officials *accountable* for their actions. Accountability is also an assumed attribute of all the models, including the Pluralist model, which defines the democratic citizen's key role as passing judgment on the performance of officials at election time. Such a judgment cannot be made effectively when the separation of powers obscures who is responsible for governmental conduct.

Responsiveness

Although democrats can sympathize with the Founders' concern for protecting minority rights and preventing majority tyranny, objectives all democrats share, the separation of powers creates a problem for responsive democratic politics. The system is incapable of distinguishing between majorities that are tyrannical and those that are not tyrannical; it frustrates all majorities, regardless of their objectives. The system creates a series of blockades at which a minority interest can prevent change a democratic majority supports. An electoral majority may send to Washington a House of Representatives prepared to enact policies they favor only to have the Senate, in which less-populated states are overrepresented and two-thirds of the senators do not have to face the electorate in a given election, vote it down. Or a president elected to office with a majority mandate for change may face opposition in either house of Congress that will prevent him from enacting the program. Or the president may be a minority instrument, employing the veto to prevent enactment of legislation — a veto that can be made override-proof with the cooperation of only thirty-four senators. Separation of powers provides a constitutional structure inherently biased against change, even when change has the support of an overwhelming majority of citizens.

The separation-of-powers system was *intended* to reduce the responsiveness of government. Because of their fear of majority tyranny, the Founders wanted to "cool" democratic passions by passing them through several independent institutions.[13] In addition, they believed in the classical liberal ideal of limited government. Separation of powers served this ideal by providing a permanent conservative bias to government; a minority could easily block the passage of new policies. Even large popular majorities in favor of a measure had to fight through numerous barriers before innovative laws could be passed. As a result, government could act in response to democratic majorities only slowly and in a limited way. Defenders of the separation of powers, including the founding fathers, usually have justified this blanket frustration of all majorities by arguing that enduring majorities backing wise and useful policies will eventually succeed. They believe the system will stop wrongheaded proposals passionately backed by a transitory majority, but if a proposal has genuine merit, it will succeed through several election cycles to bring to power supporters in all branches and then be enacted into law. As one defender puts it, the separation of powers was intended "to protect liberty from an immoderate majority while permitting a moderate majority to prevail."[14]

Separation of powers in a democratic political system, then, is based on a proposition about its consequences for democratic majorities: tyrannical, immoderate, and unwise majorities will be blocked; nontyrannical, moderate, and wise majorities will eventually succeed. Does our two-hundred-year experience with the separation of powers confirm this proposition? An easy "objective" test of this proposition would be quite difficult. Observers of the historical record are likely to differ over whether majority-backed policies that have not succeeded or were long delayed were or were not "immoderate," "unwise," or "tyrannical." An evaluation of the issue requires detailed argumentation about individual policies and historical episodes. I believe that such a detailed review of our history would show that the separation of powers has impeded the enactment of numerous moderate, just, and wise policies. For the past two hundred years, this system has worked repeatedly to frustrate and divide popular majorities. Even with the partial amelioration of the Jeffersonian model, our constitutional system has made the enactment of every policy innovation a long and protracted struggle. As a result, many popular programs and policies have failed to be enacted or have been put into place only after years of debate, discussion, and compromise, which dilutes their effects. Because of this bias against policy innovation, government *is* smaller in the United States than in other industrialized nations, but our government also provides fewer and less generous social programs than citizens insist on elsewhere.

For example, the United States is the only industrial democratic nation in the world that does not guarantee all its citizens access to health care. In other democratic countries, citizen demand for access to health care has produced a variety of government policies to provide either universal health insurance or government-subsidized health services. According to public opinion polls, the same majority preference for universal health coverage that produced such programs elsewhere has existed in the United States for several decades.[15] But, unlike in other industrial democracies, since the administration of President Franklin Roosevelt in the 1930s, minority special interests have been able to manipulate the separation-of-powers system to block numerous attempts to enact universal health insurance.[16] Although separation of powers is supposed to impede only unwise policies, in the case of health insurance it has helped produce the most complex and expensive system in the world, one that leaves approximately 44 million Americans without health coverage and many others inadequately covered.[17] But in 1994, the opponents of change again manned the roadblocks of the separation-of-powers system to frustrate President Clinton's attempt to provide much-needed reform.[18]

I could cite numerous other examples of the separation of powers impeding government responsiveness to majority preferences. The blockage of civil rights legislation by a minority of southern congressmen in the 1940s, 1950s, and 1960s; the National Rifle Association's continuing obstruction of reasonable gun-control legislation; the failure to enact meaningful campaign finance reform; the decade-long delay in enacting a minimal family-leave policy; and the inability to face up to financing Medicare and Social Security adequately are just a few. The inherent bias of the separation-of-powers structure against majorities supporting change inhibits government responsiveness to serious problems and citizen concerns. Given this system, it is not surprising that most Americans have less and less confidence in governmental institutions. The perception that "those politicians in Washington can't seem to get anything done" reflects an understanding of the inherent unresponsiveness of government. Americans need to understand that this unresponsiveness is built into the separation-of-powers structure.

Governmental unresponsiveness is most often associated with periods of divided government, but the separation-of-powers system places roadblocks in the way of policy innovation even when a single party controls both branches of government. In the past, the Jeffersonian model was a means of sometimes overcoming institutional division to enact progressive policies. In more recent years, the weakening of political party ties has undermined any president's ability to gain support even from congressional members of his own party. In the late 1970s President Jimmy Carter discovered that substantial Democratic Party majorities in both houses of Congress were not enough to enact his legislative agenda, including his major proposal for a comprehensive energy policy. The opposition of Democrats in Congress blocked many of his initiatives, sealing the reputation for weakness and incompetence that brought about Carter's defeat in the 1980 presidential election. When Bill Clinton assumed the presidency in 1993, after twelve years of divided government, many observers expected that a more politically savvy president would be able to mobilize congressional Democrats to carry out his electoral mandate. Soon after taking office, Clinton found this was not to be the case. An early flap over his signing of an executive order allowing homosexuals to serve in the military signaled what was to come. A powerful Democratic senator, Sam Nunn of Georgia, used his position as chairman of the Armed Services Committee to force Clinton to rescind his order and accept a compromise policy more in line with Nunn's views.[19] Nunn was able and willing to defy openly and publicly his own party's president because his own reelection from Georgia was in no way dependent on Clinton's success or failure as president. Nunn, who seemed to have his own presidential ambitions at the time, used the homosexual ban to send the president a message that Nunn was an independent power with whom Clinton would have to deal.

Nunn's message was only the first of several that Clinton would receive in his first months in office. Several were sent in the process of enacting his first major piece of legislation, a budget that would provide economic measures to reduce the deficit and stimulate the economy, as he had promised during the campaign. Early in consideration of the measure, the entire portion of the plan aimed at stimulating the economy had to be withdrawn because of a Republican filibuster in the Senate.[20] A fine example of the antimajoritarian logic implicit in the separation of powers, Senate filibusters allow only forty-one of one hundred senators to block the passage of legislation by preventing a vote. After the Republicans forced withdrawal of the job-creation portion of his package, Clinton had to battle with congressional Democrats because many of them insisted on protection of constituency special interests in exchange for their votes. Clinton found that most of his fellow Democrats cared little about the promises he had made to the country as a whole or about the success of his presidency, but focused mainly on how the legislation would affect their constituencies and the special interests that funded their campaigns.[21] Crucial opposition came from Senator David Boren of Oklahoma, a powerful member of the Senate Finance Committee, which had jurisdiction over the budget's tax proposals. Boren opposed a BTU tax (a kind of sales tax on energy usage that had been proposed to reduce the budget deficit) because he believed it would hurt his state's oil producers. Even after the administration withdrew the BTU tax, Boren continued to oppose the budget plan, demanding further concessions, and along with a few other key Democrats, created a key obstacle to its passage.[22] Eventually, the budget bill, substantially watered down in response to congressional demands, passed in the House by a margin of one vote and in the Senate only after Vice-President Gore cast a tie-breaking vote. This razor-thin victory would prove crucial to the nation's economy in the 1990s as the budget balancing measures enacted so narrowly in 1993 would contribute substantially to the economic prosperity in the latter part of the decade. What would have happened to the economy, and Clinton's central campaign promise, had there been one more no vote in either the House or the Senate? The separation-of-powers system almost prevented the Clinton administration from responding, even in the attenuated form of the 1993 budget legislation, to its central mandate from the voters — fix the economy.

After reviving the economy, reform of the American health-care system had been the second major theme of Clinton's 1992 campaign. In all his campaign speeches, Clinton had denounced the existing system for its failure to insure more than 30 million Americans and for its uncontrollable and escalating costs. He promised, if elected, to introduce legislation to create a system of universal health insurance that would guarantee health care for all and reduce health-care costs. When he unveiled his plan to the nation in September 1993, he was responding to clear and strong public demand that something be done to assure health care for all. Public opinion polls at the time showed strong support for his plan, and most knowledgeable observers expected that the time had finally come for enactment of universal health insurance in America.[23] But like other presidents before him, Clinton soon found the veto points embedded in the constitutional system insurmountable barriers to reforming the health-care system.

Accounts of the defeat of Clinton's health-care plan in 1994 identify a multitude of causes for the plan's failure. Strong interest-group opposition, the plan's complexity, administration mistakes in drawing up and introducing the plan, the ambivalence of public opinion, and even Hillary Clinton's prominent role are some of the reasons given for its defeat. All certainly contributed, but the political incentives existing within the separation-of-powers structure enhanced the effect of each and made building majority support for any kind of reform nearly impossible. Given the weakness of party ties and the autonomy of individual members of Congress and their ability to demand attention to even the narrowest of special-interest concerns in exchange for their votes, the passage of complex legislation such as the health-care bill, which affected so many interests, turned out to be impossible. As was the case in the flaps over homosexuals serving in the military and the budget bill the previous year, the actions of a single legislator proved critical to the health-care bill's defeat. In this case, the legislator was not a powerful senator like Sam Nunn or David Boren but a little-known member of the House of Representatives, Democratic Congressman Jim Cooper of Tennessee.[24]

Since being elected to the House in 1982, Cooper had served on the Health Subcommittee of the House Energy and Commerce Committee, where he developed a reputation for expertise on health issues. Clinton's health-care plan would have to pass the Energy and Commerce Committee if it were to advance through the legislative process, but it soon encountered trouble because of Cooper's opposition. Even before the September 1993 announcement of the Clinton plan, White House staff and Clinton himself had tried to gain Cooper's support, but to no avail. Complicating the discussions were Cooper's ties to the hospital and health insurance industries, which were providing contributions to his planned 1994 Senate campaign. At one point, when a supporter of the Clinton plan suggested to Cooper that his opposition might hurt his campaign for the Senate, Cooper pointedly disagreed, claiming the success or failure of Clinton's health-care plan was irrelevant to his Senate race.[25]

Early in the process Cooper raised objections to the Clinton plan's mandate that all employers provide health insurance, a provision essential if health insurance were to be truly universal, and he offered an alternative that fell short of insuring all Americans. During the winter of 1993 and into the spring of 1994, as the Clinton plan bogged down in the legislative process, Cooper's alternative plan gained media attention and began to undercut seriously the Clinton plan's support among other congressional Democrats. Although Cooper spoke of forming a bipartisan alliance around his alternative, congressional Republicans, seeing an opportunity to embarrass Clinton with a total defeat of health-care reform, refused to compromise. In the end, the Clinton plan, facing solid Republican opposition and unable to gain the votes of a few Democrats like Jim Cooper, was defeated in the House Energy and Commerce Committee in September 1994. Two months later, the Republicans took advantage of Clinton's unpopularity, linked to the failure to deliver on his promised health-care reform, to capture majority control of both houses of Congress for the first time in forty years.

One victim of the Republican onslaught was Jim Cooper of Tennessee, defeated decisively in his Senate race.

The 1994 midterm election, bringing Republican majorities to both the Senate and the House of Representatives, returned divided government to Washington. The Republican victory was as decisive as it was unexpected, giving the party a strong twenty-eight-seat advantage over the Democrats in the House and a four-seat advantage in the Senate. In view of this victory, Republicans interpreted the election as a mandate to carry out their "Contract with America." Although Republican congressional leaders attempted to carry out a conservative legislative agenda in response to the electorate that had brought them to power, they soon were frustrated, as Clinton had been in his first two years, because the president used his power to block their agenda. At the same time, after his failure to pass health-care reform, any hope that Clinton might be able to advance the agenda he had campaigned on in 1992 was dashed in the face of the Republican majorities. *Gridlock* was once again the predominant term used to describe national policymaking.

The faceoff between president and Congress brought about a crisis at the end of 1995 — a crisis following directly from the logic of the separation of powers. The incumbents of the two branches, each grounding its position in the popular legitimacy obtained from the electorate in separate elections, could not reach agreement on a budget. After a year of wrangling, the crisis came to a head in mid-November when the president vetoed a routine bill to increase the country's debt limit, to which the Republicans had attached amendments cutting spending on a number of programs. Clinton objected especially to increases in Medicare premiums and environmental spending cuts that he characterized as "an overall back-door effort by the Congressional Republicans to impose their priorities on our nation." In response, Speaker of the House Newt Gingrich insisted that the Republicans' position reflected their electoral mandate: "We were elected to change politics as usual...to get rid of all the phony promises and the phony excuses and to be honest with the American people."[26] Given the logic of the separation of powers, both Clinton and Gingrich could claim democratic legitimacy for their positions, but the consequences were a stalemate that produced one of the more embarrassing episodes in recent American history.

Because his veto denied the federal government the authority to borrow the money needed for its operations, Clinton was required to shut down "nonessential" government operations and lay off millions of federal employees. As an incredulous world watched, the government of the largest and wealthiest industrial democracy was paralyzed. This first shutdown would be followed by another, so between mid-November and early January, federal government operations were closed for nearly four weeks. Millions of federal workers went without paychecks during the Christmas holiday season, and millions of Americans had their benefits and services delayed.[27] Eventually, in the face of adverse public opin-

The partial shutdown of the federal government in late 1995 is reflected in the temporary closure of the Lincoln Memorial. (AP/Wide World Photos)

ion polls, the Republicans backed down from their position and a compromise was reached. Later the Republicans claimed that the disapproval they received for the shutdown was more a consequence of an effective White House public relations strategy than a fair assessment of who was to blame for the crisis.[28] They argued that their budget proposals were reasonable and that the president had refused to negotiate in good faith and had precipitated a crisis over what was a very modest difference in the rate of growth of Medicare expenditures.[29] Determining who in fact was accountable for the shutdown, as the Republicans discovered, was not easy when both they and the president shared decision-making power. That the public may have assigned blame incorrectly, as the Republicans claimed, demonstrates a consequence of how the separation of powers not only impedes responsiveness but also muddles accountability.

Accountability

The accountability of elected officials to those they represent is crucial to *representative* democracy. The famous democratic theorist Jean-Jacques Rousseau did not believe people could rule themselves through representatives because he did not trust representatives to make laws in their constituents' interests rather than in their own. Proponents of representative democracy held that Rousseau's distrust of representatives could be overcome if elected officials were required to face the electorate at regular intervals. At election time, the represented would be able to review the governmental record of their representatives and decide whether they had been well served. Between elections, elected officials would exercise their duties responsibly because they would know they would be accountable to their constituents for their performance at the next election. This system of accountability of representatives to the represented means citizens must be able to evaluate the performance of elected officials: those who have performed well will be reelected; those who have done poorly will be rejected.

The American separation-of-powers system hopelessly muddles the ability of citizens to hold their representatives accountable. Under the system, the president and Congress share responsibility for public policy and governmental performance, but they are held accountable separately. At election time, not only must citizens form a judgment about governmental performance (already a challenging task for most of us), but they must also sort out responsibility for that performance between the president and Congress (and between the House of Representatives and the Senate!). Determining this responsibility is in itself a monumental task — one that would require hours of research on separate issues — but it is made impossible by the way incumbents of both branches distort their records. The president and members of Congress routinely take credit for governmental successes while blaming the other branch for any failures.

This accountability problem is compounded during periods when the political parties divide control of the branches, as they did between 1981 and 1992. During that period, most Americans were clearly dissatisfied with how the government was handling many problems in our society. Annual governmental deficits raised the national debt to its highest peacetime levels. Government regulators failed to prevent bankruptcies of thousands of savings-and-loan associations, leaving taxpayers with a huge bailout bill. Government failed to deal adequately with such social problems as homelessness, violent crime, and ineffective schools. Any citizen dissatisfied with government performance in any of these areas and wishing to punish the responsible elected officials at election time, as the theory of representative democracy says should be done, would be frustrated.

The citizen's first accountability problem in the 1984, 1988, and 1992 elections was the difficulty in evaluating candidates' claims about their own performance. In all these elections, the Republican presidential candidates, Ronald Reagan and George Bush, blamed the Democratic majorities in Congress for problems such as large government deficits. In "running against" Congress, the Republicans adopted an obvious and often utilized strategy for an incumbent president in a period of divided government, one the Democrats had employed, for example, in the 1948 election, when Harry Truman campaigned against a "do nothing" Congress. Because Congress does share in budgetary policymaking, Reagan and Bush could persuasively argue that voters should not hold them accountable for the failure to control deficits. Instead, they asked voters to support them on the basis of policy successes, conveniently ignoring the fact that Congress had shared

also in making these policies. For example, in the fall of 1991, in a series of public appearances intended to test themes for his 1992 reelection campaign, George
Bush blamed Congress for "blocking his domestic programs," even though most
observers faulted him for not having a domestic agenda, and he claimed credit
for legislation such as the Clean Air Act, even though it had been largely a
congressional initiative.[30]

Meanwhile, Democratic congressional incumbents also sought to avoid responsibility when running for reelection.[31] They either blamed deficits or the
savings-and-loan mess on the Republican administration or claimed that, whatever the collective congressional responsibility for these problems, they *individually* had not contributed to them. Given the way the separation-of-powers
system muddles responsibility for policy, assessing the truth of such claims would
be nearly impossible for even the most conscientious citizen. Not surprisingly,
despite widespread dissatisfaction with Congress as a whole and despite growing uneasiness about many domestic issues since 1981, incumbent members of
Congress are usually reelected.[32]

If both branches of government share responsibility for policy, why shouldn't
a citizen avoid the nearly impossible task of sorting out responsibility for policy
failures and still hold officials accountable by simply voting against incumbents
in both branches at once? Such a solution might be reasonable if members of
the same political party controlled both Congress and the presidency, but when
control is divided between the parties, this approach places a dissatisfied citizen in an absurd position. A majority of citizens voting against incumbents in
both branches would punish a party's control of one branch by rewarding it with
control of the other. The logic of separation of powers — shared responsibility
for policy along with accountability through separate elections — makes holding
officials accountable for policy failure extremely difficult, if not impossible.

The separation of powers renders a muddled message, as well, when voters
seek to acknowledge policymakers' accountability for success. On the strength
of a robust economy, in 1996 Clinton handily won reelection. One might see
a Democratic presidential victory as a strong voter endorsement for the policies Clinton had pursued during the previous four years, had the Republican
majorities in both House and Senate not been returned at the same time. At
the same time Clinton was rewarded with another term, voters returned to the
other branch those who had opposed nearly all his policy initiatives during the
previous four years. Republicans had solidly opposed, for example, the Clinton
economic and budget package, including a tax increase, that many observers credited with sustaining the strong economic recovery that was the basis for Clinton's
popularity. Just as congressional Democrats had done for many years, Republicans benefited from the power of incumbency to solidify their 1994 capture of
congressional majorities, even as the voters were rewarding Clinton for his economic record. Although less than a year earlier, at the time of the government

shutdown, opinion polls had shown that voters were fed up with gridlock (and had even blamed the Republicans), the election outcome set the stage for more gridlock. Most Republican candidates in individual congressional races managed to distance themselves from the unpopular Speaker of the House and escape responsibility for "extreme" Republican leadership policies.[33]

In 1998 public opinion polls throughout the year showed Americans frustrated with Republican efforts to impeach President Clinton over the Monica Lewinsky matter. The November elections offered an opportunity to hold them accountable for this frustration, and in a marked reversal of the normal historic pattern in "off year" elections, the Republicans lost a substantial number of House seats and failed to gain seats in the Senate. Despite this reversal, the lame-duck Republican Congress proceeded to impeach Clinton and the Senate went ahead to try (and eventually acquit) him in early 1999, clearly ignoring popular will. As constitutional scholar Kathleen Sullivan has pointed out, the behavior of Congress in Clinton's impeachment turned Madison's constitutional theory on its head.[34] Instead of level-headed representatives cooling the passions of a wild democratic majority, the American people in 1998 were the level-headed ones who signaled to their passionate and partisan representatives not to pursue an unnecessary impeachment effort. Unfortunately, however, the constitutional system insulated those representatives from accountability to the electorate's wisdom, leaving the country bogged down for several months in a protracted impeachment process. Congress failed to hold Clinton accountable for his misdeeds by even a censure resolution, while Clinton's fixed and final, lame-duck presidential term insulated him from political accountability had the electorate wished to punish him through the ballot box.

Along with providing citizens an opportunity to punish their representatives for policy failures and reward them for policy successes, accountability is supposed to assure more responsible behavior from representatives between elections. The 1980s American experience with the savings-and-loan crisis and the 1990s failure to address future entitlement costs illustrate how the separation of powers undermines this aspect of accountability.

Among the most significant governmental failures of the past several decades was the savings-and-loan (S&L) scandal of the 1980s. Since the 1930s most savings-and-loan institutions, which traditionally specialized in providing home mortgages, were insured through a government insurance agency called the Federal Savings and Loan Insurance Corporation (FSLIC). Like its counterpart in banking, the Federal Deposit Insurance Corporation (FDIC), the FSLIC was intended to assure depositors of the safety of their deposits by guaranteeing them with the full faith and credit of the U.S. government. If a savings-and-loan institution became insolvent, the FSLIC insurance fund would pay to every depositor the full value of his or her deposit up to a set amount ($100,000 in the 1980s). The purpose of this system was to create consumer confidence in S&Ls and prevent disastrous "runs" on these institutions, as had occurred with the banks in the 1930s. Backing up this system was careful FSLIC regulation of the industry to assure that S&Ls made prudent loans and concentrated primarily on providing mortgages to home buyers. For fifty years, this system worked very well, supporting a successful industry. In the 1980s, however, both Republican President Reagan and the Democratic Congress supported legislation easing regulation of savings and loans while maintaining the commitment to depositors.[35] Then both parties turned a blind eye as unscrupulous investors took advantage of the new looser regulations to burden S&Ls with risky loans, usually in areas other than the S&Ls' traditional business of home-mortgage financing. When these loans went bad in the late 1980s, Congress was forced to pass legislation bailing out the industry, saddling taxpayers with a bill of approximately $500 billion to be paid over the next decade. Voters were unable to hold either political party accountable for this massive governmental failure because, through the shared power in the separation-of-powers system, both were equally responsible for it, and both parties conspired to keep the issue out of the 1988 and 1992 presidential elections.[36] The muddling of accountability permitted by the separation of powers allowed officials in both branches to act irresponsibly in their oversight of the S&L industry. All knew that citizens would never be able to hold any one branch or party responsible for the S&L mess because both were culpable.

Just as both parties were jointly to blame for the S&L debacle, both were responsible for the rising government debt of the 1980s and 1990s. Not surprisingly, with joint culpability, both parties have found the separation of powers helpful in avoiding accountability for the long-term threat of growing entitlement costs. The alarming rise in government budget deficits (the difference between annual government revenues and annual government spending) beginning in the early 1980s was a combined result of large tax-rate cuts in 1981 without comparable spending cuts and the growing cost of large entitlement programs, such as Medicare and Social Security. Experts acknowledged that controlling the deficit required a combination of tax increases and modest reductions in entitlement benefits.[37] Yet for many years, the separation of powers stalled agreement on these policy choices. Only when the danger of enormous debt far into the future helped to undermine the economy, contributing to the recession of the early 1990s, did Congress and the president begin to act, passing budget agreements in 1990, 1993, and 1997, that included both the modest tax increases and restraint on the growth of government spending economists had been recommending to bring the budget under control. These measures combined with the booming economy of the late 1990s have balanced the federal budget and produced the first federal budget surplus since 1969. This recent success, however, will be fleeting unless long-term policy decisions are made to address Social Security and Medicare spending, which are set to explode when the "baby boom" generation becomes eligible for benefits early in the twenty-first century.

Although projections of future deficits resulting from growing entitlement costs are clear, both parties have avoided developing concrete proposals to address this longer-range and more intractable problem. Both Republicans and Democrats seem caught up in tactics aimed at avoiding any blame for reducing entitlement benefits and placing blame for future shortfalls on the other party. The Republican tactic is to push unrealistic proposals to "privatize" Social Security and Medicare that a Democratic president would be sure to veto.[38] The Democratic tactic is to characterize even the most modest and reasonable cuts in entitlement benefits as attempts to eliminate popular programs. This is what Republicans accused Clinton of doing during the 1995 budget crisis, and Democratic campaign commercials in the 1996 election explicitly accused Republicans of wanting to cut Medicare and Social Security. In early 1999 the Medicare Commission, jointly appointed by the president and Congress to bridge the differences between the branches, disbanded without agreeing on a strategy for keeping Medicare solvent.[39] As different parties control the different branches, each can point the finger at the other for not addressing the problem while blocking any attempt to address it realistically. Given this failure of accountability, any serious effort to deal with future entitlement growth, which would require only modest sacrifice now, may be delayed until a crisis point is reached. Then, as in the S&L affair, neither party will be held accountable because both, from the vantage point of their respective branches, will have been to blame.

The Parliamentary Alternative

If the separation of powers inhibits governmental responsiveness to majorities and muddles accountability, achieving these democratic values would require concentration of policymaking power in a single institution, or what political scientists call unified government. In 1789 the Founders associated unified government with tyranny because the existing examples of such governments, usually ones that concentrated power in the monarchy, were clearly authoritarian regimes. Since the eighteenth century, however, a democratic variant of unified government was devised as European democrats came to power in their countries. This democratic form of unified government, called a *parliamentary system,* is the most widespread form of democratic government in the world. Among the world's most industrially advanced democracies, the United States is the only one with a separation-of-powers system rather than a parliamentary system.[40] The Founders' attempt to craft the world's first large-scale representative democracy could not draw on experience with mass-based political parties and party organized legislatures that brought about the evolution of parliamentary systems in the nineteenth century in Europe. Had they had the opportunity to consider this alternative in 1787, they might have opted for a parliamentary structure.[41] Unlike the authors of our Constitution, modern Americans are able to consider a democratic alternative to our separation-of-powers system and consider whether it might provide better opportunities to achieve responsive and account-able government. In doing so, we would be following the recommendation of Gouverneur Morris "to take counsel from experience," in this case the experience of parliamentary democracies, and identify ways to improve our constitutional structure.

In a parliamentary system, both executive and legislative powers are concentrated in a "government" composed of members of whichever party or coalition of parties has a majority in a democratically elected legislature (or parliament). This government consists of a prime minister, usually the leader of the legislative majority party, and a cabinet that the prime minister selects from among her or his legislative majority. Cabinet ministers head the various government executive departments (or ministries, as they are usually called) and, under the direction of the prime minister, supervise the day-to-day operation of the government bureaucracy. In exercising their executive roles, the prime minister and cabinet function much like the president and the cabinet in the American system except that they are simultaneously elected representatives in the legislature, a dual status that is constitutionally prohibited in our separation-of-powers system.

As legislative leader, the parliamentary government is responsible for initiating and passing all legislation. Its legislative proposals are discussed, debated, and always strongly criticized by the legislative opposition, but, with rare exception, its proposals are also enacted into law. The government's legislative program is passed because it can count on party discipline from the members of its party or coalition, who possess the majority of votes in the legislature. Thus, when a prime minister is elected to power in a parliamentary system, he or she can be certain to be able to enact the governmental agenda promised to the voters during the election campaign. Political parties play a much more powerful and important role in a parliamentary system than we are accustomed to in the United States. In the legislature, whether in the majority or in opposition, individual legislators in a parliamentary system follow the directions of their party leaders when voting on legislation. They must do so because the party leaders control their ability to run under the party label at election time. This is a major difference from the American system of primary elections, which has largely eliminated the ability of party leaders to control who runs under a party label. In a parliamentary system, any legislator who votes against the leadership can be sure to find someone chosen in his or her place for the next election. In addition, advancement to positions of governmental power, such as a cabinet post, is under the control of party leaders, providing an additional incentive for ambitious legislators to submit to party discipline.

Political parties are also more closely associated with a consistent set of public policy positions in most parliamentary systems than in the United States. Within the American Republican and Democratic parties, one finds officeholders advocating a wide variety of specific policy positions. They can do so because they are elected on the basis of their individual legislative records, not the collective record of their political party. In a parliamentary system, it is this collective record that a party member must defend when running for election; therefore, policy differences usually exist between parties, not within them. Because of the sharper definition of what a party stands for and because parties have the power to enact their promises when elected, voters in a parliamentary system focus much more on party than on any other factor at election time. National legislative elections are contests between political parties, each presenting its party program and seeking control of government to carry it out. This is very different from American elections, which involve contests between hundreds of individual legislative candidates who run on individual policy platforms, and who can promise no more than to be advocates for these policies within the complex separation-of-powers system. When a political party wins an election in a parliamentary system, it and its leader, the prime minister, control all the governmental levers of power to enact their legislative mandate. Responsiveness in carrying out the will of the electoral majority is obviously not a problem. But what about accountability? Accustomed as we are to the checks inherent in the separation of powers, Americans are apt to regard the awesome power of a parliamentary prime minister with alarm. What is to prevent such a powerful individual from using this power to pursue an undemocratic agenda? How can one be sure that a prime minister, once in office, will not act tyrannically?

The appearance of unrestrained prime ministerial power does not coincide with the reality of the political position of prime ministers in most parliamentary systems. Prime ministers are constrained and held democratically accountable in their exercise of power in three ways. First, their political parties hold them accountable. Although leaders can count on discipline from the members of their party in the legislature, these same members can collectively remove the prime minister if they become dissatisfied with his or her leadership. This happened to British Prime Minister Margaret Thatcher in 1990 when members of her Conservative Party forced her to resign because they feared her leadership would result in a defeat for the party at the next election. Second, a prime minister can lose the parliamentary majority if enough members of that majority defect to the opposition. This can come about either by some members of the prime minister's own party defecting or, in the case of a multiparty governing coalition (given party discipline, this is the more likely scenario), by one of the coalition parties withdrawing its support. Finally, and most important, citizens hold prime ministers and their governments accountable in parliamentary systems. Although they possess unified control of government while in power, prime ministers know that eventually, at the next election, they will need to defend their exercise of power to the voters. Unlike the separation-of-powers system, the parliamentary system offers no possibility of deflecting responsibility for governmental performance onto another branch of government or the opposition party. Consequently, in making every governmental decision, prime ministers and their governments must be sensitive to how these decisions will affect those who will decide at the next election whether the government should continue in power.

The contrast between how a parliamentary system and the American separation-of-powers system can hold a head of government accountable for her behavior was revealed in the controversy over President Bill Clinton's impeachment. Removing an individual prime minister from office, as the case of Margaret Thatcher shows, is easier and carries with it less constitutional significance than removal of an American president. Prime ministers are merely heads of government and do not carry with them the quasi-monarchical character of a president who also is head of state. Moreover, although prime ministers are important political leaders who tend to dominate their governments and, in the current era of highly personalized campaigning and media coverage, the primary symbol of governmental power, they remain simply leaders of a collective leadership comprised of their cabinet and party majority in parliament. While in most parliamentary systems modern prime ministers are more than "first among equals," their power derives from the collective leadership that backs them up. Therefore, if an individual prime minister is removed, for whatever reason, between elections, the collective party leadership remains in power, including the programs and policies the electorate endorsed in the last election. How different from the act of removing an American president! Since a president is elected separately from Congress and embodies alone (albeit in combination with the vice-president) the will of those voters who elected him, removing a president between elections means a reversal of the previous presidential election. In a democracy, this is an awesome decision that cannot be made easily.

The Founders understood how serious it would be to remove a president in the system they had devised, causing them to ponder long how it would be accomplished. The solution they came up with was impeachment based on a procedure developed in 18th century Britain to remove King's ministers.[42] In an era prior to the development of the parliamentary system, the King appointed government ministers whom parliament could remove only through impeachment and proof of "high crimes and misdemeanors." The process was a quasi-judicial one, although parliaments of the era often abused it to remove officials on political grounds. As the practice of the parliamentary majority appointing ministers evolved in the nineteenth century, impeachment was no longer needed. Everyone understood that all ministers, including the prime ministers, served only so long as they had the confidence of a parliamentary majority; no legal process proving "guilt" was required to be rid of them.

Impeachment and conviction in a Senate trial for treason, bribery, or a "high crime and misdemeanor" remains, however, the only means of removing American presidents between elections. This quasi-legal standard, to be administered in the quasi-judicial proceeding of a Senate trial, created the dilemma that Congress wrestled with and that distracted the country through most of 1998. While many could agree that President Clinton's conduct was reprehensible, demeaning of his office, and immoral (as even his strongest defenders said), the constitutional standard required that proof be offered that his actions constituted high crimes and misdemeanors. In the end, a majority of senators voted that they did not. Yet was his continuance in office good for the country and would he be able to exercise effective political leadership for the balance of his term?

The Advantages of Unified Government

In a parliamentary system, dealing with a prime minister found to have been involved in conduct comparable to Clinton's would have occurred on a basis more suitable to the nature of his transgressions. More appropriate political judgments, rather than quasi-legal judgments, would have governed the impeachment process. The issue would not have revolved around a determination of Clinton's individual guilt or innocence, but, for a democratic leader, appropriate considerations of his accountability to and ability to be responsive to those who had elected him, irrespective of legally established guilt.[43] His own party would have had to make a judgment regarding his political viability in light of the revelations of his tawdry sexual liaison and his attempt to cover it up. In making this judgment, party members would have needed to evaluate how his presence or absence would affect the furtherance of their political program. In doing so, they would be most sensitive to the electorate's reaction and how its decision would affect the party's future at the ballot box. What would have been the fate of a Prime Minister Clinton is impossible to predict, but it would have been determined cleanly, definitively, and much more quickly in a parliamentary system. The months of preoccupation and distraction from other issues that Clinton's impeachment engendered would not have occurred. And in the end, he would have been held accountable to those most important in this situation — the American people.

In more than just the removal of a head of government, the experience of parliamentary systems seems superior to our separation-of-powers system in providing both responsiveness and accountability.[44] Elections produce mandates that those elected have the power to carry out. Voters can select through their ballots which party's policy proposals they wish carried out and can actually expect them to be implemented. They can also hold governments accountable. Citizens in a parliamentary system are able to evaluate clearly and unambiguously whether the government has served them well or poorly. In making this evaluation, they are assisted by the political opposition party or parties, which naturally seek to expose the governing party's failures and offer themselves as an alternative. In such a system, citizens can use their strongest tool — elections — much more effectively than is possible under a separation-of-powers system. The ambiguity, confusion, and obfuscation of who is and is not responsible for government action is not possible in a unified government system.

While most critics of the separation-of-powers system would be delighted if the United States adopted a parliamentary form of government, few expect Americans would quickly embrace such a dramatic reform. Nevertheless, reformers believe that changes could be made in operating the separation-of-powers system that, while falling short of creating a true parliamentary system, could introduce quasi-parliamentary features. These reforms would permit more unified government, reviving, at the least, the possibility of the Jeffersonian model of government. In fact, most reform advocates hope that their proposals would go beyond the Jeffersonian model and assure permanent and continuing unified government.

Strengthening political parties is central to most calls for reform of the separation of powers. In both the parliamentary system and the Jeffersonian model, political parties support the effective operation of the governmental structure. Unfortunately, in 1789, the American Founders did not understand the critical role of political parties in organizing democratic government and assuring its responsiveness and effectiveness. They equated party (a word they used interchangeably with "faction") with the small personal cliques surrounding individual leaders in the British Parliament. They could not have foreseen how, as parliamentary systems were organized in Europe in the late nineteenth century, party leaders would make them the linchpin of responsible and effective democratic government. Had the Founders been able to observe the effective marriage of party politics with a unified parliamentary system, they might have decided not to separate the executive and the legislature.[45] As we have seen in the Jeffersonian model, before the ink was dry on the Constitution, they were using parties to bridge the separation between president and Congress.

Understanding this need for strong parties, many of America's most distinguished political scientists have been leading advocates of reforming and strengthening political parties.[46] In 1950, the American Political Science Association went so far as to publish an official report advocating various measures to strengthen parties.[47] If parties can be revived as strong, disciplined, and coherent political organizations, according to reformers, the separate branches can act in a unified manner, and at election time voters can both hold the governing party accountable and make clear choices between the parties. To accomplish this, party organizations would have to be given greater control over party nominations through elimination of the party primary. Party discipline would have to be imposed on legislators so that legislative parties could take unified, consistent stands on legislation. And parties would need to differentiate themselves clearly on policy issues so that voters could make a clear choice between them.

Such proposals for a "more responsible two-party system" (the title of the 1950 American Political Science Association report) have been forcefully made for many years without much impact. In fact, American political parties seem to grow steadily weaker in spite of the cries of knowledgeable reformers. Waiting for parties to reform themselves as a way to bridge the gap between the constitutionally separated branches has produced (as waiting does in Samuel Beckett's play *Waiting for Godot*) much debate and discussion but no result. It seems the separation-of-powers structure itself, although needful of strong parties to operate effectively and democratically, is a barrier to their development. As long as the president and individual members of Congress are elected independently of one another, they will seek to establish independent political bases organized around their individual political performances. Although strong and organized parties would make them more effective collectively, they would also make each individual accountable, as we have seen, for collective outcomes. Rather than risk having to answer for these collective outcomes, individual politicians prefer to go it alone and resist efforts to strengthen parties. In the past decade, a number of prominent Americans and political scientists have begun to argue forcefully for direct constitutional reform as the way to address the weakness of parties.[48] They believe parties cannot become more responsible until the electoral and institutional context in which parties operate encourages them in that direction.

Because divided government results from ticket splitting — voters choosing a president of one party and congressional representatives of another — several reform proposals seek to limit or prevent this practice. One approach to creating more coherent governing parties would be simply to prohibit ticket splitting and require the presidential candidate and members of his party running for Congress to run on a team slate. This reform would reduce the possibility of divided government because voters would choose simultaneously a president and their congressional representative with a single vote, virtually assuring the winning president of a majority in the House and probably one in the Senate. More important, it would link the political fates of all members of Congress to their party's presidential candidate. Individual congressional candidates would have to convince voters to select not only themselves but also their party's presidential candidate. Such a reform would link a representative's election to the success or failure of the party's presidential candidate as well as his or her individual voting record.

Despite its attraction for assuring more coherent government, team tickets would meet with resistance from voters, who value their traditional right to make independent choices for president and Congress, and from incumbent members of Congress, who prefer to run on their own records in the current system.[49] Since the support of Congress and voters would be needed to pass a constitutional amendment for such a reform, it is not likely to be adopted. Two alternative reforms might encourage voters not to split their tickets without prohibiting them from doing so.

One would be simply to restore the option of straight-party-ticket voting that no longer exists in thirty-one of the fifty states. In all states, providing separate party slates for all federal offices as a voting option might reduce ticket splitting. A second reform would be to hold the election for Congress, in presidential election years, two weeks after the presidential election. This would give the newly elected president a chance to appeal to those voters who just elected him to support members of his party for Congress. A system along these lines in France did help President François Mitterrand obtain legislative control for his party after both the 1981 and 1988 presidential elections.[50] A more dramatic reform would ensure presidential control of Congress by giving the president-elect's party automatic bonus seats to provide majorities in both houses. In addition to these electoral reforms, reformers suggest a number of changes in the relations between the separate branches to create quasi-parliamentary government.[51] One would be to amend the Constitution so that members of Congress could serve in the president's cabinet and head executive branch agencies. Another would require presidents periodically to submit to questions either before congressional committees or before the entire Congress, as happens in most parliamentary regimes. Some reformers also suggest that the president should have the power to dissolve Congress and call new congressional elections. This would allow a president to appeal directly to the people to elect new representatives if he thought members of Congress were an obstacle to enacting a coherent government program. The basic premise of all these proposals is that elements of parliamentary-style government can be introduced into the American constitutional structure that would retain the form of the separation of powers while instituting the reality of more unified government.

Objections to Unified Government

Americans are likely to be nervous about the reforms suggested in the previous section. The idea of institutional checks and balances is such a settled and familiar part of our constitutional history that many are likely to be worried about what we might lose in modifying the system. Even those who have been convinced that the reform could produce more responsive and accountable government still might argue that these benefits would be purchased at too high a cost. Separation of powers, even though it presents barriers to democracy, remains a useful deterrent to tyranny. Defenders of the separation of powers usually offer three arguments on its behalf: eliminating separation of powers runs the risks of increasing the likelihood of majority tyranny, losing the useful bias toward limited government inherent in the structure, and losing checks on the abuse of power.

The specter of majority tyranny was, of course, the primary rationale for the separation of powers from the beginning. But it is a rationale based on an unproven assumption: that majority tyranny is somehow a greater danger than minority tyranny.[52] The Founders, who were preoccupied with the former, set up a system that, as we have seen, actually facilitates the latter. If tyranny is the danger, instead of solving the problem, the separation of powers creates a system in which well-placed minorities can pursue their interests at the expense of other minorities or even the majority. A more productive way to avoid tyranny is to rely on the democratic ethos of citizens. As the noted political theorist Robert Dahl argues, "the protection of minority rights can be no stronger than the commitment of the majority of citizens to preserving the primary democratic rights of all citizens, to maintaining respect for their fellow citizens, and to avoiding the adverse consequences of harming a minority."[53] Also, American political history offers little evidence to support the Founders' fear of majority tyranny. Rather than a group united by a single-minded "passion or interest," majorities in American politics tend to be large coalitions representing diverse interests.[54] In a large and diverse country like the United States, even without institutional checks and balances, a governing majority will include many different groups with individuals holding overlapping memberships in many of them. In such a situation, building a majority consensus behind any policy measure will involve a process of accommodating diverse preferences and interests. James Madison realized this himself when he argued in *Federalist* No. 10 that the size and social diversity of the United States was the principal check against majority tyranny. Institutional checks and balances were only an "auxiliary precaution," but one that, I have argued, does not discriminate between tyrannical and benign majority preferences. In reforming the separation of powers as suggested above, majority rule in America can be facilitated without significant risk of majority tyranny.

Along with their concerns about majority tyranny, the Founders, being good classical liberals, were interested in limiting government. As shown earlier, their handiwork has succeeded in assuring an institutional bias in favor of limited government. Those introducing policies that will expand the role of government into a new area or activity, even when such policies are popular with a majority of citizens, are easily blocked. Realizing this, defenders of the separation of powers often accuse its critics of advocating more unified government merely as a way of promoting an activist ideological agenda.[55] This is probably true: contemporary liberals (not the classical kind) do believe a majority of citizens would support a more activist government if the restraints on political change inherent in the separation of powers were removed.

But why should one of the central issues of our time — activist versus limited government — be decided by the bias of our constitutional structure, rather than democratically through political debate, discussion, and competitive elections? Political conservatives who favor a smaller, less activist government should obtain it through open processes of political competition; they should persuade a democratic majority that such a government is in the majority's interest. Those who favor separation of powers because they support its bias toward limited government are supporting, just as the activist liberals are supporting, a particular constitutional structure because they believe it promotes their ideological agenda.

In the contemporary era, however, some conservatives have found the separation of powers to be an obstacle to their policy preferences. They have discovered that our institutional structure is biased not so much in favor of limited government as against innovation and change. Anyone wishing to expand the existing size and scope of government is at a disadvantage, but so is anyone who wishes to reduce government below the size it has reached. In the twentieth century, liberals did succeed, despite the separation of powers and employing the Jeffersonian model, to expand the responsibilities of the federal government (although, as argued earlier, not as much as has occurred in parliamentary democracies). Conservatives who came to power in the executive branch with the presidential elections of the 1980s and in the legislative branch in 1994 have found the separation of powers and divided government obstacles to their political agenda. Part of the preoccupation of many House Republicans, particularly the group first elected in 1994, with the attempt to impeach President Clinton in 1998 may have been tied to their frustration over how he blocked their political agenda. Liberals, paradoxically, have found Democratic control of the opposing branches useful for protecting established programs. If, as conservatives believe, there now exists a substantial majority in the country in favor of reducing the size of government, separation of powers is not currently a force in favor of more limited government but a structure that impedes a democratic movement on its behalf.

A third reason usually given in defense of the separation of powers is that it provides an institutional check on the abuse of power. Usually, proponents of this argument point to the important role Congress has played in investigating abuses of executive power in the past few decades. The Senate Watergate hearings, 1970s hearings investigating abuses in the FBI and the CIA, the Iran-*contra* hearings in the 1980s, and the hearings on Clinton administration campaign finance dealings are examples of a politically independent Congress looking into abuses of executive power.

I agree that a key cost in modifying the separation-of-powers system would be a reduction in the political independence of Congress in carrying out investigations such as the Watergate hearings. In evaluating this cost, one needs to weigh it against the benefits that would follow from a more responsive and accountable government. Also, one needs to consider how high the cost of the loss of institutional checks on abuse of power would actually be. Does the ability of the branches to investigate each other's activities justify, in itself, a separation-of-powers structure?

The first point that needs to be made in response to this question is that although the reforms suggested above do reduce *institutional* checks on abuse of power within each branch, they increase other kinds of checks on such abuses. In a more unified government, responsibility for monitoring governmental abuses would shift to the political opposition and the electorate as a whole. The party in opposition would have great incentive to be vigilant in looking for abuses because, once exposed, such abuses could be the basis for electoral defeat of the government and a return of the opposition to power. Since a governing party would have to take responsibility for abuses that occurred while it controlled the government, its members would have to take responsibility for any abuses of power during their tenure in office. In parliamentary systems, when incidents such as Watergate or Iran-*contra* occur, they produce governmental resignations and, often, new elections in which the electorate can pass judgment directly on the abuses that have occurred. In the United States, we rely instead on long-drawn-out hearings or judicial investigations in which the electorate is simply an observer. By the end of these investigations, responsibility for the abuses is usually unclear (not surprising, given the way the separation of powers muddles responsibility for government actions) and the resolution is obscured by complicated legal proceedings. As argued earlier in the case of Clinton's impeachment, a more unified government would shift responsibility for monitoring governmental abuse to the more democratic process of competition between government and opposition, followed by the voters' judgment.

Second, more unified government would not eliminate altogether the capacity for institutional checks on governmental abuse, especially congressional checks on executive power. Although a president would always have a supportive congressional majority under the reforms sketched above, Congress would still retain the capacity to look into abuses. In cases of serious abuse, one could reasonably expect even members of the president's own party to be concerned to investigate. Because they will be quite sensitive to the electoral repercussions of any scandal, members of a president's party will want to be seen on the right side of the issue, speaking out against abuse of power. In the Watergate affair, for example, members of President Nixon's own Republican Party convinced him to resign. In a unified government, members of a governing party would have added incentive to forestall their party's identification with scandal or governmental abuse. They would be concerned to act both within the party and in Congress to check abuses.

Finally, none of the reforms described above reduces the independence of the judiciary and its capacity to check abuse of power. Parliamentary systems do not customarily provide for the sort of independent judiciary with the power to review the constitutionality of governmental laws and actions that we have in the United States. But there is no reason why reforms to provide more policymaking coordination between the president and Congress would have to interfere with judicial independence. The current power of the U.S. Supreme Court derives from the life-long tenure of judges and widespread acceptance of the doctrine of judicial review. There is no reason why either would have to be modified if a more unified government system were adopted. In fact, recently, reformers in several countries with parliamentary systems, including Great Britain, have begun to advocate independent judiciaries on the American model. This is the one feature of our constitutional structure that seems exportable to our sister democracies in the industrial world!

DIVIDED GOVERNMENT AND the separation of powers challenge democracy by impeding responsiveness to legitimate majority interests and by muddling the accountability of representatives to citizens. The institutional checks in our constitutional structure offer many opportunities for minority interests to block needed

After the Senate Watergate hearings in 1974 seemed to threaten impeachment, President Richard Nixon resigned in a nationally televised address. (Archive Photos)

change and reform. The fact that politicians must share policymaking with those in other institutions permits them to blame others for policy failures and thereby escape accountability to the people. Stronger parties to bridge the responsibility gap between Congress and the president, the Jeffersonian formula for coping democratically with our institutions, would improve the situation, but efforts to strengthen the parties have not been successful and parties are growing steadily weaker. Both stronger parties and more democratic institutions would require fundamental constitutional revision in the direction of more unified government.

Unfortunately, democrats must realize that the sorts of constitutional reforms discussed in this chapter are not likely to be adopted easily. Among the barriers to progressive change built into our constitutional structure is a complex amendment process designed to impede change. In addition, two centuries of indoctrination concerning the "sanctity" of our constitutional arrangements have made most Americans reluctant even to consider changes, despite massive institutional failure. Although Americans seem less and less confident in the performance of their governmental institutions, they tend to want to blame the current occupants of those institutions, rather than institutional structure. Much public education will be needed to convince the American public that reconsideration, as intended by the Founders, of a portion of our constitutional arrangements — the separation of powers — might be the way to better and more democratic government.

THOUGHT QUESTIONS

1. The chapter argues that the separation-of-powers system reflects the outlook of the Protective Democracy model. Why? What about the other models? Analyze separation of powers from the perspective of each of the other models. From which perspectives can you develop arguments supportive of separation of powers and which suggest more support for a parliamentary system?

2. Suppose the Founders had adopted a parliamentary system; how would American history have been different? Pick a crucial moment from history and analyze how it might have been different had America had a parliamentary system. For example, how might Prime Minister Abraham Lincoln have handled the threatened secession of the southern states?

3. Suppose, having been persuaded by this chapter's argument, the American people amended the Constitution to create a parliamentary system; how might such a change affect the party system? Would we continue to have two dominant (Republican and Democratic) parties? Or would a multiparty system evolve? How would such a development impact responsiveness and accountability in an American parliamentary system?

4. A parliamentary system, according to this chapter, would be superior to separation of powers in achieving democratic accountability and responsiveness. But what other political values would you want to consider before adopting as momentous a constitutional change as proposed here? How would they be affected under each alternative system?

5. Political leaders in parliamentary systems, such as prime ministers, must have long experience in national government before rising to the leadership of their party and, hence, governmental power. In contrast, American presidents, because of the separation-of-powers system, can come to power with little or no experience in national government and politics. Dwight Eisenhower, Jimmy Carter, and Bill Clinton are examples of men whose first national elective office was president of the United States. What are the advantages and disadvantages of these alternative patterns of recruitment to national office?

SUGGESTIONS FOR FURTHER READING

Burns, James MacGregor. *The Deadlock of Democracy.* Englewood Cliffs, N.J.: Prentice Hall, 1963. A classic statement of the political consequences of separation of powers and how Americans have coped with them for the past two hundred years.

Fiorina, Morris. *Divided Government.* New York: Macmillan, 1991. A thorough analysis of why partisan division between the president and Congress has increased over the past four decades.

*Goldwin, Robert A., and Art Kaufman, eds. *Separation of Powers — Does It Still Work?* Washington, D.C.: American Enterprise Institute, 1986.

*Goldwin, Robert A., and William Schambra, eds. *How Democratic Is the Constitution?* Washington, D.C.: American Enterprise Institute, 1980. These two collections contain articles arguing various points of view on the extent to which the separation of powers and other aspects of the Constitution are democratic.

Johnson, Haynes, and David Broder. *The System: The American Way of Politics at the Breaking Point.* Boston: Little, Brown, 1996. Two of America's best journalists offer a blow-by-blow account of the defeat of Clinton's health-care proposal. The tale provides a close-up view of how the separation of powers works in practice to frustrate innovative and progressive policy.

*Jones, Charles O. *The Presidency in a Separated System.* Washington, D.C.: Brookings Institution, 1994.

*Jones, Charles O. *Separate but Equal Branches: Congress and the Presidency,* 2d ed. New York: Chatham House, 1999. In these two works, a renowned American government scholar defends the wisdom of the separation of powers.

Linz, Juan, and Arturo Valenzuela, eds. *The Failure of Presidential Democracy.* Vol. I. Baltimore: Johns Hopkins Press, 1994. Distinguished political scientists compare the performance of presidential (separation-of-powers) and parliamentary systems around the world and find parliamentary ones both more democratic and more stable. Linz's essay argues strongly that presidential democracies are prone to collapse and replacement by authoritarian governments.

*Mayhew, David. *Divided We Govern: Party Control, Lawmaking, and Investigations 1946–1990.* New Haven: Yale University Press, 1991. Mayhew argues that divided government has not made any difference for the enactment of "a standard kind of important legislation" (p. 4) and documents this claim with a thorough analysis of legislative enactments over the past fifty years. But he does not consider whether these enactments were responsive to democratic majorities; he ignores the accountability issue.

*Palazzolo, Daniel J. *Done Deal? The Politics of the 1997 Budget Agreement.* New York: Chatham House, 1999. A case study of legislative success under divided government.

Price, Don K. *The Unwritten Constitution.* Baton Rouge: Louisiana State University Press, 1983. Reform of the Constitution is unnecessary because of an "unwritten constitution that can be adapted by political bargaining to new needs and circumstances" (p. 149).

Robinson, Donald, ed. *Reforming American Government: The Bicentennial Papers of the Committee on the Constitutional System.* Boulder, Colo.: Westview Press, 1985. A collection of articles advocating various reforms to produce more unified government.

Sundquist, James L. *Constitutional Reform and Effective Government.* Washington, D.C.: Brookings Institution, 1986. Also two follow-up volumes published by Brookings: *Beyond Gridlock? Prospects for Governance in the Clinton Years and After,* 1993, and *Back to Gridlock? Governance in the Clinton Years,* 1995. A well-argued case for fundamental changes in the separation of powers, including an interesting history of the origins of the constitutional structure and the two-century debate it has engendered. The two follow-up volumes are based on conferences that examine Sundquist's arguments in the light of Clinton's first term.

*Presents points of view that disagree with the arguments presented in this chapter.

SELECTED WEB SITES

http://www.whitehouse.gov/ The official White House web site.

http://thomas.loc.gov/ Library of Congress site for gaining access to legislative information and all government agencies.

http://www.agora.stm.it/elections/parlemen.htm A site providing links to all the parliaments of the world.

http://www.ipl.org/ref/POTUS/jmadison.html A site on the Internet Public Library with information about James Madison and links to related sites.

CHAPTER 2

The Second Challenge: Radical Individualism

I came here to say that I do not recognize anyone's right to one minute of my life. Nor to any part of my energy. Nor to any achievement of mine.... I came here to say that I am a man who does not exist for others.

—AYN RAND

Each man is forever thrown back on himself alone, and there is danger that he may be shut up in the solitude of his own heart.

—ALEXIS DE TOCQUEVILLE

AMERICANS CELEBRATE INDIVIDUAL autonomy. This celebration can be found throughout American popular culture, as we see in the quotation from novelist-philosopher Ayn Rand's *The Fountainhead*. Rand gives these words to the novel's hero, Howard Roark, an architect who succeeds based on his individual brilliance, talents, and efforts despite social pressures to conform to the mediocrity of the broader society. In the novel, the autonomous individual is portrayed as the source (fountainhead) of all that is creative, good, and worthwhile in life; the community, in all its manifestations—government, public opinion, family, social mores—is only an impediment to be overcome. Ironically, for all her celebration of individual uniqueness and creativity, Rand repeats the commonest theme in American mass culture: the virtuous autonomous individual triumphing in the face of social pressures.

This celebration of the individual hero is also a standard formula in popular genres like the western film and the detective story. Lone cowboy heroes, for example, Shane or Rooster Cogburn or the Lone Ranger, come to the rescue of communities of hapless citizens unable to save themselves from evil criminals.

Opposite: *NRA president Charlton Heston leads that group's resistance to any restrictions on the individual ownership and use of firearms. (AP/Wide World Photos)*

And whether the detective hero is Sam Spade working out of a seedy San Francisco office or Jessica Fletcher sleuthing in the more wholesome atmosphere of Cabot Cove, the same formula is a staple. Even when the hero has the help of a cadre of loyal friends, as in the sci-fi western *Star Wars,* the climax depends on the ability of Luke Skywalker, alone, to place his bomb precisely to blow up the imperial battleship. Success and the triumph of good over evil are products of individual effort. The role of social factors in contributing to individual success (who, for instance, built Luke's starfighter?) remains in the background.

America's celebration of the individual in novels, movies, and television often carries over into our perception of the real world. Economics and politics are usually portrayed in highly individualistic terms. The individual business entrepreneur is celebrated as the source of our prosperity. The individual political hero, a Franklin Delano Roosevelt or a Martin Luther King Jr., is the author of political progress. From such portrayals, it would be impossible to know that most business people work in large hierarchical organizations, corporations, or that such historic political achievements as the New Deal and the civil rights movement were products of the efforts of millions of people.

The focus on the individual carries over into how Americans see themselves. Countless studies of American attitudes find that ordinary people are likely to see their personal successes and failures in highly individual terms. Getting into a good college or landing a good job is perceived as the reward for hard work and individual talent. Americans tend not to think how social institutions and forces, such as a good school system or a growing economy that creates good jobs, make their achievements possible. Failure is also usually attributed to individual factors. During the 1930s, for example, in the throes of the social disaster of the Great Depression, unemployed American workers were likely to blame themselves for their unemployment.[1] Like Howard Roark, most Americans see themselves as sole authors of both their achievements and their failures.

Individualism is certainly an attractive and even democratic aspect of American society. The chance for individual freedom and autonomy has been a major factor attracting immigrants to American shores. The United States is perceived throughout the world as a place where, to quote the U.S. Army recruiting slogan, you can "be all that you can be," free from the constraints of traditional social institutions that elsewhere trap people in particular social roles. Compared to many other countries, the United States is very egalitarian in the opportunities it offers ambitious individuals to use their individual initiative, talent, and energies to get ahead. Just as they were one hundred years ago, American cities today are full of individual immigrant entrepreneurs running grocery stores, small restaurants, corner bars, and laundries. The United States continues to attract people from all over the world who are eager to be free to make something of themselves.

Yet, for all its positive aspects, American individualism, as the Tocqueville quotation at the beginning of this chapter suggests, has a dark side. Along with freeing people from social constraints, individualism tends to isolate people from one another. To return to western films: The cowboy hero is also a loner. Clint Eastwood's character, "the man with no name," provides the definitive portrayal of this aspect of the cowboy hero as someone so detached from society that no one knows his name. What happens to society when individualism becomes so extreme that people do not need names for each other? Can nameless people "shut up in the solitude of their own hearts" form a democratic society?

Recognition of the dark side of individualism raises the question whether the American celebration of the autonomous individual has become so extreme that the United States has become a society of isolated individuals. Before analyzing the implications of individualism for American democracy, however, it is useful to identify the sources of American individualism in the American creed and American history.

SOURCES OF AMERICAN INDIVIDUALISM

American national identity, unlike that of most other nations, is based on a set of political ideas: the American creed.[2] People in most other nations understand their national attachment in terms of a common historical experience, usually common ethnicity, and often common religious belief. As a nation of immigrants, the United States contains a diversity of people with different histories, ethnic backgrounds, and religions. What has held the nation together is a widely held commitment to the ideals symbolized in the founding events of the nation, the American Revolution and constitutional ratification, and the principles found in the documents connected to these events. Unlike the French, who have more often been divided than united by the political ideals of the French Revolution, acceptance of the ideals of the American founding is usually considered a prerequisite to considering oneself an American, as in the requirement that new citizens learn about the creed and swear allegiance to it before they can be naturalized. Because of the ideological character of national identity, political crusades, such as McCarthyism in the 1950s, accusing citizens of disloyalty to American ideals often use the label "un-American." Accusing a German or French person of being "un-French" or "un-German" because of political beliefs would be absurd.

What are these ideals — the American creed — that define American identity? For the most part, they are the ideals of classical liberalism as defined in the introduction: limited government, the rule of law, liberty, political equality, and individualism. The political ideas of seventeenth- and eighteenth-century liberal political theorists were given, of course, a particular American cast by the founding events of the American republic. The revolution, in particular, employed the ideals of liberalism to achieve democratic ends.[3] While John Locke may have understood liberal ideals to be relevant to the political goals of English gentleman propertyholders, the American revolutionaries applied these ideals, especially political liberty, equality, and individualism, to all citizens. The American Revolution produced a democratized version of classical liberalism that became the American creed.

Of the various components of the American creed, individualism has been a powerful and distinctive influence on how Americans understand themselves and how they understand politics. Tocqueville perceived this on his visit to the United States in the 1830s. In fact, he coined the term *individualism* to describe the attitude he found among Americans. This is how he defined it:

> Individualism is a calm and considered feeling that disposes each citizen to isolate himself from the mass of his fellows and withdraw into the circle of family and friends; with this little society formed to his taste, he gladly leaves the greater society to look after itself.... Such folk owe no man anything and hardly expect anything from anybody. They form the habit of thinking of themselves in isolation and imagine that their whole destiny is in their hands.[4]

Although Tocqueville had grave concerns about the long-run effect of individualism, Americans enthusiastically embraced this outlook. A society in which individuals are in charge of their own lives, free from social constraint, became our central ideal.

American individualism derives from the classical liberal idea that the individual is at the center of political society. As we saw in the introduction, liberals believe political society exists to facilitate the individual's ability to pursue individual goals as he or she defines them. The preoccupation of the Founders, as revealed in the Constitution and *The Federalist,* with government's role in protecting individual liberty, and their concern that government be structured so that it not interfere with individual liberty, nurtured individualism. From the founding of the republic, Americans had political institutions that both protected and promoted their ability to pursue individual goals and aspirations. Individualism received further reinforcement as a capitalist market economy, also based on liberal premises, developed in the nineteenth century. Success in the marketplace required individuals to think primarily of how to achieve individual material goals. Both political and economic institutions in the United States provided a context to support the American attitude that people "hold their destiny in their own hands."

Americans have found much to value in individualism, especially the social mobility that is seen to follow from individualism. In coming to the United States, immigrants have sought to escape rigid social, class, and caste barriers that restrict choice of vocation and social status based on birth. In contrast to "the old country," the United States has been seen as a place where one makes it on one's own based on individual qualities. Such an attitude is found in the comment of a nineteenth-century celebrant of the concept of the American "self-made man," who described the United States as a place where people "can attain to the most elevated position or acquire a large amount of wealth, according to the pursuits they elect for themselves. No exclusive privileges of earth, no entailment of estates, no civil or political disqualifications, stand in their path; but one has as good a chance as another according to his talents, prudence, and personal exertions."[5] Americans have always associated individualism with the chance to get ahead based on one's own efforts, free of cultural, social, and political constraints.[6]

Americans also associate individualism with freedom to express their individuality. They value the chance to define for themselves their own ideas of what is good for them. This freedom is claimed for nearly all aspects of life. Americans expect to say, believe, live, eat, and wear whatever they like based on individual choice. Attempts to regulate individual behavior in behalf of the broader good, such as requiring the wearing of seat belts or motorcycle helmets, are always met with opposition. As long as they regard such behavior as harmless to others, Americans are quick to demand the right to do whatever they want. Many Americans would easily agree with one of the respondents to a recent survey of American young people who, when asked what was special about the United States, responded, "Individualism, and the fact that it is a democracy and you can do whatever you please."[7]

Although this respondent's claim of autonomy is extreme, it does reflect, as do all American claims of individual freedom and autonomy, a very democratic sentiment: the dignity of each individual and his or her choices about how to conduct his or her life. Such an outlook demands respect for individuals as worthy human beings no matter how they may or may not conform to dominant social mores. Americans from Ralph Waldo Emerson to the hippies of the 1960s to the computer hackers of the 1990s have claimed a right to "do their own thing" as part of their individualistic heritage. To recognize the right of individuals to choose how they conduct their lives means tolerance for a variety of lifestyles and cultural differences. In this sense, individualism stimulates openness, initiative, and creativity — all positive values supportive of a democratic society. Because so many Americans value their individual freedom from social and political constraint, those suffering from overt oppression can appeal to these individualistic values when demanding relief, as blacks and other minorities, homosexuals, and women have done. Americans readily recognize the role individualism can play in reinforcing and expanding democracy.

Unlike most modern Americans, who are likely to perceive individualism as supportive of democracy, Alexis de Tocqueville, while appreciating its value, was concerned that individualism, taken too far, could undermine democracy. He believed it could easily degenerate into a radical form of individualism that he called *egoism* — a condition that leads a person "to think of all things in terms of himself and to prefer himself to all."[8] A society of egoists, or what I call *radical individualists,* Tocqueville feared, would be vulnerable to despotism. Although individualism helped free people from external social and political constraints, it also tended to isolate them from one another and prevent them from perceiving their common interests. Isolated individuals with no concern for public affairs lose sight of common interests and fail to participate in public life. According to Tocqueville, radical individualism would erode the public-spirited mentality — what some might call *civic virtue* — necessary for the support of a free society. Radical individualists would lose the capacity to notice when a despotic power was in control of the state. Without concern for one another's freedom, individuals would be unable to act together to protect anyone's freedom. Tocqueville paints a dark picture of "men, alike and equal, constantly circling around in pursuit of the petty and banal pleasures with which they glut their souls. Each one of them, withdrawn into himself, is almost unaware of the fate of the rest."[9] In this condition, individual citizens succumb one by one to the power of a despotic state. Unable to act together to resist such power, isolated individuals will inevitably lose their freedom to it.

In spite of his fear of the effects of individualism, Tocqueville was somewhat optimistic about the future of democratic government in the United States. The American individualists he met in the 1830s had not yet succumbed to *radical* individualism. The reason for his optimism was another phenomenon he discovered on his travels: the lively civic participation of Americans in both their local governments and nongovernmental associations. He was impressed with the seriousness with which Americans involved themselves in local government, such as the town meetings in New England. Through involvement in public decision making on mundane matters, such as repair of local roads, citizens came to understand the relation between their individual well-being and that of the larger community.[10] This understanding was nurtured, as well, in the multitude of civic, religious, and business groups Tocqueville discovered running schools, building churches, organizing festivals, and providing charity. Both local government and nongovernmental associations reminded individualistic Americans of their connection to their fellow citizens. The civic involvement of Americans developed in them the proper "habits of the heart" required for the success of a democracy. By "habits of the heart," Tocqueville meant the unconscious feelings and attitudes or, as he put it, "the whole moral and intellectual state of a people" that guides their behavior.[11] For an individualistic society such as the United States, it was important that these feelings and attitudes include a sense of civic obligation and interconnectedness, or the society would easily slip into egoism. Tocqueville believed the American society he observed in the 1830s sustained the proper balance through involving individual citizens actively in public affairs. Even though excessive individualism might become a danger to American democracy, Tocqueville concluded that Americans possessed the proper antidote: civic-minded "habits of the heart."

Is what Tocqueville found true in the 1830s true of the United States today? Do Americans still possess "habits of the heart" conducive to a civic-minded outlook? I believe that we have reason to worry about the balance between individualism and civic virtue in the United States today. American "habits of the heart" have evolved in the direction of less understanding of the social ties that bind us together in a common democratic society and a more selfish preoccupation with our individual selves. Individualism seems to have become excessive to the point that Tocqueville, visiting the United States today, would probably have grave concern that our healthy democratic individualism was degenerating into the radical individualism he called egoism.

AMERICAN "HABITS OF THE HEART"

In recent years, a number of sociological studies have documented the growing radical individualism of contemporary Americans. One of the most influential, published in 1985, was *Habits of the Heart,* by a distinguished sociologist, Robert Bellah, and several of his colleagues.[12] Taking their cue from Tocqueville, these investigators interviewed several hundred middle-class Americans about their beliefs and aspirations regarding family, community life, politics, morality, and religion. What they found were people who defined every aspect of their existence in highly individualistic terms. At the same time, they seemed to have lost those habits of the heart conducive to understanding the meaning of community and the interconnectedness of social existence. Bellah and his colleagues found people who defined "personality, achievement, and the purpose of human life in ways that leave the individual suspended in glorious, but terrifying, isolation."[13]

Habits of the Heart begins with a profile of one of the study's interview subjects, under the pseudonym Brian Palmer, who exemplifies the isolation they find characteristic of many middle-class Americans. Brian is a successful businessman in his forties who has recently altered his lifestyle dramatically from one dominated by career and money-making to a more family-centered existence. A divorce and second marriage precipitated this change and came about as a result of much soul-searching on Brian's part about what gave him the most joy and satisfaction: business success or family relationships.

What the authors find important and somewhat disturbing about this change in Brian's life is the totally individualistic terms in which he justifies it. He altered his lifestyle based on "idiosyncratic preference rather than representing a larger sense of the purpose of life."[14] Having devoted his earlier life to career success, he shifted his priorities based simply on what he now sees giving him more personal satisfaction, wife and family, without any reference to "any wider framework of purpose or belief." For Brian, one's life goals are simply a matter of individual choice at a given moment and are not related to any value system outside oneself or connected with any community norms.

To Brian, how he lives his life is not connected in any way to the broader community, and this is how he thinks it should be. This outlook is revealed in one comment he makes about the virtues of living in California:

> One of the things that makes California such a pleasant place to live, is people by and large aren't bothered by other people's value systems as long as they don't infringe on your own. By and large, the rule of thumb out here is that if you've got the money, honey, you can do your thing as long as your thing doesn't destroy someone else's property, or interrupt their sleep, or bother their privacy, then that's fine ... just do your thing. That works out kind of neat.[15]

Brian's only understanding of his connection to others in his community, their only mutual interest, is that they leave one another alone to pursue their individually determined lifestyles. That he and his neighbors might have a common interest in one another's well-being — that their individual lives may, in some sense, depend on one another — seems to be a concept alien to Brian's understanding of society. Brian appears to be "shut up in the isolation of his own heart," a situation typical, according to Bellah and his associates, of many Americans.

Bellah and his associates find this sense of individual isolation to carry over into how Americans see their role as democratic citizens. First, they define their own success in terms of their individual efforts through competition in the marketplace independent of politics and government or cooperation with their fellow citizens.[16] Their personal well-being is not connected to their role as citizens. Second, they tend to think of their civic involvements in altruistic terms — a matter of voluntary service to others and the community. Such involvements are most likely to be with local community organizations, such as a Rotary Club or a local YMCA, rather than a political office, an election campaign, or a political party. Civic involvement is a matter of "getting involved" with like-minded people to do good for the community independent of one's own interests or personal well-being.

The people interviewed for *Habits of the Heart* tended to divide their conception of the larger political world between the ideal and the real.[17] They would like politics to be similar to what they experience in their civic involvements, a matter of face-to-face interaction based on a spontaneous consensus about what is good for the community. This ideal conception, which Bellah's respondents do not even label "politics," is not, however, their understanding of day-to-day politics as it is associated with national or local government. They believe that a politics of consensus is impossible in a diverse society containing different interests. They therefore conceive of the real world of politics as the "pursuit of differing interests according to agreed on, neutral rules."[18] This real world of politics is seen as a "necessary evil" and an arena dominated by political professionals. This is a world they regard with distaste, a world that individuals enter into only to pursue selfish individual or group interests. Unlike the free economic market, also a world of pursuit of selfish individual interests, the pursuit of interests through politics is seen as somewhat illegitimate because outcomes are based on "unfair" mobilization of political power. This differs from free markets, whose outcomes are perceived as a reflection of individual talent and initiative. Because politics, in contrast, is an arena "rewarding all kinds of inside connections, and favoring the strong at the expense of the weak, the routine activities of interest politics thus appear as an affront to true individualism [which rewards individuals for their own effort] and fairness alike."[19]

Because of their radical individualistic orientations, Americans, according to Bellah, are trapped between two unpalatable conceptions of politics: an ideal one, suitable when consensus occurs spontaneously between like-minded individuals, such as for the annual community fund drive; and a "realistic" one, where conflicting parties battle to achieve their selfish interests in public policy. Neither conception allows for the formulation of a common *public* good arrived at through democratic discussion among public-spirited citizens with varying interests. Neither calls attention to how the differing interests and problems of individuals may result from common interdependencies and institutional structures. In Tocqueville's terms, Americans have lost the "habits of the heart" that allow them to see how their differing interests are interrelated or how achieving a good for someone else may be connected to a good for oneself.

Another sociologist, Herbert Gans, has identified similar problems with American individualism through careful analysis of public opinion data. Like Bellah, he finds that "popular individualism" characterizes how middle-class Americans think about themselves and the world they live in.[20] Although less critical of individualism than Bellah, Gans sees similar orientations to politics and citizenship. Most middle-class Americans, he says, are wrapped up in their *microsocial* relations, their relationships with family and like-minded friends. They avoid and ignore *macrosocial* relations, that is, their ties to such formal organizations as Big Government and Big Business, even though these large formal organizations have a great influence over their microsocial relations. People feel in control of their microsocial lives even as they fail to perceive how they are buffeted by events in the macrosocial world. Because they see little relevance between their microsocieties and macrosociety, they tend not to participate in the larger society beyond observing it from afar through the news media (and this practice is declining) and voting.[21] Gans's description of middle-class Americans preoccupied with microsocial relations calls to mind Tocqueville's description of the individual disposed "to isolate himself from the mass of his fellows and withdraw into the circle of family and friends."

Although Tocqueville's observation suggests that the predominance of micro-social life is deeply rooted in American history and culture, Gans describes several social changes since World War II that have exacerbated popular individualism and severed people's relation to macrosociety, including loosening religious ties, decline of political parties and labor unions, and most important, suburbanization. The postwar explosion of the suburbs followed from the rapid rise in economic prosperity and security that occurred during this period. With increasing economic security, middle-class Americans literally moved away from the communities, urban and rural, in which they had grown up to brand-new suburbs without the common history that characterized the old community. As Gans puts it: "In the communities or subdivisions into which they moved, they learned to make friends with strangers on the basis of shared interests rather than shared upbringing or history."[22] Suburban residents not only shared interests but they also tended to share similar income levels and social status. These were very different from the communities they came from, which, while sharing a common history and perhaps ethnic identity, consisted of people of varying social status who interacted on a regular basis. As communities of choice, not common history, the suburbs were perfect for radical individualistic society. They allowed individuals to live among those people they wanted to, usually people like themselves. They also allowed individuals to choose from among different kinds of communities based on individual preference for different styles of living. The result is the "lifestyle enclave" — a community made up of individuals who come together because of a choice of a particular lifestyle.[23] Some of the earliest were retirement communities, which sprang up in Florida and the southwestern states to attract elderly retirees. These communities often exclude residents below a certain age and provide special recreational facilities, golf courses and shuffleboard courts, and social activities of interest to older people. By the 1970s, lifestyle enclaves for a variety of different kinds of people — condo developments for singles, housing developments of fundamentalist Christians, the Castro district for homosexuals in San Francisco — were springing up throughout the country.

By far, the most common lifestyle enclave is the exclusive, upper-middle-class, planned community, usually built around a golf course and protected from outsiders by private security guards. Often, in order to live in these communities, residents must join a homeowners' association that tightly regulates the kinds of homes and kinds of people (not poor) who can live there. For example, in the 1980s one such association in an exclusive community in Southern California opposed construction of forty-eight housing units for *senior citizens* on the grounds that they would "attract gangs and dope."[24] Besides controlling who can live in these communities, brick walls, security gates, and mazelike street patterns

Private security guards protect the residents of an exclusive planned community from contact with outsiders or the problems of the larger society. (Corbis)

keep outsiders out. In Simi Valley, north of Los Angeles (a community we re-visit in chapter 6), the entire valley of exclusive developments can be sealed off from the rest of the world by blocking four freeway exits. As one proud resident bragged, "You'd be stupid to commit a big crime here, because you can't get out. The police can seal this place off in 15 minutes."[25] Choosing to live in a lifestyle enclave allows residents to escape from undesirable people and "solve" the prob-lems of the larger society, such as crime and poverty, by walling themselves away from them.

There is no doubt that residents of places such as Simi Valley are proud of their communities and find their lives there comfortable. Such comments as "We like living in a place with educated people, people who live as we do" and "The people who live here share my values . . . it's a good socioeconomic climate — con-servative, but not stuffy. It's one of the few communities left where you can go shopping and not get hit up by people wanting money" reflect such satisfaction.[26] In fact, such residents seem more willing to support their communities, through taxes to improve local public schools or special homeowners' assessments to pay for security guards, than we normally associate with individualistic Americans.

The reason may be found in the attitudes toward politics that Bellah and his associates discovered. In homogeneous lifestyle enclaves, individualistic residents can practice their ideal brand of consensus politics among like-minded individuals. Because interests, incomes, and values are so similar, there is minimal conflict and no need to work to accommodate differences. But Tocqueville would be alarmed that this is also not an environment conducive to developing democratic "habits of the heart." Learning such habits requires communicating with different sorts of people, seeing different points of view, having the capacity to empathize with someone else's problem. Cutting themselves off in lifestyle enclaves may allow people to satisfy individual aspirations, but it also promotes a radical individualistic outlook that undermines their capacity to understand, participate in, or even care about the larger macrosociety. Can such people be good democratic citizens?

THE FLAWS OF LIBERTARIANISM

Many readers, at this point (especially if they are individualistic Americans), may not be concerned about the upsurge of radical individualism among Americans. Many will question whether radical individualism, Tocqueville's (and the author's) fretting notwithstanding, is a problem for a democracy. After all, isn't democracy about people being able to live their lives as they see fit? You may, as Ayn Rand's Howard Roark would, consider the liberty Brian Palmer and the residents of Simi Valley have to be the "authors" of their own lives evidence of the success of American democracy, not a threat to it. Why should democratic citizens have to be concerned about an abstraction like the "public good" if they choose not to be? If some people freely choose to do good works for the less fortunate or concern themselves with macrosocial issues, fine; but why is there a need for everyone to be so concerned? As long as people obey the law and do not interfere with the rights of others, what difference does it make whether or not they possess public-spirited "habits of the heart"? Shouldn't a real democracy be mainly about preventing community institutions, especially government, from interfering with what individuals choose to think, say, and do?

These rhetorical questions reflect a political ideology known as *libertarianism*. A political ideology is a somewhat systematic set of prescriptions about how government and political life should be organized. While radical individualism is a diffuse set of cultural values that orient people toward the whole range of their experience, libertarianism provides a more specific road map for organizing a society to reflect and promote radical individualism. Libertarians believe that people are and should be radical individualists, that is, individuals existing independent of and free from obligations to the rest of society. A good government is one that facilitates the ability of individuals to make their individual choices about how they live their lives. Libertarians favor a minimal government whose principal role is protecting individual rights and which itself must not interfere with those rights. In the economic sphere, this implies a free-market economy with little or no government regulation. In the social sphere, it means individuals free to do whatever they want, from taking drugs to playing the violin, without government interference, as long as their behavior does not harm or violate the rights of others. According to the libertarians, the obligation of citizens to participate in or support the broader community or public good is minimal. In fact, many libertarians would question the concept of the public good beyond the aggregation of individual goods. As long as individual liberty and autonomy are preserved, the public good is achieved.[27]

Libertarianism, obviously, should strike a chord among individualistic Americans. Some readers may find in the previous paragraph a precise summary of their own personal ideology. In fact, one can find libertarians across the political spectrum in the United States, among people who call themselves liberals and those who say they are conservative, among Democrats and Republicans. Libertarians who call themselves liberals are usually people mainly concerned with protecting social and political rights, such as free speech and privacy, and they probably belong to the American Civil Liberties Union (ACLU). Conservative libertarians are more likely to focus on economic rights and to promote free-market economics, and they probably voted for Ronald Reagan and Steve Forbes. What these groups have in common is concern to limit government interference with individual behavior. For the past two decades, a Libertarian Party has nominated candidates to national political office who run on a platform advocating a pristine form of libertarianism encompassing both economic and social liberties.[28] The Libertarian Party advocates dismantling nearly all government programs; the decriminalization of all drugs, prostitution, and pornography; the elimination of nearly all business regulation; and reducing the size of the military. Although few libertarians belong to or subscribe to the tenets of the Libertarian Party, it takes seriously the central premise of libertarianism: a truly democratic society is precisely one in which individuals have maximum freedom to pursue their own goals independent of others in society.

In this section, I argue that this libertarian view of society is flawed. It fails to take into account the many ways individuals are inevitably connected to and dependent on one another and on society as a whole. A society in which people concern themselves only with pursuing their individual goals and do not take responsibility for the whole community could not survive. Because we live in society, we cannot avoid being concerned with others and the good of the collectivity.

One demonstration of the limitations of the libertarian vision of society is to evaluate it in terms of its own goal: the achievement of individual interests and aspirations. Social scientists have devised a number of logical "thought experiments" to show that, in certain situations, totally self-interested individuals

Burglar A's Options

	Keep Quiet	Snitch
Keep Quiet	Cell A Both keep quiet and both go free	Cell B A gets 5 years while B gets 20 years
Snitch	Cell C B gets 5 years while A gets 20 years	Cell D Both get 5 years

Burglar B's Options

Figure 2.1 The Prisoner's Dilemma

cannot achieve even their individual interests without the cooperation of others. One of the simplest and most famous of these is the *prisoner's dilemma.*

Imagine two self-interested partners in crime picked up by the police on suspicion of a rash of burglaries. The police do not have any concrete evidence to convict the prisoners unless they can convince one of them to snitch on his accomplice. Just as in good cop shows on television, the prisoners are separated from one another at the police station and are not allowed to communicate. Each is separately offered the same deal: "Snitch on your friend and admit your crimes, and we'll let you cop a plea. If you don't talk and your friend does, you'll draw the maximum sentence." Figure 2.1 shows the dilemma each burglar is in.

Obviously, both burglars would be best off if they both kept their mouths shut (cell A). Without a confession, the police cannot convict either of them and both will go free. But neither prisoner can be sure whether his partner will break under the questioning and cop a plea. If this happens, whichever burglar keeps quiet will do hard time (cells B and C). Since the burglars cannot cooperate and agree in advance to keep quiet, the most rational decision for both burglars would be to snitch (cell D). This outcome is less desirable than going free, but it is the only way that each prisoner, pursuing his individual self-interest independent of cooperation with the other, can be sure to avoid the worst outcome—a jail term of twenty years. The value of the prisoner's dilemma is that it illustrates the flaw in our intuitive sense, especially that of individualistic Americans, that the best strategy to succeed is to "look out for Number One." Often in the real world we find ourselves in situations like that of the imaginary prisoners: if we look out only for ourselves and ignore the well-being of those around us, we will end up falling short of what we could achieve through cooperation. For example, the political scientist Paul Brace argues that the prisoner's dilemma applies to the strategies individual American states need to develop to promote economic development.[29]

In recent years, many state governments have behaved like our burglars. They have competed vociferously to attract businesses to their states by offering big tax breaks and subsidies. Businesses, as one might expect, have taken advantage of this situation by getting neighboring state governments to engage in a bidding war in offering such incentives. In some instances, the result has been a state's winning the bidding war to the detriment of its economic development. The incentives it had to offer to attract the businesses exceed the economic benefits the businesses actually bring to the state. At the same time, by lowering tax rates to attract business, the states lose out on revenues to invest in public services, especially education, which support economic development. In the long run, needed public investment in economic growth declines everywhere, eventually hurting even those that competition between states for business is supposed to benefit: business firms and those they employ. Most economic development specialists today argue that cooperation between states to promote economic development is a better long-run strategy for all states. Through cooperation they can devise policies that place them in cell A in the prisoner's dilemma.

The prisoner's dilemma shows that failure to cooperate with others in pursuit of one's individual self-interest may result in "suboptimization": failure to achieve as much as could have been achieved through cooperation. Another common thought experiment suggests that failure to cooperate may result in more than suboptimization; it can lead to disaster.

Imagine a common grazing land that is home to several families of ranchers. Each family maintains a separate herd of cattle but relies on turning them out into the common pasture to fatten them for market. (Incidentally, reliance on common grazing land remains a major form of ranching in much of the American West today.)[30] Being rugged individualists, each family of ranchers relies on itself to make its living and is not in the habit of communicating with its neighbors, who are also its competitors, about individual business decisions. Being good libertarians, all the ranchers regard any attempt to regulate any aspect of how they run their ranches as a violation of their individual property rights.

One day, while rounding up calves for branding, Rancher Jill notices quite a few bare patches in the pasture and sees that the family's cattle are thinner than last year. She realizes that the common pasture is being overgrazed; there are too many cattle on the land. When she gets back to the ranch house, she calls a family council to decide what to do. What will the family decide? If it acts rationally and in its individual self-interest, the family will decide to buy more cattle to add to the grazing land. When the other families discover the problem, they will do the same. Very quickly, the grazing land will be destroyed, and all the families will be out of the ranching business. This is the *tragedy of the commons*.

The tragedy of the commons follows inevitably from the logic of the situation. This is the case even though the best solution, obviously, would be to limit the number of cattle allowed on the land to its grazing capacity. Such a solution, however, would require some sort of cooperation among the ranchers. They would have to agree collectively to limit the size of their herds and develop some institutional mechanism to enforce the agreement. Since our libertarian ranchers oppose all collective regulation, however, they can respond to the situation only by changing their individual behavior. In the case of reliance on the common grazing land, an example of what economists call a "common pool resource," this will always lead to abuse and the eventual depletion of the resource. If any of the ranch families decided individually to limit its herd, it would see its competitors take advantage of that decision by adding to their herds. The only solution is to grab for oneself as much use of the common pool resource as possible before it is all gone.[31]

The tragedy of the commons shows that with common pool resources, the ability of individuals to pursue their individual self-interest independent of and oblivious to one another has to be regulated. If it is not, the individual well-being of all will suffer. This insight is applicable to a whole range of human experience and practical policy problems. Environmentalists are especially sensitive to the tragedy of the commons because the environment is our largest and most obvious common pool resource. Consider clean air. Factories that emit pollutants into the air cannot be expected to limit such pollutants voluntarily on their own initiative. Cleaning emissions increases production costs and places a factory that does so at a competitive disadvantage to those that do not. The ability to manufacture products by polluting the air instead of cleaning up emissions is a common pool resource that smart factory managers will use to their advantage if left free to do so; factories that lower production costs by polluting will win out in competition with those that do not. In this case, free-market competition leads inevitably to the tragedy of the commons. The only way such pollutants can be limited is if government, or some other collective institution, regulates the individual's liberty to pollute.

I have dwelt on the prisoner's dilemma and the tragedy of the commons because, aside from their applicability to interesting policy problems such as air pollution or economic development, they underscore the limits of the libertarian view of society. In the prisoner's dilemma, a libertarian orientation undermines the ability of individuals to maximize even their own self-interest. In the tragedy of the commons, libertarianism leads to disaster. These insights suggest that a society of even radical individualists must be sensitive to the necessity of collective action if it is to be successful. In a democracy, an understanding of how individual success is related to cooperation with other individuals is a valuable habit of the heart for all citizens. Such an understanding leads democratic citizens to think about how their own interest relates to the interest of others. Only with this understanding can tragedies of the commons be avoided and prisoners' dilemmas resolved. Unfortunately, because of our radically individualistic culture, both often ensnare us.

Another way that libertarians and radical individualists misunderstand the relationship between individuals and society is in their conception of liberty. Libertarians, like most Americans, tend to think of liberty as freedom from external constraints on individual behavior. According to this concept, I am free whenever government, or other social institutions, do not prevent me from pursuing my individual goals. Freedom means being able to use my property as I wish, speak my mind, practice my chosen profession, live where I want, and worship as I please. Liberty is only in danger when social institutions, especially government, interfere with my ability to do these things. The libertarian perspective assumes that the absence of constraints on individuals satisfies the requirements of liberty.

I, along with many political philosophers, would argue that the concept of liberty is more complex than simply freedom from constraints on my behavior.[32] Even in a political system that imposed no constraints on my freedom, such freedom would mean nothing unless I also possessed the means to exercise it. *Freedom from* external constraints is only one side of liberty; *freedom to* exercise it is the other. This latter side of liberty implies individuals possessing the capacity and power to act. Possession of "freedom to" is a product of community resources and social institutions that provide the capacity to exercise one's freedom. A government that does not prevent me from writing what is on my mind, worshipping as I please, or choosing my own profession is essential for liberty. But the absence of such prohibitions means little to me if I have no writing instruments, there are no churches, and there are no jobs. The availability of these things depends on living in a community that makes them available.

Tyrants understand well these two sides of liberty. In the former Soviet Union, for example, although political dissidents were often imprisoned for criticizing the regime, the main limitation on freedom of expression was through state control of all media. The ability to publish or disseminate ideas was denied to all but regime supporters. Without the ability to take advantage of liberty, the absence of constraints on liberty has little value.

Of course, a libertarian would point to the Soviet media monopoly as the problem in my example and not in his conception of liberty: Allow free speech *and* free ownership of media, then true liberty of individual expression will exist. Such a view ignores, however, the extent that free speech, even in a free-market society, depends on social institutions. The widespread dissemination of one's ideas requires access to media outlets such as newspapers, television, radio, publishing firms, and the Internet. Even in the absence of a government monopoly of media outlets, individuals who want to communicate ideas to more than a small circle of friends will need to utilize social institutions. The ability of the owner of a television station, for example, to exercise free speech depends on social networks: the past efforts of those who invented television technology, the widespread ownership of television sets, plus the cooperation and expertise of employees. The emergence of the Internet and the ability of individuals to disseminate their ideas through their own individual web pages seems to offer new opportunities for speech free from dependence on the social networks required by previous technologies. The evolution of this new medium, however, shows the inevitability of social influence over access. Social institutions will define who can access the computer hardware and software needed to use the Internet; what rules access providers, such as America Online, will use in governing access; what browser software is easily available and how it might channel access; and what governmental regulations will govern use of the medium. *Freedom to* express one's ideas will always exist, no matter what the technology, within a fabric of social institutions.

The more complex understanding of individual liberty as both freedom from *and* freedom to underscores the degree to which an individual's freedom depends on the support of others and society. All one's freedoms depend on a structure of social institutions that provides the means to exercise them. College students, exercising their individual freedom to learn, provide a good example of the need for social support to practice freedom. The freedom to pursue higher education would mean nothing if such social entities as colleges and universities did not exist. Their existence is the result of contributions of resources, some going back many years, of many individuals. Admission to a college is a product, in part, of individual talent and effort, but access to elementary and secondary schools is crucial for developing talent. And, for most of us, an important prerequisite of freedom to learn is the support of a nurturing family that provides us the wherewithal to learn throughout our schooling. Declaring that no government should prohibit some individuals from acquiring an education does not mean that even strongly motivated and ambitious individuals will be able to learn. Freedom to be educated requires a supportive social environment.

The prisoner's dilemma, the tragedy of the commons, and the understanding of liberty as freedom to as well as freedom from — these paradoxes and self-contradictions undermine the libertarian conception of the autonomous individual. Individuals require more than simply freedom from others and society to attain their goals. Individuals require social support and the cooperation of others if they are to live successful and productive lives. Recently, social scientists have employed the concept of *social capital* to describe the social networks, norms, and trust that benefit individuals.[33] They argue that the development of social capital improves the ability of individuals to cooperate for mutual benefit. In a study of regional governments in Italy, the political scientist Robert Putnam discovered that regions with "strong traditions of civic engagement" such as high voter turnout, lots of active community groups, and high levels of awareness of public affairs had effective governments and were economically prosperous.[34] These regional governments administered successful programs for economic development, child care, environmental regulation, and health clinics. Citizens were largely satisfied with their government's performance. In contrast, in regions lacking these characteristics, social capital was low. Citizens had a "stunted" conception of citizenship, regarding "public affairs [as] somebody else's business — *i notabili,* 'the bosses,' 'the politicians' — but not theirs."[35] In these regions, mainly in Italy's impoverished southern region, regional governments were failures: "inefficient, lethargic, and corrupt." Putnam argues that the presence or absence of social capital is deeply rooted in the differing histories of the regions going back to the Middle Ages. Successful regions had old heritages of civic solidarity built on "guilds, religious fraternities, and tower societies for self-defense." Unsuccessful regions had heritages of remote despotic government. Social capital, Putnam concludes, "seems to be a precondition for economic development, as well as for effective government."

Putnam identifies three key characteristics of social capital that support good government and economic success: generalized reciprocity, trust, and past success at collaboration. *Generalized reciprocity* is the willingness of an individual to come to the assistance of someone in need with the understanding that the needy individual will return the favor at some future time. This is the ethic of the frontier barn-raising common in nineteenth-century rural America. When a new family arrived in a community, neighboring farmers would organize a day-long welcoming celebration that featured building a barn for the new family. The recipient of the barn would then be expected to participate in such barn-raisings for future community members. The tradition of barn-raising was a form of social capital that helped each individual farmer to prosper but also increased the chance that all community members would succeed and none would become a burden on the community. Acts of generalized reciprocity contribute to the development of *trust* between individual community members. Such trust develops "networks of civic engagement" that can be drawn on when cooperative effort is needed, whether for day-to-day public projects or in emergencies. Both trust and generalized reciprocity become historically rooted over time as individuals in a community *collaborate* successfully. This provides the community with a stock of self-perpetuating and self-reinforcing social capital that can be drawn on to solve a wide variety of problems. In his study of Italian regions, Putnam found that regions possessing large amounts of social capital seemed successful in all areas of social existence: culture, economics, and politics; communities without social capital seemed to fail in everything.

It is important to understand that the concept of communities possessing so-cial capital is quite different from the idealized vision of a consensual community that the Americans whom Bellah interviewed desired. Communities do not need to be made up of totally like-minded individuals, as in Simi Valley, to build social capital. Trust, reciprocity, and a history of successful collaboration can be devel-oped among individuals with differing values, income levels, race or ethnicity, and aspirations. The idea of social capital is that it lubricates relations among in-dividuals so that individual differences that might interfere with cooperation do not. Just like Tocqueville's "habits of the heart," social capital connects disparate individuals.

Since completing his study of the importance of social capital in Italy, Robert Putnam has turned his attention to examining the state of social capital in Amer-ica, and his findings suggest reason for concern. In a 1995 article, "Bowling Alone: America's Declining Social Capital," Putnam presented evidence of a decline in membership in civic groups ranging from fraternal organizations to bowling leagues.[36] His brilliant title referred to his discovery that, although the number of individuals who bowled regularly increased in the 1980s, membership in bowling *leagues* declined. Putnam's phrase "bowling alone" cleverly captured the idea that Americans were becoming less willing to associate with one another in the types of groups that observers such as Tocqueville praised as nurturing citizenship. While Putnam's findings have not gone unchallenged — his critics claim that his analysis focused too much on traditional organizations rather than on new forms of association — his work has made an impact because it reflects many people's everyday experience, and his findings are consistent with many other studies, such as Bellah's, that document rising interpersonal distrust and radical indi-vidualism.[37] The recent report of the National Commission on Civic Renewal, funded by the Pew Charitable Trusts, developed an index of "civic health," a con-cept similar to Putnam's social capital — based on data on political involvement, interpersonal trust, group membership, crime incidence, and family structure. Figure 2.2 summarizes the Commission's finding, showing that American civic health declined significantly between the early 1970s and the early 1990s.[38] A par-ticularly ominous aspect of this decline in American social capital is the decline in generalized social trust among American young people. Young Americans' lack of social trust, according to a recent study, is linked to rising materialism which itself is rooted in rising individualism and declining religious commitment.[39] Several dramatic, violent incidents in schools — such as the Columbine High

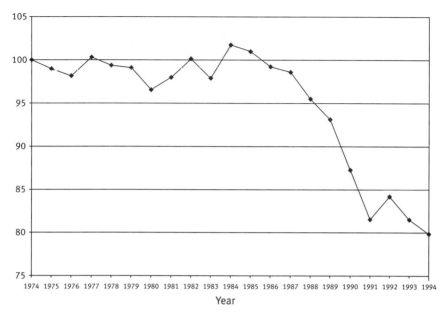

Figure 2.2   The Index of National Civic Health (INCH)

Source: National Commission on Civic Renewal, update to "A Nation of Spectators Repent," 27 September 1999,
http://www.PUAF.umd.edu/civicrenewal/inch/INCHupdate.PDF.
Note: The year 1974 is a baseline, set at 100.

School shooting in Colorado — may reflect the restlessness and disconnectedness of American youths, even in affluent communities. Distrust in government is so high in 2000 that many Americans refuse to respond to census questionnaires.[40] While much additional research into changes in America's social capital is needed, the findings of Putnam and others suggest that radical individualism has worn away the fabric of social connections that support democracy.

The concept of social capital, like the other concepts discussed in this section, implies a more complex understanding of individuality than in either the radical individualism of many Americans or libertarian ideology. Libertarians see individuals as atomized, existing independent of one another. In fact, the autonomous individual existing independent of social constraint is their ideal. Social institutions, especially government, and the community of other individuals, are external forces apart from the individual. Yet the concepts of social capital, the prisoner's dilemma, the tragedy of the commons, and liberty as "freedom to" suggest that this conception of the individual is unrealistic. Individuals, as the Greek political philosopher Aristotle said, are *social* beings. Robert Bellah makes the point eloquently:

> We find ourselves not independently of other people and institutions but through them. We never get to the bottom of ourselves on our own. We discover who we are face to face and side by side with others in work, love, and learning. ... And the positive side of our individualism, our sense of the dignity, worth, and moral autonomy of the individual, is dependent in a thousand ways on a social, cultural, and institutional context that keeps us afloat.[41]

As social beings, the beneficiaries of those social institutions that nurture us, we also have a moral obligation to help and support those institutions, including political ones.[42] Libertarianism's myopic focus on the individual free of external constraint ignores this individual moral obligation to other individuals and society.

This more complex understanding of individuals should cause concern about the radical individualism of Americans described earlier in this chapter. If Bellah and his colleagues, Gans, and other social commentators are correct about the recent evolution of American culture, individual Americans are less and less aware of their dependence on others and social institutions. Radically individualistic Americans may be becoming like the burglars caught in the prisoner's dilemma or the ranchers living on the common grazing land — unable, because of their individualistic blinders, to perceive the advantages of cooperation. The dominance of the conception of liberty as freedom from constraint may prevent them from supporting social institutions, such as public schools, that give meaning to those freedoms. Ignorance about their dependence on society may lead Americans to deplete the social capital required for successful economies and governments. If these things come to pass, Americans will have lost the "habits of the heart" Tocqueville thought were required for successful democratic government.

Unfortunately, certain tendencies in contemporary politics indicate that our radically individualistic political culture may be having this effect. First, the way we discuss politics seems to be dominated by "rights talk," which gets in the way of resolving important public problems. Second, narrow selfish interests have come to dominate public policymaking so that attempts to achieve broader public aims are nearly impossible. Both developments make our politics pathological and Americans cynical about democracy.

OUR PATHOLOGICAL POLITICS OF RIGHTS AND INTERESTS

Americans are not shy about asserting their rights. Much of our politics involves individuals or groups entering the public arena to demand recognition or protection of a right. Pro-choice women demand the right to have an abortion, pro-life women the right to life of the fetus. Smokers claim a right to smoke, nonsmokers the right to smoke-free air. Labor union members assert their right to strike, businesses their right to hire replacements for striking workers. "I demand my rights"

In his radical crusade to assert an individual's "right to die," Dr. Jack Kevorkian defies a cease-and-desist order to his assisted suicide activities. (AP/Wide World Photos)

is perhaps the commonest phrase in our politics. In the United States, "rights talk" is our predominant form of political discourse.[43]

The American rights tradition is closely linked to our understanding of constitutionalism and democracy. Surveys show that when asked about the content of the Constitution, most Americans refer to the Bill of Rights. When asked to identify the meaning of American democracy, young Americans refer to rights and freedoms.[44] Naturalization ceremonies for new citizens emphasize the rights that citizenship confers on them.[45] This preoccupation with rights reflects, is consistent with, and reinforces American individualism.

A concern for rights is also essential to and consistent with democracy. Individual rights to participate, express one's views, assemble for political purposes, and receive due process from government are necessary conditions for the existence of democracy.[46] Also, the assertion of individual rights can be a claim for recognition as a member of a democratic community. In the United States, the assertion of rights has been the principal means groups have used to gain inclusion as citizens. To demand a right and have the community recognize it symbolizes inclusion as an equal member of a democratic society. This is a device black Americans, women, and others have used and continue to use to gain democratic power in American society. The possession of rights establishes an individual or group as a legitimate participant in democratic processes. Progress toward making the United States more democratic over time has been largely a process of universalizing rights — bringing more individuals and groups into the democratic community.

Although rights and rights talk have been instruments for expanding democracy, the political theorist Benjamin Barber points out that, in recent years, the democratic and social character of rights has tended to be ignored as rights have become "privatized."[47] Although a democratic understanding of rights recognizes their social character — the fact that rights are rooted in membership and participation in a democratic community — contemporary Americans seem to consider their rights as a private possession unrelated to their political involvement. Americans increasingly claim rights, but feel under no obligation to participate in their enforcement. As Barber points out, small-town citizens nowadays demand the right of fire protection but refuse to join the volunteer fire department.[48] The radical individualism of Americans seems to blind us to the link between rights and democratic processes.

The radical individualism of American rights talk tends to undermine effective democratic politics.[49] While concern for and protection of rights is an important concern in a democracy, American rights talk has trivialized rights. Traditionally, the assertion of rights has been confined to claims for recognition of freedoms fundamental to democratic citizenship, such as free speech or the right to a fair trial. Nowadays, people tend to turn every want or political demand into a demand for recognition of a right. Assertions of a right to smoke, to carry an assault rifle, to view cable television, or not to wear a motorcycle helmet are a few examples. These are all concerns that may need to be addressed as a matter of public policy, but equating them with such rights as free speech, which are fundamental to democratic liberty, cheapens the more fundamental rights. Moreover, discussing all public policy in terms of the existence or absence of a *right* is not the most useful approach to resolving public issues. Assertions of claims to a right result in arguments about whether or not such a right should be recognized, rather than a consideration of what is in the public interest.

Because individualistic Americans tend to think about public policy issues in terms of individual rights, no public policy issue is immune to a rights claim. In recent years, these claims have included demands for animal rights and even the rights of inanimate objects. To cite an extreme example, a legal scholar in California has argued for the rights of sand as a way of protecting beaches from development.[50] Such an issue needs to be addressed in terms of collective values, such as public responsibility for the environment and preserving it for posterity. But because our individualistic culture impedes our ability to address issues in such terms — because we have become more comfortable with "rights talk" than with discussions of the public interest — proponents of an issue try to formulate it in terms of a right. They know such formulations gain more serious consideration from individualists used to thinking in rights terms. Sadly, such trivialization of rights also serves to reinforce our radical individualism and undermines our capacity to think about the public interest. To assert rights in regard to every political want fuels a circular process in which a radically individualistic outlook encourages rights claims validating, in turn, an even more individualistic orientation.

Along with trivializing rights, the privatization of rights has led to assertions of rights without consideration of responsibilities. Because American individualists have tended to see their rights as a kind of private property, rights have become individual claims on government and the rest of society without consideration of the responsibilities that accompany rights. For example, Americans demand the right to a trial by a jury of their peers, but few are willing to serve on juries.[51] Yet no right can exist unless citizens take responsibility for assuring it.

Failure to perceive the relationship between rights and responsibilities seems to characterize Americans' understanding of their role as citizens. In a recent study, when college students were asked to describe what being a citizen means, most immediately mentioned rights, but few believed having those rights required political participation on their part. As one young man said, "Being a citizen is your God-given right. Politics doesn't have anything to do with being a citizen."[52] Without taking responsibility for participating politically to protect citizenship rights, this young student certainly will need God's assistance if his rights are to last long.

Demanding rights without accepting the responsibilities that go with them has affected how individuals perceive their relation to government. By understanding citizenship as merely the possession of a bundle of individual rights, people begin to think of themselves solely as clients whose rights must be serviced. They do not feel any more responsible for producing these services than they would for producing the programs they watch on television. Government is perceived as an institution totally independent of themselves that must provide services to which their rights entitle them. A lone rights-bearing citizen does not perceive her or his role as a democratic citizen to take responsibility for these rights and participate in their provision.[53] The extent to which people have come to misunderstand their connection to government is illustrated by the comment of a participant in a television talk show on the savings-and-loan crisis; she argued that *taxpayers* should not have to pay for the S&L bailout, the *government* should![54] For this citizen, all sense of democratic participation in and responsibility for government has vanished; this citizen may still believe in government *for* the people, but *of* and *by* the people have become no more relevant than if she were referring to McDonalds hamburgers.

To conceive of democratic government as merely a servicer of rights creates severe obstacles for identifying what the *public* interest is on a particular problem. One obstacle is the tendency to assert individual rights in such absolute terms that weighing broader public concerns in regard to an issue becomes impossible. The politics of gun control provides a dramatic example of such rights absoluteness. Interpreting the Second Amendment "right to bear arms," which most constitutional scholars interpret as a right to form public militias, in totally individualist terms, the National Rifle Association (NRA) has deployed this right to resist enactment of any restrictions on the individual ownership and use of firearms. It has opposed regulation of even the most dangerous forms of weaponry, such as semiautomatic assault rifles, on the grounds that the absolute individual right to bear arms overrules any concern for the danger to public safety that the easy availability of these weapons presents. For the NRA, the purported right to guns takes precedence over any other public consideration — even the millions of deaths and injuries caused by firearms each year and the mounting insecurity most citizens feel about the burgeoning arsenals of weapons on the nation's streets. The success of the NRA in blocking more effective gun control reflects its lobbying skills and its strategic use of legislative campaign contributions. But its success reflects, as well, the resonance of rights talk in our political culture, which tends to privilege any claim of an individual right when public policy problems are addressed. A more balanced, less rights oriented, less individualist approach to such issues as gun ownership would seek to balance legitimate individual interest in access to guns, for legitimate purposes in sports and recreation, with important broader concerns such as public safety. But our radically individualist culture tends to privilege absolutist rights claims and inhibits our ability to formulate reasonable balances between individual and public interests.

Rights talk also impedes identifying the public interest because of our propensity to formulate nearly all political conflicts in terms of conflicting rights. Resolving conflict becomes impossible when one absolute, irreconcilable individual right is deployed against another. This has been the reason why formulating public policy regarding abortion has been so frustrating and disruptive in the United States. Americans have formulated the issue in terms of a woman's right to privacy versus an unborn fetus's right to life, neither of which can be acknowledged without violating the other or denying the legitimacy of the other.[55] Rather than focus simply on these logically irreconcilable "rights," a more useful approach might be to examine the social context within which abortions occur. What are the financial, personal, and psychological conditions that make pregnancies "unwanted"? What public policies might relieve women of the individual burden our society imposes on them for childbearing and childrearing? Attention to such questions might lead to the formulation of policies for birth-control education, pregnancy and child-care support, facilitation of adoption, and family nurturing, which would reduce the number of abortions while preserving women's legitimate concern for control over their lives. Such an approach is not likely to solve the many complex moral conflicts raised by the abortion issue, but it would offer both pro-life and pro-choice groups the means of addressing many social issues surrounding the abortion issue on which they could agree.[56] Unfortunately, our radically individualist rights talk gets in the way of discussing these issues.

One side effect of American rights discourse is excessive judicial involvement in policymaking. Because policy issues are framed in terms of recognition of individual rights, partisans of a particular side to an issue often go to court to win policy victories, rather than debate issues in the legislature. Although courts and judges are important democratic tools for adjudicating disputes, determining guilt or innocence, and protecting constitutional rights, democrats need to be concerned about their use as policymaking instruments. Public policymaking involves balancing and reconciling a myriad of wants, needs, demands, and interests — including the public interest. As discussed in the introduction, the democratic presumption is that this reconciliation produces the long-term good of everyone when all citizens participate in discussing and deliberating about them, whether directly or through representative institutions. In the United States, courts are not participatory institutions, nor are judges democratically elected officials: judges are usually appointed for life to insulate them from political pressures, and courts are supposed to make decisions on the basis of legal criteria and concepts, usually in language inaccessible to laypeople, rather than on the basis of public opinion. While these characteristics are highly desirable for adjudicating disputes and trying those accused of crimes, they produce undemocratic policymaking. When policy issues are brought to court, judges are forced to behave as philosopher-kings, weighing competing interests and demands while taking into account their interpretation of the public interest. In doing so, they may be wise and benevolent, just as monarchs or dictators may be, but the idea of democracy is that determining the public interest is best left to the widespread participation of all. Because our rights discourse too often leads to judicial resolution of public policy issues, democracy is more than undermined, it is abandoned.[57]

Of course, not all public policy issues are left to the courts; most are addressed in legislative assemblies such as Congress, state legislatures, and city councils. Within these assemblies, however, the predominant manner in which representatives address these issues leaves much to be desired from a democratic point of view. The American radical individualist culture encourages most Americans to think primarily in terms of their individual self-interest, rather than the public interest, when thinking about public policy. "Looking out for Number One" seems to have become many Americans' only orientation to political issues. Whenever public policy proposals are raised, the automatic reaction is to ask, "How am I helped or hurt by this proposal," not, "Is this proposal good for the country (or town or state)?" Legislative representatives face overwhelming pressure from both their constituents and organized special interests to protect individual and group self-interests when considering legislation; any orientation to the broader public good is totally up to them.

Our recent political history is replete with examples of the politics of self-interest overwhelming attempts to deal with public problems. Representative (and political scientist) David Price tells of his chagrin in the face of self-interested reaction to his support for catastrophic health insurance in 1988.[58] In that year, Congress enacted major legislation to expand Medicare coverage to include long-term nursing-home care for the elderly. Although senior citizen groups had been major proponents of the legislation, when Congress imposed increased Medicare premiums to pay for the expanded coverage, these same groups were outraged. Price tells of his frustration with the reaction of some of his constituents, who, in meetings in his district, would express strong support for catastrophic coverage but also oppose any method of paying for the program. One constituent, in fact, told the congressman that, as a citizen, he felt no obligation to consider alternative ways to pay for the program—that was the congressman's job! It seems this constituent presumed his role as citizen to involve only looking out for his own self-interest.

Given the pervasiveness of radical individualism, the attitude of Price's constituent seems to be widely shared in contemporary American politics. Many Americans are quick to consider how public policies affect their individual rights and interests but are unable to think of themselves as responsible members of the sovereign people with an obligation to be concerned with the public interest. According to the political theorist Joseph Tussman: "The citizen, in his political capacity... is asked public, not private questions: 'Do we need more public schools?' not 'Would I like to pay more taxes?' He must, in this capacity, be concerned with the public interest, not with his private goods."[59] When citizens lose the capacity to think about public issues in the terms Tussman describes, solving public problems becomes extremely difficult, if not impossible. Any proposal to solve a public problem is not evaluated or discussed in terms of its capacity to address the overall problem; it is subjected only to self-interested scrutiny by various groups to see how their interest is affected. The "politics of special interests" familiar in any day-to-day account of national politics in Washington reflects this orientation. The existence of thousands of organizations and lobbyists in the national capital whose sole purpose is to monitor how legislation affects particular narrow interests seems quite normal once one assumes politics to be solely about self-interest. Political success, in this context, is a matter of what you can get for your group without any consideration of how the broader public interest is affected. To hesitate to defend one's narrow interest could bring disaster, as other self-interested groups would move to take advantage of such hesitation. Politics, overall, becomes a matter of all groups fighting for themselves, like sharks feeding on a carcass, while the public interest is left to take care of itself.

Given the largely self-interested orientation of most citizens and groups to politics, the burden of looking out for the broader public interest is placed on elected officials. Their ability to do so is limited, however, because there are few rewards for doing so. Failure to respond to self-interested demands will result in loss of political support. Moreover, when politicians attempt to pursue the public interest, they are likely to be suspected of a self-interested motivation. In a self-interested political culture, all political actions or proposals will be assumed to be selfishly motivated. This phenomenon is evident in the cynical approach of most journalistic commentary on politics. Little attention is given to the substance of policy proposals or the consequences of the actions of political figures. Journalists tend to focus on how actions support the political appeal and ambitions of political figures and the purported self-interested motivation behind those proposals.[60] In the face of special-interest pressures, self-interested constituent demands, and a cynical press, it is not surprising that few politicians nowadays consider pursuit of the public interest to be their main concern. A successful political career is more likely to be had serving a particular interest and watching out for its concerns than attending to the broader public interest. Politicians who set aside the narrow concerns of their constituents for the broader good of the country, who turn aside offers of special-interest political action committee (PAC) funds, or who devote their time to pushing public-spirited ideas are not apt to last long in office. This does not mean that skillful, public-spirited politicians never put the public interest ahead of selfish interests, it only means that public-interested behavior is likely to be rare. A political system that privileges self-interested political behavior and expects it is likely to get it.

Our pathological politics of rights and interests follows from the radical individualism of the political culture. As long as Americans understand their relationship to political life primarily in terms of the pursuit of individual goals, they will turn to politics and government only to protect what they consider a right or to promote a selfish interest. The growing radical individualism that Bellah, Gans, and others have documented encourages a politics of rights deadlock and an unbridled pursuit of self-interest. As Tocqueville would have expected, citizens who have lost the "habits of the heart" that tie them to the broader community will think of public policy solely in terms of how their individual selfish interest is affected. They will demand services from government while refusing to support taxes to pay for them, yet not be able to perceive the contradiction between the two positions. That an astronomical national debt, decaying roads and bridges, and squalid public schools seemed to be permanent conditions in the United States at the end of the twentieth century follows. Democratic citizens who are "shut up in the solitude of their own hearts" may have some success for a time in watching out for their rights and interests, but unless the broader public sphere is attended to, eventually even individual interests will be ignored, and rights will vanish.

AMERICAN RADICAL INDIVIDUALISM challenges democracy in several ways. Most fundamentally, it erodes the habits of the heart that tie democratic citizens to one another and promote civic virtue. The relationship between radical individualism and civic-minded habits is circular. The more individuals see themselves as isolated and the more they are preoccupied with their own individual goals, the less they will participate in public affairs or support the public sphere. As participation declines and the public sphere atrophies, individual isolation grows and individuals understand less about their interdependence with others. In short order, the society becomes merely an aggregation of isolated individuals whose mentality cannot encompass a larger society outside themselves. In this infertile ground, as Tocqueville understood, democracy is in peril.

In a society of radical individualists, libertarian ideology tends to dominate all political discussion. Citizens are obsessed with their individual rights and interests and are unable to perceive the need to balance these rights and interests against the public good. Just as the radical individualist culture undermines civic virtue, libertarian ideology impedes enactment of civic-minded public policy. Policymakers become trapped in the prisoner's dilemma, unable to communicate with one another and cooperate in order to make all better off. Essential investments in social capital are neglected in favor of short-term self-interested gain. A deteriorating public sphere and weak social institutions fail to provide the social support that would empower individuals to take advantage of their freedom. Libertarians underestimate the importance of community in providing the foundation for liberty.

I have argued here that Americans are too radical individualist and libertarian for the good of American democracy. Our political culture is biased in favor of individual desires over social needs, private interests over the public interest, and individual liberty over community. The criticism of this bias is not meant to denigrate the importance of individual interests and liberty for democracy. A society that failed to provide individuals with a measure of autonomy to pursue their individually determined goals could not be classified as democratic. But the goals of individuals need to be in balance with the needs of the community.

Bringing about a better balance between community and the individual in the United States requires a more communitarian approach to politics.[61] Such an approach challenges the libertarian view that individuals are completely autonomous authors of their own existence; instead, it regards people as products of the many communities, from their families and neighborhoods to the national community, in which they live. Unlike the libertarians, who understand only freedom from community-imposed constraints, communitarians understand that human freedom and dignity require the support of a network of social institutions. A communitarian approach would seek to nurture and protect such institutions, rather than letting them decay as libertarians have. Instead of a libertarian preoccupation with rights, communitarianism emphasizes the need to balance rights with responsibilities, if rights are to be preserved.

A more communitarian influence in American democracy will not be easy to establish. Radical individualism pervades our culture, and it has strong historic roots. Also, careful balancing will be necessary to prevent a pendulum swing toward community from going too far. Authoritarians have often used the preservation of the community as an excuse to abolish individual liberty and impose a single set of community values and norms. Even when democratic institutions are maintained, too much concern for community solidarity can be as great a threat to democracy as excessive individualism. While too much individualism may be a challenge to American democracy, too much community and too little individualism seem to be major challenges in Japan.[62] Balancing American individualism with a greater concern for community and the public good must be done with a judicious concern for preserving the virtues of individualism.

THOUGHT QUESTIONS

1. To what extent might the "radical individualism" decried in this chapter be simply a reflection of a self-interested human nature? Or is a self-interested outlook, itself, a social product—a consequence of a radical individualist culture?

2. Is it realistic to expect people to approach public issues in the disinterested way advocated by Tussman (p. 86)? Can you identify examples from history, news accounts, or your own experience when people seem to have placed the broader public good ahead of their individual self-interest?

3. On p. 82, the author makes a distinction between "trivial" and "fundamental" rights (e.g., right to smoke versus right to due process). What seems to be the basis for this distinction? How would we distinguish a claim to a fundamental right from a claim that is trivial? What criteria are implied in this chapter? Do you agree that this distinction is possible?

4. Do you find anything attractive in the outlook of Brian Palmer (pp. 65–66)? What advantages might there be to a society made up of Brian Palmers? Do these, possibly, offset the disadvantages emphasized in this chapter?

5. If radical individualism is as pervasive in modern America as this chapter argues, can anything be done to counteract it? Are there practical reforms that might encourage Americans to adopt more communitarian outlooks? Or do we need to find ways to adjust our conception of democracy somehow to accommodate radical individualism?

SUGGESTIONS FOR FURTHER READING

Bellah, Robert N., Richard Madsen, William M. Sullivan, Ann Swidler, and Steven M. Tipton. *Habits of the Heart: Individualism and Commitment in American Life.* Berkeley: University of California Press, 1985. This classic diagnosis of American radical individualism is must reading for anyone interested in understanding contemporary American life. The authors have written a follow-up volume that suggests some reforms: *The Good Society.* New York: Vintage Books, 1992.

Ehrenhalt, Alan. *The Lost City: The Forgotten Virtues of Community in America.* New York: Basic Books, 1995. A description of life in Chicago in the 1950s, emphasizing not nostalgia but the advantages and disadvantages of a more communitarian time and place.

Elshtain, Jean Bethke. *Democracy on Trial.* New York: Basic Books, 1995. An analysis of the weakening of democratic civil society and civility in America today.

Etzioni, Amitai. *The Spirit of Community: Rights, Responsibilities, and the Communitarian Agenda.* New York: Crown Publishers, 1993. Sociologist Amitai Etzioni is one of the founders of a new communitarian movement in the United States that seeks to balance excessive American individualism with more concern for community values. This book sets out the principles of the movement. Communitarians publish a quarterly journal entitled *The Responsive Community.*

Glendon, Mary Ann. *Rights Talk: The Impoverishment of Political Discourse.* New York: Free Press, 1991. A thorough analysis of the political consequences of the American preoccupation with individual rights and the simultaneous neglect of community responsibilities. Included are many comparisons of American rights talk with how other democracies address rights issues.

*Hayek, Friedrich A. von. *The Road to Serfdom.* Chicago: University of Chicago Press, 1944.

*Hayek, Friedrich A. von. *The Constitution of Liberty.* Chicago: University of Chicago Press, 1978. Hayek's works provide a systematic and persuasively argued case for the libertarian position.

Putnam, Robert. *Bowling Alone: The Collapse and Revival of American Community.* New York: Simon and Schuster, 2000. Putnam makes his case that Americans do not involve themselves in the civic realm as they once did and provides some concrete suggestions for bringing them back in.

*Schudson, Michael *The Good Citizen: A History of American Civic Life.* New York: Free Press, 1998. A thoughtful history of differing American conceptions of citizenship since colonial times. Schudson sees the current preoccupation with rights not as a corruption of civic life, but as the latest, enriching layer in Americans' continually evolving understanding of democratic citizenship.

Slater, Phillip. *The Pursuit of Loneliness.* Boston: Beacon Press, 1990. Originally published in 1970, this is one of the most thoughtful analyses of American culture to emerge from the turmoil of the 1960s. Slater believes that individualism provides the key to understanding all of America's ills — from militarism abroad to dysfunctional families at home.

Tocqueville, Alexis de. *Democracy in America.* Edited and abridged by Richard D. Heffner. New York: Mentor Books, 1956. This shortened version of Tocqueville's classic provides a good introduction to his work.

*Presents a point of view that disagrees with the arguments presented in this chapter.

SELECTED WEB SITES

http://www.Puaf.umd.edu/civicrenewal/ The official website of the National Commission on Civic Renewal, including all its reports and briefing papers.

http://www.gwu.edu/~ccps/ The Communitarian Network, sponsored by Amitai Etzioni, puts one in touch with the latest communitarian thinking.

http://www.cato.org/ The leading libertarian think tank provides a reasoned defense of the libertarian point of view as well as practical policy proposals.

http://www.ksg.harvard.edu/~saguaro/ This is Robert Putnam's project for exploring how civic participation can be renewed.

CHAPTER 3

The Third Challenge: Citizen Participation

> *The political activity that pervades the United States must be seen in order to be understood. No sooner do you set foot on American ground than you are stunned by a kind of tumult.*
>
> —ALEXIS DE TOCQUEVILLE

DO WE AMERICAN citizens participate too much or too little for the good of our democracy? To many readers, this may seem a silly question. Of course there is too little participation! As hundreds of editorials have reminded us after recent presidential elections, nearly half of the eligible electorate fails to go to the polls in these quadrennial opportunities to exercise the right to vote. In midterm congressional elections, voter turnout has dropped to about one-third of eligible voters during the past couple of decades. Turnout in state or local elections held at times that do not coincide with the biennial national elections is usually even lower; turnouts of less than 10 percent of eligible voters are not uncommon. For many commentators, such low turnout rates, in themselves, represent an apathetic, politically disinterested citizenry offering inadequate support to our democratic institutions. The fact that turnout rates have been steadily declining for the past thirty years portends, for some, an alarming prospect for the future survival of American democracy. If fewer and fewer citizens participate in as fundamental a democratic institution as elections, these commentators ask, how can our democracy remain healthy?

Although a focus on voter turnout suggests a politically detached and increasingly apathetic citizenry, other developments seem to indicate the opposite. At the same time that voter turnout has been declining, the country seems to have experienced an explosion of citizen activism. During the 1970s, 1980s, and 1990s,

---

Opposite: *The Rev. Martin Luther King Jr.'s "I Have a Dream" speech energized the 1960s civil rights movement. (AP/Wide World Photos)*

more and more Americans have been getting involved in grassroots citizens' groups organized around a host of public issues. Representing themselves with colorful acronyms such as ACORN, COPS, and BUILD, these organizations have begun to play an important role in the politics of many local communities. At the national level, groups knitting together local activists organized around such important national issues as environmental protection, consumer protection, abortion, taxes, and civil rights, among many other issues, place tremendous pressure on elected representatives at all levels of government. And not content simply to lobby representatives, citizens have taken direct control of legislation with increasing frequency. In states that permit it, use of the voter initiative and referendum to allow citizens to vote directly on issues has expanded steadily for the past two decades. Larger numbers of citizens than ever are prepared to put their time and energy into promoting causes they believe in and, sometimes, take direct responsibility for enacting their preferences into law.

From the perspective of elected lawmakers, the citizen participation issue has two faces. On one side, fewer citizens seem interested in showing up to vote representatives into office. On the other side, once in office, elected representatives are beleaguered with citizen activists monitoring every vote and ready with vociferous demands on every conceivable issue. This second side of participation has led some political analysts to worry about excessive participation, despite declining voter turnout. These analysts are concerned because our representative institutions have become overloaded with too many demands from an overly active citizenry. This overload has made it impossible for them to deliberate calmly and devise good policies for the entire society. So, from the point of view of "overload" on elected representatives, too much participation may be the larger problem for our democracy. In order to sort out these contradictory features of citizen participation in American politics, it is necessary to examine how the various trends in participation are affecting the ability of the system to satisfy the prescriptions of democratic theory. How does the nature of participation in contemporary American politics affect our ability to achieve the fundamental values of political equality, liberty, and popular sovereignty? This examination begins with a brief review of contradictions in democratic theory regarding the appropriate role of citizen participation in a democracy. I then summarize what political scientists know about the nature and extent of political participation in the United States. Alternative evaluations of these findings from the point of view of democratic values are then discussed. And, finally, I present my own views on the state of participation and democracy.

CITIZEN PARTICIPATION AND DEMOCRATIC THEORY

As we discussed in the introduction, a major disagreement among democratic theorists revolves around the citizen's role in a democracy. The Developmental/ Participatory variants of democratic theory assert the need for an active citizenry to be fully participant in all aspects of government if democracy is to be healthy. This view contrasts sharply with the more passive citizen role prescribed in the Protective and Pluralist variants. For these theorists, low levels of citizen participation and participation restricted to limited roles are signs of democratic health. What is the basis for this disagreement over the impact of citizen participation on democracy?

Democratic theorists who advocate the need for high rates of participation believe that participation promotes healthy democracy in two ways. First, widespread participation ensures that public policy will reflect the public good of all and not just the interests of a few. Second, through political participation citizens learn how to be good democratic citizens capable of understanding what is in the public good. According to the Developmental/Participatory theorists, if democracy is to produce government policies reflecting the interests, preferences, and concerns of everyone, the meaning of popular sovereignty, then everyone needs to participate in influencing those policies. Participation, in other words, is an "instrument" for getting what one wants from government; those who fail to use the instrument will be ignored.[1] A healthy democracy involves all in determining government policy because only then will a public good encompassing all be achieved. This participation must include voting in elections, but it must also include vigorous citizen activity between elections to ensure that representatives pay attention to everyone.

More than simply an instrument of popular sovereignty, participation, for Developmental/Participatory theorists, is an end in itself. It is a mechanism for educating good democratic citizens. According to this view, one learns democracy by practicing it. The process of participation allows people to learn about public issues, to become more aware of public needs and the needs of their fellow citizens. In sum, participation is a way of acquiring "civic virtue." As John Stuart Mill put it, "among the foremost benefits of free government is that education of the intelligence and of the sentiments which is carried down to the very lowest ranks of the people when they are called to take part in acts which directly affect the great interests of the country."[2] Another great democratic theorist, Alexis de Tocqueville, believed that political participation trained people in the necessary values of democracy best if it involved direct participation in making policy and responsibility for public policy. That is why he admired New England townships in his visit to the United States.[3] Through direct participation in governing their towns, Tocqueville thought, New Englanders acquired the "republican spirit" needed in governing the nation as a whole. Citizens deliberating on matters of local concern, such as building a road, learned how to listen and understand the needs of their fellow citizens and reach a consensus on the broad needs of the community. For advocates of citizen participation, the capacity of citizens to look beyond their individual self-interest to the larger needs of the community is crucial to a healthy democracy and can be learned only through participation. If citizens do not participate, they not only lose their opportunity to gain attention for their own concerns, but they also fail to acquire the capacity to understand the needs of others and the community. A democracy in which many citizens do not possess this civic virtue will not be a successful democracy.

As we have seen, advocates of a more participatory democracy, while embracing the importance of voting participation, believe that opportunities to participate beyond simply voting are needed if the civic virtue of citizens is to be realized. Many emphasize the importance of participation in contexts in which citizens can deliberate face to face with one another and determine policies directly. Like Tocqueville, Participatory theorists look to direct citizen involvement in local institutions, such as town meetings, as important arenas for learning how to be good democratic citizens. Within representative institutions, they insist on the importance of direct citizen monitoring of representatives as critical to the proper functioning of those representatives. A citizenry that participates only by voting occasionally in elections will not learn completely the democratic lessons that participation should provide. Only direct engagement in debating and, to some extent, deciding public issues will teach the civic virtue that all citizens of a democracy can and must possess.

Proponents of the Protective/Pluralist models are much more skeptical about the capacity of all citizens to acquire civic virtue. They believe democracies must rely primarily on the civic virtue of representatives, with most citizens confined to the role of participating in the selection of good leaders. In *Federalist* No. 10, James Madison argues that one of the advantages of representative democracy over direct democracy, as existed in ancient Athens, is that "the public voice, pronounced by the representatives of the people, will be more consonant to the public good, than if pronounced by the people themselves."[4] This greater emphasis on representatives as responsible for healthy democratic politics leads to a very different outlook on the proper level of participation needed in a good democracy.

According to this alternative view of participation, the lack of participation of even a large proportion of citizens in politics is not a problem for democracy. Protective/Pluralist theorists regard nonparticipation as a sign of stability in democratic regimes and evidence that citizens are content with the policies their representatives have decided for them. Elections are, of course, important for assuring the legitimacy of representatives' decisions, and all citizens in a democracy must have an equal right to participate, but if some citizens opt not to exercise that right, democracy is in no way diminished. As long as democratic rights to participation are assured, those citizens, even if only a minority, with intense interest in public issues will make their concerns known to representatives at the ballot box and between elections. If large numbers of citizens remain quiescent in response to the policies representatives enact, it must be because the nonparticipants are generally satisfied with those policies.

For the Protective/Pluralist theorists, dangers to democracy arise when too many citizens become active. If nonparticipation is a sign of citizen contentment and regime stability, sharp increases in participation indicate that something is wrong. These theorists worry that high levels of participation will lead to more conflict than democratic politics can handle. This conflict will interfere with the ability of representatives to work out reasonable compromises to solve societal problems. Moreover, Protective/Pluralists worry that citizens who choose not to participate in normal times may not possess a sufficient commitment to democratic values. When aroused, they will be prone to support authoritarian solutions to public problems. The increase in protest and participation that preceded the rise to power of the Nazis in Germany in the 1930s is often cited as evidence to support this claim.[5] In sum, too much democracy creates more conflict than representatives can easily resolve, and it brings into democratic politics authoritarian elements of the population who are intolerant of democratic compromises.

The division among democratic theorists about the appropriate role of citizen participation in a democracy suggests competing criteria for evaluating the level and amount of participation in contemporary America. Later on in this chapter, these criteria are used to assess whether the state of American political participation is or is not a challenge to democracy. Before that can be done, we need to look at some empirical information about how much and why Americans participate.

CITIZEN PARTICIPATION IN THE UNITED STATES

Analyses of levels of political participation in the United States usually focus most of their attention on voting. This concern is appropriate for those of us worried about democratic values. For each of the democratic models discussed in the introduction, elections are seen as a crucial mechanism for assuring popular sovereignty in a representative democracy. By voting in elections, individual citizens are able to participate in the exercise of sovereignty. Universal suffrage and a one-person, one-vote system assure that this participation is distributed equally among all citizens. Whatever other inequalities may exist in society, the equal right to the ballot is supposed to provide all citizens with the capacity to influence their representatives. When some citizens fail to exercise their right to vote, thoughtful observers are correct to question the degree to which government by the people can exist.

If voting in elections were the principal criterion for measuring the health of democracies, the United States would be on the critical list. Among industrial democracies, the United States ranks next to last in average voter turnout in recent elections (see figure 3.1, p. 98). Even if we focus only on presidential elections, which create the most interest and excitement among the public, U.S. voter participation is extremely low. In 1996, about 49 percent of all eligible voters turned out to vote for president.[6] This was the lowest turnout of voters in a

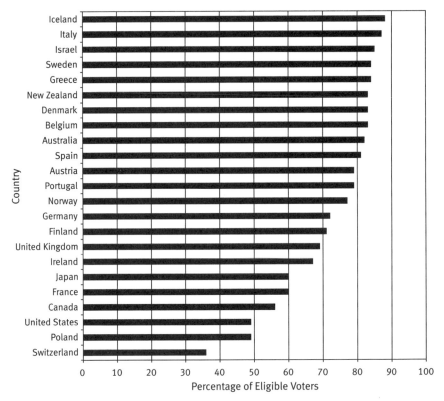

Figure 3.1 Voter Turnout in Selected Industrial Democracies, 1990s

Source: International Institute for Democracy and Electoral Assistance,
www.idea.int/turnout/.
Note: Percentages are for most recent legislative election.

presidential election since 1924. More alarming than the low level of turnout in comparison to other democracies has been the trend in turnout in the United States. Between 1960 and 1988, there was a slow but steady decline in presidential election turnout, with the exception of a slight increase in 1984 (see figure 3.2). A substantial increase in turnout in the 1992 presidential election — to 55.2 percent of eligible voters — offered a hopeful sign that the decline in turnout had bottomed out. Even so, nearly half of eligible voters in 1992 chose not to claim their right to vote, hardly an indication of a surge in participation. In 1996, the 1992 surge proved to be temporary, as turnout of eligible voters dipped to an abysmal 49 percent. The trend has been down, likewise, in midterm congressional elections: in the early 1960s nearly one-half of eligible American voters turned out for those elections; by 1998, only 36 percent did so.[7]

Often when I present these statistics to my students, many of whom have

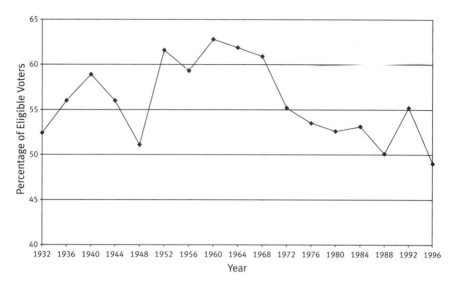

Figure 3.2 Voter Turnout in U.S. Presidential Elections, 1932–96

Source: U.S. Department of Commerce, Bureau of Census, *Statistical Abstract of the United States* (Washington, D.C.: Government Printing Office, 1993), 284. Estimate for 1996 by Center for the Study of the American Electorate.

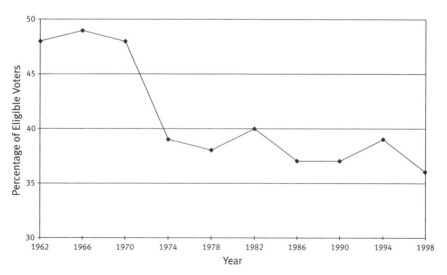

Figure 3.3 Voter Turnout in U.S. Midterm Congressional Elections, 1962–98

Source: Center for the Study of the American Electorate.

recently turned eighteen and are looking forward to their first opportunity to exercise the right of suffrage, they are amazed that so many of their fellow citizens decline to vote. They ask how so many people seem unable to devote a few minutes every few years to such a simple form of participation. Nonvoting, for my students, is an unambiguous indicator of a lazy and apathetic citizenry. As I explain to them, before one draws a hasty conclusion that all nonvoters are lazy and apathetic, one needs to think more carefully about the costs and benefits of voting to the individual. We are all acquainted, especially those of us who have taken Economics 101, with how calculations of costs and benefits affect one's willingness to engage in a particular activity. I hate to get up early and I detest exercise, but every morning I pay the significant cost, to me, of getting up for an early-morning jog because I value the anticipated benefits of long-term good health and a slimmer waistline. Some students may view reading a political science textbook in these terms — as a costly chore that may pay off in the benefit of a good grade. Although we do not often think of political participation in this way, analyzing the costs and benefits of voting is a good approach to understanding why many people do not vote.

At first glance, voting seems like a cost-free activity; it involves nothing more than showing up at the polling booth for a few minutes every year. Surely the benefits of such a simple act will always outweigh the costs. But if we think carefully about the costs and benefits of voting, we can begin to understand why this may not always be the case. First, although the costs of voting are not usually very high (unless you live on a ranch in Nebraska fifty miles from your polling place), voting is not a cost-free activity. Some time must be found on election day to go to the polls. For college professors (and students) with flexible schedules, this may be fairly easy, but for many people, for example, those juggling two jobs, with kids to fetch at the day-care center and dinner groceries to pick up, voting can involve considerable schedule rearranging. Even if they vote only once every four years, busy people may consider whether what they gain from voting is worth disrupting their normal routine. In addition, intelligent voting, surely the goal of a democracy, involves much more than simply showing up at the polls. One must spend time finding information on which to base one's vote. Learning about the candidates and election issues, and forming one's own opinion, will require at least some time reading newspapers and watching television news shows to acquire necessary information. Again, for busy people, this may be a considerable cost.

In the United States, voting involves more than showing up at the polling place and acquiring information. Before one can vote, one must register to vote. This is an added cost to voting, and one that is quite high in some states. It may involve a special trip to a county courthouse, not usually open on weekends, to fill out a registration form, although because of the federal "motor voter" law (discussed in detail later), voter registration at motor vehicle offices has simplified the process for many. Nevertheless, those who may have failed to register while licensing their vehicle still must make a special trip before an election. Most states require that this be accomplished a specified number of days before the election, a significant barrier to potential but busy voters who may not focus on the election until it draws near. And most states require people to be resident in a particular locality for a specified time in order to register, a problem for people who move frequently. As we later see, registration requirements seem to be a major factor in raising the cost of voting.

Even taking into account its costs, voting still is a relatively low-cost activity, especially in comparison to other activities that most people seem to find time for, such as participating in church services, going bowling, or attending a rock concert. Nevertheless, the cost-benefit perspective demands evaluating costs in relation to the benefits of voting, and when we think about voting benefits, we can begin to see how some people may decide that they are not worth even the relatively low voting costs.

One benefit an individual might expect from voting is the opportunity to influence an election outcome, and ultimately public policy, in the direction of her or his preference. Democratic theory assumes this sort of benefit exists when it connects individual suffrage with popular sovereignty. But what is the probability that my individual vote will, in fact, determine an election outcome? In a national presidential election in which millions of other voters participate, this probability is clearly minuscule. Whether I show up on election day or not will not likely make a difference in the outcome of a presidential election. If the benefit I am seeking from voting is a chance to determine an election outcome and thus see that my individual preferences are taken into account when the election is over, the value of this benefit is extremely low. In fact, it will almost never equal even the low costs of voting.

The value of voting benefits in relation to voting costs becomes even lower if we take into account what political scientists call the "paradox of collective action." This paradox is rooted in the peculiar way the relationship between costs and benefits is affected when benefits are collective rather than individual. When I take my morning exercise, the benefits I earn are mainly individual—they contribute to my good health and my slim waist (although my family and friends may also derive some pleasure from seeing me fit and healthy). If I want the benefits of exercise, I can get them only by paying the costs. If I pay the costs, I know I will personally gain the benefits. The benefits I gain from voting are quite different. Election outcomes provide collective benefits rather than individual ones. The benefits I may derive from the victory of candidate A over candidate B will be shared with everyone else in society who benefits from such an outcome. If I benefit from the tax cut candidate A promises, so will all other taxpayers. Moreover, I benefit from the tax cut *whether or not I pay the cost of voting*. Unlike the benefits of my exercise, which I get only if I pay the costs, failing to show up to

UNIVERSITY OF WALES LIBRARY SWANSEA

vote for my favored candidate A does not prevent me from enjoying the tax cut if candidate A wins. Likewise, if I show up and vote for candidate A and a majority of voters choose candidate B, I must suffer with high taxes even though I did my bit to get them cut.

This collective nature of election outcomes should affect how I calculate the costs and benefits of voting. Since the probability that my individual vote will determine an election outcome is so small and since I must live with the outcome whatever it is, I am always better off not paying the low costs of voting — even, paradoxically, when I highly value the benefits I might derive from an election outcome. From my individual point of view, if I do not vote but my candidate wins, I get the benefits of the election outcome without paying any cost. If I do vote, but my candidate happens to lose, I have paid the costs of voting but have not gained any benefits. Given this situation, from a purely individual cost-benefit perspective, nonvoting is always more reasonable than voting. Understanding the logic of the "paradox of collective action" leads one to ask, not why so many people do not vote, but why so many do!

The reason many of us vote, of course, is that we do not calculate the costs and benefits of voting precisely in the way I have described them. Although some of us may pretend sometimes that our one vote makes a difference in an election outcome, most voters are realistic enough to know that an individual vote is not going to determine who wins or loses. But people do not necessarily value the benefit of voting in terms of their individual impact on the outcome or the concrete ways a particular outcome will affect their self-interest.

For most of us, the benefits of voting are symbolic and expressive. I vote in every election because I believe voting is a duty of citizenship in a democratic society. My vote symbolizes my participation in a crucial process that I value very highly. In addition, I usually feel strongly about the competing candidates in a particular election, and voting is a way for me to express my support for the candidate I favor. My vote is an expression of solidarity with my preferred candidate and the millions of other people who support that candidate. To vote for my preferred candidate is a way of saying, "I am the sort of person who believes in the things my candidate represents." Satisfaction from such solidarity comes whether one's candidate wins or loses and may continue to provide expressive opportunities long after the election is over. This expressive satisfaction is revealed in the bumper stickers that often appear in the middle of the term of an unpopular incumbent: "Don't Blame Me, I Voted for [the incumbent's previous election opponent]!" For most voters, going to the polls means more than just influencing the election in a way that serves their interest; it is also a way to feel part of a central symbolic ritual of democracy and to express support for a particular political orientation.

Symbolic and expressive benefits, unlike the effects of an election outcome on the public, are individual rather than collective benefits. I derive the benefit simply by showing up at the polls, no matter what the election result. We can now see how, even from a cost-benefit standpoint, some people might calculate the costs of voting from their point of view in relation to the individual expressive and symbolic benefits and decide to vote. If the benefits to be derived from voting are individual and not collective, there is no "paradox of collective action," and reasonable people will sometimes value the benefits of voting more than its costs. The puzzle posed a few paragraphs ago as to why people bother to vote is largely solved. It is also reasonable to assume that many voters, especially in the face of the powerful symbolic and expressive incentives to vote, do not always think clearly about their potential individual impact on election outcomes. The "paradox of collective action" is not typically part of most civics curricula and is not a concept most voters think about. Consequently, many voters may calculate incorrectly how their vote relates to how they may benefit from election outcomes. This collective benefit illusion added to the individual benefits of voting suggest that many voters may calculate that benefits exceed costs when it comes to voting.

To sum up, then, because many voters will not weigh benefits as they should if they understood clearly the voting paradox and because voting provides individual benefits, many people will weigh the costs of voting against its benefits and decide to go to the polls. At the same time, if we think of voting as a cost-benefit decision, we can understand that some citizens may decide that the benefits of voting are not worth the costs and will stay home on election day. This understanding, however, leads to another puzzle: Why do voters and nonvoters sum the costs and benefits of voting in a given election differently? In other words, what determines who votes and who does not?

Political scientists have found two sets of factors important in determining voter turnout.[8] The first set, *social-psychological* factors, refer to how social status and attitudes affect whether or not one votes. The second set, *legal-institutional* factors, involve the legal rules associated with voting and the governmental and political institutions that organize elections.

Among the social-psychological factors, the most important is the socioeconomic status (SES) of individual voters. People with high SES, usually measured by income, level of education, and occupational status, are much more likely to vote than those with lower SES. Of the components that define socioeconomic status, education is most strongly related to voting. This is not too surprising, considering how education is likely to affect the costs and benefits of voting. The acquisition of election information — who the candidates are, what their stances on issues are, how their positions relate to one's own ideology and interests — becomes easier as one becomes more educated. A college graduate will not have to devote much time to following an election campaign in order to assimilate the information needed to cast a vote. Someone with very little education, however, may find deciphering the front page of a newspaper a daunting and time-consuming task. Also, because more highly educated people are more likely to hold higher-status jobs, which provide more autonomy, they will find getting a few minutes off from work to go to the polls much simpler than an assembly-line worker will.

But it is in the area of voting benefits that educational level probably plays the more important role. Schooling exposes a person to indoctrination regarding the duties of citizenship. Moreover, educated people are apt to read newspaper editorials and magazines promoting the importance of voting. Education also provides people with confidence that their ideas matter; thus they are likely to obtain satisfaction from the expressive benefits of voting. High levels of education are also associated with certain attitudes linked to the propensity to vote. Numerous studies show a strong relationship between voting and a series of attitudes such as an interest in politics, feelings of involvement with political affairs (demonstrated in reading about politics in newspapers and news magazines or watching television news), feelings of political efficacy ("What I think and do makes a difference"), and partisan attachments.[9] Educated people are more likely to vote because education contributes to holding positive political attitudes, lowers information costs, and promotes symbolic and expressive satisfaction.

The impact of social-psychological factors on voting participation strongly skews this participation in the United States in the direction of wealthier citizens. All these factors are strongly associated with one another and seem to follow from access to economic advantages.[10] The wealthier one's family, the more likely one will be highly educated. Education leads to higher incomes and better jobs and the capacity to educate one's own children. Along with a good education and high status, one picks up positive attitudes toward politics and a strong interest in following public affairs. A person with such experiences will weigh the costs and benefits of voting differently than will economically disadvantaged citizens. Consequently, the overall or "aggregate" impact of how social-psychological factors affect each individual's propensity to vote is to produce an electorate that is more affluent than the general citizenry. Although the right to vote is equally distributed in the United States, the actual practice of voting is unequal.

These social-psychological determinants of voting interact strongly with the other set of voting determinants, the legal-institutional. The rules and organizational context in which voting takes place tend to raise the costs of voting for most voters. Unlike many other democracies that schedule elections on holidays or provide workers with time off for voting, American elections invariably occur on workdays. The need for potential voters to register in order to be qualified to vote constitutes the greatest single barrier to voting for most people. The principal difference between voter turnout in industrialized democracies where a large percentage of citizens vote and in the United States is the existence of registration requirements. If one compares voter turnout in the United States with other countries among all *registered* voters rather than all *eligible* voters (which includes people who are not registered), then the United States no longer ranks at the bottom of democracies but somewhere in the middle.[11] Turnout in U.S. presidential elections was 76 percent among *registered* voters in 1992 and 63 percent in 1996 (compared to 55 percent of *eligible* voters in 1992 and 49 percent of eligible voters in 1996).[12] Clearly, many of those who do not vote are unable to do so because they are not registered.

Why does voting registration make such a difference in voter turnout in the United States and not in other democracies? In the United States, unlike in all other democracies, voter registration is an individual rather than a governmental responsibility.[13] In other democracies, government bureaucracies are charged with the task of identifying, prior to election time, who is eligible to vote. In many countries, governments issue all residents identity cards, which indicate voter eligibility. On election day, citizens simply show their identity cards in order to be admitted to the polling booth. Democracies without identity cards, such as Great Britain and Canada, conduct canvasses before each election to determine voter lists.[14] For Americans, registration requires individuals to overcome state-government-imposed bureaucratic obstacles. So, unlike in other democracies, registration in the United States is subject to the same individual cost-benefit calculations as are involved in voting.

Not surprisingly, the social-class bias of voting affects registration. All the factors mentioned above that deter less affluent, less educated, and lower-status citizens from voting operate to discourage registration. Given the complicated nature of registration, the class bias is compounded, since the cost of registration in time and effort is even higher than showing up at the polling place on election day. Most registration laws, with their minimum residency requirements and preelection cutoff dates, also discriminate against the less affluent, who tend to change their residence more often than their better-off fellow citizens. In 1993 Congress enacted the National Voter Registration Act, or "motor voter" law, aimed at simplifying registration. The new law requires states to provide their citizens with the opportunity to register to vote by mail and at automobile registry offices (hence "motor voter") and other state offices that citizens regularly visit. Although only partially implemented by 1996, "motor voter" seems to have increased somewhat the number of registered voters, but it obviously did not increase actual voter turnout in either the 1996 or 1998 elections.[15] Given more time, "motor voter" may produce registration rates comparable to other democracies and reduce the social-class bias in American voting participation. Meanwhile, registration laws will continue to be a factor in the low turnout in the United States compared to other democracies and make voting participation more strongly skewed in favor of the more affluent than in any other democracy.[16]

Aside from comparisons with other democracies, we can see the impact of complex registration procedures on turnout if we study our own historical experience. During most of the nineteenth century, voter turnout was much higher than it is today. Two developments resulted in the enactment of restrictive registration laws and other barriers to voting around the turn of the century. First, in the South, white elites passed a variety of measures aimed at preventing blacks from voting. These restrictions required potential voters to pay a poll tax or pass a literacy test in order to register, provisions that prevented poor whites as well as poor blacks from exercising their right of suffrage. Consequently, voter turnout in the South dropped to only about 20 percent of the eligible electorate by the 1920s.[17] In the North, a simultaneous development served to erect barriers to the participation of some voters. Progressive reformers, concerned with the corruption of political party machines, won the enactment of voter-registration statutes to prevent voter fraud.[18] However laudable the Progressives' intentions, these statutes raised the cost of voting and discouraged turnout.

In their zeal to stamp out political party corruption, the Progressives succeeded in bringing about another legal-institutional change that undermined turnout. Various reforms, such as party primaries and civil service reform, greatly weakened the organizational strength of political parties. Yet strong, well-organized political parties had been a major factor in mobilizing voters. The weakening of political parties that the Progressives set in motion has continued throughout this century (a matter explored in more detail in the next chapter) and has effectively eliminated the capacity of political parties to mobilize voter turnout. At the same time that complex registration laws increased the cost of voting for individual voters, an institution that could have helped individual supporters to overcome these costs — the political party — lost its capacity to do so.[19] Political party mobilization in European democracies, particularly on the part of labor and social democratic parties, are a major factor in both raising overall voter turnout and bringing lower-SES voters to the polls.

In summary, several factors discourage a large proportion of Americans from voting. Most important seem to be registration laws, which place the burden for qualifying to vote on the individual citizen. These laws seems to be a heavy cost for many potential voters. And institutions, such as political parties, that might have assisted voter registration have ceased to play this role. With voting participation left up to individual calculations of costs and benefits, individual social-psychological factors become key determinants of who votes. Because nearly all the attributes associated with the propensity to vote — from education to positive feelings about politics — are more likely to be present among the more affluent, the electorate is not representative of all citizens. In the United States, elections are increasingly a ritual in which only the economically comfortable play a part.

One puzzle for political scientists is why voting participation has gradually but steadily declined since 1960. Given what we know about general determinants of voting participation, one might have expected participation to have increased over the past forty years. Potential voters are better educated now, and the Voting Rights Act of 1965 eliminated significant barriers to voter registration of blacks in the South, among whom turnout has increased. In spite of these factors, which would seem to promote higher turnout, something else seems to be producing continued turnout decline. Lower turnouts in the 1970s were often attributed to the effect of the Twenty-sixth Amendment, which lowered the voting age from twenty-one to eighteen in 1972 (younger citizens are less apt to vote than older ones), bringing into the electorate the large "baby boomer" generation. But when the trend continued, even as boomers reached middle age in the 1990s, political scientists had to search for other explanations.

One systematic study attributes most of the decline in voting to a decline in citizens' confidence in their ability to influence government (political efficacy), less interest in political campaigns, and less political partisanship.[20] All these factors suggest voting decline is rooted in people's feelings of connection to the political system. More Americans are choosing not to vote because they feel disconnected from politics and do not think it is especially relevant to their lives. The continuing decline in political parties as voter-mobilization institutions contributes to these feelings of disaffection. Also, as is discussed more fully in the next chapter, citizens' disgust with the increasing triviality of election campaigns turns them away from politics. Voter disenchantment with politics and increasing detachment from political parties seemed to contribute to the extremely low turnout in the most recent elections, overpowering the "motor voter" law's increase in registration.[21] One careful study provides convincing evidence that negative media coverage of politics has fostered public cynicism that, in turn, has suppressed participation.[22] Whatever the precise reasons for turnout decline, its effect has been to produce an active electorate that is better off economically than American citizens as a whole.

The factors that affect voting participation influence other forms of electoral participation as well, except that even fewer citizens engage in these activities than vote. Only about one-third of citizens report discussing elections and trying to persuade others how to vote during presidential election campaigns.[23] Other, more intense activities, such as working in campaigns, attending meetings, and giving money, involve even fewer citizens. Unlike voting, however, participation in these other forms of electoral activity has not declined over the past few decades; about as many people attend election rallies, give money, and try to persuade their neighbors today as did so thirty years ago. The exception seems to be wearing campaign buttons and putting bumper stickers on cars — items in short supply in recent years because campaigns must spend most of their money on television advertising. Also, Americans are not significantly different from the citizens of other democracies in their propensity to engage in these other election activities.[24] But these other more intensive forms of participation are even more likely than voting to involve the more affluent. Based on their study of all forms

Demonstrators in the streets of Seattle voice their protests against the global influence of the World Trade Organization. (AP/Wide World Photos)

of voluntary political participation in America, political scientists Sidney Verba, Kay Schlozman, and Henry Brady conclude that "the public's voice is often loud, sometimes clear, but rarely equal."[25]

The most common form of electoral participation is voting for representatives, but over the past two decades, many Americans have had increasing opportunities to vote issues of concern to them directly into law. Voter initiative and referendum, devices allowing citizens to pass laws directly, are a legacy of the same Progressive era that so greatly weakened political parties. At the beginning of this century, many states enacted constitutional procedures permitting citizens to initiate proposals for new laws through the circulation of petitions and to vote directly in an election to enact such proposals. At present, about half the states permit the initiative and referendum.[26] This form of direct democracy allows citizens to bypass their elected legislators and seize for themselves the right to pass laws.

Citizens' use of the initiative and referendum is more common today than even a few years ago. It is now typical for more than two hundred referenda to be on ballots throughout the United States in an election year.[27] Referenda take in a range of political concerns, from seat-belt laws to prayer in schools. Among the issues with greatest governmental impact have been initiatives in several states, most notably California's Proposition 13 and Massachusetts's Proposition 2½, to limit the ability of elected representatives to raise taxes, and initiatives to limit the terms of elected representatives. Both political liberals and conservatives have used the referendum device to enact issues of concern to them. In the past couple of decades, although participation of all voters declined, citizen activists participated vigorously in putting issues directly on the ballot. The picture of citizen apathy that appears when we look at voter turnout statistics is at odds with the willingness of some citizens to be more active than ever in asserting their rights to direct democracy.

Another trend at odds with declining voter turnout is the rise in citizen activism. Since the 1960s, more Americans have been willing to devote time to participation in causes and movements in which they believe. This can be seen in both the rise of grassroots citizen activism and the increase in the number of national public interest and citizen groups. To some extent, this rise in citizen activism is a legacy of the protest movements of the 1960s, such as the civil rights and antiwar movements. Experiences with these movements provided Americans with models for mobilizing ordinary individuals to influence political events. Although most of us associate the citizen mobilization of the 1960s with liberal causes, the spirit and tactics of these movements have inspired conservative activism as well, such as the Right-to-Life movement, which consciously models itself on the civil rights movement.

In many local communities, groups of citizens have been engaged in what author Harry C. Boyte has called a "backyard revolution" — the formation of citizens' groups organized around local issues: preventing crime, improving schools, protecting consumer rights, and forcing toxic-waste cleanup.[28] Sometimes these efforts lead to the formation of permanent community organizations in which ordinary citizens participate to produce far-ranging changes in their communities. One such organization is Communities Organized for Public Service (COPS) in San Antonio, Texas. Formed in 1974 in San Antonio's Mexican American barrios, COPS brought together citizen leaders from church parishes, PTAs, Boy Scout and Girl Scout groups, and women's clubs to find ways to participate effectively in influencing local government.[29] COPS concentrated initially on such mundane but important neighborhood issues as pressuring the local government to pave streets and install street lights in the poor neighborhoods of San Antonio's west side. Soon, however, the organization's clout was utilized in behalf of broader issues. By the early 1980s, these citizen activists had changed the city charter to permit more adequate representation of all citizens, elected a majority on the city council (formerly dominated by local business interests), and elected San Antonio's first Mexican-American mayor.[30] According to Boyte, this kind of successful citizen activism has flowered in many other cities, producing a nationwide network linking grassroots organizations with colorful acronyms: CAP in Chicago, UNO in Los Angeles, OCO in Oakland, and BUILD in Baltimore.[31] This network, organized under the auspices of the Industrial Areas Foundation founded by the famous community organizer Saul Alinsky, has formed twenty-four organizations in seven states.[32]

Although many grassroots citizens' movements focus on groups representing poor people and more liberal political agendas, citizen activism spans the political spectrum. In fact, some of the more successful grassroots movements have promoted conservative causes. The various taxpayers' revolts of the 1970s and 1980s all had grassroots components that energized many ordinary citizens to work for state tax limitations. The classic was the movement to pass Proposition 13 in California, which was led by a colorful real estate entrepreneur, Howard Jarvis. Fueled with business funding, the Proposition 13 movement mobilized many Californians to volunteer their time and work actively to promote passage of the amendment.[33] Opposition to government taxes has been one of the more effective issues for mobilizing citizen activism in recent years.

The new citizen activism has not always been benign. The bomb at the federal building in Oklahoma City on 19 April 1995 that killed 168 people brought to the nation's attention a network of right-wing militias that seems to have nurtured this vile act. Press reports following the attack educated many Americans about the growth in recent years of small groups of paranoid activists organizing private armies and undertaking military training to prepare for armed conflict with the federal government. Like the citizen activists described above, militia members join with fellow citizens on behalf of shared political beliefs, but, in this case, the beliefs derive from far right, usually white supremacist ideologies and paranoid conspiracy theories, rather than a concern to improve local communities. Besides the militias, some activist groups have taken otherwise legitimate political aims, such as opposition to abortion, concern for the environment, or advocacy of more effective AIDS policy to fanatical extremes.[34] They adopt tactics as offensive as possible and physically threatening to their opponents in order to attract publicity to their cause. While the activists believe that their goals justify such tactics, their approach to public issues is no more conducive to the civil discourse required in a democracy than the threat and use of violence by the militias. Luckily for democracy, so far, militia violence and extremist tactics have been only a sideshow in the backyard revolution of grassroots citizen activism.

In addition to a rise in local citizen activism, the past few decades have produced a rise in national organizations mobilizing their members on behalf of public causes or issues. Common Cause, the Sierra Club, Mothers against Drunk Driving (MADD), and the Children's Defense Fund all provide vehicles for citizens throughout the country to participate in various ways in promoting public causes.[35] For many members of these organizations, participation is limited to contributing dues and following the lobbying activities of the national organization in the literature it distributes. Others are more actively involved; they join organized letter-writing campaigns to legislators or participate on the boards of directors of the organizations' local affiliates. Again, while commentators often focus on the rise of liberal advocacy groups, such as Norman Lear's Citizens for the American Way, many citizen advocacy groups have promoted conservative causes. Groups opposing government spending and taxes, such as the National Taxpayers Union, or opposing abortion rights, such as the National Right to Life Committee, are as much a part of the rise in citizen activism as are groups on the left. As with direct democracy through the initiative and referendum and grass-roots citizen activism, the increase in citizen involvement in national advocacy groups cuts across ideological lines.

The new citizen activism does offset somewhat the picture of growing citizen disenchantment and apathy in the United States portrayed when declining voter participation is discussed. While many citizens are participating less in the simplest form of participation, voting, some citizens have become much more active in promoting their views directly to government. The seemingly contradictory picture described at the beginning of this chapter of a citizenry simultaneously more apathetic and more active in the past few decades becomes more understandable. Fewer Americans vote, but more Americans than in the past join and participate in organizations that promote specific political views.

Before understanding this new activism as fulfilling the Developmental/ Participatory vision of an active citizenry, three cautions are in order. First, the new citizen activism is still confined to a very narrow sector of the American population, and it is a sector that is much more affluent, on average, than most Americans.[36] As the earlier discussion of the costs and benefits of participation suggests, one should not expect very many citizens to be willing to pay the rather high costs of citizen activism unless benefits are also high. Survey evidence suggests that only a very small number of citizens are willing to pay the costs of citizen activism. Although from the perspective of a member of Congress seeing an explosion of groups lobbying on a wide variety of issues and receiving a mountain of postcards pressuring for a vote on a particular issue, millions of citizens seem involved as never before, but these citizens constitute a very small proportion of a country of 250 million people. Only a minority of Americans belong to a membership organization, even when one includes such nonpolitical groups as the Elks.[37] The proportion fueling the new citizen activism is a minuscule part of the overall American citizenry. Also, as one would predict from the earlier cost-benefit analysis, affluent citizens are better able to pay the costs of participation than are the less affluent. Citizen activism, despite the inclusion of "backyard" groups of poorer people, is skewed overall even more in the direction of the highly educated and affluent than are less costly forms of participation, such as voting.[38]

Second, as is detailed in chapter 5, powerful, well-funded elite groups, particularly business corporations, have developed sophisticated techniques to use both direct democracy and the appearance of genuine citizen activism on behalf of their special interest goals. In states such as California where referenda are common, corporate interests routinely hire paid signature gatherers to place

Petitions generated by a lobbying group opposed to the 1999 turnover of the Panama Canal pile up near the steps of the Capitol. (AP/Wide World Photos)

initiatives on the ballot and then fund advertising campaigns to pass them. For example, Philip Morris funded a campaign a few years ago to pass what appeared to be an antismoking initiative, but with small print provisions that actually weakened the state's existing antismoking legislation.[39] Similarly, citizens who attempt to use referenda as a tool to regulate corporate interests must be prepared to counter expensive opposition media advertising. Rather than being a tool that the Progressives hoped would empower ordinary citizens, referenda, in an era of expensive and sophisticated mass media communication, have become more of a tool for wealthy special interests. Another way in which what appears to be genuine citizen activism is really a tool for wealthy interests occurs in so-called "astroturf" campaigns. Using direct mail, television advertising, and toll-free 800 numbers, lobbyists, acting on behalf of wealthy interests, generate huge volumes of mail to congressional offices.[40] Such campaigns are intended to give the impression of genuine grassroots concern, but it is concern artificially generated by the lobbyists.

Third, while some of the new activism has involved groups, such as COPS, that are concerned with a wide range of issues and requiring sustained time commitments, most citizen activism has involved people mobilized around narrow issues whose involvement consists mainly in writing checks. While the extent of member involvement in group activities varies and nearly all have local affiliates, paid professionals run most of the national citizens' groups mentioned earlier, such as Common Cause. The typical group member need devote little time or effort to the group's activities other than responding to funding solicitations. Such groups offer little opportunity for developing the civic skills and "social capital" nurtured in the nonpolitical associations so important to observers such as Tocqueville and Putnam, as described in chapter 2. While some commentators see the rise of new citizens' groups as a substitute for the decline in membership in civic groups that concerns Putnam, the more limited involvement that they require is cause for skepticism.[41] Furthermore, because they mobilize their members around a single or narrow range of issues, such groups may not stimulate broader concern for public affairs among most group members or do much to stimulate general political participation. While intense concern for drunk driving or abortion or the homeless is laudable, it does not necessarily produce the actively involved citizens envisioned in the Developmental or Participatory models.

PARTICIPATION AS A CHALLENGE TO DEMOCRACY

What sort of challenge does this rather contradictory picture of citizen participation in the United States pose for our democracy? Do Americans participate too much or too little for the good of democracy? How does the amount and quality of citizen participation in America influence the quality of our democracy? Among thoughtful observers of trends in participation, there are three different responses to these questions. One response is to worry that the increasing use of such direct democracy devices as the initiative and referendum and the rise in citizen activism are undermining representative institutions. A second focuses on the class bias in voting participation and the consequent exclusion of many citizens from democratic politics. And a third response decries the limited opportunities for citizens to participate in a meaningful way in deliberating on public issues.

A number of commentators on recent American political history have expressed concern that pressures from an active citizenry prevent elected governmental officials from making the "hard choices" and "imposing the necessary medicine" to solve our problems. A Harvard political scientist, Samuel Huntington, made such an argument in a now-famous essay published in a report of the Trilateral Commission in 1975.[42] According to Huntington, a "democratic surge" of participation that began in the 1960s was threatening the "governability of democracy" in the United States. Protest demonstrations, social movements, the mobilization of campaign workers for political candidates ranging from Eugene McCarthy to Barry Goldwater, and the rise of citizen advocacy groups such as Common Cause were having adverse consequences for stable democratic politics.

Politicians were forced to respond to this citizen participation by increasing the level of governmental activities, specifically higher levels of expenditures for social programs. At the same time, increased participation constituted a challenge to government authority, preventing politicians from imposing the "hard" decisions necessary to make government effective in solving problems. Huntington feared that this "democratic distemper" — increased government activity combined with a reduction in government authority — had two dangerous consequences.[43] First, a growth in deficit spending, which was caused by expanded government spending not accompanied by increased taxation, created a fiscal crisis in the economy. Second, in the wake of the Vietnam War, the government lost its capacity to impose sacrifices, such as the draft and high levels of military spending, needed to maintain national security. Government was thus "overloaded" with democratic demands from all sides, leaving no capacity to formulate effective policy to address domestic and foreign policy challenges. The only solution, for Huntington, was "a greater degree of moderation in democracy."[44]

As readers of the first section of this chapter can readily see, Huntington's analysis is grounded in the Protective/Pluralist orientation to democracy. Citizens participating too actively in making demands on their representatives will interfere with effective elite policymaking. By the 1980s, Huntington moderated his position somewhat, noting a moderation in the democratic surge of the 1960s and the capacity of the Reagan administration to renew a more aggressive foreign policy posture.[45] Other commentators have taken up his concerns, however, pointing to the explosion of deficit spending under Reagan.[46] In fact, these observers argue that the 1981 Reagan tax cuts that created the mammoth deficits were an outgrowth of the citizen tax revolts beginning in California with Proposition 13 in 1978. Reagan responded to popular pressure to cut taxes but was unable, because of equal popular pressures, to cut spending to offset the tax reduction.[47] The difficulties that Reagan's successors had in controlling deficit spending through the mid-1990s were seen as a continuing consequence of popular pressure interfering with the ability of elected elites to impose "hard choices." More recently, the reluctance of both the Clinton administration and congressional Republicans to propose either tax increases or benefit cuts to address projected shortfalls in Social Security and Medicare financing in the next century is attributed to fear of mobilized pressure groups such as the American Association of Retired Persons (AARP).

Overload theorists assume that policymaking in a democracy is solely the responsibility of elected representatives. In their view, effective policymaking requires insulating representative institutions from popular democratic forces. When popular pressures are too great, representatives are unable to forge the compromises needed for the public good. As was Madison's belief, overload theorists expect representatives, not the public at large, to be the guardians of the public good. If you assume that responsibility for the public good lies with elected elites, rather than with the people, keeping the people away from too direct an involvement in policymaking becomes, ironically, a requisite for healthy democracy.[48]

While some political analysts worried that too much political participation constrained necessary policy choices, others emphasized how declining voter participation facilitated the conservative policy shifts of the past two decades. Beginning in the late 1970s, federal policymakers were altering government policy in favor of business interests and more affluent Americans. Deregulation of business, a less progressive tax code, antiunion labor policies, and cutbacks in social programs for the poor have been the staples of government policymaking for many years now.[49] President Clinton's remark that the "era of big government is over" signaled an admission that both major parties endorsed these policy trends. Of course, ending big government came at the expense of the less affluent, while "middle-class" but expensive programs, such as Medicare and Social Security, have remained largely untouched. Since the late 1970s, government seems to have been quite capable of imposing "hard" decisions on poor and working-class Americans, while the more affluent have benefited greatly from government programs.[50]

For some observers, this conservative policy shift was possible only because of the underrepresentation of workers and the poor among the electorate and the politically active. Richard Cloward and Frances Fox Piven, for example, point to the lack of support in public opinion for most of the conservative agenda. Reducing big government succeeded electorally because voting participation was confined to the more affluent parts of the population.[51] For example, one study found the voting preferences of nonvoters to be so different from those who voted that the election of Republican President Ronald Reagan in 1980, a key event in propelling the subsequent antigovernment shift, would not have occurred had voter turnout been higher.[52] According to these analyses, politicians from the 1970s through the 1990s could not have been elected had they been required to sell these conservative policies to a more highly mobilized electorate. The more extreme class bias of other forms of participation, such as contributing to campaigns or contacting representatives, distorts the public voice even further in the direction of policies favoring the more affluent.[53]

The argument, then, is that low rates of citizen participation and the class bias of this participation produce policies that are not representative of the preferences of the entire citizenry. Politicians can safely ignore poor and working-class citizens when enacting policies because they know the less affluent are not among the politically active. According to some observers, the long-term "demobilization" of the working-class electorate since the imposition of registration and other voting barriers at the beginning of this century has been a major factor in preventing the emergence of a genuine labor or social democratic party in the United States.[54] In Europe, such parties are common and have been a major factor in mobilizing voters in behalf of more generous social welfare policies. People who do not vote in the United States have precisely the social and economic character-istics of those who support left-wing European parties. Higher voter participation rates would provide political support for such social programs as universal health insurance, which public opinion polls show a majority of Americans favor and which has existed for years in all other industrial democracies.[55] The long-term conservative bias of American public policy is a reflection of the strongly skewed class bias of voting participation.

There is some evidence that modern political campaigns have adjusted to declining participation rates and even encourage the trend in order to simplify campaigning.[56] As political consultants have become more influential in shaping modern campaigns, they have applied many of the techniques used in market-ing commercial products to "selling" political candidates. One of these lessons is the importance of targeting messages to those most likely to "buy" one's prod-uct. Smaller, less diverse electorates are easier to target than larger, less predictable ones. As one political scientist describes this orientation: "Political marketing maxim number one: the fewer people voting, the easier it is to sell a candidate."[57] In this context, negative, foolish campaigns that disgust voters and discourage them from voting become a conscious tactic to facilitate selling the candidate. Because less educated and less affluent voters are less likely to participate to begin with and are more easily discouraged, these techniques increase the bias of appeals to the more affluent. Modern campaign techniques, like the longer-term trends of voter demobilization, are likely to increase the extent to which the participatory electorate is unrepresentative of the citizenry as a whole. Under these conditions, public policy is not likely to reflect in a democratic manner the preferences of all the people. Elections have ceased to be an instrument of popular sovereignty.

The third and final concern about how the character of American political participation undermines our democracy focuses not on who participates but on how participation is organized. As we saw earlier in this chapter, democratic the-orists of both the Developmental and Participatory persuasions emphasize the educational importance of the experience of political participation for forming good democratic citizens. For John Stuart Mill and Alexis de Tocqueville, citizen deliberation on public affairs was key to the maintenance of a successful democ-racy. Deliberation meant discussing public issues, listening to alternative points of view, arguing one's position, and through this process forming a consensus or, at least, a majority outlook on what was good for the community. For some ob-servers of contemporary American politics, our main participation problem is the absence of real deliberative opportunities for citizens. For most citizens, political participation is usually an isolated individual act largely disconnected from inter-action with others, particularly those who might think differently about issues. As is described in more detail in chapter 4, participation in elections involves passive observation of campaigns leading to an individual decision to vote. Although some of us may discuss an upcoming election among family and friends, we are primarily passive observers of the contest between the participants as it is reported in the media. The marketing model presented earlier accurately reflects the role most voters have been assigned in modern campaigns — selecting the preferred candidate "product" after individual evaluation of the alternatives. The process provides little real opportunity to deliberate with fellow citizens about public issues.

The lack of deliberation opportunities in the election of representatives is duplicated in other forms of participation: voting on referenda, supporting interest or advocacy groups, and even responding to public opinion polls. Public opinion expert Daniel Yankelovich calls this the "missing concept" in American democracy.[58] Deliberation on public issues has ceased to be part of the citizen's role; only experts and elites participate in shaping actual policy decisions. Without appropriate deliberative institutions, citizen opinion on issues becomes an aggregation of individual snap judgments without the thoughtfulness, weighing of alternatives, and genuine engagement with an issue that democracy requires.[59] This explains why public opinion polls reveal seeming contradictions, such as overwhelming support for expenditures for public services along with overwhelming opposition to the taxes needed to pay for them. As long as citizens are not actively engaged with public issues, they do not have to face the tradeoffs necessary to cope with them.

At the same time, governing elites exploit contradictions in public opinion on behalf of their own policy agendas. What is missing in American democracy are public institutions through which citizens can deliberate on public issues and form considered judgments. Without them, elites will disregard public preferences when actually formulating policy, even while selectively using public opinion to legitimize the elite's agenda. This missing concept in American democracy leads to the growing alienation of many Americans from the political system. The feeling that political decisions are made without regard for the concerns of ordinary people is common in the United States today, and many citizens link it to the absence of mechanisms for deliberating on public issues.

Americans' frustration with the absence of meaningful structures for deliberation and participation was the central finding of a Kettering Foundation study conducted in 1990 and 1991.[60] Citizens' groups in ten cities probed what a cross section of Americans thought about their role in the political system. Far from being apathetic, the Kettering study participants were anxious to participate in a constructive way in public life. To their chagrin, the participants felt "pushed out" of a political process dominated by politicians and special-interest lobbyists. Sound bites and negative attacks were perceived as dominating public discourse.[61] Most important, debate on public issues was remote from citizen concerns and offered no opportunity for citizen involvement. As one participant said, "I'm never aware of an opportunity to go somewhere and express my opinion and have someone hear what I have to say."[62] Ordinary citizens seem to share the democratic theorists' concern that our democracy does not offer structures for citizen deliberation and involvement in public decisions.

PARTICIPANTS IN THE Kettering study would surely find Huntington's preoccupation with participatory overload in American politics bizarre. Instead of feeling involved in pressuring elected representatives, the Kettering respondents perceived representatives as remote figures imposing choices over which the ordinary citizen had no control. Analysts who emphasize the class bias of voting participation would also take issue with overload theorists. To what extent, they would ask, are the pressures on representatives and policy gridlock really the consequence of democratic pressures? Perhaps the problems overload theorists are concerned about, particularly the failure of elected elites to address problems effectively, are a consequence of disagreement among factions of the privileged few who have ready access to policymakers?

I believe that Huntington and the other overload theorists fail to make a sound case that our contemporary policy problems stem from an excess of democratic participation. First, they do not show that policy failures, like the inability to reduce government debt or assure the financial health of Social Security, are the consequence of popular pressure rather than the demands of privileged elites. In fact, the tax cuts and defense spending increases that were largely responsible for massive deficits through the mid-1990s resulted from the demands of business interests and conservative ideologues, not the public.[63] Policy gridlock seems less the result of democratic overload than a consequence of the influence of the privileged. Second, over the past decade, policymakers have been able to make the "hard choices" and impose "sacrifices" that the overload theorists thought impossible, at least regarding programs that benefit the poor and the working class. Social welfare cutbacks and economic policies have diminished the standard of living of less affluent Americans while enormously benefiting the rich (see chapter 6).[64] Instead of being constrained by participatory pressures, elected elites felt free in the 1980s and 1990s to impose sacrifice on those segments of the population unable to participate effectively on their own behalf.

Finally, the overload theorists, in my opinion, accept only partially the democratic ideal; their outlook has more in common with that of authoritarian critics of democracy than with the mainstream of democratic theorists. Their focus on the need to limit popular interference with elite decision-making assigns ordinary citizens too limited a role. Like authoritarian critics of democracy, overload theorists distrust the majority of citizens. They want them to participate only in legitimizing elite decisions, not in forming those decisions. Even in a representative democracy, this is too restrictive a role for citizens. A core value of democracy is the equal capacity of all people to govern themselves. Although for the sake of efficiency in representative democracies everyone does not get involved in making laws on a day-to-day basis, some involvement of as wide a range of the citizenry as possible can only enhance the ability of representatives to formulate policy effectively in the public interest. As the Kettering study participants understand better than the overload theorists, the future health of our democracy lies not in keeping citizens out of government decision making but in finding practical mechanisms for improving their ability to participate.

A first step in organizing more effective citizen participation in our democracy must be to reduce the strong class bias in participation. Reform of the one mode of participation most easily available to all people, voting, is surely the place to begin. Students who sense that a 50-percent participation rate in presidential elections cannot be good for democracy are correct. Because nonvoters and voters are different, a restricted electorate cannot reflect the range of preferences and concerns needed in a democracy. Reductions in voting participation barriers, such as simplifying registration procedures or holding elections on work holidays, are needed to make elections more representative. Enacting reforms such as automatically registering people with driver's licenses is one approach. Whatever the particular reform, the basic change needed is for state governments to take responsibility for identifying eligible voters and drawing up voter lists as is done in all other industrial democracies. Making voting participation less costly for all will increase the level and representativeness of voting participation in elections.

Beyond raising voting participation levels, improving democracy requires enhancing the quality of participation. Structures must be developed to address the need identified in the Kettering study for involving citizens more directly in making decisions affecting their lives. This involvement must mean more than simply registering the preferences of isolated individuals in referenda and public opinion polls. Participation in the actual deliberation on public issues needs to spread beyond the legislative chambers, think tanks, and media that dominate public discussion today. Several proposals have been made to bring citizens more actively into policy deliberations. One popular approach is to utilize advances in electronic technology, sometimes referred to as "teledemocracy," to interconnect citizens in electronic town halls for the purpose of discussing public issues. Another suggestion is the "deliberative opinion poll," in which a random sample of citizens is not asked for individual opinions on an issue, as in a conventional poll, but is brought together in a central place to debate and discuss an issue before registering an opinion. The purpose of this approach is to measure public opinion that reflects thoughtful deliberation on issues.[65] An equally persuasive model is the sort of deliberation on local issues promoted in the Industrial Areas Foundation (IAF) citizens' groups discussed earlier. One of the main differences between these groups and other examples of citizen activism is that the IAF encourages groups to do more than mobilize citizens in behalf of individual issues. It seeks to create ongoing mechanisms for debating and discussing a broad range of issues, even issues that are not of immediate and direct concern to group members.[66]

Whatever the precise mechanism advocated, these examples suggest a hopeful beginning in this country of attempts to develop more meaningful structures of participation. In the conclusion, some of these attempts are examined and critiqued in more detail. Finding ways to expand participation and improve the opportunities for citizens to deliberate directly on public issues is an exciting challenge facing our democracy.

The underlying theme of this chapter has been the need for a democratic system that does more than merely guarantee its citizens the right to participate. In the past two hundred years, providing this right to all has been a serious challenge to our democracy. Only in the twentieth century, for example, did women and black Americans win participation rights. Over the past few decades, such laws as the 1965 Voting Rights Act, when properly implemented, have helped ensure participation rights. While remaining vigilant about protecting rights to participate, partisans of democracy need to shift their attention to creating structures for making the participation of all effective in determining government policy. Until we find ways to make all citizens active participants in deliberating and controlling the decisions that control their lives, democracy in the United States will remain incomplete.

THOUGHT QUESTIONS

1. If, as this chapter shows, nonvoters are less educated, less interested in public affairs, and less knowledgeable about politics than current voters, would increased participation necessarily enhance the quality of American democracy?

2. Some people hope that new media technology promise to enhance democratic deliberation and participation through such activities as electronic town halls and Internet discussion groups. How might such new forms of participation be organized? Would they necessarily strengthen deliberation or might they pose a new challenge to democracy?

3. Political parties play an important role in mobilizing voter participation in other democracies and once did so in the United States. Do you think public policies to encourage political parties to play this role again are desirable? Or do you think nonpartisan organizations, such as the League of Women Voters, are more appropriate organizations for encouraging citizen participation?

4. Would you favor, as this chapter implies, the government's assuming responsibility for automatically registering all eligible voters, as occurs in some other democracies? Should other measures to simplify ballot access, such as voting on holidays, be adopted?

5. As we see in the introduction to this book, The Pluralist model sees nonparticipation as potentially positive and even as indicative of citizen satisfaction and contentment with the political process. Based on what you learned in this chapter, what do you think of this argument?

Suggestions for Further Reading

Boyte, Harry C. *The Backyard Revolution: Understanding the New Citizen Movement.* Philadelphia: Temple University Press, 1980. A well-written account of the growth of grassroots citizen activism.

Conway, M. Margaret. *Political Participation in the United States.* 2d ed. Washington, D.C.: CQ Press, 1991. A leading textbook that reviews the existing political science literature on why and how citizens participate in politics.

Cronin, Thomas. *Direct Democracy.* Cambridge: Harvard University Press, 1989. A thorough analysis of the history and current status of the initiative, referendum, and recall in the United States. Includes a discussion of how these institutions affect democratic values.

*Crozier, Michel, et al. *The Crisis of Democracy.* New York: New York University Press, 1975. A publication of the Trilateral Commission that articulates the thesis of participatory "overload."

Piven, Frances Fox, and Richard Cloward. *Why Americans Don't Vote.* New York: Pantheon Press, 1989. A careful documentation of how governmental policies, especially registration laws, have been effective in demobilizing the American electorate in the twentieth century.

Rimmerman, Craig A. *The New Citizenship: Unconventional Politics, Activism, and Service.* Boulder, Colo.: Westview Press, 1997. A review of the variety of new citizen activism of recent decades and an analysis of its implications for American democracy.

Verba, Sidney, Kay Lehman Schlozman, and Henry E. Brady. *Voice and Equality: Civic Voluntarism in American Politics.* Cambridge: Harvard University Press, 1995. A detailed study based on an extensive survey of Americans about their political participation, documenting the extent to which political participation is skewed on behalf more affluent Americans. But it also confirms Tocqueville's insight that involvement in associations, particularly churches, teach citizens crucial civic skills.

* Presents a point of view that disagrees with the arguments presented in this chapter.

Selected Web Sites

http://www.kettering.org/ An organization that seeks novel ways to involve citizens in political life.

http://www.idea.int/turnout/ International Institute for Democracy and Electoral Assistance provides detailed information about electoral participation around the world, including the latest turnout statistics.

http://www.rockthevote.org/ The MTV-inspired organization that seeks to involve young people in politics.

http://www.vanishingvoter.org/ The Vanishing Voter Project of the Shorenstein Center at Harvard's Kennedy School of Government provides polling data on the level of citizen interest in political campaigns and views toward reform.

CHAPTER 4

The Fourth Challenge: Trivialized Elections

The key to democracy is a system of government by discussion. A good discussion can draw out wisdom which is attainable in no other way.
—A.D. LINDSAY

ELECTIONS ARE CONSIDERED the essential institution in the modern conception of democracy. Nowadays, scholars, journalists, and ordinary people tend to identify democratic political regimes by the presence or absence of competitive elections to fill government offices.[1] The Schumpeterian definition of democracy as "a competitive struggle for the people's vote" has come to dominate the conventional classification of which countries have democratic governments and which do not. Rarely do knowledgeable commentators delve beyond the mere presence of elections to examine other aspects of society that might bear on the extent of a country's democracy. As long as there seems to be free and open electoral competition in a given country, the existence of elections equals democracy.

The ancient Greeks would have regarded this modern equation of democracy with elections as very strange. In democratic Athens, most officials were selected by lot, not election. The Athenians thought selection by lot superior to election as a democratic device because it gave every male citizen — remember that the Athenians excluded women, slaves, and foreigners from their democracy — an equal chance and right to serve in office and reflected the equal capacity of all men to carry out state policy.[2] According to the Greek philosopher Aristotle, elections, in contrast to selection by lot, were *aristocratic* institutions because they allowed electors to choose the "best" people (*aristoi*) for public office, rather than the ordinary citizen who would be chosen in a lottery.[3]

Opposite: *Texas Governor George W. Bush's early fund-raising success made him a prohibitive favorite to win the Republican Party's presidential nomination in 2000. (AP/Wide World Photos)*

This concept of elections as aristocratic devices is revealed in an important exception to the selection-by-lot rule in ancient Athens: the election of generals. Because nearly all citizens were also soldiers with combat experience, the Athenians were keenly aware of the need for talent and experience in military leaders. This was one area of government where the efforts of amateurs could not be tolerated, so the Athenians elected their generals. Yet it is important to note that Athenian democrats regarded elections even in this instance as a *deviation* from democratic practice, and it was one that made them nervous. They worried that elected generals would use the popularity shown by their election to claim power for themselves. In order to prevent this abuse, the Athenian Assembly elected generals for short terms of office and punished them severely if they ignored the wishes of the Assembly. For the ancient Greeks, elections were dangerous to democracy.

The difference between the Greek concept of elections as nondemocratic devices and the modern concept derives, obviously, from the difference between Athenian *direct* democracy and modern *representative* democracy. In ancient Athens, the essential democratic institution was the assembly of all citizens. The Assembly discussed, debated, deliberated, and made all public policy decisions; it reflected directly, through its own actions, the will of the people. Public officials were merely instruments for carrying out Assembly decisions, and though they often had discretion in implementing policy — just as modern bureaucrats have discretion — they had to answer directly to the Assembly for their actions. In modern representative democracy, elected officials are chosen, not to carry out policy, but to debate, discuss, deliberate, and make public policy. Given this very different role of the public official in a representative democracy, elections have a different and important *democratic* function.

Under the logic of representative democracy, the responsibility for public decision making, which in classical Athens was lodged in the Assembly, is shared between citizen voters and their representatives. Election is the mechanism that makes the system democratic, that is, it assures rule by the people. While Athenian citizens could rule directly by attending the Assembly, citizens of a representative democracy must use the tool of a democratic election to exercise their rule. If government is truly democratic, elections must not only occur but they must be able to serve the democratic purpose of involving all citizens in the policy deliberations of their representatives. In terms of A.D. Lindsay's idea quoted at the beginning of this chapter, elections must contribute to the "government by discussion" that is the essence of democracy.

In this respect, elections must take on the characteristics of the classic Athenian Assembly if they are to be effective democratic institutions. Because elected officials are not mere civil servants but representatives with actual decision-making power, elections provide the crucial link between citizens and representatives in democratic governance. Elections in which governing officials are chosen are not necessarily, then, in themselves indicators of democracy. For elections to be democratic, they must provide citizens a chance to join the public policy discussion and guide their representatives' public policy decisions.

In this chapter I argue that for elections to be democratic they must meet three essential criteria. First, democratic elections in a representative democracy must provide the opportunity for the equal representation of all citizens. To the extent that certain citizens or groups are advantaged in their ability to influence election outcomes, elections are less than fully democratic. Second, elections must be mechanisms for deliberation about public policy issues. In a representative democracy, citizens cannot deliberate and make policy directly, as the citizens of Athens did; citizens in modern democracies must rely on their representatives to make the ultimate decisions. But this does not mean that citizens cannot share in democratic deliberation. Well-designed and well-run elections can be occasions for deliberating about what policies government should pursue. To the extent that they do so, they are democratic. And, third, if elections are to be democratic, they must control what government does. There must be a link between election outcomes and the policies government eventually enacts. If elections cease to determine what happens, the people no longer govern.

Unfortunately, recent elections in the United States have fallen short of meeting these criteria. This chapter argues that American elections are increasingly unrepresentative because special interests, PACs, and wealthy individuals have come to dominate electoral competition. Deliberation about public policy issues facing the country has become impossible as the sound bite, entertainment-oriented media coverage, and candidate manipulation of symbols have come to dominate campaigns. And, finally, election outcomes have become less and less important for determining policy, which is now made increasingly in the bureaucracy, the courts, and congressional committee rooms. Although the United States satisfies well the simple criterion of selecting millions of public officials through competitive election, the criteria of truly democratic elections are far from being achieved. In the United States, elections have become a major challenge to our democracy, rather than an indicator of it.

EQUAL REPRESENTATION

In ancient Athens, political equality was guaranteed to every citizen, not through the right to vote, but through the right to speak to the Assembly, a right the Greeks called the *isegoria*. When matters of public policy were debated, each citizen could be sure that his preferences were given consideration because he could stand up and state them directly to his fellow citizens. Of course, not all citizens spoke on each issue; prominent Athenian orators tended to dominate debates and articulate positions to which large numbers of their fellows would give assent. But every citizen knew that if no one expressed how he felt on an issue, he had direct recourse — to stand up and say what he believed. In addition, debate on matters of public concern took place outside the Assembly — in shops, the public square, and marketplaces — as well as within.[4] Undoubtedly, arguments put forth in these areas carried over into the Assembly and enhanced the equal representation of citizen views when public decisions were taken. In the small-scale democracy of Athens, equal recognition of the right to be heard was sufficient to ensure democratic outcomes. Simply by speaking up, the Athenian citizen could seek to influence political outcomes.

In modern representative democracies, the equivalent to the Athenian *isegoria* is the equal right to vote. Voting rights are a political resource distributed equally to all citizens, irrespective of wealth or social status, and according to the theory of representative democracy, they provide each citizen with a capacity to influence public decisions. In a large society without elections, people would be able to influence government only through private actions, whether bribery, flattery, or private petition. The ability to influence government in this nondemocratic setting would be grossly unequal, reflecting inequality in political resources. Elections under universal suffrage, by contrast, are a public institution for influencing the conduct of government officials within which everyone has the same power: one vote. If elections are conducted fairly and if they control the actions of public officials, they give every citizen an equal chance to determine what government does. According to one analysis, "elections, by introducing a formal, public means of influencing official conduct, can compensate for private inequalities in political resources."[5] To do so, however, elections must provide equal representation.

Unlike ancient Athens, the vote cast in a mass representative democracy, involving millions of voters, vastly complicates the achievement of equal representation. While individual Athenians could make their preferences known and influence public debate in the marketplace and the Assembly, individual citizens of representative democracies can only pull the lever of a voting machine and hope it translates into an expression of their preferences. Clearly, for the right to vote to lead to equal representation, more than millions of voters pulling voting levers in isolation is required. Some mechanism has to exist to lend coherence to these millions of votes and structure them to provide majority control of government. Individual voters must be able to act in concert with like-minded citizens to send clear signals about their policy preferences as they vote for their representatives. Voters organized to act in concert are the functional equivalent of hundreds of Athenian citizens in the Assembly responding with their applause to the convincing argument of a fellow citizen. The equal right to vote alone cannot provide equal representation; it must be exercised through an election process that provides meaningful choices and channels for translating votes into the expression of political influence.

Since the beginning of representative democracy, political parties have provided the means of structuring equal representation. As the political scientist E.E.

Schattschneider once put it: "modern democracy is unthinkable save in terms of parties."[6] Unthinkable because some way has to be found in a mass democracy to bring together millions of voters with diverse concerns and interests to form a broad governing majority. Individuals are represented when they have the potential of contributing to that majority, and parties have been the traditional mechanism through which such majorities are brought to life. In addition, by organizing government, parties can make the electoral majority they represent effective in formulating policies that reflect the preferences of the individuals and groups who support the party.

Ideally, parties perform three vital functions that lead to promoting equal representation.[7] First, they select candidates for office and mobilize voters to create a link between individual citizens and government. Parties in a democracy, because they can win office only by attracting the votes of a majority of citizens, will seek to select candidates who can represent the preferences of a majority and will attempt to organize voters around policy issues that address broad public needs. Since every vote can be of value in contributing to winning a majority, democratic political parties will compete to attract votes through the support of policies that address the preferences, needs, and concerns of all voters, regardless of wealth or social status. Second, on winning office, the political party provides the structure around which government can be organized to implement a winning party's campaign promises. As shown in chapter 1, this is a particular challenge for the American separation-of-powers system, but, as was also argued earlier, overcoming the institutional barriers to enact majority preferences has involved always using party, as in the Jeffersonian governing model. For all representative democracies throughout the world, political parties remain the universal mechanism for organizing governments to enact the will of electoral majorities. Third, when parties are in charge of what happens in government, they can be held accountable for what happens. Again, as discussed in chapter 1, this empowers voters. Through the use of party label, citizen voters can pass judgment on the performance of elected officials: rewarding them with continuance in office if they have addressed majority concerns and throwing them out of office in favor of an alternative party if they fail. According to the ideal of party government, if all these functions are performed, the right to vote can lead to equal representation.

Of course, no political parties in actual representative democracies have satisfied perfectly this ideal vision of party government. The American historical experience with the bossism of urban political machines and political party corruption has deviated often from the ideal vision sketched in the previous paragraph. Nevertheless, no other mechanism besides parties has been developed anywhere that structures the votes of millions of individual citizens to provide representation. As I argue here, without strong political parties, alternative means of structuring votes are likely to develop that bias representation in the direction of the rich and powerful much more than parties do.

For all their potential faults, the democratic virtue of political parties is that they are mechanisms for collecting votes; their power depends on the number of votes they gather. The fact that each citizen in a representative democracy has a vote makes her or him, because of that fact alone, worthy of attention from party leaders. Whatever other attributes or resources a citizen might have — wealth, education, status — the possession of a vote alone gives even the poorest and weakest a measure of influence through a political party. This is why, in the United States one hundred years ago, political party workers stood on the docks to organize arriving immigrants. It is also why, in the evolution of nearly all democracies, vigorous party competition has resulted in the expansion of suffrage as parties in power granted the vote to additional groups of voters in hopes of enlisting them among party supporters. The democratic significance of political parties can be understood more clearly if we examine the increasing inequality in representation that has resulted as political parties have declined as an electoral force in American elections.

The decline of American political parties is a political phenomenon that American political scientists have documented thoroughly. As the world's first mass representative democracy under universal white male suffrage, the United States in the 1830s was where the modern, mass-based political party was invented. Throughout the balance of the nineteenth century, the dominant Democratic and Republican parties organized voters and competed to control government. Urban party machines integrated millions of immigrants into American political life and along with their rural counterparts oversaw the emergence of an industrial society. Nineteenth-century elections were well-organized affairs in which tightly structured precinct and ward organizations kept in contact with individual voters and turned them out to vote in massive numbers. During the twentieth century, beginning with Progressive attacks on machine bossism and corruption, the role of political parties in organizing elections steadily diminished. First, civil service reform and the government bureaucracy's assumption of traditional party functions, such as running elections (printing ballots, setting up voting booths, etc.) and providing social welfare, eliminated patronage resources that nineteenth-century parties had used to reward supporters. Second, the direct primary took away from party officials, party conventions, and party caucuses the crucial power to choose who ran under the party label. Although primaries were first introduced in some states at the beginning of the twentieth century, they only gradually became the dominant means of selecting party nominees. As recently as 1968, Hubert Humphrey gained the Democratic nomination for president without entering a single presidential primary; he accumulated sufficient support from delegates chosen at state party conventions and caucuses to win. By 1972, this had become impossible for presidential aspirants in either political party as most states enacted comprehensive primary laws, and by the end of the 1970s, nomination to nearly all elective offices in the country required winning primaries. Third, as voters became more educated in the post–World War II period, the strength of their attachment to parties declined. More voters identified themselves as independents or as only weakly attached to either party, and they were more willing to split their tickets between the parties at election time. Suburbanization contributed to these weakening attachments as voters left the environment of the densely structured urban party organization. In the suburbs, the traditional precinct-ward organizational structures never took root.

In the United States today, political parties have become largely marginalized as election vehicles. Because state election laws continue to make ballot access easier for party nominees and because enough voters retain party identification to give such nominees an automatic pool of support, candidates for office still seek the party label, but attaching the label tends to be all that parties contribute to the process. Modern campaigns have become candidate centered rather than party centered. Individual candidates build their personal campaign organizations, using professional campaign managers and funds they have raised themselves. With the latest marketing techniques, they sell themselves to the voters using paid campaign advertising and attracting media attention. Party attachments tend to be deemphasized, and party officials, as opposed to personal campaign advisers, are not involved in the process. Unfortunately for democracy, this new candidate-centered style of campaigning has undermined equal representation.

Candidate-centered campaigns go through several typical steps. Tracing these steps, in contrast to how party-centered campaigns are organized, can illustrate how modern campaigns cannot provide equal representation. The essential four steps are deciding to run for office, raising campaign funds, building a professional campaign organization, and marketing the candidate to the voters.

In contemporary candidate-centered elections, deciding to run for office involves initially what political analyst Alan Ehrenhalt calls the "mirror test."[8] The prospective candidate gets out of bed one morning, looks in the mirror, and says, "I want to be a United States senator (or governor or mayor or president)." After passing the mirror test, becoming a successful candidate is a matter of proceeding to step 2: raising campaign funds. This self-selection of candidates is a far cry from candidate selection in party-centered election systems. In those systems, party leaders play a crucial role in selecting and recruiting party candidates. Usually, this process requires candidates to spend many years working their way up through lower-level political offices, learning the role of being a representative and absorbing the traditions and policy orientation of the party. Before former British Prime Minister Margaret Thatcher attained that post, for example, she had spent nearly thirty years in politics: as a local Conservative party official, then nearly a decade as an ordinary member of Parliament, followed by another decade serving in various cabinet posts (in either the government or in the Conservative "shadow cabinet" when the party was in opposition).[9] In the past, although never in as structured a manner as in Great Britain, American politicians also had to

Reform Party rivals Donald Trump and Minnesota Governor Jesse Ventura demonstrate that little or no previous political experience is now required of candidates for national or local office. (AP/Wide World Photos)

work their way up through party ranks. Since candidate self-selection has become the norm, however, candidates for major office have sometimes won with little or no previous political experience. In the 1996 presidential election campaign (including the primaries), three of the major candidates — Ross Perot, Patrick Buchanan, and Steve Forbes — had never been elected to public office. Prior to his election to the presidency, Bill Clinton had never held national office, although he had extensive experience as governor of Arkansas. If previous national political experience is no longer a requirement for a presidential candidate to be taken seriously, it is not surprising that many lesser posts in Congress and in state and local governments are now routinely filled by politically inexperienced individuals.

This sort of candidate self-selection is harmful to equal representation because, without party involvement, individual voters have no involvement in the candidate choices they will be presented with at election time. When party leaders and party processes select candidates, this selection is made by people who are in a position to do so because they have succeeded in winning past elections and have been previously successful in choosing candidates who have won the electorate's endorsement. In a well-organized, party-centered system, one would not achieve a position of leadership without some success at providing representation. In selecting party candidates, attention would have to be paid to more than simply an individual candidate's personal ambition. Running for the party would require commitment to the party's political platform, which, if the party is to be electorally successful over the long run, must be responsive to voter concerns. In this case, voters could evaluate an individual candidate's campaign promises and platform in the light of the historical track record of the party and its effectiveness in carrying out its promises. In candidate-centered campaigns, in contrast, candidates can create out of thin air brand-new platforms that are not grounded in any previous historical experience, leaving voters with very little basis to evaluate the candidate's actual commitment to promises. Finally, because party-centered campaigns tend to field candidates with long personal track records, voters can judge candidates on the basis on their past performance as representatives, something that is impossible when candidates have a limited history.

The second step in contemporary candidate-centered campaigns is raising campaign funds — the step principally responsible for the destruction of any possibility of equal representation in contemporary politics. Once a candidate passes the mirror test, his or her viability as a candidate depends on the ability to raise the money to finance the next two steps — hiring a professional campaign staff and marketing the candidate to the voters. Under existing federal campaign finance laws, there are three principal sources of funds to finance a campaign for Congress or the presidency: the candidate's personal resources, political action committees (PACs), and contributions from individuals.[10]

Personal riches are the most accessible source of campaign financing. In 1976, the Supreme Court ruled that the expenditure of one's personal funds on one's election campaign was protected speech under the First Amendment, effectively preventing any legal limits on personal financing of campaigns. Not surprisingly, in the light of this ruling, more and more individuals who put themselves forward as candidates in recent elections are wealthy individuals, the most noted examples being billionaire Ross Perot and publishing magnate Steve Forbes. The 1996 Republican presidential primary campaign demonstrated the potency of an individual fortune for making someone a major political contender. Despite his lack of previous political experience, Forbes's spending of $37.5 million from his personal fortune, more than was spent by any other contender for nomination as presidential candidate with the exception of the eventual winners — Dole and Clinton — allowed him to catapult himself into contention, even though he entered the race later than the other major candidates.[11] Forbes's deep pockets allowed him to return to mount another well-funded campaign for the 2000 nomination. The Forbes and Perot phenomena prove that a friendly mirror and deep pockets are all that are required to make wealthy individuals significant contenders for political office.

If a prospective candidate does not have a large personal fortune, another important source of campaign funds is a PAC. PACs have become major sources of funds for congressional and presidential campaigns since the passage of the

Federal Election Campaign Act of 1974. This "reform" legislation set limits on the amount of funds individuals could contribute to individual campaigns and prohibited direct corporate contributions. To get around these limitations, big business and other groups began to use PACs, allowed under the law, to funnel contributions to candidates. Although corporations cannot contribute directly to campaigns, the law allows the formation of a political action committee composed of executives from a given corporation. Each PAC member is able to give up to $1,000 to the PAC, and each PAC can give up to $5,000 to a single campaign. In addition to corporate PACs, there are PACs representing particular professional groups, such as doctors and lawyers, labor unions, and even individual politicians. For example, Ronald Reagan promoted his presidential candidacy in the 1970s through his own personal PAC, called "Citizens for the Republic," which contributed to the campaigns of Republican members of Congress and state and local candidates.[12] Newt Gingrich used the same tactic in the late 1980s and early 1990s, supporting Republican candidates with his personal GOPAC. After 1994, when they gained a majority in the House, grateful Republicans were eager to elect their benefactor Speaker.[13] Although the limits on what a single PAC can give to a candidate seem to be a restraint on PAC influence over a given candidate, PAC managers have learned how to leverage their funds effectively to maximize their influence. Most significant is cooperation among the PACs of individual firms in a single industry to target their funding at candidates considered friendly to their industry's interests. In addition, congressional lobbyists and interest-group representatives are usually involved in coordinating PAC contributions and following up to pressure PAC fund recipients when relevant legislation is under consideration. After becoming the congressional majority in 1994, House Republicans began aggressively to solicit business PAC contributors to shift their contributions from the Democrats to the party now in control of the House, an effort that succeeded as Republicans raised more PAC money than the Democrats in both 1996 and 1998.[14] This conversion confirmed the relationship between PAC contributions and who holds the power in Congress.

Despite the $1,000 individual limit on federal campaign contributions, individual contributions remain an important source of funds for prospective candidates. Candidate entrepreneurs willing to work hard at cultivating a few hundred wealthy individuals can raise substantial amounts despite these limitations. Although a few hundred sounds like a large number, it is only a small fraction of the hundreds of thousands of voters in a typical congressional district, and candidates are not limited to their own districts in seeking contributions. In recent years, individual contributions have become an increasingly important factor as certain industry lobbyists devised the strategy of "bundling" individual contributions to get around the $5,000 limitation on PAC contributions to a single campaign. Bundling involves coordinating individual contributions up to the $1,000 limit from numerous individual executives in a given industry. One study

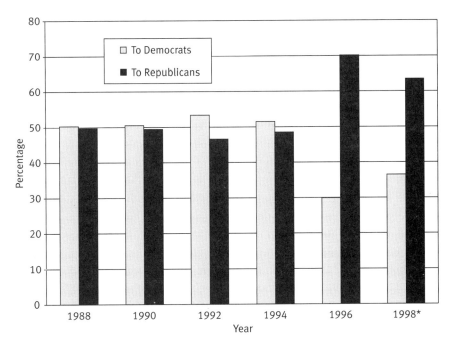

Figure 4.1 Business PAC Contributions, 1988–98

Source: Center for Responsive Politics, http://www.opensecrets.org/pubs/whopaid/pacs/
business.htm.
Note: Based on data released electronically by the Federal Election Commission on
1 October 1998.
*Estimate

of 1990 congressional campaigns found that some industries gave more money
to individual candidates using bundled funds than PAC funds.[15] Bundling was
a major source of campaign funds in the 2000 presidential primaries, especially
for Republican nominee George W. Bush, who had received 50,000-plus bundles
from twenty-five different corporate donors by November of 1999.[16]

This second step toward mounting a political campaign amounts to a "hidden election" for office that determines the actual electoral choices voters will
have.[17] Before any polls are taken or any votes are cast, wealthy individuals and
interest groups and PACs select with their contributions who the credible candidates for office will be. Success in this hidden election is crucial to mounting
a campaign and getting media attention, which tends to evaluate the credibility
of candidates based on the amount of campaign funds they have raised.[18] This
early fund-raising success can be crucial to later electoral success. For example,
Bill Clinton's lead in the campaign for funds before the Democratic presidential
primaries in 1992 was a critical factor in his ability to survive setbacks early in the

process, such as the bad publicity over alleged extramarital affairs, his draft record, and his defeat in the New Hampshire primary.[19] Lack of campaign funds, by contrast, forced Paul Tsongas to drop out of the race in March, although he had won six primaries, including New Hampshire, and three caucuses. Money also played a crucial role in Clinton's 1996 renomination as he raised large amounts of campaign funds early in the process to discourage any challengers.[20] Unlike other recent incumbent presidents, such as George Bush in 1992 or Jimmy Carter in 1980, Clinton's money advantage saved him from a debilitating primary campaign. Vice-President Al Gore followed this strategy for his 2000 presidential campaign, raising such a large campaign war chest that, a year before the first primary election, all his competitors, with the exception of former Senator Bill Bradley, had dropped out of the race.[21] On the Republican side, Texas Governor George W. Bush was so successful in the hidden election of fund raising for the 2000 Republican primaries that, nine months before the first primary vote, his opponents were forced to cut back their campaign efforts because of a shortage of campaign funds.[22] As in presidential primaries, electoral success in congressional elections and in state and local races depends largely on whether a candidate can raise the funds in the hidden election to mount a credible campaign.

From the perspective of equal representation, the hidden election sharply biases the election process in favor of that very small and wealthy portion of the electorate that contributes to political campaigns. As pointed out in chapter 3, political participation declines rapidly when one moves to forms of participation beyond voting; only an extremely small proportion of the electorate contributes money to election campaigns. Moreover, wealthy individuals and those promoting special interests dominate this group, so those who participate in the hidden election for campaign funds are far from representative of the electorate at large. In an analysis of the zip codes of contributors to the 2000 presidential election contenders, Public Campaign, a nonprofit, nonpartisan organization dedicated to campaign finance reform, found that residents of a handful of wealthy neighborhoods, such as Manhattan's Upper East Side, Beverly Hills, California, and northwest Washington, D.C., provided the bulk of individual campaign donations, and, not surprisingly, residents in these same neighborhoods funded the 1996 campaign.[23] Before most voters can be represented through their electoral choices, the hidden election in effect restricts those choices to candidates who pass muster with the rich and the special interests.

If a candidate succeeds in the hidden election, the next step is to hire a team of professional campaign consultants to organize the campaign. Although the use of campaign consultants employing modern public relations methods to market candidates dates back to the 1930s, only in the past two decades have these professionals come to dominate campaigning at all levels. In the early 1960s, only a handful of such consultants worked in campaigns; now there are thousands.[24] Nowadays, professional consultants are standard participants in nearly all congressional campaigns and many state and local ones. Before the era of professional campaign consultants, a candidate for office would turn to a friend or associate with experience working in previous campaigns in the particular locality to handle campaign organization. Often, these individuals would be party officials or have close ties to the local party organization. They shared loyalty between the individual candidate they were supporting and the broader political community of which they were a part. Whether their candidate won or lost, they remained in the community where their candidate ran and continued to be involved in the politics of the area after the election was over. In a party-centered campaign, winning office was only the start of the campaigner's attachment to a candidate. Of equal concern was that the elected candidate perform well in office so that the candidate and fellow party members could win future elections.

The relation between candidates and professional campaign consultants is more of a business arrangement than a political alliance. Consultants work directly for individual candidates, not political parties. They come into a state, a locality, or a congressional district to run a campaign; after the election, they are off to the next campaign job. With limited ties to the jurisdiction, their focus is solely on getting their candidate/client elected, not the long-run well-being of the community in which the campaign is run. Unlike campaign advisers in a party-centered campaign environment, the consultants' professional success depends only on winning elections, not on successful governing after the campaign is over. Nor are campaign consultants and the candidates they serve concerned, necessarily, with the long-run well-being of a political party and the long-term citizen interests it represents. The use of professional campaign consultants has become another factor undermining parties because it provides candidates with an avenue to office independent of any party connection. Since party primaries are now the principal means of acquiring nominations, a candidate using the services of a good campaign consultant can gain a party nomination without any prior commitment to the party or its principles.[25] Once elected, such candidates are not likely to give party ties or connections to other elected representatives much thought when making policy. In legislative bodies, such as the U.S. Congress, this situation has made it almost impossible to build the broadly representative coalitions necessary for governing. Governments and legislatures made up of independent political entrepreneurs provide the perfect formula for policy gridlock.

Once a candidate picks a campaign consultant, the next step is marketing the candidate to the voters in a manner similar to selling a product. Modern campaign consultants use all the techniques of the advertising and public relations worlds to market candidates. Sophisticated public opinion polls identify the concerns of the electorate, direct mail is used to raise additional campaign funds and make contact with carefully targeted groups of supporters, and a media strategy is designed to present an image of the candidate attractive to what the polls say voters want. Nowhere in this marketing approach to campaigning is there a concern for or need to develop a strategy for *representing* voters. Modern campaigns focus on projecting favorable images of the candidate, rather than on gaining support for a mix of policies. For the campaign consultants and their clients, getting the citizen's vote in a particular campaign through image manipulation takes precedence over developing long-term support through effective representation. This marketing approach to campaigns contrasts with party-centered campaigns. Before the era of candidate marketing through campaign consultants, parties organized campaigns based on deep, long-term ties between citizens and their representatives. First, partisan appeals relied heavily on citizen identification with the party based on past experience with the party and its candidates. Party identification is a long-term attachment grounded in evaluations of how a particular party has represented the interests and concerns of citizens. When citizens have a sense of how a party has or has not represented them in the past, they are less susceptible to the manipulation of candidate images during a particular campaign. With the decline of party identification, citizens have lost the reference point it provides in evaluating a candidate, much as a brand name provides a reference for evaluating a product, and, consequently, they are left to judge a candidate's representative capacity solely on the basis of glitzy advertisements.

Second, the decline of parties has meant an end to the important role they usually played in linking candidates and voters organizationally during campaigns. Modern candidate-centered campaigns are carried out exclusively through television, with either campaign commercials or campaign events staged for television coverage. Party-organized rallies and block-by-block canvassing of voters are relics of a Jurassic era in American politics. So too are party campaign volunteers committed to the broad goals and aims of the party, rather than the ambitions of a particular candidate. Campaign consultants still use campaign volunteers but recruit them solely on the basis of attachment to an individual candidate and have no need for them between campaigns. Party volunteers, by contrast, provide a continuing representative link between elections.

The decline in the electoral role of political parties and the rise of candidate-centered campaigns have enhanced the importance of the media. In the absence of party structures for communicating with voters, candidates depend on media access to present themselves to voters. Beyond the access they can purchase in campaign commercial time, they also need favorable attention to their candidacies in news programs and, more recently, in talk shows and other general entertainment formats. From one point of view, this situation is advantageous to political entrepreneurs — they have direct access to voters through the media without the intervention of political party bosses — but they are now at the mercy of newspeople and media stars as to how much attention their candidacies will receive.

In recent years, the media have come to play an extremely important gatekeeper role, along with participants in the hidden election, at the beginning of electoral cycles in determining who is identified as a credible candidate for office.[26] Party leaders played this gatekeeper role in the past, selecting credible candidates based on their political experience and their capacity to represent the party, its policy commitments, and the broad coalition it must satisfy to elect its candidates to office. In performing their gatekeeper role, newspeople use different criteria in deciding who the credible candidates are — criteria that are less relevant to representation. Recent studies show that the media are likely to select candidates based on their success at raising campaign funds (enhancing the importance of the hidden election), the celebrity status of potential candidates, incumbency, and personal qualities and foibles that will provide for entertaining coverage.[27] Although these criteria may not be very relevant to the candidate's ability to provide equal representation to voters, media coverage has been an important factor influencing, especially in the early stages, presidential primaries and many congressional, state, and local races.[28]

Another way in which contemporary candidate-centered campaigns distort representation is through declining electoral competitiveness, especially in congressional races. Since the 1970s, numerous observers have documented the growing advantage incumbents have in defending themselves against electoral challenges.[29] An important factor in incumbency advantage is the incumbent's ability to raise campaign funds. The special interests that finance elections tend to give more to incumbents than to challengers because they want commitments from those most likely to win. This greater access to money only reinforces the natural advantages of incumbency, such as name recognition and previous service to constituents. Beginning in the late 1970s, many congressional incumbents utilized the rise of PACs to build huge campaign war chests to deter campaign challenges. The links between incumbents and campaign contributors had a twofold impact on equal representation. First, it made incumbents especially beholden to special-interest contributors. Second, in reducing the competitiveness of campaigns, it took away from ordinary voters the main lever they have to assure themselves of representation: a realistic opportunity to choose between alternative candidates in a competitive election. As the reelection of incumbents became routine, any need for officeholders to be responsive to voters diminished, while their dependence on big PAC and other campaign contributions to keep elections noncompetitive increased.

The 1998 congressional races confirmed the advantage of incumbents in fund raising and its value in assuring their reelection.[30] In House races, incumbents raised an average of four times the amount of funds that challengers raised. In the 401 districts where incumbents ran, 395 (98.5 percent) won. In only 58 of the races did incumbents face challengers who came close to being financially competitive, that is, who could muster at least half of what was available to the incumbents. Even in these "financially competitive" races, 52 (90 percent) of the incumbents won. In the only 6 races nationwide where challengers managed to beat incumbents, they were able to do so because their average spending matched that of the incumbent. The situation was similar in 1996 when those few challengers who won did so by matching the spending of incumbents. Commenting on the 1996 result, columnist Paul Starr pointed out that in 1996 there were two elections: the campaign for money and the campaign for votes, and a "challenger who lost the 'money' election, as 95 percent did, had slim chance of prevailing in the people's election."[31]

The new candidate-centered campaigns, with their use of professional campaign consultants and sophisticated media techniques, have increased dramatically the costs of campaigns. Election campaigns, at all levels of government, cost about $300 million in 1968; by 1988, they cost $2.7 billion — a ninefold increase in twenty years.[32] The Center for Responsive Politics reports that 1996 spending on races for the presidency and Congress alone exceeded $2.2 billion; when state and local races are added to this figure, the 1996 election was the most expensive ever.[33] Because of the increasing costs, the hidden election for campaign contributions becomes more important as candidates for office work harder and longer to raise funds. No one can hope to gain office, or keep it, unless the concerns of those who fund campaigns are addressed. Candidate commitments to contributors rarely involve an outright promise to do something specific for the contributor; more often, the commitments involve agreeing not to support a specific piece of legislation that will harm the contributor's interest. A recipient of support from the pharmaceutical industry will promise to oppose any health-care reform that involves controls on drug prices; a beneficiary of oil and gas industry contributions will promise not to support an energy tax. Commitments to look out for these narrow interests make it difficult to craft broad governing reforms for health care or deficit reduction, contributing to the governmental deadlock of recent years.[34] Representation of the broad public interest continually must stand aside for representation of the narrow concerns of campaign contributors.

In 1996 and 1998, candidates from both political parties exploited a new source of campaign funds — "soft money" — in a manner that turned national political party organizations into a major source of funds, although in a way that diminished the parties' democratic character. As pointed out earlier, the federal election law has imposed limits on how much individuals and PACs can contribute to any one campaign, and certain kinds of contributions, such as direct contributions from corporations and labor unions, are prohibited. But in the same 1976 Supreme Court decision that prevented the Federal Election Commission from regulating expenditures that individuals, such as Ross Perot, spend on their own campaigns, the Court also excluded from regulation "issue advocacy" advertising sponsored by organizations operating "independently" of a particular candidate's campaign organization. Even if the ads provided information that was obviously favorable or detrimental to a particular candidate, as long as they did not expressly say to vote for or against a particular candidate, they were considered protected speech under the First Amendment and therefore free from regulation. In the 1980s, a number of organizations, such as the Christian Coalition, had exploited this loophole to run ads supportive of groups they favored. But a new wrinkle was added in 1996 as both the Republican and Democratic parties employed this loophole to raise money for issue-advocacy ads in support of their candidates.

Although the parties had begun exploiting this loophole as the campaign year approached, their activities received a green light in June 1996 when, in a decision addressing the issue of political party issue advertising, the Supreme Court said that the free speech exclusion from regulation applied fully to political parties just as it did for any other organization engaging in "uncoordinated" campaign activities. The parties redoubled their efforts to raise and spend this unregulated soft money. By November, they had raised nearly $300 million in soft money, which was spent to support both the presidential and congressional candidates.[35] Since this money was totally unregulated, the parties were free to ask corporations and other "fat cat" donors to give funds in any amount they wished, and they did. The list of the largest 1996 soft-money contributors includes many of America's largest corporations. Most disturbing is that many of the largest contributors had direct and specific interest in government policy decisions that would be made after the election, such as Philip Morris ($2.2 million to the Republicans), which was concerned about regulation of smoking; AT&T ($550,000 to the Republicans), Walt Disney Co. ($870,000 to the Democrats), and MCI ($540,000 to the Democrats), all with interest in telecommunications legislation.[36] By exploiting the soft-money loophole, corporations are able to contribute directly to political parties and indirectly to candidates in a way prohibited to them for most of this century. Both parties aggressively raised soft money for the 1998 congressional elections, doubling the amounts raised in 1996.[37] As fund raising heated up for the 2000 elections, most experts predicted a new high in soft-money contributions easily surpassing one-half billion dollars.[38]

Given this book's argument that renewed party involvement is crucial for more equal representation in elections, this enhanced involvement of party organizations in campaign fund raising could be seen as a positive development for democracy. Unfortunately, the manner in which soft money is raised and spent amounts to a perversion of the parties' democratic role. Instead of acting as democratic instruments for collecting votes, the parties have behaved as plutocratic instruments for collecting money. Soft money has made the parties simply another way for moneyed interests to funnel money to individual candidates. As table 4.1 (p. 140) shows, the use of soft money has increased inequality in the campaign finance system, for the bulk of soft money comes from the wealthiest contributors. At least in 1996 and 1998, the parties' use of soft money did little to alter the candidate-centered nature of campaigns. Parties simply served

Table 4.1 Large and Small Soft-Money Contributors:
Number of Contributors versus Amounts Raised, 1995–96

Contribution	Total Raised Democrats Republicans (in millions)		Percentage of Money	Number of Contributors	Percentage of Contributors
0–$1,000	$1.3	$7.0	3.6	19,670	71.3
$1,001–$10,000	10.2	10.4	8.8	5,009	18.2
$10,001–$50,000	24.5	23.3	20.6	1,907	6.9
$50,001–$100,000	19.6	20.2	17.1	523	1.9
$100,001 and up	54.2	61.9	49.9	487	1.8
Total	$109.8	$122.8	100.0	27,596	100.1

Source: Adapted and reprinted from *Dollars and Votes: How Business Campaign Contributions Subvert Democracy,* by Dan Clawson, Alan Neustadtl, and Mark Weller, by permission of Temple University Press. © 1998 by Temple University. All rights reserved.

as another source candidates could access to support their otherwise independent campaigns. The Democratic Party fine-tuned this system in recent congressional campaigns with a "tally system." Once individual contributors to a Democratic candidate's campaign had made the maximum allowable hard-money contribution, they would be invited to make an additional soft-money contribution to the Democratic Party, which would be tallied to the candidate, directing that amount of "independent" expenditures to that candidate's campaign.[39] Federal campaign law, as interpreted by the Supreme Court, with the legal fiction that party expenditures must be "independent" of individual campaigns, serves as an additional barrier to the parties' playing a truly democratic role. Until the parties can join their candidates into a coherent organization that appeals collectively for votes rather than money, and that can truly link ordinary citizens to party members in office, the parties will not be fulfilling their democratic role.

Campaign commitments to those who contribute money to the hidden election have had a particularly harmful effect on Congress. According to the political scientist Lance Bennett, in the 1980s the combination of professionalized campaigning and the need for large amounts of cash to support it turned Congress into a veto institution.[40] Any major legislation, whether proposed by a Democratic or a Republican president, to address a broad national problem was picked apart in Congress as each member sought to block any provision that adversely affected big contributors. Both Bush and Clinton faced this obstacle in fashioning budgets that would reduce the budget deficit. Congressional commitments to the health-insurance industry and drug companies seriously constrained Clinton's attempt to provide for national health insurance. Finally, as we saw in chapter 3, the decline of parties and citizen disillusion with the contemporary system of public campaigning has contributed to declining voting participation. Smaller electorates mean increasingly unrepresentative electorates, because nonvoters are likely to be poorer and of lower social status than voters. Even after the hidden election has biased electoral choices in favor of wealthier citizens, the actual vote further biases the choice in the direction of the better-off because they are overrepresented in the subset of citizens who actually participate.

In sum, the decline of party-centered campaigns and the rise of candidate-centered ones undermine the potential for campaigns to provide equal representation. Candidate-centered campaigns, with their reliance on professional campaign consultants and expensive marketing techniques, need to make commitments to narrow, moneyed, special interests to raise the funds needed for expensive campaigns. Contributors in the hidden election have representational clout well beyond that of the ordinary voter. As candidate-centered campaigns have come to replace party-centered campaigns, they have undermined the broadly representative role parties have played in democracies. Parties cannot fulfill their function of bringing together diverse groups of citizens in governing coalitions when they have become merely labels for self-selected candidate entrepreneurs. Finally, once in government, these independent entrepreneurs cannot formulate coherent policies representative of electoral majorities without party ties to hold them together. Given their electoral independence from one another, candidate entrepreneurs have little incentive to cooperate with one another when governing. Without such cooperation, citizens are not going to see their concerns and needs represented and translated into public policy.

DELIBERATION

From what we know of life in ancient Athens, political discussion was lively, intense, and constant. In a society in which citizens made decisions directly in the Assembly, debates and arguments about public decisions were at the center of public life, and no decision was taken without extensive deliberations both within and outside the Assembly. These deliberations were face-to-face affairs as persons with various points of view confronted one another directly. Participants also knew one another personally and could weigh arguments according to the personal reputations for wisdom and intelligence of those who made them.[41] In a predominately oral culture without the equivalent of modern newspapers or other media, political deliberations were unmediated, that is, communication came directly from the participants without the need to learn of them through written reports. The purpose of these deliberations was reaching a public decision that would be taken by majority vote in the Assembly. Constructive debate and talk leading to democratic decision on public issues were a natural part of small-scale, direct, face-to-face democracy in Athens. Obviously, no large-scale representative democracy can come close to recreating the intense public deliberation of ancient Athens. From the point of view of the typical citizen of a representative democracy, political arguments, by necessity, must be made at a distance; they must be mediated by either written or electronic means; and participants are not likely to be intimately acquainted. Nevertheless, election campaigns in representative democracies do offer citizens the potential to observe and participate in public deliberations. If campaigns illuminate alternative points of view on serious issues and feature debates among those views, they can provide a context for public deliberation in which citizens can participate with their votes. In order for this to happen, the discourse of election campaigns needs to provide real contention among various viewpoints on public issues; candidates need to articulate clearly issue positions and address directly the views of their opponents, and the media need to report extensively on these contending views in a manner that assists voters in making judgments about them.

According to this ideal, elections are institutions for peaceful conflict over public issues resolved at the ballot box after careful deliberation over alternative courses of action. The candidates running for office represent in their platforms and position papers the concrete policy alternatives under deliberation. When a majority of voters choose one set of candidates over another, they are using the election to confer a majority decision about what courses of action the newly constituted government should take. In a representative democracy, the directions given in an election, in contrast to the decisions of the Athenian Assembly, do not provide detailed directions to elected representatives; the responsibility for actual legislation lies with the representatives. If open, reasoned debate and deliberation occur during the election, however, election outcomes offer resolution to fundamental political conflicts and provide a decision regarding the overall direction of government policy. Unfortunately, the reality of campaign discourse and electoral politics in the contemporary United States deviates dramatically from this ideal. In fact, many election observers believe campaign discourse has become useless as a means for public deliberation on important issues. Consequently, elections provide little resolution to public conflicts and contribute little to the capacity of election winners to govern.

Unlike the citizens of Athens, American voters depend on the media as sources of information about politics, including election campaigns. In recent years, political scientists have studied intensely how both the print and electronic media cover election campaigns, and their findings do not suggest that newspapers, magazines, or television provide information conducive to citizen deliberation. Although much popular commentary in recent years has focused primarily on the failings of television coverage of election campaigns (the main source of campaign information for most citizens), political scientists find few differences between the way newspapers and television report campaigns. Newspapers tend to provide more details, but both tend to say similar things in similar ways about campaigns—little of it of much use for deliberation.[42] The first problem is that, surprising as it seems, too little attention is given to elections. Only about 15 percent of national news coverage during presidential election years is devoted to covering the national campaign, and this percentage has been shrinking over the last three presidential campaigns.[43] Television news reports largely ignore campaigns for lesser offices, such as campaigns for the House of Representatives and for state and local positions. Most voters receive most of their information about these races from campaign commercials.

In the coverage provided, little information is conveyed that is relevant to deliberation on issues. One problem is the phenomenon of the "incredible shrinking sound bite" — the amount of time provided in television news programs for candidates to state their positions on issues. In 1968, television evening newscasts provided candidates with an average of 42 seconds of uninterrupted time to communicate their views; by 1988, the sound bite had shrunk to 9 seconds; during the 1996 presidential election, it had dropped to 8.2 seconds.[44] The pressure on television news organizations to concentrate information in smaller and smaller bites prevents communicating much more than slogans. Beyond shrinking sound bites, very little of media election coverage and commentary discusses policy issues. One study of election coverage in national news magazines found policy issues to make up only 17 percent of campaign coverage; the bulk of the coverage was of the campaign game — the "horse race" and candidate strategy and tactics.[45] This journalistic "schema" or "frame" of elections as a strategic game between opposing campaign teams not only diminishes discussion of issues, it distorts discussion of issues on the rare times when they are raised. Rather than portray candidate issue statements as serious proposals for addressing the country's problems, the strategic game frame treats issue statements as merely positions taken to attract the support of a particular constituency.[46] Although candidates do seek political support based on their issue positions, campaign speeches and policy positions also offer voters information on what candidates intend to accomplish if elected. Studies show that voters are intensely interested in learning about candidate issue positions as a way of evaluating the candidate's capacity to address real problems, even though the journalist's strategic frame lets little of that information get through to them.[47]

When journalists do report on issues, little information is conveyed that would contribute to constructive deliberation. The media, especially television, tend to ignore broad social and economic policy issues because of their complexity and the difficulty of simplifying and dramatizing them.[48] The media prefer narrow controversial issues such as gun control or abortion, which permit them to dramatize conflict between the opposing candidates. Or, more often, they create "issues" out of campaign gaffes or scandals at the expense of substantive policy discussion. An incident early in the Democratic primary campaign in 1992 revealed the journalistic treatment of issues. On a day when candidate Bill Clinton gave a comprehensive speech at Georgetown outlining his policy priorities, one of his opponents, Senator Bob Kerrey, happened to be caught unawares by an open mike telling an off-color private joke to a friend. The Kerrey gaffe led the news and dominated election coverage for several days, while Clinton's speech was hardly mentioned. Even the *Washington Post,* a highly reputable newspaper known for its serious coverage of national affairs, devoted one inside page story to the Clinton speech, but four stories plus an editorial to Kerrey's joke.[49] The tendency of the media to frame election campaigns as strategic games focuses coverage on campaign tactics, conflict, and gaffs and away from serious analysis of issues. Since so little serious issue information sifts through to voters, elections provide little opportunity for them to deliberate about how to address the country's problems.

A major factor contributing to this inadequate news coverage of elections is the need to make the coverage entertaining. Commercial networks and newspapers in the United States are business enterprises that seek to make money for their owners. To do so they must attract customers for their product, and the formula they use is to entertain and amuse. As television news producers, for example, have discovered that viewers find fast-paced programs more entertaining, they have devised programs that move quickly through shorter stories: shrinking sound bites are the result. The same need to entertain forces reporters to seek out dramatic stories, hence the emphasis on personality and gaffes over issues. And when issues are covered, controversy and confrontation are the criteria used to select issues, rather than their substantive importance to the country's future. Longer stories, which place issues in context and provide information for evaluating the issue positions of candidates, are rarely on television because producers fear they will not hold the attention of viewers. According to some media critics, the fast-paced entertainment-oriented news coverage of television has conditioned viewers to want this kind of news. News producers who fear that viewers are not interested in complex discussions of issues may have turned this fear into a self-fulfilling prophecy. As television viewers are presented with fast-paced superficial coverage, they come to expect this approach. Neil Postman, a leading media analyst, argues that television "has made entertainment itself the natural format for the representation of all experience... [because] all subject matter is presented as entertaining."[50] The emergence of tabloid "news" programs, such as *A Current Affair,* which blatantly seek the sensational over serious coverage, may be a reflection of how trends in conventional news programs have shaped viewer tastes. These tabloid programs in turn are placing increasing pressure on the conventional news programs to sensationalize in order to attract viewers. All the major networks now have their own versions of tabloid-style programs, such as *Prime Time Live* or *Dateline NBC,* that mimic the sensationalism of the tabloids. Competition with entertainment channels on cable has reduced the major networks' audience share, leading them to inject even more entertainment value to their news coverage. One response has been the creation of all-news cable channels such as MSNBC and CNBC ("all Monica, all the time") that specialize in nonstop reports on the latest scandal, rather than political substance. Local news programs also are caught in a downward spiral of competition with the tabloids and one another to present sensational, entertaining stories to the point that coverage of public issues, unless they relate to political scandal, are ignored completely. During elections, voters are going to find very little information on television that is useful for deliberating on public issues.

Unfortunately, the production values of television news and cable have carried over in recent years to the print media. The creation of *USA Today* was a watershed in the conscious attempt to imitate television news in its design. The paper prints extremely short news stories providing basic information, much like what one would hear in a televised news report. The use of color and graphics likewise reflects a desire to make the news entertaining and appealing, but with much loss in substantive information. Since the appearance and success of *USA Today,* mainstream newspapers, including such prestigious ones as the *New York Times* and the *Washington Post,* have experimented with similar formats. Although these changes may be a necessity to attract readers in an electronic age, they have undermined the political discourse of campaigns and the possibility of useful deliberation.[51] The bites of information voters are receiving in both print and electronic media are just not sufficient for constructive political discourse.

Not surprisingly, candidates for office have adjusted their style of campaigning in response to the style of media coverage. They attempt to manipulate the coverage to their advantage using techniques that, while effective in winning votes, do nothing to advance coherent deliberation on public policy. Instead of seeking to win votes in a direct debate with opponents on what policies are needed for the country, modern campaigns are exercises in image manipulation. Campaign managers attempt to manufacture positive images of their candidates and, through the use of negative advertising, negative images of opponents. The basic approach is to strike a "responsive chord" with the electorate, that is, to convey a message that resonates with concerns already present in the electorate in order to stimulate a positive or negative reaction.[52] Nothing in this approach relates to raising or discussing serious policy issues; the point is to stimulate an emotional response to obtain votes.

Campaign consultants have developed striking the responsive chord in voters into a fine art. In the 1988 presidential campaign, Bush campaign manager Lee Atwater drew on a minor incident from the gubernatorial record of Bush's opponent Michael Dukakis to associate the Massachusetts governor with a black criminal named Willie Horton. During Dukakis's tenure as governor, Horton had raped a woman while on a weekend furlough from the Massachusetts state prison. Although Dukakis had no direct involvement in the decision to furlough Horton, Atwater discovered in precampaign focus groups that people reacted strongly against Dukakis when they heard the Horton story. When the Bush campaign ran negative ads featuring Horton's mug shot, voter's fears about crime

Former Democratic Senator Bill Bradley plays upon his previous career as a professional basketball player to strike a responsive chord with primary voters. (Newsmakers)

and violence and, for some whites, racial prejudice provided the basis for a strong anti-Dukakis response that proved very effective.[53] In 1994 congressional Republicans further perfected the responsive chord technique in using polling and focus groups to identify the precise words they should include in their "Contract with America" to obtain favorable voter response. Although the Contract included concrete legislative proposals that the Republicans attempted to enact, campaign consultants designed the wording of the Contract to maximize positive voter response to Republican candidates.[54] Democrats, too, rely on campaign consultants to devise the precise images for striking a responsive chord. In 1996 Clinton turned to master image manipulator Dick Morris for help with his reelection campaign. Morris provided daily polling reports identifying the precise themes and words that Clinton should use to elicit a positive voter response. According to campaign insiders, Morris's polling analysis influenced nearly everything Clinton did prior to the election, including where he spent his summer vacation![55] For consultants like Morris, political campaigns are opportunities for image manipulation, not serious democratic deliberation. Furlough ads, campaign contracts, and vacation choice were all simply packages "of stimuli whose sole purpose was to win the elections."[56]

Unfortunately for democratic deliberation, similar packages of stimuli have come to dominate contemporary campaigns. Candidates and their professional consultants manufacture series of images to be presented in the media in order to strike responsive chords with the voters. Campaigns feature "war rooms" to devise responses to the campaigns of opponents and endless efforts to "spin" events in ways favorable to the candidate. Rather than write speeches to advance reasoned arguments about public policy, professional speechwriters build them around pithy phrases and slogans that can fit the sound bites of the television news programs. Media events are staged to attract media coverage and strike a responsive chord with voters, such as Bush at an American flag factory or Dukakis riding in a tank in 1988 or the innumerable Clinton/Gore bus tours in 1992 and 1996. Promises are made that the candidates know are unrealistic ("No new taxes"). Even the televised candidate debates are primarily opportunities to project images and strike poses rather than discuss public policy issues seriously. Both candidates and the media focus on who "won" the debate, rather than what was said, and winning or losing is defined in terms of major gaffes, such as Dukakis's failure to show emotion in response to a hypothetical question about his wife's rape, or memorable put-downs, such as vice-presidential candidate Lloyd Bentsen's "You're no Jack Kennedy" remark to Dan Quayle, or humorous slogans, such as Ross Perot saying, "I'm all ears." Presidential candidates are now so sensitive to the need to avoid gaffes that, by the 1996 campaign, Clinton and Dole were prepared so well to avoid mistakes that the debates seemed scripted and bland. Not surprisingly, the 1996 debates failed to attract much voter attention, gaining the lowest viewing audience (about one third of viewers) in thirty years.[57]

Voters cannot even be sure that candidates actually believe what they say in debates or speeches. Debates are thoroughly rehearsed and scripted as much as possible in advance. Because of the use of professional speechwriters, voters cannot be sure that candidates have ever even "thought the words they have spoken."[58] In fact, there is some evidence that candidates do not take their campaign claims very seriously. According to an article in the *New Yorker* published in fall 1992, former Soviet Premier Mikhail Gorbachev said that George Bush warned him before the 1988 presidential campaign not to pay any attention to anything Bush might say about the Soviet Union during the election campaign; it would just be campaign rhetoric and not reflect Bush's real thinking about Gorbachev and U.S.-Soviet relations![59] Even though the American stance toward Soviet liberalization was a major policy concern in 1988, Bush proceeded to say very little about it; instead, he concentrated on ritualistic denunciations of Soviet power and the need to maintain America's defense strength (as did Dukakis) in line with his warning to Gorbachev. Bush clearly had no intention of involving American voters in any deliberation regarding U.S. policy toward the then-crumbling Soviet state.

The 1988 presidential campaign, as previous examples suggest, reached a nadir in trivialized campaign rhetoric. During and after the campaign, many commentators criticized the mindlessness of the candidates' campaign appeals and the poverty of the media coverage. These critiques pointed out the irrelevance of most of the issues featured in the campaign — furloughs, the Pledge of Allegiance, and Dukakis's purported liberalism — and noted the absence of any discussion of such truly serious issues as the S&L scandal or the impending end of the Cold War. After the election, many news organizations critiqued their own performance and vowed more substantive coverage and the avoidance of candidate manipulation. Opinion polls indicated that voters were especially dissatisfied with the campaign, which the low voter turnout confirmed. Were opportunities for issue deliberation any better in 1992?

Most analyses suggest that the 1992 presidential race did offer some improvement over 1988.[60] Candidates refrained from blatant manipulations, such as the Willie Horton ad. More real issues were discussed, and the media paid more attention to them. Part of this improvement may have been the result of widespread voter disgust with the 1988 campaign. All participants may have concluded that the approaches of 1988 would not sell to 1992 voters. In one of the more interesting innovations of the campaign, candidates, especially the Democratic primary candidates and Clinton and Perot during their general election campaigns, attempted unmediated contact with voters through appearances on televised town meetings and talk shows. The improved campaign resulted in increased voter satisfaction and a small increase in turnout.

The 1996 campaign, however, failed to continue the innovative uses of alternative media tried in 1992, as the candidates pursued more conservative and conventional campaigns. The story of media coverage in 1996 was its failure to spark public interest in the campaign, a probable factor in the low voter turnout.[61] As in the past, reporters focused most of their coverage on the strategic "horse race." Even when substantive issues were raised, it was usually in terms of their impact on campaign strategic dynamics, not their substance. For example, when Steve Forbes proposed a flat tax during the Republican primary, most coverage focused on whether the issue would be an effective tactic to advance Forbes's campaign, not whether it was sound economic policy.[62] Campaign coverage in 1996 was noteworthy also for its overwhelmingly negative portrayal of the candidates — more negative than the candidates' descriptions of each other.[63] Television coverage was so uninspiring that it became the object, itself, of TV coverage. Matthew Robert Kerbel tells of an NBC News report entitled "Feeding Frenzy" that described television coverage of the New Hampshire primary as a "mindless video game." This report, however, seemed to have no impact on NBC's continuing participation in the very "frenzy" that its report deplored.[64]

The campaign manipulations and media coverage described so far suggest that American elections provide little opportunity for democratic deliberation. At election time, citizens are mere observers of a spectacle that means to entertain them in order to attract their votes but offers no opportunity for them to join in debates about policy directions.[65] Political communication during elections makes no effort to create coalitions behind "governing ideas." According to the political scientist Lance Bennett, "missing almost entirely is any sort of give and take exchange through which social groups, parties, and candidates might develop mutual commitments to a broad political agenda."[66] By abandoning substantive exchanges on policy issues that matter, election campaigns have diminished campaigns as a democratic device. They may remain the means by which Americans choose the individuals who govern them, but because of the dearth of deliberation, their outcomes provide little indication of how voters expect to be governed. Small wonder, then, that elections seem to have ceased to be effective devices for democratic control of government.

CONTROL

Given the poverty of electoral discourse in American elections and the absence of deliberation about important issues, the meaning of electoral outcomes is always in doubt. Neither winners nor losers are required to draw specific policy lessons from election outcomes. In this situation, elections have begun to lose their capacity to control what happens in government. Elections decided on the basis of sound bites, debate gaffes, and campaign image manipulation fail to resolve the political conflicts going on in society. All sides to fundamental conflicts can easily point to the irrelevance of what went on in the election to their particular concerns. Nor do elections empower anyone's governing agenda when they cease to play the role of building a governing coalition behind a specific agenda. Elections that fail to send those holding government office clear direction permit those officials to set that direction themselves, independent of the democratic electorate's control.

To use the example of Athenian democracy once again, the contemporary American situation contrasts sharply with the control Athenian citizens exercised over public action through the Assembly. Public deliberations conveyed precise directives of the citizenry's will to those officials charged with carrying out policy. As participants in those deliberations, officials knew from direct experience what decisions they were to execute. They were also subject to direct intervention from the Assembly if their actions deviated from what was intended. In addition, the Athenians provided for annual audits of official actions to evaluate whether they conformed to Assembly intent.[67] Punishment was immediate and severe if official misconduct was discovered. During the period of democratic rule in Athens, there was no question that democratic institutions were in control of public policy. Unfortunately, the same cannot be said of the foremost American democratic institution — elections. In recent years, a number of political scientists have begun to question whether elections continue to play a major role in controlling public policy. As one recent book title puts it, *Do Elections Matter?*[68] It has become a serious concern. Since elections do not provide clear policy direction, nonelected officials and processes unconnected to elections have come to play an increasingly important role in making important policy decisions. Bureaucratic agencies and the courts have become the arenas in which policy questions unaddressed in election campaigns are decided.

One area where much policy responsibility has been ceded to nonelected bureaucrats is the making of national economic policy. Since the 1970s, several presidents and Congress have been unable to formulate coherent policies to manage the national economy. Because of the ambiguity of election outcomes, elected representatives have not had a political mandate to deal with major economic problems, whether the spiraling inflation of the 1970s or the sluggish economy of the early 1990s. Candidates have sought election based on promises to address these issues, but once in office, they find themselves unable to agree on specific policies. Since members of Congress and the president are elected as independent political entrepreneurs, all claim the right to interpret the election as endorsing whatever specific approach to solving economic problems they happen to favor. The inconclusiveness of elections interacts with the institutional deadlock of the separation-of-powers structure to create a stalemate.

Without effective action on the part of elected officials, the Federal Reserve Board, an appointed body designed to be insulated from electoral pressures, led by its chairman, has taken control of much of the responsibility for economic policy. When Congress and the president failed to come up with an effective policy to stem inflation in the late 1970s, Federal Reserve Board Chairman Paul Volcker stepped in and imposed stringent controls on the nation's money supply, which restricted the availability of credit and pushed up interest rates. While this approach proved effective in bringing down inflation in the 1980s, it did so at the cost of a massive recession and unemployment for millions of Americans. Alternative approaches to inflation control or approaches that might have balanced controlling inflation with other policy goals, such as maintaining high employment, could not be undertaken because elected officeholders did not possess the electoral mandate to enact them. Chairman Volcker stepped into a policy vacuum, but not with the policies a democratic citizenry would have chosen. Partisans of democracy should be concerned when a poll of European business people, cognizant of the important role of the Federal Reserve in recent years, listed an unelected official, the chairman of the Federal Reserve, as the second-most-powerful American after the president.[69]

In 1990 a similar policy deadlock, this time over how to bring the country out of a recession, again left the problem in the hands of the Federal Reserve. With Congress and the president unable to agree on how to stimulate the economy and the huge budget deficit, which itself was a consequence of electoral and institutional deadlock, inhibiting enactment of stimulative spending programs, the Federal Reserve attempted to stimulate the economy through lower interest rates. Unlike the attack on inflation in the 1980s, this had only modest effect, as the recession stretched into the longest since World War II. Only when the president and Congress agreed on fiscal policy aimed at budget balance beginning in 1993 did the economy begin to revive. Interestingly, as the economic boom of the 1990s proved to be the longest sustained period of economic growth since World War II, many observers credited Federal Reserve chairman Alan Greenspan, rather than elected officials, and looked to him to maintain prosperity. Whatever the effect of its actions, the prominence of the "Fed" as principal economic policymaker in recent years is a feature of the decline of elections as the controlling determinant of these policies. This absence of electoral control means, given the logic of representative democracy, that the people have lost control of the policies that govern their economic affairs.

Just as the growing importance of the Federal Reserve is a reflection of elections' failure to play their proper role in a representative democracy, the increasing use of the judiciary to make important policy decisions reflects the decline in electoral control. Often, analysis of the policymaking role of the Supreme Court and the other federal and state courts focuses on arguments about judicial activism versus judicial restraint. Rarely do these arguments about judicial philosophy consider that the growing policy role of the courts may result less from the attitudes of judges and more from the propensity of everyone to bring to the courts policy issues that remain unresolved in the electoral arena. As elections fail to bring cloture on serious social conflicts over abortion, the status of minorities and women and gays, or the need to protect the environment, the parties to these conflicts turn to the courts. While judicial policymaking in the 1960s and 1970s was associated with liberal social policies, such policymaking has not been confined to social issues, nor has it been exclusively a practice of liberal judges. In the early 1980s, for example, a federal judge supervised one of the most significant economic and business developments of the decade — the breakup of the AT&T telephone monopoly. This decision, which went well beyond merely dividing AT&T into several "Baby Bells," dictated much of American telecommunication policy well into the future, including regulation of the development of such new technologies as fiber optic networks.[70] Amazingly for a representative democracy in which elections are supposed to be controlling, these decisions were made without the participation of any elected officials and with virtually no discussion during election campaigns.

Along with empowering nonelected officials, the weakness of elections as institutions for resolving political conflict has increased the importance of other forms of political combat. According to political scientists Benjamin Ginsberg and Martin Shefter, revelation, investigation, and prosecution (RIP) to discredit political opponents have become substitutes for beating them in election contests.[71] Using both the media and the judiciary, politicians raise questions about the behavior of public officials, often in congressional hearings; call for investigations into improper behavior; and then seek prosecution for misconduct. Congressional Democrats perfected these techniques, most notably in the Watergate affair, to attack political opponents in Republican presidential administrations. In the Reagan and Bush years, several officials were subject to such treatment, including EPA director Anne Burford Gorsuch, Attorney General Edwin Meese, and Defense secretary nominee John Tower. By the mid-1980s, Republicans were responding in kind with RIP attacks on House Speaker Jim Wright and majority whip Tony Coelho for accepting improper campaign contributions.

When they gained control of Congress in 1995, Republican legislators subjected the Clinton administration to the kind of RIP attacks the Democrats had used against Clinton's Republican predecessors. They subjected his nominees to demeaning attacks, leading several to withdraw their nominations. House and Senate committees sought to embarrass the president and his wife through prolonged and expensive hearings on the Whitewater affair. Multiple special prosecutors were appointed to investigate several prominent members of the administration, including the secretaries of Agriculture, Commerce, and Interior and even the president himself over Whitewater. Republican political activists sought to embarrass the president further by encouraging a former Arkansas state employee, Paula Jones, to sue the president for sexual harassment, the first time in history that a president had been sued for personal actions that occurred before he took office.[72] Ultimately the Paula Jones suit and the investigation by Whitewater Special Prosecutor Kenneth Starr came together to expose Clinton's tawdry affair with Monica Lewinsky. The subsequent scandal and Clinton's awkward attempt to conceal his affair led to the ultimate RIP attack — a presidential impeachment, the second in American history.

The Senate's failure to convict President Clinton and remove him from office was an outcome consistent with most RIP attacks. Although sometimes serious misconduct leading to punishment or removal from office is uncovered, few of the RIP investigations in recent years have uncovered serious wrongdoing. In the multiple investigations of the Clinton administration or the prior inquiries into the conduct of the Bush and Reagan administrations, few accusations have been proven. The Watergate scandal was historically exceptional in actually uncovering a serious abuse of power and resulting in a presidential resignation. What is interesting about RIP from the standpoint of representative democracy is not whether investigation of official misconduct has uncovered real abuse, but the fact that it has come to substitute for electoral pressures in framing political conflict. As elections have become indecisive events, political combatants use accusations of impropriety as weapons to undermine the power of opponents and their ability to enact their preferences into policy.

The failure of elections to control what government does derives from both the inequality of representation and the absence of meaningful deliberation in contemporary elections. As argued earlier, elections are a mechanism to "compensate for private inequalities in political resources."[73] In the absence of elections, powerful private interests will find some way, whether through bribery or flattery, to influence government officials. When officials are truly subject to the will of the electorate, however, they are under control of a mandate each voter has had an equal hand in producing. As special interests have come to undermine equal representation in elections, this increases their capacity to influence officials independent of elections. In the infamous case of the "Keating Five," five U.S. senators received large campaign contributions from Charles Keating, owner of a large southwestern savings-and-loan corporation. In Senate hearings and later at his own trial on securities fraud, Keating revealed that the purpose of his contributions was to gain, with the senators' assistance, access to and influence with the Federal Home Loan Bank Board, which regulated S&Ls.[74] For Keating and many other big campaign contributors, contributions are not for influencing election outcomes as much as they are investments in access to the bureaucracy, where the important decisions affecting their interests are made.

The powerful interests that provide money for modern campaigns do so, primarily, to prevent elections from controlling what government does. As long as elected officials are constrained by promises made in the hidden election not to enact legislation adverse to the interests of their big contributors, they have an incentive to delegate decision making to the bureaucracy and then intervene selectively on behalf of wealthy and powerful contributors. In much the same way, meaningless campaign rhetoric keeps discussion of major issues out of election campaigns. When these important issues eventually are dealt with — in congressional committees, the bureaucracy, or the courts — their resolution is left to well-placed and powerful interests with access to those arenas. Keeping deliberation on important issues out of the visible public arena of electoral politics empowers those with access to the less visible arenas where the final decisions are made. In this way, the absence of meaningful campaign deliberation reinforces biased representation, both of which undermine the control of elections over government policy.

FOR ALL OUR celebration of elections as the touchstone of representative democracy, the practice of electoral politics in the contemporary United States falls far short of what democratic theory requires. Contemporary practice meets none of the three criteria for democratic elections listed earlier in the chapter. The decline of political parties, the hidden election, and modern campaign techniques all undermine equal representation in elections. By the time the ordinary voter pulls the voting lever, the powerful special interests that have structured the ballot have left the voter with very little meaningful choice. To the extent that there is a choice between candidates, the trivial rhetoric of modern elections obscures choices relevant to important issues. Elections decided on sound bites, negative campaign commercials, and sensationalized exposure of personal character flaws provide no meaningful direction of government. As long as candidates need not discuss what truly matters to voters to get elected, they need not pay any attention to the electorate when governing. As a result, elections make less and less difference to what government does. Decisions on important issues are made increasingly out of public view, in legislative committees, the bureaucracy, and the courts. In a representative democracy, the degree to which elections fall short of satisfying the criteria of democratic elections defines the extent to which government fails to be truly democratic.

The criteria of equal representation, deliberation, and control are demanding ones. Elections in the United States have never satisfied these criteria completely, nor do elections in other representative democracies. The failure to satisfy these criteria, in itself, is not the challenge facing American democracy today. Making elections democratic institutions is a continual struggle in democracies, one that can never be fully won. The challenge that current electoral practice poses for American democracy is that the struggle to make elections democratic institutions seems to have been largely abandoned. Democrats should hope that however short of the democratic ideal elections fall, they are at least evolving toward it. Unfortunately, Americans' recent experience with elections suggests that we are regressing from the democratic ideal. The challenge to our democracy is to reform our electoral institutions so that they once again evolve in a democratic direction.

A number of reforms might assist in restoring the democratic evolution of elections. One obvious one would be to end the power of special interests and powerful individuals to limit choice in the hidden election. An expanded system of public financing of elections combined with provision of free media access would be a major improvement. Currently, some public funds are provided for presidential election campaigns, but much funding in presidential primary elections and all funding in congressional races are raised in the hidden election. Full public funding of campaigns would undercut the power of special-interest money. Such funding also would need to be combined with limits on campaign spending to prevent an extravagant burden on taxpayers. One way to reduce campaign costs would be to provide free media access to major candidates, thereby eliminating the most expensive part of the campaign. Devising a fair and democratic system for allocating public campaign funds and determining who obtains media access would be complex, but many European democracies have devised such systems.[75] Elections are a *public* institution for assuring democratic governance; they can succeed in this role only with *public* funding.

Revitalizing political parties is another crucial element in making elections operate democratically. As argued earlier in this chapter, only when strong competitive political parties contest elections are ordinary citizens able to make meaningful election choices. After several decades of gradual party decline, party renewal would require a variety of reforms involving changes in how parties are organized, changes in election laws, and changes in the attitudes of voters.[76] Parties need to develop organizational mechanisms for keeping in contact with voters to replace the old precinct and ward structures of the past. Party expert Larry Sabato suggests that parties should build structures to provide ordinary citizens with help in gaining access to government services, expand their fund-raising and campaign assistance to candidates, and engage in public education geared at strengthening their ties to voters. Funneling the public funding of campaigns through parties would be a critical factor in promoting party renewal. Reform of primary laws needs to limit or eliminate primaries as mechanisms for nominating candidates in favor of such processes as party caucuses or conventions that allow party activists a more deliberative role in choosing party nominees. But, as argued in chapter 1, party renewal cannot occur unless it is combined with reform of the separation-of-powers structure. A governing party needs to be able to obtain unified control of government when it wins office so that voters can easily hold government accountable.

Reforming parties and campaign finance methods will not happen quickly; party building will require years of effort, and campaign finance reform must overcome intense opposition from incumbent officeholders.[77] In the meantime, the political theorist James S. Fishkin suggests an intriguing way to improve public deliberation in presidential election campaigns.[78] He proposes bringing a random sample of voters to a single spot, perhaps a university campus, early in the presidential nominating process to meet with prospective candidates. Over a period of several days, the voters would meet the candidates, hear their campaign speeches, and have an opportunity to question them. All these events would be televised to a national audience. In addition to meeting the candidates, the group would hear from experts on various issues affecting the country and, most important, would have an opportunity to discuss and debate among themselves. At the end of the period, the voters would be polled on their opinions of the presidential candidates. Fishkin calls this a "deliberative opinion poll" because, unlike conventional polls, which are mere aggregations of responses that isolated individuals make to questions, this poll would come after the sample of citizens had an opportunity to listen and talk among themselves about the candidates and the issues. Fishkin hopes this event, if well publicized, could be a major factor influencing the presidential campaign and bringing an element of deliberation to the process. Similar deliberative polls could be used in congressional, state, and local elections.

Innovative ideas for making elections more democratic cannot succeed, however, unless citizens are more aware of why and how elections are deficient. Citizen discontent with election processes has been well documented in recent years and is reflected in the success of antipoliticians such as Ross Perot. But making elections more effective instruments of democracy will require more than voting for folksy demagogues. As this chapter argues, effective democratic reform must begin with an understanding of what makes elections democratic instruments. Electoral reforms must promote more equal representation, citizen deliberation, and the control elections have of government officials. To meet this challenge of democracy, we must remember that elections alone do not guarantee democratic government. Only elections organized to empower ordinary voters satisfy democracy's promise.

> ### THOUGHT QUESTIONS
> 1. This chapter argues that candidate-centered campaigns are less democratic than if political parties had a stronger role in organizing campaigns. Think about this issue in terms of your own congressional representative. Do you think that you would be better represented if congressional candidates in your district ran under a party-organized campaign instead of one organized and run by individual candidates? Would some types of representation be enhanced and others diminished?
>
> 2. One way to enhance party control of election campaigns would be to eliminate primary elections and allow party organizations to choose their candidates. Would you favor such a reform? What are the pluses and minuses of choosing candidates for office through primary elections?
>
> 3. In the landmark 1976 case *Buckley* v. *Valeo,* the Supreme Court ruled that campaign contributions were a form of free speech and thus protected by the First Amendment, thereby overturning any mandatory controls on the amount of money spent in campaigns. Do you agree with the Court that campaign contributions deserve protection under the First Amendment? Can you think of reasons why limits on spending might be justified?
>
> 4. This chapter argues that democratic elections need to provide opportunities of citizen deliberation on public issues. Is this a realistic expectation in modern America? Can you come up with any suggestions for how deliberation might be successfully integrated into modern election campaigns?
>
> 5. The intervention of the judiciary in setting policy in a variety of areas such as civil rights, the environment, abortion, and business regulation is presented in this chapter as undermining electoral control of these policy areas. Is diminishing electoral control in these areas necessarily undemocratic? Think about this issue from the point of view of a racial or ethnic minority, a gay person, a pregnant woman, or an environmental activist.

SUGGESTIONS FOR FURTHER READING

Alexander, Herbert E. *Financing Politics: Money, Elections, and Political Reform.* 4th ed. Washington, D.C.: CQ Press, 1992. The definitive analysis of how our complex system of campaign financing works.

Edelman, Murray. *Constructing the Political Spectacle.* Chicago: University of Chicago Press, 1988. According to this book, all the political world's a stage and citizens are mere spectators, especially at election time.

Fishkin, James S. *Democracy and Deliberation: New Directions for Political Reform.* New Haven: Yale University Press, 1991. A critique of American elections as deliberative institutions with intriguing proposals for reform.

Ginsberg, Benjamin, and Martin Shefter. *Politics by Other Means: The Declining Importance of Elections in America.* New York: Basic Books, 1991. A detailed account of how elections have become practically irrelevant to government policymaking.

Jamieson, Kathleen Hall. *Dirty Politics: Deception, Distraction, and Democracy.* New York: Oxford University Press, 1992. A thorough and authoritative critique of how recent American elections have been conducted.

*Morris, Dick. *Behind the Oval Office: Winning the Presidency in the Nineties.* New York: Random House, 1997. Clinton's 1996 campaign strategist provides a professional's perspective on American elections.

*Polsby, Nelson W., and Aaron Wildavsky. *Presidential Elections.* 10th ed. New York: Chatham House, 2000. While not uncritical of American elections, these leading political scientists see them as fairly effective democratic institutions.

Pomper, Gerald M., ed. *The Election of 1996.* Chatham, N.J.: Chatham House, 1997. The best among several anthologies analyzing the 1996 elections, with thoughtful essays on every aspect of the election.

Sabato, Larry J. *PAC Power: Inside the World of Political Action Committees.* New York: Norton, 1985. A path-breaking study of how PACs work.

Vote for Me: Politics in America. Produced by Louis Alvarez, Andrew Kolker, and Paul Stekler. Film distributed by The Center for New American Media, 524 Broadway, 2d floor, New York, N.Y. 10012. This entertaining and educational film documents how elections, at all levels, are conducted in America today.

White, John Kenneth, and Daniel M. Shea. *New Party Politics: From Jefferson and Hamilton to the Information Age.* New York: St. Martin's Press, 2000. A comprehensive review of the important role parties have played in the history of American democracy, with keen insights into renewing them as democratic institutions.

*Presents a point of view that disagrees with the arguments presented in this chapter.

SELECTED WEB SITES

http://la.utexas.edu/research/delpol/cdpindex.html Site of James Fishkin's Center for Deliberative Polling provides latest information on deliberative polling experiments, including video clips.

http://www.commoncause.org/ Information about campaign finance expenditures and latest news on attempts at reform.

http://www.vote-smart.org/ Election news plus specific information on candidates for office. Look up your congressperson!

http://www.opensecrets.org/home/index.asp The Center for Responsive Politics provides detailed and up-to-date information on campaign contributions and lobbying. Look up your congressperson here too!

http://www.publiccampaign.org/index.html Public Campaign is a nonprofit, nonpartisan organization working to reform the campaign finance system.

CHAPTER 5

The Fifth Challenge:
The "Privileged Position" of Business

The flaw in the pluralist heaven is that the heavenly chorus sings with a strong upper-class accent.

—E.E. SCHATTSCHNEIDER

The large private corporation fits oddly into democratic theory and vision. Indeed, it does not fit.

—CHARLES E. LINDBLOM

THE PLURALIST MODEL of democracy, described in the introduction, has been influential as an interpretation of American democracy. In fact, many of the political scientists who developed the model in the middle of the twentieth century considered it a concrete description of democracy as actually practiced in the United States. American politics was widely viewed as group politics in which a wide variety of interests interacted to influence government policy. In both textbooks and journalistic accounts, interest groups were portrayed positively as vehicles of democratic representation. As groups competed with one another to influence election outcomes or lobby for the passage of legislation, they represented the interests and concerns of virtually all Americans. No one group held a dominant position in American society.

This chapter is a critique of this central assumption of the Pluralist description of American politics. I argue that one can identify a dominant group in our politics: business. More specifically, I present evidence that people who control large business corporations dominate our political processes and largely control public policy outcomes. Although the United States is a highly diverse society with a lively variety of groups, some even organized as "interest groups" in order

Opposite: *Microsoft chairman Bill Gates looms large in the booming information technology business, despite charges of monopolistic abuses. (Newsmakers)*

to influence government, Big Business is a special group. Unlike other groups, it has a "privileged position" in U.S. politics.[1] This chapter describes the nature of that privileged position and how this situation impedes democratic politics.

Before I develop this argument, however, we need to revisit the Pluralist model and see how political scientists deployed it in the 1950s and 1960s as a description of how American politics worked.

AMERICAN POLITICS AS PLURALIST HEAVEN

For many political scientists writing in the post–World War II period, the Pluralist model provided a realistic description of how American democracy works. Books such as David Truman's *The Governmental Process,* published in 1951, focused on the activities of interest groups as the key to understanding how American public policies were actually formulated.[2]

The starting point for this analysis of American democracy was the diversity of American society and the lively associational life of Americans, a phenomenon Tocqueville remarked on as early as the 1830s. Certainly little empirical investigation was required to demonstrate that American society contained lots of different groups with varying preferences on public policy issues. Farmers, businessmen, workers, fishermen, retailers, manufacturers, poor people and rich people, pro-lifers and pro-choicers, environmentalists and those opposed to excessive environmental regulation — this is just the beginning of what would be an extremely long list of politically relevant groups in America. And as the Pluralists could easily document, many of these groups organized into formal interest groups for the purpose of influencing government. A brief perusal of the Washington, D.C., telephone book (or that of any state capital) will yield the names of many such groups. Through careful observation of the actual process of government, Pluralists documented the important role of these organized interest groups in influencing the day-to-day formulation of legislation.[3]

Whereas earlier observers of American politics had often characterized such influence as the undemocratic activity of "special interests," political scientists such as David Truman celebrated group politics as the essence of American democracy. Truman formulated three key concepts to demonstrate the democratic character of American politics: rules of the game, potential group, and points of access.

By "rules of the game," Truman meant the variety of procedures, formal and informal, in American politics that ensure a wide variety of societal interests will be able to influence government. Elections, free speech, the rights to assemble and to petition, press scrutiny, and politicians' sense of fair play create a context in which many different groups may form, promote their points of view, and have a chance for a fair hearing from government. In such a context, no one group in society will be able to develop a privileged position in government because opposing groups would quickly form to counter such a group. There can be no "special" interests when the rules of the game make government responsive to any and all interests. Truman argued that the group process itself protects the rules of the game and the governmental openness they assure. Any attempt to undermine the rules of the game on behalf of a special interest would produce retaliation from other groups, the general citizenry, and government officials such as the president, congressional leaders, and judges. For the Pluralists, public officials have a special responsibility to protect the rules of the game.[4]

Clearly, elections are a crucial part of the rules of the game because they provided for the continuing responsiveness of governmental officials to a wide variety of interest groups. Pluralist descriptions of American politics characterize politicians as brokers who make deals among various conflicting groups. Politicians seek to broker deals because they want the widest possible support at election time. Given the openness of the political process, a strategy favoring the preferences of one special interest over others will be too risky for most politicians. Instead, in formulating public policy, they will attempt to craft compromises that reflect as much as possible the preferences and interests of a wide variety of groups. Such a strategy is most likely to assure a politician's reelection and ensures the democratic character of public policy. According to Truman, the influence of what he called "potential groups" also promotes politicians' incentives to craft democratic policies. As a realistic observer, Truman understood that groups differ in the degree to which they are effectively organized. On any given policy issue, it is possible that some affected interests may be too weak and disorganized to be represented directly in the negotiation of policy compromises. But even though potential groups are not directly represented, policy compromises will take their interests into account because, given the openness of the system, "if [potential groups] are too flagrantly ignored, they may be stimulated to organize for aggressive counteraction."[5] Over the long run, governmental policy will democratically represent not only all the formally organized groups lobbying directly on issues but also the relatively unorganized.

Contributing further to the widely representative character of American democracy is the nature of our governmental structure and the many "points of access" it provides. Truman praised the separation of powers and federalism, as well as political parties and the bureaucracy, as offering different groups multiple opportunities to be represented in decision making. This means different groups with different political resources can be represented in different parts of the governmental structure. Some groups will find political party leaders responsive to their needs; others may find parties uninterested but can turn to the courts. Multiple points of access ensure that almost any group can find a way to have its interest represented.

In the years since Truman and others formulated it, this Pluralist description of American democracy has been subjected to thorough criticism from a wide variety of viewpoints. A complete review of these arguments would divert us from the central concern of this chapter.[6] I mention only two of them that I think undermine significantly the Pluralists' claim that group politics results in democratic politics. First, Pluralists have never been able to substantiate the empirical claim that interest-group politics in the United States is actually representative of all citizens, yet a demonstration is required if we are to accept the claim that such politics is democratic. In fact, careful empirical studies, examined in more detail later, show that interest groups represent only a small proportion of Americans. In the everyday policymaking process, the play of group pressures leaves out many citizens.

Of course, Truman realized this problem and tried to get around it with the concept of potential groups, but this is an inadequate solution. First, responsiveness to potential groups cannot be empirically tested because, by definition, the demands of these interests remain unarticulated. If no potential group rises up in reaction to policy, does that mean, as the Pluralists claim, that the interests of that group have been addressed or, as a critic might argue, that the group lacks the capacity to organize even in the face of action adverse to its interests? The absence of response could indicate either interpretation. Second, even if we were to concede that politicians sometimes anticipate provoking the ire of potential groups and may therefore respect their interests when making policy, it seems unlikely that this would be a frequent occurrence. In the face of direct and sometimes conflicting pressures from *organized* interests, it seems more plausible that policymakers will usually be too preoccupied with these interests to give much thought to the *unorganized*. But merely occasional attention to the needs of potential groups falls far short of satisfying the standards of democratic theory.

A second major flaw in the Pluralist description is that it underestimates the significance of inequalities in political resources on the part of even organized groups. Pluralists do not deny that political resources — for example, money, organizational leadership, group cohesiveness, and size — affect the ability of groups to influence policy. Instead, they argue that these resources are widely distributed among different groups, and no systematic bias exists in favor of a particular group or set of groups. Some groups may have lots of money, but others can balance that resource by the size of their membership. Small groups with few members can gain attention by the cohesiveness of their membership and the skills of their leaders.

This chapter challenges this claim. Its argument is that one group in society does monopolize political resources and can exact a response from the political system in a way that no other group can. The political power of business in American society provides convincing refutation of Pluralist descriptions of democratic group politics. Furthermore, business power, although always a decisive influence in American politics, seems to have been increasing in recent years, and this increase constitutes a major challenge to the future of American democracy.

BUSINESS: THE "PRIVILEGED" GROUP

The position of political privilege accorded to business has two faces in American society. The first face is the more familiar one. It involves business and groups representing business actively manipulating the political system through lobbying, elections, and media propagandizing to attain their political objectives. As I later show, business has overwhelming political resources that make it virtually unbeatable whenever it decisively mobilizes to move government on its behalf. The second face of business power is more subtle and is one that most of us rarely think about. It involves the power business wields over society and the political system without needing to seek actively to influence them. This is the privileged position we give to business when we opt, in a capitalist market economy, to give business leaders autonomous power to make society's crucial economic decisions.

The first face of business power, the predominant role of business groups within the governmental process, has received thorough documentation from political scientists and journalists.[7] In this chapter, I can provide only a brief summary of this literature in terms of three different aspects of this open face of business power: business predominance in lobbying policymakers, the role of business in financing elections, and the propagation of ideas and messages favorable to business in the media, schools, and universities.

Group theorists were correct in describing the day-to-day politics of public policymaking, both in Congress and the bureaucracy, as a politics of group pressures. A wide variety of groups actively seek to influence legislation and regulations.[8] What is significant about these group pressures, however, is not, as Pluralist group theorists would have us believe, the representativeness of these groups; instead, it is the extent to which these groups represent one societal interest: business. A variety of different groups represent business. First, some business groups represent the broad general interests of all businesses and are especially active on legislation dealing with issues that affect the entire business community, such as general tax legislation, labor laws, and overall business regulation. The three most powerful groups in this category are the U.S. Chamber of Commerce, representing federations of about 250,000 business members nationwide; the National Association of Manufacturers (NAM), representing the nation's largest industrial firms; and the Business Roundtable, made up of the CEOs of the 200 largest U.S. corporations. Although these groups have distinct policy agendas, they usually unite and coordinate their activities when it comes to matters affecting business as a whole. For example, in 1978, they were quite effective when they organized a massive lobbying effort to defeat the labor law reform bill that would have facilitated labor union organizing.[9]

Second, about a thousand trade and commodity organizations represent different segments of the business community. These include groups such as the American Bankers' Association, the National Association of Home Builders, and the National Association of Wheat Growers. Although the last sounds as if it should be classified as a farmers' group, it, like most commodity groups, includes agribusiness and food-processing firms along with some family farmers. Trade associations concentrate on policies aimed specifically at a particular segment of industry, as when the American Bankers' Association organized a massive grassroots lobbying campaign in the early 1980s to defeat a congressional attempt to institute tax withholding of profits from stock dividends and savings accounts, as occurs with wages. This classic effort involved widespread advertising in the mass media and the distribution of postage-paid postcards in banks across the country that bank depositors could mail to their members of Congress. The proposed legislation was defeated in short order.

A third and increasingly important form of business representation is the direct Washington presence of individual corporations. Sometimes, in the case of the five hundred largest corporations, this involves corporations with Washington offices employing large staffs lobbying full time on legislation affecting corporate interests. More often, this representation involves the retention of one of the many Washington law firms specializing in lobbying or specialized consultants with Washington experience and connections. With their deep pockets, large corporations can hire the most skilled and well-connected lobbying experts. Microsoft's $3.7 billion lobbying budget in 1998 brought to its lobbying team the services of Michael Deaver, Ronald Reagan's renowned campaign adman; Haley Barbour, former Republican National Committee chair; Ralph Reed, former Christian Coalition director; Mark Penn, a top pollster to the Gore presidential campaign; two former staffers to House Majority Leader Dick Armey; and former Democratic Congressmen Vic Fazio and Tom Downey.[10] Notice that Microsoft's lobbying team covers the full political and ideological spectrum, including well-known Republican conservatives such as Reed and Deaver and Democratic liberals such as Downey and Fazio. Corporations seeking influence cover all political bases in buying support.

These three kinds of business groups account for most of the interest-group activity in Washington, D.C. A recent study of the seven thousand or so groups active in the nation's capital found that corporations, trade associations, and general business organizations (including foreign business) accounted for 70 percent of all groups with Washington representation.[11] By contrast, labor unions accounted for 1.7 percent of groups, social welfare groups and those representing the poor .6 percent, and citizens' groups 4.1 percent. This same study documented a large increase in overall interest-group activity between 1960 and the 1980s, including an increase in citizens' groups and those representing the poor.

Nevertheless, the increase in the number of business groups has outpaced these other groups so that business dominates the group process more now than it did thirty years ago.[12]

Business has become quite sophisticated in linking its Washington lobbying activities to efforts to generate the appearance of grassroots support for its concerns.[13] In recent years, business and trade associations have fine-tuned their procedures for influencing individual members of Congress.[14] For example, the U.S. Chamber of Commerce maintains a list of Key Resource Personnel (KRP) — people living in each congressperson's district with personal access to the member. KRPs are mobilized to call on their "friends" in Congress on issues of concern to the Chamber of Commerce. Businesses employ sophisticated "astroturf" campaigns to generate phone calls, postcards, and letters favorable to their concerns. In 1993, the National Restaurant Association defeated an attempt to reduce the tax deduction on business meals with a television advertising campaign that included a toll-free telephone number to patch calls directly to Senate offices. Usually, consultants screen such calls to make sure that only opinions favorable to business interests get through.[15] Because influencing legislation is now more costly and time-consuming than ever, groups with more resources and expertise are stronger than ever.[16]

Business advantage in the world of political lobbying depends, of course, on the receptivity of those being lobbied: elected officials. Election campaign contributions are one way in which business groups can assure a friendly reception when they come calling to influence legislation. Obviously, business is not the sole source of campaign contributions in the United States, but just as business dominates the universe of lobby groups, it dominates the universe of campaign contributions. Since the passage of the 1974 amendments to the Federal Election Campaign Act, which limited how much individual "fat cat" contributors could give to individual campaigns, a major source of election campaign funding has been political action committees.[17] PACs are simply groups organized for the express purpose of collecting funds to contribute to candidates. Under the 1974 reform, a PAC can give up to $5,000 to a candidate for any one campaign but can contribute to as many candidates as it wishes. In 1998, of the 3,798 PACs registered with the Federal Election Commission, 1,682 (44 percent) were corporate PACs whose sources of funds were executives of individual corporations.[18] If you add to the number of expressly corporate PACs, the 821 "membership" PACs, most of which represent trade associations, business dominance of the PAC universe grows to 65 percent. Business dominance is reflected as well if one examines the actual expenditures of PACs (see figure 5.1, p. 166). In 1998, when labor spent a total of $44.6 million on election campaigns, the combination of corporate and trade association PAC spending was $144.4 million.[19] Business PAC money not only supports congressional and presidential primary races but, increasingly, is invested in state and local political campaigns.

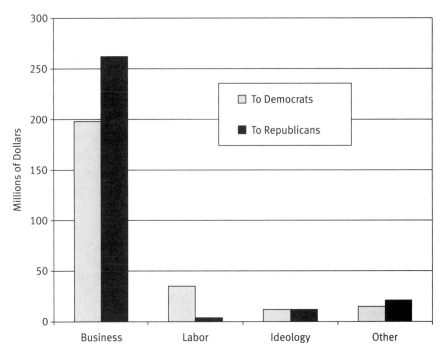

Figure 5.1 Business, Labor, and Ideological Contributions, 1997–98

Source: Center for Responsive Politics, http://www.opensecrets.org/pubs/whopaid/bigpic/ sumo5.htm.
Note: Totals include all contributions to federal candidates and political parties, as categorized by the Center. Based on data released electronically by the Federal Election Commission on 1 October 1998. (Contributions were given primarily from 1 January 1997 to 30 June 1998.)

Of course, as described in the preceding chapter, PAC spending is only part of the campaign spending picture in contemporary campaigns. The increasingly important role of "soft money" in the past two elections has served to increase the importance of corporations as sources of campaign financing. Figure 5.1 indicates this overwhelming corporate advantage. Also, soft money has allowed simpler and more direct corporate access to campaigns. Although federal campaign laws throughout the past century prohibited direct corporate contributions to candidates, the essentially unregulated character of soft money now permits corporations to support their favorite candidates, in any amount they wish, directly from the corporate treasury. During the past two election cycles, major corporations have taken full advantage of this new opportunity. In 1996, corporations funneled $140 million in soft money to campaigns, outspending labor's $9.2 million fifteen to one. Corporate soft money dominance continued in the

1998 congressional elections, as table 5.1 (pp. 168–69) shows. The top fifty soft-money contributors that year were overwhelmingly large corporations, with only two labor unions making the list. In addition, businesses were most active in coordinating individual contributions through the "bundling" of top corporate executives and major stockholders. With soft money and bundling, corporations can now buy direct access to top officeholders in a way never before possible.

Key questions relating to business influence are, What does all this money buy? To what extent do campaign contributions ensure public policies favorable to business? The answer to these questions is complex, for concern about campaign contributors is only one of several factors, among them ideology and personal experience, that influence an elected official's stance on an issue. Studies by political scientists have not been able, for example, to establish a direct relationship between the flow of PAC money and roll-call votes in Congress.[20] Nevertheless, most studies show that contributions provide contributors with *access* to elected officials, and as political scientist Larry Sabato states, "political analysts have long agreed that access is the principal goal of most interest groups, and lobbyists have always recognized that access is the key to influence."[21]

Business campaign contributions, then, buy the ability of business representatives to be heard when public policy is formulated. This access does not guarantee that business groups can dictate decisions, but it ensures that business preferences will be taken into consideration — insurance that many other groups in society do not have. As Senator Robert Dole put it when asked to explain why the Reagan budget cuts of the 1980s seemed to fall most heavily on the poor: "There aren't any Poor PACs or Food Stamp PACs or Nutrition PACs or Medicare PACs."[22] Unlike the poor, business can be sure that government officials will listen to its concerns because business provides the campaign contributions officials need.

Although access is probably the primary benefit that business buys with its campaign dollars, considerable anecdotal evidence suggests it often gets more. Contributions seem to be an effective means of influencing members of some congressional committees. According to one sociologist, Amitai Etzioni, a crucial vote to relax auto-emission regulations in the House Committee on Energy in 1982 reflected the influence of corporate contributions. Automobile manufacturers, through their PACs, had given $160,000 to the campaigns of committee members; those voting to relax emission controls received five times what members voting to maintain controls received.[23] In 1999, after a massive lobbying campaign from the banking, insurance, and securities industries, Congress repealed the depression-era Glass-Steagall Act, which had protected consumers by keeping these three industries distinct from one another.[24] Under the new legislation, firms in these three industries will be allowed to merge, allowing an acceleration of the growth of mega-banks providing one-stop shopping for

Table 5.1 Top Soft-Money Donors, 1997–98

Contributor	Total	To Democrats	To Republicans	Industry
Philip Morris	$1,779,845	$292,823	$1,487,022	Tobacco
Amway Corp.	$1,312,500	$0	$1,312,500	Retail Sales
AT&T	$844,743	$280,240	$564,503	Telephone Utilities
American Financial Group	$735,000	$175,000	$560,000	Insurance
RJR Nabisco	$701,422	$132,572	$568,850	Tobacco
Bell Atlantic	$683,169	$180,300	$502,869	Telephone Utilities
Blue Cross/Blue Shield	$671,950	$109,375	$562,575	Insurance
Freddie Mac	$625,000	$125,000	$500,000	Real Estate
Walt Disney Co.	$596,778	$294,503	$302,275	TV/Movies/Music
Travelers Group	$587,829	$169,000	$418,829	Insurance
Buttenwieser & Assoc	$570,000	$570,000	$0	Education
Communications Workers of America	$561,250	$561,250	$0	Industrial Unions
BellSouth Corp.	$542,606	$263,027	$279,579	Telephone Utilities
Chevron Corp.	$531,160	$166,300	$364,860	Oil & Gas
Loral Spacecom	$526,000	$526,000	$0	Telecom Services & Equipment
MCI Telecommunications	$519,090	$218,565	$300,525	Telephone Utilities
Pfizer Inc.	$516,550	$80,000	$436,550	Pharmaceuticals/ Health Products
Atlantic Richfield	$510,456	$170,500	$339,956	Oil & Gas
Enron Corp.	$505,500	$77,000	$428,500	Oil & Gas
Tobacco Institute	$499,700	$130,200	$369,500	Tobacco
Boeing Co.	$475,350	$190,800	$284,550	Air Transport
Slim-Fast Foods/ Thompson Medical	$450,000	$410,000	$40,000	Food Processing & Sales
Joseph E. Seagram & Sons	$437,675	$204,689	$232,986	Beer, Wine & Liquor
Bristol-Myers Squibb	$434,975	$100,300	$334,675	Pharmaceuticals/ Health Products
Waste Management Inc.	$420,525	$102,500	$318,025	Waste Management
US West Inc.	$417,000	$97,000	$320,000	Telephone Utilities

stock trading, insurance, and traditional banking services. Along with repealing the Glass-Steagal regulations, Congress substantially weakened requirements that banks invest in poor communities under the Community Reinvestment Act. To obtain these changes the three affected industries invested, according to the Center for Responsive Politics, $175 million in federal campaigns between 1997 and 1999. This money was carefully targeted to key members on the congressional banking committees, such as Texas Republican Senator Phil Gramm, chairman of the Senate Banking Committee, who received a total of $2.07 million from the three industries between 1993 and 1998. In addition, these industries spent collectively $163 million on direct lobbying for the legislative changes.

Big Business also uses its resources to influence public opinion. The most direct approach is advertising to promote probusiness views and cast doubts on

Table 5.1 Top Soft-Money Donors, 1997–98 (continued)

Contributor	Total	To Democrats	To Republicans	Industry
JW Childs Assoc.	$415,000	$0	$415,000	Securities & Investment
Williams & Bailey	$410,000	$410,000	$0	Lawyers/Law Firms
Tiger Management Corp.	$400,000	$0	$400,000	Securities & Investment
Connell Co.	$400,000	$400,000	$0	Food Processing & Sales
AG Spanos Development	$395,000	$0	$395,000	Real Estate
Tele-Communications Inc.	$391,000	$196,000	$195,000	TV/Movies/Music
Union Pacific Corp.	$384,700	$50,300	$334,400	Railroads
SBC Communications	$381,911	$158,061	$223,850	Telephone Utilities
CSX Corp.	$375,750	$49,000	$326,750	Railroads
AMR Corp.	$373,207	$153,521	$219,686	Air Transport
Archer-Daniels-Midland Co.	$373,000	$163,000	$210,000	Agricultural Services/Products
Time Warner	$371,000	$181,000	$190,000	TV/Movies/Music
Sprint Corp.	$370,043	$153,465	$216,578	Telephone Utilities
Goldman, Sachs & Co.	$368,250	$310,000	$58,250	Securities & Investment
Federal Express Corp	$365,000	$56,500	$308,500	Air Transport
Intl Brotherhood of Electrical Workers	$362,660	$362,660	$0	Industrial Unions
Ernst & Young	$361,066	$222,300	$138,766	Accountants
Microsoft Corp	$359,316	$95,000	$264,316	Computer Equipment & Services
Brown & Williamson Tobacco	$355,000	$20,000	$335,000	Tobacco
UST Inc.	$354,592	$53,583	$301,009	Tobacco
Prudential Insurance	$349,720	$141,945	$207,775	Insurance
Anheuser-Busch	$346,657	$152,207	$194,450	Beer, Wine & Liquor
Amoco Corp.	$345,000	$95,000	$250,000	Oil & Gas
Metropolitan Life	$341,500	$206,500	$135,000	Insurance

Source: Center for Responsive Politics, http://www.opensecrets.org/pubs/whopaid/soft/topdonors.htm.

opposition views. Beginning in the late 1970s, major corporations greatly increased their expenditures for these purposes and focused much of their attention on attacking government regulation of business.[25] Mobil Oil was in the forefront of these efforts with the use of "advertorials" — corporate editorials placed in purchased space on the op-ed pages of newspapers. These Mobil columns usually avoided promoting the narrow policy agenda of the oil industry; they concentrated instead on criticizing "big government" and more general concerns of business. Advertorials are increasingly targeted directly at those business wants to influence. One study shows increasing use of high-cost probusiness advocacy ads in publications read mainly by policy elites in Washington, such as the *National Journal* and *Congressional Quarterly Weekly.*[26] The Business Roundtable found the Capitol Hill newspaper *Roll Call* an effective vehicle for an ad directed at the congressional community to prevent expansion of mental health benefits.[27] Whether the audience is the general public or key policy elites, business uses its resources to shape opinion relevant to its concerns.

The 1990s witnessed a shift away from the more general themes of op-ed advertorials to the use of television advertising to promote the specific political agenda of business corporations. Such advertising proved to be a major factor in the debate over Clinton's health-care reform proposal. One such ad, funded by the health insurance industry, featured a pair of middle-aged actors playing two worried Americans, Harry and Louise, discussing over their breakfast toast how the Clinton plan would undermine their access to quality health care. Targeted to the districts of members of Congress undecided on the Clinton plan, they generated substantial mail that turned crucial votes against health reform. Since the success of Harry and Louise, other industries have funded similar television ad campaigns on issues ranging from tort law reform to the balanced budget amendment. Usually, these ads exhort viewers to contact their congressional representatives, generating the appearance of a spontaneous grassroots uprising on a particular issue.[28] Without the resources to mount a countercampaign, those opposing an industry's position on an issue are unable to present an alternative view to the public.

Along with direct promotion of business interests through corporate advertising in the media, corporations try to influence the country's public policy agenda through the support of public policy "think tanks." These are private research establishments employing hundreds of scholars who write books and articles on public policy issues. Although think tanks have a variety of ideological agendas, the overwhelming number of them are business funded and, not surprisingly, churn out policy proposals favorable to business. Organizations such as the Heritage Foundation, the American Enterprise Institute, the Hoover Institution, the Cato Institute, and the Manhattan Institute receive their funding from big corporate donors and produce scholarly studies designed to promote ideas favorable to business.[29] Even the Brookings Institution, one of the oldest think tanks and traditionally one with a reputation for supporting liberal scholars, has shifted its line in a more conservative direction in recent years in response to corporate funding. Sometimes businesses seek to generate favorable studies related to immediate concerns, as Microsoft did in early 1999 by contributing to the Hudson Institute and the Heritage Foundation, both of which published analyses of antitrust law supportive of the company's position in the Justice Department's antitrust suit against it.[30] Through support of think tanks, business buys intellectual support and research favorable to probusiness policies and a probusiness ideological climate.

In addition to dominating the production of information about public policy, business controls citizen access to information through its ownership of the

Corporate CEOs Stephen Case, Gerald Levin, and Ted Turner celebrate a proposed AOL/Time Warner merger, creating the largest media conglomerate ever. (Reuters Newmedia Inc./Corbis)

media. Newspapers, magazines, television and radio networks, and publishing houses are themselves businesses and, not surprisingly, project probusiness views. Moreover, the wave of mergers and acquisitions in business in the 1980s tended to place control of the mass media in large business conglomerates. One study estimates that most of the mass communication industry is now concentrated in about twenty giant holding companies.[31] Usually nonmedia businesses dominate these media conglomerates, and these business interests have a direct interest in the content of information that is reported through their media outlets. For example, the television network NBC is part of a business conglomerate including the industrial giants Radio Corporation of America (RCA) and General Electric (GE), making it one of the largest business enterprises in the United States.[32] Both RCA and GE are among the largest defense contractors in the country, along with diverse interests in many other areas. NBC executives, who produce both news and entertainment programming, have to be mindful that NBC profits are tied to the well-being of these industries.

So far, this discussion has outlined various aspects of only one face of business power. Lobbying power, electoral influence, and media manipulation are direct and obvious ways in which business exercises its power in society. The second face of power, emphasized by such analysts as Charles Lindblom, is more subtle and sometimes goes unnoticed, but it is essential to business's privileged position.

This is the power business obtains through society's view of private property and its willingness to interpret control of giant business corporations as merely the exercise of property rights.

According to Lindblom, in order to understand how property rights lead to the "privileged position" of business, one must understand that the laws that confer and protect property rights amount to a grant of public authority.[33] They give to business owners and managers "authority over society's resources," authority they exercise without any democratic control. This authority is exercised in two arenas: within the business enterprise itself and outside it, over society.

American business enterprises are not normally organized democratically. Our legal system and business managers assume that managers have the right to decide how work will be organized and what rules workers will follow. For the minority of workers protected by union contracts, there are sometimes limits placed on the authoritarian control of management, but the range of unrestrained management power remains wide even in unionized firms and is nearly absolute in nonunion ones. Authoritarian control of the internal operations of business is usually justified as necessary for the sake of efficiency, but, however justified, it removes from democratic control many decisions that directly affect the daily lives of most citizens.

Outside the firm, business managers make numerous decisions that greatly affect the lives of citizens, independent of any control by democratic processes. They have virtually autonomous authority to determine how production will be organized and where it will occur. Will products be manufactured on assembly lines or by small groups of workers who complete an entire product? What technologies will be employed? Will robots replace workers? Will the factory be located in Indiana, Georgia, or Mexico? Business managers are not required to seek the approval or advice of either government officials or citizens when they make these decisions. The same applies to decisions about the social consequences of production and the use of products. Within some constraints imposed by government regulation (constraints business seeks to keep at a minimum through deployment of its power), its decisions about what to produce and how to produce it have far-reaching consequences for society. Pollution levels, along with health and safety hazards resulting from products, are to a great extent determined by business managers. Will automobiles have airbags? Will guns be sold? Will hamburgers be wrapped in styrofoam? These decisions are left, in the main, to business.

More fundamentally, the doctrines of private property and the free market mean depending on private business managers to decide how society's resources will be allocated to alternative investments. Should investments in alternative forms of transportation emphasize mass transit or private automobiles? Since the 1920s, American business has directed most investment into the automobile industry and away from mass transit. The auto and tire industries went so far as to buy up existing trolley-car systems in many cities and destroy them, thereby encouraging the sale of cars and buses.[34] In the United States, government left the development of much of the current system of transportation to "the market," which meant, in effect, to business.

Leaving important societal decisions to "the market" means dividing authority for important social decisions between two sets of rulers. In any capitalist market system the question Who rules? has to be answered: Government officials *and* businessmen.[35] The decisions of government officials may be subject to the control of democratic processes, such as elections; those of businessmen are not. Yet, in many respects, the decisions left to business have more direct significance for most of us than those made by government. This significance gives business tremendous leverage, in turn, over government decisions. The result is a privileged position for business.

The way in which General Motors (GM) carried out its decision to close many of its factories around the country in 1992 illustrates the privileged position of business in action. In February, GM announced it would be closing twelve plants in the U.S. and Canada, a move that would affect 16,300 workers, as the first phase in a decade-long process to shut down a total of twenty-one plants.[36] A relatively small number of GM executives made these decisions in secret, without any participation from GM workers, national government officials, or citizens or local governments in the communities where the plants were located. (The *New York Times* reported that GM CEO Robert C. Stempel telephoned President Bush before the public announcement, as a courtesy, to tell him of the plan. It did not report whether Stempel asked the president, the nation's elected chief executive, his advice or opinion.) Although these decisions were made in private by "private" business executives, one can imagine no government official's decision in recent years (including Bush's Persian Gulf War decision) that would have as far-reaching an impact on American society. Beyond the nearly 17,000 workers directly affected by the decision, thousands of other workers in the communities where the plants were located would lose their jobs as these plants ceased purchasing supplies and workers no longer had wages to spend. Local communities would lose millions of dollars in tax revenues and thus would be forced to close schools and cut back public services. Ultimately, the quality of life of millions of people would be lowered as a consequence of these decisions. Yet our "democratic" society gives to people like Stempel complete autonomy to make such decisions without even informing anyone of the basis for the decision.

In announcing the decision, Stempel said "worldwide" events and poor economic performance of the automaker necessitated the decision. He did not, however, reveal any information about the facts and analyses that led GM to address these problems by closing plants or explain why particular plants were chosen to be closed. Nothing was revealed about what alternatives were considered or whether some other way might have been found, a way less devastating to the well-being of the workers and communities involved, to make the corporation more competitive. There was also no attempt to explain how or why GM had become so noncompetitive or whether previous decisions by Stempel and his fellow executives might in any way be related to the current necessity for such drastic action. Any notion that such democratic values as responsiveness or accountability might, in any way, be related to decisions with such a broad public impact were absent from corporate statements and media discussion of the GM action. GM executives decided what would happen, and so it did.

As this illustration shows, people who are able to make decisions that will have such an impact on society exercise a large share of authority in society. One cannot imagine any decision that any mayor in the various towns affected by the GM decision would make that would affect their communities more. But the privileged position of business involves more than this ability to make socially relevant decisions in the economy. This ability affects how influence over the totality of social decision-making authority, including governmental decisions, is shared between business executives and elected governmental leaders. Because of the importance of their decisions for the well-being of communities, business leaders have important leverage over governmental decisions. Whenever public officials consider policies involving taxation or public services, they must be very attentive to the effect of these decisions on business. Since the community's well-being is so dependent on business decisions to invest in the community by opening new factories or not closing existing ones, public leaders must make sure that nothing they do alienates business and leads to community disinvestment. In fact, realizing their situation, most astute public servants devise various inducements, such as tax breaks and subsidies, to encourage business to invest in their communities. They avoid raising taxes to finance generous social services to ensure that business will not consider moving to communities with lower taxes. No business lobbying is necessary to produce these favorable decisions. Intelligent public officials know without being told what they must do: Keep business happy. If, perchance, citizens somewhere elect to office people who are resistant to automatic probusiness policies, a corporate threat to move a local firm elsewhere suffices to change the "business climate."[37]

The offer of such inducements was involved in the GM reorganization. Two months before the announcement of plant closings, GM executives revealed a small bit of information about their plans. They said they were considering closing one of two plants producing large rear-wheel-drive cars: one in Ypsilanti, Michigan, and one in Arlington, Texas. The announcement set off a wave of inducement offerings in both communities as each tried to convince GM officials to keep its plant open. Ultimately, Arlington won, offering, among other things, a package of tax abatements in an enterprise zone that just happened to be placed in the area surrounding the GM plant, and Texas Governor Ann Richards promised to buy a thousand GM cars for state use.[38]

The Ypsilanti-Arlington competition reveals the essence of business's political privilege. Most citizens and groups must bring their cases to elected officials in order to influence public policy. Nonprivileged actors must compete with other groups for a favorable decision and try to persuade elected representatives, and often the public at large, of the wisdom of their position on an issue. Business is different. It can sidestep the process of group interaction and competition that Pluralists describe and merely announce its decision regarding the disposition of its economic resources. Such an announcement, by itself, will cause public officials to act on business's behalf. As in the GM case, elected government officials will devise public policy inducements to get business to serve the community interest. Business does not have to plead or cajole elected officials to get favorable public policies; it gets to pick the best offer. No other group in the "pluralist heaven" has such a privilege.

Economic globalization has served to enhance further business leverage over politicians to extract policies favorable to its interests. Free trade agreements such as the North American Free Trade Agreement (NAFTA) and the General Agreement on Tariffs and Trade (GATT) have facilitated the movement of business production to anywhere in the world. The international organizations that make the rules for this new global marketplace, the World Trade Organization (WTO), the World Bank, and the International Monetary Fund (IMF), are sensitive to the privileged position of multinational corporations. Business investment capital is free to travel around the globe in search of such conditions as low wages, government subsidies, and policies discouraging labor unions, all of which maximize profit opportunities. In the new global marketplace, American workers in places like Ypsilanti and Arlington find themselves competing not only with each other but with workers in Monterey, São Paulo, and Shanghai. Not only governors and mayors, but presidents and prime ministers must be mindful of pleasing business interests if their people are to prosper.

Developing countries of Asia and Africa have discovered that the jobs that multinational corporations bring come at price — the country's ability to control its own affairs. One example is Malaysia, which has experienced rapid economic growth in recent years because many electronics and semiconductor firms, such as Motorola, have established assembly plants there.[39] A docile workforce of poor rural village women manufacture silicon chips and the other high tech products of the computer age for a fraction of the wages that would have to be paid in Silicon Valley. Government leaders in Malaysia understand that policies favorable to the electronics multinationals are essential to keep them, so they deliver. The semiconductor industry enjoys a blanket "tax holiday" of five to ten years for any plants opened in the country. More ominously, electronics workers are prohibited from organizing labor unions. Malaysia benefits from foreign investment, but its democratic evolution and control of its own destiny is held hostage to business requirements. As a U.S. undersecretary of commerce put it, "So Malaysia is stuck. It could lose the electronics industry overnight if it makes the wrong move."[40] Unfortunately for Malaysians, further evolution toward more democratic politics is one such "wrong move."

WHY BUSINESS PRIVILEGE IS A THREAT TO DEMOCRACY

Business's position of privilege in American society threatens our democracy in at least four ways. First, and most obviously from the preceding discussion, business privilege means that, contrary to the claims of the Pluralists, the full range of political interests in society are *not* equally represented. Second, business power restricts the agenda of policy alternatives seriously debated and discussed when public policy is formulated. Third, business power undermines the development of an effective democratic citizenry. And, fourth, business privilege results in substantive policies that are contrary to the needs and interests of a majority of Americans.

Political equality is a central value of all the models of democracy presented in the introduction. The strength of the Pluralist model as a model of democracy is its argument regarding the representative role of groups. Because, as the Pluralists claim, no group is privileged, the opportunity of all groups to influence public policy satisfies the democratic value of political equality. The reality of business privilege refutes this depiction of American group politics. Business can deploy its political resources and exploit its position in the economic structure to assure it an unequal position in the group universe. Given its position, no policy can be made democratically with the concerns and interests of all citizens given equal weight. In sum, the demonstration of business privilege, in itself, shows how the unequal representation of interests prevents the achievement of political equality when American public policy is made.

But the incompatibility of business privilege with democracy goes beyond its advantage in influencing the outcome of public policy debates. A more fundamental threat is the ability of business to bias the policy agenda so that only alternatives that take into account its interests are ever seriously considered. Even before debate on any public policy begins, the discussion is biased so that business privilege is assured. Lindblom identifies two mechanisms through which business structures the agenda to its advantage: "circularity" and "the market as prison."

Even from its position of privilege, one could imagine a situation in which business in a democratic society would occasionally face challenges to its goals. In the United States, nonbusiness groups and citizens in general are free to formulate or support political positions contrary to the interests or even the privileged position of business. One might expect, then, considerable conflict when policies bearing on business privilege are considered or when the preferences of business are opposed to those of other groups. Sometimes, business leaders might need to deflect the preferences of a democratic majority to ensure governmental response to their particular needs. Imagine, however, a different sort of situation for business, one in which nearly everyone in society seems to prefer policies that favor the interests and preferences of business. In this case, business would rarely face political opposition, because what it wanted was what everyone else in society wanted. When government leaders formulated policy, they would seem to respond to popular preferences, but in doing so, they would be serving the interests of business.

According to Lindblom, this latter situation is often true in capitalist market societies such as the United States. The genuine coincidence of citizen policy preferences and business preferences is not accidental, however, nor does it arise from the coincidence of citizen interests and those of business. It occurs because of the ability of business to indoctrinate the rest of society into wanting what business wants. The result is a circular process in which "people are indoctrinated to demand...nothing other than what a decision-making elite [government and business leaders] are disposed to grant them. The volitions that are supposed to guide leaders are formed by the same leaders."[41] Business control of media messages and their influence over other opinion-molding institutions, such as schools, permit such indoctrination.

The most important indoctrination from business's point of view is that which serves to preserve its privileged position.[42] This is accomplished in two ways. First, business persuades citizens to overlook business's privileged position by equating that position with the preservation of democracy. This is the aim of messages in the media, schools, and from business and government elites that associate the preservation of private enterprise with personal liberty, national sovereignty, and democracy. In newspaper articles, publicity, and school curricula Americans are taught that democracy means "our free enterprise system." Any challenge to business autonomy is equated with a challenge to the liberty of all Americans.

Second, business molds public opinion to keep any challenge to the privileged position of business off the political agenda. It promotes silence on major issues of "politico-economic" organization that might raise questions in people's minds about the appropriateness of business privilege. Such issues as how much autonomy corporations should have, what is an appropriate distribution of income and wealth, the role of labor unions, or worker participation in enterprise decision making are deemed too radical to merit serious discussion. Thus the absence of any serious discussion of them on television, in newspapers, or in college courses suggests that they are "unimportant" to society. For example, in the

Corporate logos dominate a new baseball stadium jointly funded by taxpayers and business sponsors. (AFP/Corbis)

early 1980s the Public Broadcasting System (PBS), which, because of cutbacks in government funding, is largely dependent on corporate contributions, canceled a planned series on the history of the American labor movement because corporate sponsors did not consider it "one of our priorities."[43] With such control over cultural production in our society, business ensures the absence of inquiry into ideas, issues, or even history that might challenge its dominance.

More subtle even than "circularity," the market system itself provides a built-in bias in favor of business preferences. This bias grows directly out of the privileged position business holds. Since in a private market system we give to businessmen the responsibility for most economic decisions, any attempt to enact a reform or impose any cost on business will have an immediate negative impact on the economy. If, for example, a community seeks to reduce pollution by requiring local businesses to clean up their emissions, some businesses may decide to move their local production facilities to communities with less stringent pollution controls, producing unemployment in the more environmentally conscious community. The immediate and direct economic pain of increased unemployment will deter most communities from serious democratic deliberation about pollution controls. In this example, the market acts as a sort of prison that restricts the range of democratic deliberation and control to those policies that will not adversely affect business.

Thoughtful readers might object that the situation just described does not represent a limitation of democracy or the "market as prison" but merely the reality of tradeoffs between competing social goals. Any society, whether it has a market economy or not, must cope with the tradeoff between the desire for a clean environment and the need for economic production. Some kinds of production will always produce pollution; communities must decide what they value more, jobs or a pristine environment. Is not the need for a local community to consider the adverse economic affect of environmental regulation merely a reflection of a natural reality?

This question indicates the subtle way the market imprisons policymaking. It assumes that communities control democratically the full range of decisions related to tradeoffs between competing social goals, like the one between a clean environment and economic productivity. In a fully democratic society this would be true. But given the privileged position of business in a market society, business managers control the economic side of the tradeoff. How a community might respond to the adverse effect of environmental controls on productivity is outside the control of democratically chosen government officials. In their deliberations, government officials can only anticipate and cope with the response of business to attempts to regulate. Since a whole range of reforms — from raising business taxes to support needed public services to environmental regulation — may elicit immediate negative economic consequences, prudent government officials avoid them.

A third way in which business power undermines democracy relates to the "developmental" aspect of democracy. As discussed in the introduction, many democratic theorists, especially those advocating the Developmental and Participatory models, have valued democracy because they believed it promotes the development of good, fully human, people. Through participation with their fellow citizens in collectively solving community problems, people have an opportunity to develop their capacity to deliberate, communicate, form critical judgments, and control their lives. According to Participatory theorists, only democratic participation allows people "to realize . . . their dignity and powers as responsible agents and judges."[44]

This concern is related to the discussion in chapter 2 of Tocqueville's comment on the necessity for the proper "habits of the heart," or political culture, for democracy to succeed. In that account, the challenge that American individualism poses for democracy is discussed. In such an individualist culture, Tocqueville believed that political participation was an important means of promoting good citizenship values. Through direct experience with self-government in town governments, Tocqueville thought that Americans honed the active, non-deferential skills that promoted effective democracy throughout the system. If Tocqueville was correct that the practice of democracy is needed to promote a democratic outlook in citizens, then the lack of participation permitted by authoritarian structures in society may undermine this outlook. This is the danger the authoritarian structure of business poses for democracy.

The authoritarian structure of business is a serious impediment to democracy given the extent to which the workplace dominates the lives of most Americans.[45] Most of us spend our entire working day in an authoritarian environment where we are usually required to follow orders uncritically. From the point of view of the Developmental and Participatory models, this experience can only undermine our capacity to be effective democratic citizens after we leave work. Much of our lives goes on within the confines of authoritarian business institutions that actively discourage participatory discussion, independent thinking, critical analysis, and skepticism regarding authority. As long as business is organized in an authoritarian manner, citizens' opportunities to develop the character that democratic theorists associate with a democratic citizenry will be severely restricted and perhaps undermined.[46]

A final reason why business power is a threat to contemporary American democracy results from a new divergence between the substantive economic interests of business elites and those of a majority of Americans. In the past decade, in response to an increasingly competitive international economy, American corporations have developed strategies that enrich top corporate managers and wealthy stockholders but tend to lower the standard of living of most Americans. American business elites have opted to shore up corporate profits in a competitive marketplace by lowering wage costs. This strategy includes pushing down the wages of American workers, shifting much industrial production abroad to low-wage countries, and downsizing corporate employment. Since the late 1970s, American business has sought and received a mixture of government policies — most important are trade agreements like NAFTA and GATT — that support this strategy.

For most of the twentieth century, the success of U.S. corporations and a rising standard of living were tied together. The large business corporations that emerged at the beginning of the century both produced and sold their products largely in the domestic economy. As Henry Ford realized when he raised the wages of his workers to the unheard-of level of $5 a day, workers would not be able to buy mass-produced industrial products, and corporations would not earn profits, unless higher wages allowed them to buy. When some of his business friends criticized Ford for bidding up wages and raising their costs of production, Ford replied with a subtle truth about the interdependency at the heart of a mass consumption economy: If he kept costs low by not raising wages, he said, "Who would buy my cars?"[47] As long as business elites understood this reality, there was no fundamental conflict between the economic interests of business and those of most American citizens. A rising standard of living for most Americans meant growing corporate profits, and vice versa. This linkage was a key reality of American prosperity in the two decades following World War II. A few hundred core corporations, giants such as General Motors, General Electric, and U.S. Steel, dominated the U.S. economy and that of the world.[48] Although these corporations sold their products throughout the world, their principal market was the United States. Business leaders readily identified corporate success with the success of the whole nation. This was reflected in corporate slogans, such as U.S. Steel's "As steel goes, so goes the Nation," and in the remark of GM President C.E. ("Engine Charlie") Wilson: "For years I thought what was good for our country was good for General Motors, and vice versa. The difference did not exist."[49]

In many respects, Wilson and U.S. Steel were correct: rising corporate profits coexisted with steadily rising living standards. Between 1945 and the early 1970s, the U.S. standard of living doubled.[50] This doubling was based on rising worker productivity, which grew at 2.7 percent annually.[51] Corporate profits kept pace, providing an after-tax rate of return on investment of about 10 percent.[52] During this period, managers of the largest corporations readily accepted the presence of well-organized labor unions and endorsed contracts providing steadily increasing benefits and wages. These contracts added stimulus to higher wages and benefits throughout the economy, distributing a portion of the gains from economic productivity to nearly all Americans. Although economic inequality persisted and many of the poorest Americans were left out of the overall prosperity, the trend was in the direction of lessening income inequality until the mid-1970s. (For more detail on income inequality, see chapter 6.)

In recent decades, this happy identity between American corporate success and a rising standard of living for Americans was broken. The principal cause was declining corporate profits brought on by greater international competitiveness. By 1979, the rate of return on corporate investments had dropped from 10 percent to about 5 percent.[53] In both domestic and international markets, U.S. corporations had vigorous competition from their Japanese and European counterparts. Most firms responded to this situation by adopting a strategy that was beneficial to the balance sheets of individual firms but has undermined the rising standard of living of many American workers.

Economists Bennett Harrison and Barry Bluestone have identified the two basic elements of corporate strategy since the late 1970s to cope with international competition.[54] The first they call "zapping labor," that is, reducing worker wages and benefits to lower production costs. This involves transferring manufacturing plants abroad to low-wage countries instead of investing in domestic manufacturing. In the shadow of shuttered American factories, American workers can be made to accept contract concessions under the threat of permanent loss of their jobs to foreign workers. Central to this element of corporate strategy has been an aggressive campaign against labor unions that has radically reduced the proportion of organized workers in the workforce. Trade agreements like NAFTA and GATT have given corporate bosses tremendous leverage to keep wages low and prevent labor organizing because workers now know that companies can easily transfer their jobs to workers anywhere in the world.

The second element in corporate strategy involves financial manipulations in what is sometimes called the "casino economy." Rather than invest in new plant and equipment, corporations have used their capital to buy and sell one another. Mergers and acquisitions, encouraged by favorable tax laws and the invention of such novel financial instruments as "junk bonds," have delivered enormous paper profits to corporate elites without contributing to future economic productivity. In fact, in most instances, the paper profits came at the expense of American factory workers who lost their jobs when the paper entrepreneurs acquired their factories, closed them, sold off the assets, and took away huge profits for themselves. Such corporate restructuring, in combination with the transfer of manufacturing abroad, has resulted in what Harrison and Bluestone have called the "deindustrialization" of America. The most concrete manifestation of this has been the loss of millions of high-wage blue-collar manufacturing jobs that delivered the high living standards of the post–World War II generation. Because business elites have chosen this strategy to compete in the international marketplace, the traditional link between corporate success and the well-being of most citizens no longer exists. As the political economist Robert Reich writes:

> Neither the profitability of a nation's corporations nor the success of its investors necessarily improve the standard of living of most of the nation's citizens. Corporations and investors now scour the world for profitable opportunities. They are becoming disconnected from their home nations.[55]

To support their ability to "scour" for favorable investments and pursue their corporate strategies, business owners used their privileged political position in the 1980s and 1990s to enact public policies supportive of their interests. The entire mix of policies characteristic of the past two decades, even under the Democratic Clinton administration — tight monetary policies, lower taxation of business, economic and social deregulation, lower social spending, privatization, and relaxed labor laws — facilitated both zapping labor and the casino economy. Foreign trade policy encouraging globalization complemented these domestic policies and strengthened business leverage to suppress wages and ensure favorable business "climates" everywhere. At the same time, business used its privileged position to resist public investment in physical infrastructure and worker education and training, which could form the core of an alternative economic strategy to cope with the internationalization of our economy.[56] Of course, given how the American corporate elite and rich investors prospered in recent years, there was little incentive for them to worry about alternatives that would be more favorable to the standard of living of the majority.

This policy bias in favor of business and owners of financial capital has protected the financial well-being of the wealthy and produce a stagnant standard of living for the average worker in both good times and bad.[57] The recessions of the early 1980s and 1990s dealt a severe blow to most workers who suffered from unemployment and declining wages. High interest rates, corporate downsizing, and factory closings — all justified in the name of increasing business efficiency — protected corporate profits and asset values from the effects of economic decline. During periods of prosperity in those decades, the benefits from growth fed corporate profits and wealth but provided only crumbs to the average worker. Despite the booming economy of the past few years, with corporate profits and stock prices reaching record heights, average family incomes have continued to stagnate, with most people getting by through working extra hours and increasing household debt. In 1997, inflation-adjusted earnings of the median worker, despite five years of steady economic growth and increases in worker productivity, remained 3.1 percent lower than they had been in 1989.[58] Just as record low unemployment, an increase in the minimum wage, and real wage growth began to deliver an improved standard of living to ordinary workers in 1999, the Federal Reserve intervened to slow growth by raising interest rates.[59] While justified as necessary to relieve inflationary pressures in the economy (although economic indicators continued to show no sign of inflation), the Fed's action would serve to constrain the growth of wages. In the new global economy, higher wages for ordinary workers is bad for business.

The danger to democracy deriving from business privilege in this new context can now be clearly seen. Although business privilege in the United States has always been a threat that undermined our democracy, until recently the exercise of this privilege, however objectionable on theoretical grounds, was consistent with substantial material benefits for most Americans. In pursuing their own interests, business elites supported policies that resulted in improved living standards for nearly all. Now, the disparity between what business wants and the needs of most citizens highlights the danger of people trusting their fate to the benign rule of an elite. As long as business maintains its political privilege, it appears more and more likely that public policies will continue to benefit this elite at the expense of the majority. Perhaps at no time in American history has the division between elite interests and those of a democratic majority been as sharply at odds as in the current era. If business elites continue to exercise their traditional political privileges, policies conducive to providing a high standard of living for all are not likely to be enacted. Only a truly democratic movement organized to counter the privileged position of business can restore the American dream.

Objections to the Privileged-Position-of-Business Thesis

Not all political scientists accept a privileged position for business as an accurate portrayal of business's political role, and many, writing from a Pluralist perspective, disagree that business has exercised privileged power in recent times.[60] They generally raise two objections to the thesis. First, they point out that Big Business does not always win. Sometimes legislation and policies that business vociferously opposes are enacted and adopted. How can this be, if business has such a privileged position? Second, they object to the implication of the argument that business is a monolithic interest. They argue that on many important public policy issues, businesspeople and corporations often are divided and seek alliances with nonbusiness groups. Conflict over policy, they argue, usually involves opposing coalitions, each containing business and nonbusiness groups.

In his book *Fluctuating Fortunes: The Political Power of Business in America,* David Vogel makes both of these arguments based on a history of business political power between 1960 and the 1980s.[61] Vogel sees in this period major fluctuations in business power, rather than consistent business privilege. The early 1960s, he agrees, can be characterized as a period of business privilege, but by the late 1960s, the mobilization of labor, consumer, civil rights, and other liberal groups overwhelmed organized business. He focuses particularly on the enactment between 1969 and 1972 of a series of laws over stringent business opposition. These included such measures as the creation of the Environmental Protection Agency, the Occupational Safety and Health Administration, and the Consumer Product Safety Commission; the enactment of progressive tax legislation; a reduction in the oil-depletion allowance and price controls on oil and gas; a ban on some cigarette advertising; and the enactment of auto safety standards.[62] Vogel portrays the mobilization and resurgence of business power in the late 1970s, which some analysts use to document business privilege (as I do), as merely a defensive action on business's part in response to the serious setbacks of the previous period. According to Vogel, business, like any interest group in a pluralist system, succeeds when it organizes and promotes its agenda effectively, but loses, like any other group, when its opponents mobilize more effectively.

In my opinion, there are a number of serious flaws in Vogel's analysis. First, he assumes that occasional business legislative defeats somehow refute the privileged-position thesis, and yet those who advocate the thesis readily admit that extraordinary public mobilization can sometimes overcome business privilege. Since the emergence of truly "big business" as part of the industrialization in the late nineteenth century, there have been a number of periods when movements of mass mobilization have succeeded in enacting restraints on business power: The Populists in the 1880s promoted railroad regulation and antitrust laws; the Progressives enacted food, drug, and fair trade regulations in the early twentieth century; laws legitimized labor-union organizing during the New Deal;

and new social regulations emerged in the late 1960s. Yet what all these periods have in common is how rare and extraordinary they are in comparison to the norm of business dominance. Even Vogel himself admits that "during this century the years when business has been relatively powerful have been more numerous than those when it has not."[63] Over the nearly thirty-year period he studies, Vogel focuses on a brief three years during which business suffered legislative defeats. Those of us more convinced of the privileged power of business focus instead on the longer and more constant period of business dominance.

A second problem with Vogel's critique arises when one examines the so-called defeats business suffered during the 1969–72 period of liberal mobilization. Some of the legislation passed during this period actually received business support. As Vogel admits, the creation of the EPA received strong business backing because business saw the environmental movement as a benign alternative to the demands of the then-burgeoning youth, black power, and antiwar movements (a view shared within the Nixon White House, which sponsored the legislation).[64] Besides, the creation of the EPA was a consolidation of existing agencies and imposed no new mandates on business, and corporations trusted the Republican administration to be sensitive to their interests when environmental laws were implemented.

This awareness of the importance of implementation points to another aspect of business legislative "defeats." Even though mass mobilization may result in antibusiness legislation, business can count on its privileged position to permit it to undermine legal implementation in the bureaucracy and the courts. This is an old story in American politics, exemplified, for example, by the railroad industry's reaction to the creation of the Populist-supported Interstate Commerce Commission in the 1880s. This agency, created to control railroad abuses, was quickly "captured" by the industry and used to protect railroad profits.[65] Because of their superior resources, businesses can hire the lawyers and lobbyists needed to intervene, when regulations implementing legislation are made, to see that business interests are protected.[66] The automobile industry used this tactic very effectively during the 1970s and 1980s to delay implementation of many of the safety and environmental standards enacted during Vogel's period of business legislative defeats.[67] Business knows that when in the full light of democratic debate such legislation is drafted, it must accept defeat for its preferred position, but it will be able to recoup its losses, behind closed doors, when regulations are drafted.

Finally, a close look at the antibusiness victories of the 1969–72 period shows no fundamental losses in relation to the central concerns of business, those relating to its continued privileged position in the economy. Business could easily absorb increased government oversight in the areas of environmental, consumer, and worker safety. In fact, increased federal government responsibility in these areas provided certain advantages for business. It relieved business of the need to comply with highly variable and, in some cases, more stringent state government regulations. It also permitted business to deflect responsibility away from itself and on to the government for environmental and safety disasters; inept government regulators, rather than corporate managers, could be blamed when disasters occurred. None of the legislation from 1969 to 1972 touched on central business concerns, such as its relations with labor or its control of the economy. When liberal and labor groups tried after 1976 to enact government planning to guarantee jobs (the Humphrey-Hawkins Act) and labor law reform, business mobilized rapidly and effectively to deliver decisive defeats.[68] Where issues central to the preservation of business privilege are concerned, business can mobilize effectively; none of these issues surfaced in the 1969–72 period of liberal ascendancy.

Vogel ends his book on an odd note for someone convinced of the variability of business power. Impressed with the strength of business mobilization in response to the minor setbacks of the 1969–72 period, he wonders whether the "fluctuations" in business power in the future will be as wide.[69] In fact, he points to growing international competition as a factor that will reinforce business political power, an analysis consistent with my discussion in the previous section.[70] Vogel feels that fluctuations in business privilege may occur but that the future portends a reinforcement in business privilege.

Critics of the privileged-position-of-business thesis misconstrue it, as well, when they point out the political divisions in the business community. The argument of this chapter does not deny that different firms and segments of industry have different interests and preferences or that business fights over these differences in the political system. In fact, the Pluralist model of group interaction describes fairly well how the political system handles these disputes. Our politics are replete with squabbles within business. For example, in recent years, one of the nation's large polluters, Waste Management, Inc., a garbage disposal firm, contributed millions of dollars to environmental organizations and advocated stringent and complex waste disposal regulations opposed by most of the rest of the industry.[71] Its motive was to drive out of business its smaller competitors, who would have a difficult time meeting the costs of the regulations. Environmentalists should not count on continued Waste Management support once this objective is realized.

In 1996 competing business interests clashed in pluralist fashion over telecommunications policy.[72] As Congress considered the first major rewrite of telecommunications regulations since the 1930s, all the affected business interests, including regional Bell operating companies ("Baby Bells"), long-distance providers (e.g., AT&T), the cable television industry, major broadcast networks, and the computer software industry, lobbied intensively on behalf of their particular concerns. All reinforced their lobbying efforts through record contributions in that year's election campaign. The result was classic pluralist bargaining over the legislation with the resulting Telecommunications Act of 1996 reflecting compromises among the conflicting interests of these major industries. Absent from the process was the broader public. Republican Senator John McCain described the bill as "protective of all the interests with the exception of the consumer. That's why we are seeing increasing phone rates, increasing cable rates, consolidations and mergers, and little if any increase in competition."[73] In the year following enactment of the legislation, which substantially loosened government regulation of the cable industry, cable rates rose 8.5 percent, over four times the rate of inflation.[74] The case of the Telecommunications Act reveals pluralist politics to be a privileged game for Big Business, but one ordinary citizens are not able to play.

The need to settle such conflicts among themselves may account for why business elites support the democratic "rules of the game" that are so important to the Pluralist model. These elites do not want any one business interest using government power against other business interests. Government brokering among business interests can produce compromises that recognize competing business interests. And businesses may seek out nonbusiness allies for their internecine battles. But these conflicts among businesses and their use of alliances do not mean nonbusiness interests are brought in on an equal footing. As in the Waste Management example, nonbusiness groups are likely to be temporary allies while businesses pursue their particular agenda.

Most important, business conflict ends when it comes to fundamentals. The central insight of the privileged-position-of-business thesis is its recognition that business can prevent raising basic questions about its economic role. On questions of government economic planning or labor relations, when fundamental business prerogatives are at stake, business presents a united front. That businesses disagree on peripheral matters does not undermine the central claim of business privilege.

THE PRIVILEGED POSITION of business is at odds with the Pluralist description of American politics. The overwhelming political resources of business, combined with its special economic role, demolish the Pluralist vision of a democracy of group competition. The competition cannot be democratic when the game is biased so decisively in favor of one of the competitors. Moreover, business privilege relieves business of the need to compete. We turn over to business elites the responsibility for key economic decisions with far-reaching implications for the public good. In making these decisions, business leaders perform a public policy-making role without the need to answer to the broader public. The Pluralist model pictures interest groups approaching government officials with demands that their interests be considered when policy is made. With respect to business, this picture is reversed. Instead of business petitioning government policymakers, elected government officials petition business decision makers with favorable policies to induce business to act for the good of the community. The "flaw" in the Pluralist model is its failure to accommodate this privileged position of business.

More than undermining the Pluralist description of American politics, the privileged position of business raises fundamental questions about the scope of democratic politics. Americans readily agree on the need for government to be "of the people, by the people, and for the people," but business decisions with impacts on the public good far beyond those of most government decisions are placed outside the sphere of public control. If we are to pay serious attention to democratic ideals, this customary definition of the proper scope of democratic politics needs to be revised. Demanding public control of governmental policy-makers but denying the public the right to influence business policymakers seems increasingly arbitrary from a democratic point of view.

The philosopher Michael Walzer tells an interesting story about the railroad-car magnate George Pullman that illustrates the arbitrary nature of how Americans define the scope of democracy.[75] In 1880 Pullman founded and built a town: Pullman, Illinois. The town was designed to be a totally planned community for housing the workers in Pullman factories. Along with housing for about 8,000 workers, the town contained a hotel, schools, shops, a library, a theater, and a church — all owned and controlled by George Pullman. Pullman ruled his town in an authoritarian manner, just as he ruled his factories. As sole proprietor of the town, the railroad magnate thought it his right to govern the people in the town as he saw fit. He imposed autocratic rules detailing the behavior of town residents, rules that a private police force enforced. Although the quality of housing was good and the community was a more pleasant place to live than workers of the time were used to, Pullman residents lacked any control over the rules that governed their lives in the community. Their subordinate situation as Pullman town residents was identical to that as Pullman factory workers, and the peculiar absence of democracy in Pullman soon attracted public attention.

In 1885 an article in a popular magazine of the day, *Harper's Monthly,* described the town as "unAmerican...benevolent, well-wishing feudalism."[76] Pullman's autocracy was deemed at odds with American democratic values. Americans were supposed to be able to govern their communities themselves, not live by the rules of one man. In 1898 the Illinois Supreme Court agreed with this viewpoint and demanded that the Pullman Company divest itself of the town and that it be given a democratic government. While the court would not have found Pullman's rule over his factories a problem for democracy, it found his rule over the town to be "incompatible with the theory and spirit of our institutions."[77]

Walzer raises a democratically interesting question about this story: "Most observers seem to have agreed that Pullman's ownership of the town was undemocratic. But was his ownership of the company any different?"[78] Both town and company were products of Pullman's entrepreneurial vision, both were built with his capital, both residence in the town and employment in Pullman's factories were voluntary on the part of residents and workers, in both town and company the residents and workers derived concrete benefits — good housing and wages — in return for submission to Pullman's rules; but only in the town did the arrangement seem at odds with democratic principles. As Walzer's question suggests, our customary expectation that democracy is relevant to the governance of geographic entities and not corporate ones may be arbitrary. If democracy is good for towns, why not factories?

An understanding of the privileged position of business calls attention to this question. It is a question Americans need to address in an era when Big Business decisions seem at odds with the well-being of the rest of us. Taking democracy seriously in the new century will require ways of reining in corporate power. Just as the abolition of aristocratic privilege was a prerequisite for democracy in the eighteenth century, twenty-first-century democracy may require the abolition of business privilege. Some suggestions about how this might be done must await the discussion of solutions to the challenges of democracy in the concluding chapter.

Thought Questions

1. Businesses often claim that their campaign contributions are meant to assure "access" to legislators rather than to influence specific votes. If this is true, and if we elect legislators with integrity, is there any reason to be concerned about contributors seeking an opportunity to make their case regarding legislation affecting their interests?

2. Would you favor more community control over business decisions to invest or leave a local community? Or should these decisions be left solely to business owners and managers?

3. This chapter's conclusion implies that we should expect to control corporations democratically just as we expect to run a city democratically. How could this be done? Would you favor introducing democratic control of corporations? Who should be represented and how?

4. Lindblom sees business "privilege" following logically from the decision-making autonomy that businesses are assigned in a capitalist market economy. Is this a reasonable price to pay for the economic advantages of a market economy? Are you willing to limit democracy in exchange for material prosperity?

5. This chapter argues that authoritarian business structures — and those of other social institutions such as schools — undermine our capacity to learn how to be good citizens. Is this argument consistent with your own experience as a student and/or employee? What expectations do you have about your ability to influence decisions where you work?

Suggestions for Further Reading

Greider, William. *One World, Ready or Not: The Manic Logic of Global Capitalism.* New York: Simon and Schuster, 1997. Provides a detailed account of how the global economy increases the power of business while undermining the ability of ordinary people around the world to control their fates.

Harrison, Bennett, and Barry Bluestone. *The Great U-Turn: Corporate Restructuring and the Polarizing of America.* New York: Basic Books, 1988. Analyzes the growing divide between economic strategies that are good for Big Business profits and what is good for the standard of living of most Americans.

Kuttner, Robert. *Everything for Sale: The Virtues and Limits of Markets.* New York: Knopf, 1997. Provides a clearly written argument about how the capitalist market system works and how it must be regulated if it is both to work well and to provide prosperity to all.

Lamare, James W. *What Rules America?* St. Paul, Minn.: West, 1988. A detailed review of how Big Business organizes itself and how it exercises its power.

Lindblom, Charles E. *Politics and Markets: The World's Political-Economic Systems.* New York: Basic Books, 1977. An analysis of how market and government command systems differ from one another, detailing the advantages and disadvantages of each. In his analysis of market systems, Lindblom develops the "privileged position of business" thesis. A challenging but rewarding book for students who want to understand how the world works.

Mills, C. Wright *The Power Elite.* New York: Oxford University Press, 1956. While the Pluralists were celebrating the democratic character of American politics in the 1950s, one of America's most famous sociologists was writing this little book documenting how elites, including business leaders, manipulate our democracy to their advantage. A classic and "must reading" for serious students of politics.

*Novak, Michael. *The Spirit of Democratic Capitalism.* New York: Touchstone, 1982. Unlike this book, which questions the compatibility of capitalism and democracy, Novak believes the two are not only compatible but essential to one another.

Ricci, David. *Community Power and Democratic Theory: The Logic of Political Analysis.* New York: Random House, 1971. A clearly written summary of the several variants of Pluralist theory, including a superb critique.

Schattschneider, E.E. *The Semi-Sovereign People: A Realist's View of Democracy in America.* New York: Holt, Rinehart and Winston, 1960. This political science classic by a great political scientist presents a theory about the interaction of interest groups and political parties that takes issue with most of the Pluralist description of American politics. Each page is packed with fascinating propositions about politics.

Schlozman, Kay Lehman, and John T. Tierney. *Organized Interests and American Democracy.* New York: Harper & Row, 1986. The authors provide a comprehensive look at how interest groups, including business groups, go about influencing public policy.

*Vogel, David. *Fluctuating Fortunes: The Political Power of Business in America.* New York: Basic Books, 1989. Vogel argues that the political power of business is usually exaggerated.

West, Darrell M., and Burdett A. Loomis. *The Sound of Money: How Political Interests Get What They Want.* New York: W.W. Norton, 1999. An up-to-date account of the means special interests use to get their way in Washington. Includes detailed case studies of recent legislative battles.

*Presents a point of view that disagrees with the arguments presented in this chapter.

SELECTED WEB SITES

http://www.bog.frb.fed.us/ Web site of the Federal Reserve Board.

http://www.soc.american.edu/campfin/ Another site documenting business contributions to campaigns.

http://www.epinet.org/ The Economic Policy Institute offers studies and analysis of the impact of globalization on the economy plus general information on economic issues.

http://www.brtable.org/index.cfm Site of the Business Roundtable, a lobbying group of the CEOs of America's largest businesses. Take the pulse of what is on the mind of Big Business.

CHAPTER 6

The Sixth Challenge: Inequality

No novelty in the United States struck me more vividly during my stay there than the equality of conditions.

—ALEXIS DE TOCQUEVILLE

That democracy and extreme economic inequality form, when combined, an unstable compound, is no novel doctrine.

—R.H. TAWNEY

ON THE AFTERNOON of 29 April 1992, a jury in Simi Valley, a small suburban town northwest of Los Angeles, returned a verdict acquitting four Los Angeles police officers charged with beating a black man named Rodney King. This verdict shocked most Americans who had seen repeated telecasts of a bystander's videotape of the officers savagely pounding King. In spite of this graphic visual evidence of police brutality, the police officers' defense lawyers managed to convince the all-white, suburban, middle-class jury that the beating shown on the tape was justified as a means of controlling a violent criminal. Within hours of the verdict, the people living in South-Central Los Angeles, only a few freeway minutes but a cultural world away from Simi Valley, responded with three days of intense rioting resulting in 5,383 fires, 58 deaths, 16,291 arrests, and $785 million in damages.[1] Over the next days and weeks, the media presented numerous discussions and analyses of the riot. Most of them portrayed the King verdict as the spark that ignited underlying social forces. Many observers identified the resentment that people in the South-Central neighborhood felt toward the Los Angeles Police Department as a major factor in the rioting. People in the area had experienced directly the kind of police brutality inflicted on King and had looked to the

---

Opposite: *The sensational murder trial of O.J. Simpson exposed a wide racial divide in reactions to his eventual acquittal. (Reuters/Vince Bucci/Archive Photos)*

King trial to vindicate their sense of injustice about their own treatment. When the trial failed to provide this vindication, they reacted with irrational rage.

But analyses of the riot quickly moved beyond viewing it as the result of bad police-community relations. For many observers, the riot came to represent a consequence of the growing inequality in American society. The sharp contrast between the world of Simi Valley and that of South-Central Los Angeles called attention to how divided American society is becoming. South-Central resembles rundown urban areas throughout the country. Its citizens, predominately black and Hispanic, but also white and Asian, share the woes of poverty, unemployment, crime, and drugs. It is a world where police helicopters patrol every night, shining their spotlights down to search for drug dealers and to intimidate gang members. It is a world of the American nightmare.

For the American dream, one needs to go north over two mountain ranges to the world of Simi Valley — a community of planned suburban subdivisions, green golf courses, and backyard pools. It is a world of leisure and tranquility where streets have been consciously laid out in mazelike grids to confuse and trap any criminals from outside.[2] Its mostly white citizens earn incomes well above the national average, send their children to excellent, well-funded public schools, and, even during recessions, are not likely to be unemployed. Although they share a common citizenship with the people of South-Central Los Angeles, Simi Valley residents inhabit an entirely different world.

It is not surprising, given the cultural distance between them, that the people of Simi Valley and those of South-Central Los Angeles would not perceive white police officers beating a drunk and disorderly black man the same way. Living in insulated enclaves expressly designed to protect them from invasions by the likes of Rodney King, the Simi Valley jurors were probably predisposed to give the benefit of the doubt to white police officers over a poor black victim. In South-Central Los Angeles, everyday experience with an increasingly arrogant police force that harasses people while providing little real protection from crime and violence elicited automatic sympathy for King and uncontrollable rage at the verdict. Viewed in the light of the contrasts between the two communities, both the verdict and the riot become understandable. The stark differences between the day-to-day existence of people in Simi Valley and those in South-Central Los Angeles have produced in our society two worlds with little contact, comprehension, or empathy. Alarmingly for our democracy, the Simi Valley/ South-Central Los Angeles contrast can be replicated throughout the United States.[3]

At the time, the South-Central L.A./Simi Valley contrast seemed partly a reflection of the recession from which the economy was just emerging in 1992. Conflict between the haves and the have-nots seems strongest in times of economic distress. Candidate Bill Clinton's campaign slogan that year, "It's the economy, stupid," appealed to both the public's worry about America's overall economic doldrums and the inequality that seemed to be one of their consequences. In the years since, as we have seen almost a full decade of continuous economic growth and a record-breaking stock market, many observers have been surprised at how little economic prosperity has altered the contrast in economic prospects between the citizens of South-Central L.A. and Simi Valley. A hard fact of the current economy has been the degree to which the benefits from economic prosperity have gone, almost exclusively, to the Simi Valleys of America and missed the South-Central L.A.s. Despite the lowest levels of unemployment in two decades, median wages grew so slowly that they did not recover their 1989 level (the year prior to the last recession) until early 1999.[4] This ten-year lag in recovery of wages meant that the gap between the rich (whose incomes depend less on wages) and poor continued to grow in the 1990s.

This chapter explores the dangers of this contrast for the future of American democracy: Can political democracy survive this growing social inequality? Although the subject of the danger of inequality to democracy is an old concern of democratic theory (as Tawney says in the quotation at the beginning of this chapter), it is a relatively new concern about American democracy. Of course, social inequalities, particularly racial inequality, have always existed in American society. Nevertheless, from the beginning of the republic, American egalitarianism — despite the contradictory presence of slavery and then racial segregation — seemed to stand out in comparison to other societies. This was the observation of such nineteenth-century European visitors as Alexis de Tocqueville, who made equality the central theme of his classic *Democracy in America.* Moreover, whatever inequalities have existed in our society seemed to diminish over time. The historical experience of many immigrants who arrived in this country poor, who experienced discrimination and hardship, but who over time acquired wealth and eventually political power, has been, for many, the definition of the American dream. Even our most troublesome and disruptive inequality, that of race, seemed, until the past decade, to be diminishing.

Over the past few years, this historical confidence in the progressive decline of social inequality has collapsed. Americans have found inequalities of race and gender deeply embedded in their institutions despite the civil rights and women's movements. Economic inequality has been on the rise; the standard of living for many seems to be falling. Public opinion polls show that Americans worry that their children will live less well than they — a novel development in our history. In comparison to other industrial countries, the United States is no longer the model of social and economic equality.[5] What sort of challenge does growing inequality pose for American democracy?

The first section of this chapter examines the importance of the concept of equality, both political and social, in democratic theory. Next, I review some empirical evidence of growing economic inequality in the United States and persistent racial inequality, focusing in particular on the position of black Americans. Finally, I discuss some implications of these inequalities for the future of democracy and how we might address them.

EQUALITY AND DEMOCRATIC THEORY

Political equality, the idea that all people are equally qualified to rule, is the core value of democratic theory and the source of democracy's radicalism. From the time of the ancient Greeks, proponents of democracy have justified democracy by pointing to people's shared capacity to make the political and moral judgments that governing requires. They have been skeptical of all formulas for justifying the power of some elite or elect group of people because of the elite's alleged superior wisdom or virtue. This skepticism about elite rule has been a radical position because, for most of humanity's history, an existing governing elite has formulated elaborate doctrines to explain why it alone was qualified to rule and to ridicule the concept of political equality. To believe that ordinary people have the capacity to govern themselves has led ordinary people — whether American farmers in 1776, French *sans culottes* in 1789, or the black residents of the South African township of Soweto in the 1980s — to revolt against those in power. These revolutions have required not only seizing power from ruling elites but also refuting their philosophical claims that they had some right to rule others. What arguments have proponents of elite rule used to justify their power?

Over the centuries, a wide variety of doctrines have been advanced to "prove" why some group of people or some superior individual should rule over others. Divine right, racial superiority, aristocratic blood, or the superior insights of the revolutionary vanguard have been some of the formulations of the underlying notion that some group has special qualities that ordinary people do not, which justifies its power. All these arguments are based on the assumption that certain people have the special knowledge required to govern the community.[6] Whether this knowledge is divinely granted, inherited, or derived from the study of revolutionary dogma, all arguments against political equality assume some special knowledge is needed to govern the polity, and only certain people are capable of acquiring that knowledge. To deny such a political elite the right to rule, according to these arguments, is to accept inferior government.

This argument is central to one of the oldest works of Western political philosophy: Plato's *Republic*. In his description of the best polity, Plato gave complete responsibility for governing to philosophers trained from birth in the art of government. This training would give to these philosophers the special knowledge and capacity to make appropriate political judgments and produce justice for all. Just as one would turn to a well-trained shoemaker skilled in the art of shoemaking when seeking a good pair of shoes, one should look to a well-trained philosopher skilled in the art of government when seeking good government. For Plato, people are no more equal in their capacity to govern themselves than they are equal in their ability to make good shoes.

In a famous passage in the *Republic,* Plato has his protagonist, Socrates, present a parable of a ship to illustrate the folly of political equality. Imagine, says Socrates, a ship in which every sailor claimed equal capacity to take the helm although none had any special training in navigation.[7] This would produce a long and dangerous quarrel over control of the vessel, resulting in eventual control by an incompetent helmsman. Who would want to sail on such a ship? For Plato, democracy is like this ship because of the effect of political equality. The lesson of his parable is that no reasonable person would want to live under a condition of political equality any more than one would want to travel on a democratic ship.

As many democratic theorists have pointed out, the flaw in Plato's reasoning is that the ship parable does not distinguish between technical competence and political competence.[8] Political judgments are concerned primarily with the ends and purposes of government; what we should *do,* more than the technically best way to accomplish something. In the parable of the ship, Socrates never mentions where the ship he describes is going, but politics is often about the ends, the destinations of polities, rather than the technical details of getting there. Although special technical expertise may be required in government, as it is to run a ship, this technical knowledge is neither required nor especially helpful in determining destinations. Even democratic sailors are foolish to quarrel over who takes the ship's helm; there is nothing undemocratic in recognizing the need for navigational expertise, which sailors do not possess equally.[9] But in a democracy, political equality means the equal capacity to make judgments about political ends. Democratic sailors, whatever the range of inequality in navigational expertise, are equally capable of debating whether the day's sail should be devoted to whale watching or finding the best spot for snorkeling. When democrats claim that people are *politically* equal, they mean all people possess a roughly equal capacity to evaluate alternative courses of action from their particular perspective and make political judgments.

But why are people equal in making political judgments? Might not some people, like Plato's philosopher-kings, possess superior knowledge about the ends of politics as well as the technical details? One way to think about this question is to imagine turning over to the philosopher-kings a contemporary public problem and think about how they would handle it. Take, for example, the serious problem of the massive government debt accumulated over the past two decades. What would happen if the American Economics Association (an appropriate group of philosopher-kings for this issue) were given responsibility for solving this problem? Would they be able to handle it better than democratically elected leaders?

The first difficulty economists would face is deciding whether or not government debt is, in fact, a problem. Perhaps more than most Americans, the economics profession is divided over the degree to which the national debt threatens our economy. Some say our $4 trillion debt poses a serious threat to future economic growth; others say the debt is not that great in relation to the overall size of our economy and therefore is not a threat; still others take various positions in between. Knowledge of economic science, in itself, does not provide unambiguous guidance regarding how to evaluate a concrete political issue like the national debt. Like most social phenomena, the operation of the national economy is very complex, and economics, like all social sciences, offers no certain answers about how it operates. After all the expert opinion is reviewed and evaluated, political judgments about public problems come down to intuitive guesses about which expert prescriptions to choose. Democracy assumes that the intuitive judgment of ordinary people, given the uncertainty about how the world works, will likely be as good as that of experts.

What is true about identifying public problems is even more true, once problems are identified, about choosing policy solutions. Experts nearly always disagree about policy proposals on complicated issues such as the debt because such proposals involve predictions about the future. Will future economic growth be large enough that the debt will gradually disappear, or are concrete policy steps, such as allocating a portion of all future budget surpluses to paying down the debt, required to deal with it? Even economists cannot be certain, because of the limitation of their science, how future economic growth will affect the national debt. Because of this uncertainty, there are likely to be different schools of thought within the profession recommending different courses of action.

Besides predictions about the future impact of alternative policy options, any policy solution will always involve value choices. Should we reduce the debt by raising taxes or by cutting spending? The answer rests in part on expert predictions about which is likely to be more effective in reducing debt, but it also requires judgment about what citizens value more: money in their pockets or government services? When we begin to consider alternative spending cuts, the role of value judgments becomes more obvious. Should we cut defense spending or spending on education? Such a choice involves a decision about what people value more: a high-level security from foreign dangers or educating their children. What increase in military insecurity is acceptable in return for better-educated youngsters? The democratic option assumes ordinary people to be equally capable of making such judgments; the advice of experts does not help us, once they determine the probable consequences of alternative courses of action, to choose which set of consequences we are willing to accept. Furthermore, political equality, in contrast with the philosopher-king position, assumes individuals are more competent to judge for themselves what they want, at the level of the kinds of value choices just described, than is any expert. Equal citizens in a democracy bring to political decision making their individual judgments about what they want, something they know best.[10] Democratic decision making involves a process of discussion among these individuals until a consensus, or at least a majority opinion, is reached on what they collectively want to do. The theory of democracy makes room for the advice of experts, just as the sailors and passengers on a democratic ship need the navigational skills of the captain, but, in a democracy, the decision about where we are going requires judgments about the uncertain future and value choices that all people are competent to make.

While democrats agree on the central value of political equality, the relationship between political and social equality in a democratic society remains controversial. To say that people ought to have equal rights to political participation does not necessarily require that they be equal in any other way. In fact, vast inequalities among citizens in social status, wealth, and lifestyles can be found in all countries claiming to be democratic. Can these inequalities safely coexist with political democracy, or do they interfere with the ability of people to govern themselves as equals? To what degree does the democratic ideal of political equality require a measure of social and economic equality?

The response to these questions is usually framed in terms of the debate between *equality of opportunity* and *equality of condition*. Proponents of equality of opportunity argue that democracy and social inequality are compatible depending on the source of those inequalities. If they arise from a political elite using its political power to give themselves special economic and social privileges denied others, then they are not only inconsistent with political equality, but they result from its absence. A truly democratic polity would not likely give an elite special privileges. If, however, some individuals become wealthier than others and acquire higher social status through their own intelligence, initiative, and luck, there is no conflict with political equality. As long as the political rules of the game are the same for everyone, if some are able to succeed better than others, and inequality results, there is no cause for concern. For proponents of equality of opportunity, political equality assures that government will make the rules of economic and social competition fair for all. Unequal success under these rules does not challenge democracy as long as the rules are fair.

Proponents of equality of condition question whether true equality of opportunity can exist when there are large differences in wealth and social status in society. From this point of view, abstract assurances of equal opportunity have little meaning when comparing the actual opportunities a child growing up in South-Central Los Angeles has compared to one in Simi Valley. Existing differences in social and economic status translate automatically into differences in opportunity. A society of political equals would seek ways to narrow these differences as part of providing everyone with equal opportunity. The very existence of social inequalities, then, is probably an indicator of political inequality. Only a society where some have less political power than others would accept large social and economic inequalities. Proponents of the equality of condition also emphasize the ease with which economic and social privilege can erode political equality. They insist that people with social and economic advantages use these advantages to acquire greater political power and, inevitably, bias the rules of the game in their favor. Social inequality leads directly to political inequality and then to inequality of opportunity.

Equality of opportunity and equality of condition provide different vantage points for evaluating social and economic inequalities in a society. The former seeks to evaluate them in terms of their causes, the latter in terms of their effects. A democratic commitment to political equality is consistent with either, depending on where one wishes to focus one's attention. Neither point of view alone is very satisfactory for understanding the relationship between social and political equality in actual societies. The debate assumes a sharper distinction between the two sorts of equality than has actually been true historically when people have struggled to establish democratic government.

In nearly all movements to establish democracy, democrats have seen the struggle for equality as embracing both political and social equality perceived simultaneously as both equality of opportunity and equality of condition. The historian Gordon Wood argues that this was the case with the American Revolution.[11] "Equality," argues Wood, was "the most radical and powerful ideological force let loose in the Revolution."[12] The American revolutionaries sought to break down the sharp hierarchical social distinctions of colonial society and replace them with the concept of republican citizenship. This was obviously a political concept — a demand for political equality — but because political and social statuses were so closely related in prerevolutionary America, it also implied an abolition of all statuses.

This concern for equality did not mean the American revolutionaries wanted to level society, to make everyone the same economically. According to Wood, equality of opportunity was clearly the revolutionaries' aim. At the same time, the revolutionaries thought eliminating the hierarchical structures obstructing equality of opportunity would lead, over time, to greater equality of condition.[13] Rough social and economic equality, they thought, would be essential for political equality. Only rough equality of property holding, as in Thomas Jefferson's vision of the independent yeoman farmer, would ensure that no citizen would become dependent on someone else. Economic dependence was thought to be incompatible with the free exercise of citizenship.[14] In addition, rough equality "made possible natural compassion and affection and that bound everyone together in a common humanity" — a condition conducive to equal political participation.[15] As a result of the revolution, political and social equality were intertwined in American minds as "ordinary Americans came to believe that no one in a basic down-to-earth and day-in-and-day-out manner was really better than anyone else."[16] By the 1830s, Alexis de Tocqueville found equality of condition a distinctive characteristic of the American democratic society.[17]

The interrelationship Wood finds between political and social equality in the American Revolution seems to be characteristic, to some degree, of all "transitions" to democracy.[18] All usually involve displacing from power an elite that has used its political privilege to assure itself of economic and social privileges. During the democratic revolutions since 1989 in Eastern Europe and the former Soviet Union, for example, denunciation of the social privileges of the former Communist elite — the dachas, special stores, and vacation retreats — has accompanied the introduction of democratic processes. In some countries, a major concern has been to prevent the former elite from using economic and social privileges obtained under communism to establish a privileged position for itself under democratic capitalism. In democratic revolutions everywhere, the egalitarian sentiment of democracy seems based on a notion of equality embracing both political and social equality. Equality in a democracy means "no more bowing and scraping."[19]

The relationship between social and political equality in democratic revolutions suggests a need to examine their interrelationship in societies, such as the contemporary United States, that claim to be mature democracies. To what degree does our society retain the revolutionary sentiment that "no one is better than anyone else"? Does there remain a sense of "common humanity" characteristic of a society of rough equals and necessary for a successful democracy? Or have social and economic inequalities grown to such an extent, as the Simi Valley/South-Central Los Angeles example suggests, that our democracy may be threatened?

Before we can discuss these questions, we need to examine more carefully the extent of social inequality in the United States today. Like many other societies, American society is pervaded by inequalities of various kinds — gender, culture, linguistics, sexual orientation, organizational status, physical capacity — which undermine political equality. All these social inequalities are important barriers to achieving the level of political equality necessary in a democratic society. For example, social structures that place American women in an inferior status in the economy, in the family, and in many organizations impede their ability to participate equally with men as citizens. The significance of this inequality is obvious in the extreme gender imbalance in supposedly representative bodies, such as the U.S. Congress, despite women's gains in recent years. Full understanding of how social inequality impedes political equality and democracy requires sensitivity to the wide variety of forms inequality takes. In this brief chapter, however, I have chosen to concentrate on two that are particularly troubling for the future of American democracy because they appear to have been worsening in recent years. First, the trend toward increasing inequality in wealth and income during the past two decades challenges our central myth about the nature of American society: the American dream. Second, racial inequality, the persistent divide between black and white Americans, has deep roots in our history. Of all the social inequalities that challenge American democracy, these two are likely to be the most explosive.

Increasing inequalities of wealth and income challenge the American dream of material prosperity and social mobility. (Archive Photos)

THE END OF THE AMERICAN DREAM?

Our most enduring myth is the myth of the American dream. It is a myth, not in the sense of a fictional story, but in the sense of a symbolic representation of some fundamental expectations Americans have about the character of their country and their own place in it. The American dream is a story about ordinary people striving for material success and social acceptance in a new kind of society where such striving is actually rewarded. Unlike other societies, where rigid social hierarchies reserve independence, wealth, and power to a select few, the America of the American dream is a place where no system of social stratification stands in the way of individual success. In one popular variant of the myth, a poor immigrant arrives alone on our shores without resources, but in a few short years, through hard work, provides a comfortable living for his family; within a generation, his children become educated professionals, sometimes wealthy, and, perhaps, state governors or even president. Another variant is simply a mental picture of an entire nation living in neat, well-kept, single-family houses surrounded by equally neat, well-kept lawns, sending their children to cheerful neighborhood public schools, barbecuing on weekends in their backyards when they have not gone on an excursion in one of the family automobiles. The American dream, in short, is a vision of individual and collective material prosperity.

Like all myths, the American dream contains, within the many stories that define it, different components. Central are the expectations of material prosperity and social mobility. The myth assumes greater wealth and higher income can be had and can be more widely distributed than has been possible in other societies. Consistent with the individualist bias of our culture, the myth assumes individual effort and striving to be the source of prosperity, but the absence of social barriers to mobility provides the context in which individuals do, in fact, gain their rewards. Implicit in both expectations is an assumption of rough equality in society.

Equality does not mean, within the symbolism of the American dream, a society of absolute equality and sameness. The link between individual effort and social mobility requires a system of differential rewards. Nevertheless, the American dream emphasizes that the potential for material success and social mobility is available to all. In the United States, there are no castes or limits on particular groups' gaining access to even the best opportunities. And it is a vision of society in which material differences between people do not sharply divide them from one another: no snobbism here. The ideal of the comprehensive American high school in which children of the rich and the poor are educated together, rather than the exclusive prep school, epitomizes the American dream.

The reality of American society has never conformed to the vision presented in the American dream. It is a myth and, like all myths, although it is grounded in a basic reality, it does not accurately reflect the historical experience of all Americans. Like all societies, American society has had its inequalities, its prejudices, and its own system of stratification. There have always been exclusive prep schools along with public high schools. Immigrants arriving in the United States have found not just "streets paved with gold," but also discrimination and abuse. The shameful treatment of African Americans forced to dream their American dreams in the cargo holds of slave ships represents the most glaring contrast between myth and reality. Yet for all these failures of existing reality to live up to the myth, one of the sources of its strength results from the fact that the American dream has been about a *dream* for the future, not existing reality. Poor immigrants, hard-scrabble farmers, and even former slaves could dream the American dream in filthy, unheated tenements and dirt-floor shacks because its focus was on aspirations for the future. Existing inequalities, within the dream, were seen as carryovers from the past; the future promised steady progress toward the equal, inclusive society the dream describes. In sum, the American dream provides a series of promises about the trajectory of society. Throughout our history, it has promoted expectations that we are moving together toward greater prosperity, more mobility, and greater equality than can be found today. That people perceived such a trajectory over the course of their own lives, even when those same lives may have fallen short of attaining the "dream," has solidified the myth in American consciousness. This is why the growing perception, in the past few years, that the trajectory of society may have shifted from greater equality to greater inequality is such a profound shock. The prospect of more, rather than less, inequality in the next generation calls our culture's central myth into question and cannot help but challenge the future of our democracy. This challenge is all the greater because it comes at the end of a period, the thirty years that followed World War II, when the reality of American life seemed on the verge of attaining the American dream for all.

The years between 1945 and the early 1970s in the United States produced the longest and greatest expansion of economic prosperity in human history. Ordinary Americans were the direct beneficiaries of this prosperity as the real (inflation adjusted) median family income doubled between 1945 and 1970.[20] Unlike most families today, the typical family during this period had one breadwinner whose single income was sufficient to deliver a steadily increasing living standard. A young man (most family breadwinners during the period were men) starting his working life at age twenty-five in 1950 or 1960 could count on doubling his income by the time he reached age thirty-five.[21] Given this explosion of prosperity, the real experience of most families involved moving to a roomy house in the sunny suburbs with a two-car garage (filled, of course, with two cars), a back-yard barbecue (perhaps next to a swimming pool), in a neighborhood filled with similar families — just like the American dream.

Increasing prosperity was spread widely among Americans, producing a dramatic reduction in the level of income inequality. One of the ways in which social scientists analyze income distribution is to look at how total national income is distributed among different fifths of the population (quintiles) ranging from the poorest fifth to the richest. Tracing shifts in this distribution over time (see table 6.1) shows that between 1947 and 1969, although the overall distribution remained very unequal, the income share going to all but the richest fifth of the population increased. Naturally, the gains of the bottom four-fifths of the income distribution came at the expense of the richest fifth, who lost more than 2 percent of their share of national income. This was true, as well, at the very top of the distribution: the richest 5 percent lost nearly 2 percent of its share of national income. Even the poorest Americans gradually increased their share of national income by half a percentage point.

The shift toward greater income equality is even more dramatic if we consider the percentage of families earning various levels of income. In 1947, immediately following World War II, 97 percent of Americans earned less than $10,000 per year (in 1984 dollars); about one-third earned less than $2,500.[22] Most Americans were concentrated at the lower end of the income distribution. By the early 1970s, this situation had changed substantially, as most families moved into the middle class. By 1973 the proportion of families earning less than $10,000 (again, in constant 1984 dollars) had been cut to 39 percent, as 42 percent moved into the $10,000 to $20,000 category, and the remaining 20 percent earned more than $20,000. Most dramatically, the proportion at the bottom,

Table 6.1 Family Income Distribution, 1947–98 (in percentages)

	Poorest fifth	2d fifth	3d fifth	4th fifth	Richest fifth	Richest 5%
1947	5.0	11.9	17.0	23.1	43.0	17.5
1959	4.9	12.3	17.9	23.8	41.1	15.9
1969	5.6	12.4	17.7	23.7	40.6	15.6
1974	5.5	12.0	17.5	24.0	41.0	15.5
1979	5.2	11.6	17.5	24.1	41.7	15.8
1984	4.7	11.0	17.0	24.4	42.9	16.0
1988	4.6	10.7	16.7	24.0	44.0	17.2
1992	4.4	10.5	16.5	24.0	44.6	17.6
1994	4.2	10.0	15.7	23.3	46.9	20.1
1998	4.2	9.9	15.7	23.0	47.3	20.7

Source: U.S. Census Bureau, *Current Population Reports,* Series P-60, No. 146 (April 1985), table 17, and No. 184 (September 1993), table B-7; updates from U.S. Census Bureau, *Historical Income Tables — Families,* table F-2, http://www.census.gov/hhes/income/histinc/ f02.html.

earning less than $2,500, had declined to 4 percent, about one-tenth of what it had been in 1947. The family income distribution had shifted from one with most families at the lower end to one with most concentrated toward the middle. In terms of family income, the American dream's vision of more people sharing in the general prosperity was the reality of the thirty postwar years.

The early 1970s brought an end to this growing equality, and by the early 1980s, the proportion of families in the lowest income levels began to increase — a trend that continued through the 1990s.[23] By 1992 the gains of the poorest Americans had been wiped out (see table 6.1), and what was even more alarming, the distribution of income among quintiles of the population looked much like it had in 1947. One congressional study found that between 1977 and 1990 the richest fifth of Americans saw their incomes go up 15 percent, while the poorest Americans saw a 7 percent decline in their incomes.[24] This meant that the United States was much more unequal in the 1990s than it had been twenty years earlier. In 1979 those Americans in the top 5 percent of income earners earned thirteen times what those in the bottom 5 percent earned. But by 1996 someone in the top 5 percent of the income distribution earned *twenty-three times* the income of someone in the bottom 5 percent of the distribution.[25] In contrast to the American dream's picture of a steady march toward widespread prosperity, American reality seemed to be moving backward.

By 1992 more analyses showed the very rich had pocketed most of the economic gains of the Reagan years. A Congressional Budget Office study showed that the top 1 percent of Americans, families earning an average of $559,800 a year, gained 77 percent of the growth of income between 1977 and 1989.[26] Over the same period, the poorest 40 percent of families, those earning less than

$20,000, saw their earnings decline. Even when one looks at after-tax income (taxes are normally thought to reduce the incomes of the rich relative to poorer people), 60 percent of income growth went to the richest 1 percent of families. These trends continued throughout the 1990s. A variety of factors — favorable tax laws, a booming stock market, high interest rates, rising real estate prices — accounted for the explosion of rich people's incomes. An additional element was the generosity American corporations showed in their compensation to upper-level executives compared to average workers. In the middle of the recession in 1991, the compensation of corporate chief executives reached a historic high, with 407 executives receiving more than $1 million for a year's work.[27] One corporate CEO received $75 million. Overall, top corporate executives earned 120 times the pay of the average worker in their companies in 1990, compared to only 30 times as much in the 1970s. The economic boom of the 1990s widened this gap, as average CEO annual compensation rose to an astronomical $11.9 million in 2000.[28] Even though only part of the story, this shift in the compensation of those running corporations compared to their employees symbolizes the shift toward greater income inequality over the past two decades.

Up to now, we have looked at statistics on changing incomes to see the trend toward greater inequality. Another, and in some ways more significant, way to measure this trend is to look at wealth statistics. Social scientists label wealth as things people own — stocks and bonds, houses and other real estate, bank accounts — minus, of course, their debts; income represents the money coming into a household over a fixed period of time in the form of wages and salaries, interest earned, business profits, and dividends. The distribution of wealth is in some ways a better measure of societal inequality than income distribution. Incomes can vary greatly from year to year because they can be affected by short-term events: someone wins the lottery, another person is unemployed for part of the year, someone else sells a house and retires to Florida. In comparison to income, wealth distribution tends to be more stable, and because wealth earns future income, it is a good measure of future living standards.

During the past two decades, wealth became more concentrated in the hands of the richest families. As figure 6.1 shows, between 1983 and 1995 only the top 5 percent of the population saw their net worth increase. Everyone else lost ground, especially the bottom 40 percent who saw nearly an 80 percent decline in wealth. As of 1997, the top 1 percent of the population controlled 40 percent of net wealth, the next 4 percent about 22 percent, leaving the remaining 95 percent of the population with only a bit over one-third of total national wealth.[29] Figure 6.2 shows that wealth today is more concentrated than it has been since the 1920s and is more concentrated than in any other industrial nation.[30] Unlike in the 1920s, when wealth was more equally distributed in the United States than in Europe, wealth today is less concentrated in major European countries than in the United States. By 1992 the wealthiest 1 percent controlled 37 percent of U.S.

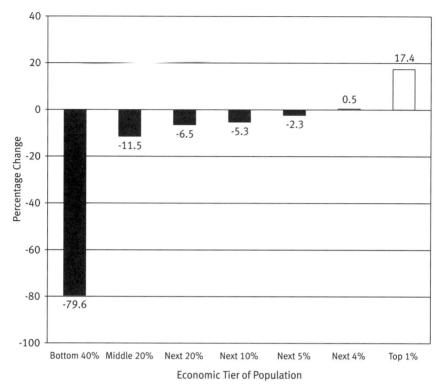

Figure 6.1 Change in Average Household Net Worth, 1983–95 (in percentages)

Source: Chuck Collins, Betsy Leondar-Wright, and Holly Sklar, *Shifting Fortunes: The Perils of the Growing American Wealth Gap* (Boston: United for a Fair Economy, 1999), 7. Based on data collected by economist Edward Wolff. (United for a Fair Economy, 37 Temple Place, Boston, MA 02111; 617-423-2148; www.ufenet.org)

wealth compared to (in 1986) 26 percent of French wealth, 18 percent of British, and 16 percent of Swedish.[31] The concentration is most significant at the heart of the productive economy. The wealthiest 1 percent of Americans can assure themselves of high future incomes through their ownership of more than 60 percent of business assets and securities: stocks, bonds, and trusts. As a *New York Times* article reporting these findings noted, such a huge concentration of wealth "flies in the face of" Tocqueville's observation, in the United States of the 1830s, of "the general equality of condition among the people."[32]

While the rich got richer in the past two decades, the poor got poorer. As one might expect, the poor suffered serious setbacks in the severe recession of the early 1980s and in the less severe one of the early 1990s. Recessions tend to affect those at the bottom of the income distribution most because unskilled workers earning low pay tend to get laid off sooner during a recession and in greater numbers than do skilled workers. But the poor suffered especially in the last two

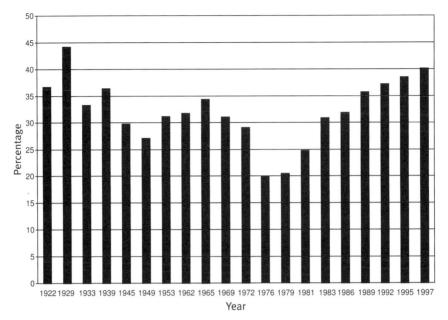

Figure 6.2 Percentage of Total Household Wealth Held by Wealthiest 1 Percent, 1922–97

Source: Chuck Collins, Betsy Leondar-Wright, and Holly Sklar, *Shifting Fortunes: The Perils of the Growing American Wealth Gap* (Boston: United for a Fair Economy, 1999), 10. Based on data collected by economist Edward Wolff. (United for a Fair Economy, 37 Temple Place, Boston, MA 02111; 617-423-2148; www.ufenet.org)

recessions because, unlike previous periods of economic growth, the rapid economic expansions in the 1980s and 1990s passed them by. Fewer than 12 percent of all Americans were poor in 1979, but in 1997, even at the height of an economic boom, 13.3 percent were poor.[33] In an analysis of the Reagan boom of the 1980s, Brookings Institution economists David M. Cutler and Lawrence F. Katz estimate that had the boom "trickled down" to the poor, in the manner of previous periods of expansion, the proportion of people in poverty should have dropped below 11 percent.[34] Unlike what happened in the 1950s and 1960s, when economic prosperity cut the poverty rate in half, economic growth during the Reagan years failed to produce the kinds of jobs that lift people from poverty. At the same time, Reagan administration cutbacks in social programs reduced the value of the safety net that, in the 1970s, cushioned the loss of income of the poor. Much the same seems to have occurred for most of the jobs created in the 1990s boom, as the social safety net also has continued to erode.

While the rich got richer and the poor got poorer, middle-class incomes stagnated and the middle class shrunk. Economists Bennett Harrison and Barry Bluestone call this the phenomenon of the "declining middle."[35] Defining middle income as families earning between $20,000 and $50,000, they report that this group dropped from 53 percent of the population in 1973 to 47.9 percent in 1984. While some of this decline resulted from families leaving the middle class by moving up (1 percent), most (4.3 percent) fell out of the middle class and into poverty. The typical "Ozzie and Harriet" family — a single earner in a male-headed family with two children — suffered especially during this period, with a 7.4 percent drop in its median income.[36] The American dream of everyone becoming middle-class now seems to be growing farther from American reality.

What accounts for this collapse of the American dream? How can the phenomenon described here — growing inequality, prosperity only for the rich, a declining middle class, increasing poverty — be explained? Economist Frank Levy, in *The New Dollars and Dreams: American Incomes and Economic Change*, identifies three factors that seem to account for this rising inequality: slow productivity growth, structural economic change favoring workers with high levels of education and skills, and declining economic and political power of average workers relative to owners of capital.[37]

In an earlier version of his work, Levy provides a brilliant demonstration of how growing inequality is related to a stagnant economy. Before 1973, the United States experienced a twenty-seven-year economic boom. During this period, inflation-adjusted wages grew by about 2.5 to 3 percent per year, delivering rising incomes to millions of workers; since 1973, wages have stagnated. This has had a direct effect on average family incomes, which grew 30 percent during the 1960s and 1970s. The postwar boom was a classic period of a "rising tide," overall economic growth, "lifting all boats," improving the standard of living of everyone. This expansion occurred because of increased economic productivity — the economic value produced by each hour of labor. Between 1947 and 1965, productivity grew each year an average of 3.3 percent. After 1965, the rate of growth began to decline, producing an average rate of only one percent between 1973 and 1996.[38]

Levy connects this decline in productivity and stagnant growth to the "inequality of prospects" they have produced for pre- and post-1973 workers.[39] Before 1973, wages rose so fast that workers readily accumulated the material components of the American dream: a house, automobiles, college education for the kids, and a savings account. Rising wages put millions of poor families over the threshold into a middle-class standard of living. Since 1973, families that achieved the American dream in the earlier period have the advantages of job seniority, low-interest fixed-rate mortgages, savings rather than debt, and, if retired, inflation-adjusted Social Security payments. Economic growth also funded a more generous welfare state, represented primarily in increasingly generous Social Security and Medicare benefits. Workers entering the workforce since 1973 have had a more difficult time, as the price of the American dream escalated.[40] Because of stagnant wages, two family members must work to attain a standard of living close to that of the previous generation; more expensive houses and home mortgages mean a higher level of debt and little opportunity to accumulate savings. Families with only a single wage earner, usually a woman, have been pushed further and further behind in the new economy. The median income for families headed by a single woman in 1995 was only $17,170, with more than 44 percent of such families earning less than $15,000.[41] These families have been especially vulnerable to rapid declines in their incomes during the recessions of the past three decades, while workers in the previous generation rode out recessions without significant loss to their long-term earning power. Economic stagnation over the past twenty years has meant diminished life-cycle earnings for the post-1973 generation. By the 1990s, this has begun to show in greater vulnerability to falling into poverty at the lower end of the income distribution and feelings of economic insecurity in the middle.

Along with the overall decline in productivity, the structure of the economy has changed since the early 1970s, altering the kinds of jobs it is producing. In the post–World War II period, most people improved their standard of living because they were able to get jobs in the core manufacturing industries of the economy. These were usually unskilled or low-skilled assembly-line production jobs but nevertheless were good-paying union jobs. These were jobs that allowed workers to acquire suburban homes and put their kids through college. They also provided substantial stimulus to the entire economy, creating more good-paying nonmanufacturing jobs, as workers spent their union-protected wages in their communities. Since the early 1970s, the economy has stopped producing these "routine production jobs," as Robert Reich calls them; instead, it has been eliminating them.[42] Between 1973 and 1986, about 1.7 million of these jobs were lost.[43] Much of the decline in manufacturing jobs is a consequence of corporations having moved production abroad to countries where wage rates are lower. In the face of the decline in manufacturing and Third World wage competition, unions have seen their membership drop precipitously, from representing nearly a third of the workforce in the 1960s to only 17 percent of workers in 1989.[44] International wage competition and union decline have meant a drop in the wages paid in those remaining routine production jobs. Ordinary people's access to good jobs paying good wages, the former source of access to the American dream, is vanishing.

This transformation in the structure of the labor force has profoundly altered the structure of economic opportunity in America. According to Reich, jobs in the current economy can be divided into three categories: routine production jobs, service jobs, and symbolic analyst jobs. Routine production jobs, including many white-collar middle-management jobs in industry, are being lost to low-wage areas abroad. Most of the jobs being created in the economy are service jobs, ranging from McDonald's hamburger flippers to real-estate salespersons, which, with some exceptions, pay low wages. Symbolic analysts are people such as scientists, engineers, some lawyers, investment bankers, even university professors —

people who earn their living through problem solving and analysis. They possess specialized knowledge and, more important, the skills to design new products, develop new industries, and organize production. In the economy of the future, according to Reich, only symbolic analysts will be able to compete in the international marketplace and, along with workers who directly support their efforts, earn high wages.

Reich describes a society in which substantial inequalities are deeply embedded in the labor force to a much greater extent than was true in the thirty years after World War II. In the 1950s, the typical high school graduate could go to the local factory and find a permanent, blue-collar, "routine production" job paying a high enough wage to raise a family in the middle class. The same factory also recruited college graduates, even those with mediocre academic records, for a large number of middle-management supervisory positions. In the 1990s, both the high school and the middling college graduate are likely to find the factory gates closed, with a "moved to Mexico" sign hanging on them. Both must turn to the service sector, where jobs can be found but at much lower wages. Even with two wage earners, families cannot look forward to the rising standard of living over their lifetimes their parents found, and they may not be able to attain an equivalent level of comfort. For those who fail to obtain a high school degree, the outlook is bleaker: poverty or, at best, occasional low-wage work. The jobs such people held twenty to thirty years ago will be filled with high school and college graduates. Only the best and the brightest, the top college graduates, many of whom must acquire graduate and professional degrees — Reich's symbolic analysts — can hope to obtain good-paying jobs, look forward to rising incomes over their lifetimes, and become upwardly mobile. The American dream will be reserved for them.

Some evidence for this sharp division in the workforce is beginning to emerge. Over the past two decades, the relation between level of education and income, a relationship that has always been strong, has become stronger.[45] Between 1973 and 1987, the average wage of someone without a high school diploma declined 18 percent, from $19,562 to $16,094 (in 1987 dollars); wages for high school graduates dropped 12 percent, from $31,677 to $27,733. Only college graduates saw their wages grow, but by a small amount, from $49,531 to $50,115. What is more significant for Reich's argument is that the gap between the wages of high school and college graduates doubled over this period. The value of education, a prerequisite for approaching the status of symbolic analyst, has clearly grown — a positive development, perhaps, from the point of view of rewarding educational effort, but one that will increase inequality of life prospects and access to the American dream among workers.

At the same time that slow growth in productivity and a changing economy were widening the gap between rich and poor, the power position of average workers within both the economy and the polity prevented them from claiming a fair share of the economy's fruits. The declining power of unions denied workers the clout to negotiate contracts with their employers that would gain them higher wages. With fewer union-organized workers, corporations were free to lower production costs by reducing real wages and benefits while taking larger profits for their shareholders. In the new global economy, workers feared pressing for higher wages because they could lose their jobs altogether if their employers moved their jobs abroad. As described in chapter 5, corporations became increasingly adept at using this threat to keep wages low. Combined with this weakness within the economy, government policy increasingly reflected the preferences of investors over wage earners. Although, as pointed out earlier, the wage gap between workers with different levels of education has grown, all workers have seen a decline in wages relative to the workers of the late sixties, no matter what their level of education. Even recent college graduates could expect lower compensation in their new jobs than did the previous generation of workers.[46] This phenomenon may account for the many reports that the so-called Generation X has a pessimistic outlook toward the future.

According to economist James K. Galbraith, the stagnant wages after 1973 were a direct result of an overall shift of government economic policy from promoting full employment, a strategy that encouraged the growth of real wages and hence declining inequality after World War II, to promoting historically high average interest rates, ostensibly to "fight inflation" but in reality to guarantee a high return on capital.[47] Presidents and Congress, since the early 1970s, have ceded control of macroeconomic policy to the Federal Reserve Board and its powerful chairmen, such as Paul Volcker and Alan Greenspan. Their abandonment of this control is partly due, as argued in chapter 1, to the barriers divided government in this period has presented to agreement on fiscal policy. In filling the policymaking gap, the unelected Federal Reserve Board has been most responsive to business interests, particularly the banking industry, rather than the needs of average workers. Whenever rising wages have begun to deliver real gains to workers, the Fed has intervened in the economy to raise interest rates as a means of slowing the economy, resulting in higher unemployment and lower wages. On several occasions—the mid-1970s, the early 1980s, and the early 1990s—sharp Fed-induced interest rate increases have plunged the economy into deep recessions producing unemployment and underemployment, particularly for those workers earning below the median wage. The periods of economic growth after these recessions have not been robust enough to allow those workers to recover the losses they sustained during the recessions. And whenever the economic recoveries begin to raise real wages substantially, the Fed, citing fears of future inflation, raises interest rates, as it did in the summer of 1999. Galbraith argues that the cumulative effect of these policies has been to direct the fruits of economic growth to the rich by keeping wages low and assuring owners of capital that inflation will not erode their gains. As a result, the rich get richer and the poor poorer.

A homeless man outside New York's World Trade Center offers a poignant reminder of inequality in the midst of prosperity. (Corbis)

Other policies have reinforced these economic policies to dampen wage gains. Because Congress has been reluctant to raise the minimum wage, it has lagged far behind inflation for the last three decades. Even when Congress finally raised the minimum to $5.15 per hour in 1996, that rate was still well below the $6.50 per hour it would need to be to restore its 1968 purchasing power.[48] Policies regulating labor unions, especially National Labor Relation Board decisions under the Reagan and Bush administrations, have contributed to union decline. Social programs, from welfare to housing, have been cut to the bone in the name of deficit reduction, yet these tend to support the incomes of the lower-wage workers. Finally, trade policy, as represented by NAFTA and GATT, has supported globalization and its depressing impact on wages. The combined effect of these policies, Galbraith argues, should lead us to regard stagnant wages and increasing economic inequality much more as the result of conscious public policy decisions than as uncontrollable economic forces. Viewed in this light, we can connect policies biased in favor of wealthy Americans to upper-class dominance of the political process, through their campaign contributions and lobbying access. Galbraith's thesis connects inequality directly to the challenges to democracy described in previous chapters.

In the early 1990s, in the aftermath of the South-Central L.A. riots and in the midst of economic recession, the media began to call attention to rising inequality and the threat it posed to the American dream. *Newsweek's* March 1992 issue titled "America's Lost Dream" and the 1991 *Philadelphia Inquirer* series called "America: What Went Wrong?" raised the issue explicitly. Politicians in the 1992 presidential campaign also raised the issue. Unfortunately, the economic prosperity of recent years seems to have pushed the inequality issue from the public agenda, even though that prosperity has not appreciably diminished inequality. As the 2000 presidential campaign approached, politicians seemed to be ignoring the issue. Even so, most Americans continued to be aware of growing inequality and blocked social mobility in contemporary America. A myriad of issues, from growing consumer debt to family breakdown, reflect the fact that many wage earners cannot keep up financially even in times of overall prosperity. Most people can see the changes described in this section in their own lives: lower wages, lost jobs, and homeless people in their communities. More important, they raise questions about the underlying optimism of the American dream — that we can expect steady progress toward greater equality and prosperity for all in the future. Nowhere has this optimism been shattered more than in the area of race relations.

THE PERSISTENCE OF RACIAL INEQUALITY

Conflict over race has been the central conflict in American political history, a conflict that underlay the Civil War, our bloodiest military conflict, and nearly divided the nation in two. The conflict's importance relates to how racial inequality in our history has been so glaringly at odds with the central tenets of the American creed and the promise of the American dream. The subservient status of black Americans has been a historical contradiction to the Declaration's commitment: "All men are created equal." To a great extent, and in a manner that no other group has had to experience, slavery and then racial segregation flatly denied one group of Americans access to the American dream. Overcoming the contradiction between the status of black Americans in American society and the myth of the American dream and the principles of the American creed *is* the "American dilemma."[49] At the time of the civil rights movement in the 1950s and 1960s, many Americans hoped that the American dilemma was on the verge of resolution. The mobilization of black and white Americans to eliminate legal segregation in the South, culminating in the 1964 Civil Rights Act and the 1965 Voting Rights Act, promised that, at long last, blacks too would have access to the American dream. Expectations at this time coincided with the optimistic strain of the myth: although black Americans remained unequal to whites in their access to the American dream, the end to legal segregation would gradually eliminate this inequality. Affirmative action programs were devised to accelerate this process. Tragically, more than thirty years later, the American dilemma remains far from resolved. The growth in social inequality has thwarted blacks' hopes for equality with whites. The American dream of the 1960s has been replaced with frustration and, once again, has increased division over how we are to cope with our racially divided society.

Like most broad-brush impressions of social phenomena, this perception in recent years of a growing gap between black and white Americans is too simple to capture the complexity of trends in race relations. Journalists Thomas and Mary Edsall detect two contradictory tracks of race relations since the civil rights revolution.[50] One is a track of progress toward integration and acceptance of blacks, and black culture, into the mainstream of American life. The end to legal segregation and societal efforts to promote integration have benefited many individual black people, especially those of the middle class. Three decades ago, elite institutions in business, government, the media, and academia were exclusively white. Today, many blacks are full participants, holding leadership positions in these institutions. One can point to specific individuals as evidence of this transformation: the former chairman of the Joint Chiefs of Staff General Colin Powell; Supreme Court Justice Clarence Thomas; media personalities Bryant Gumbel and Bill Cosby; movie director Spike Lee; numerous big-city mayors; the late Secretary of Commerce Ron Brown; and many others. The pre–civil rights movement America of the 1950s would never have seen blacks in such prominent positions.

The progress toward integration goes much further than the presence of individual blacks in token positions of prominence. During the past forty years there has been an explosion in the size and prospects of the black middle class. Between 1950 and 1990, while the black population doubled, the number of blacks employed in white-collar jobs increased ninefold.[51] Black families in the top quintile of the income distribution saw their incomes rise faster than those of white families in the top quintile.[52] Better-off nonwhite households have made some gains, also, in closing the wealth gap with whites.[53] Whereas most talented young black people in the past were consigned to seeking higher education at black colleges and could look forward to professional careers in a limited number of positions serving the black community, today elite universities compete to attract talented black students, and when these students graduate, they find places in prestigious law firms, hospitals, business firms, and universities. Although blacks remain far from fully represented in positions of prominence and in elite institutions, concentrating on the progress that middle- and upper-class blacks have made over the past forty years would support the American dream of a progressively more equal society in the future.

Tragically, the Edsalls point to a second, opposite track of American race relations that tends to dominate popular, particularly white, perceptions of black Americans. Since the 1960s, while middle-class blacks have experienced acceptance and social progress, poorer blacks have suffered from greater exclusion and increasing deprivation. Segregated in the urban ghettos of our cities, members of what scholars now call the "underclass" seem farther away than ever from access to the American dream. Although the underclass contains people of all ethnic backgrounds, the popular image of this group is strongly associated with blacks.[54] Blacks are frequently associated as well with such underclass behaviors as crime, welfare dependency, illegitimacy, and drug abuse. Often-repeated statistics about blacks, such as the high rate of out-of-wedlock births among black teenagers, the large proportion of black men in prisons, the murder rate among young black men, high rates of black unemployment, and the high incidence of black drug abuse, plus sensational press coverage of gang violence and crime in black inner-city communities, reinforce this association.

Although at times exaggerated, these statistics and images of the underclass record the reality of increasing destitution for the poorest black Americans. While upper-income blacks outpaced whites in income growth over recent decades, the reverse is true for the poorest quintile of blacks, whose income fell further behind that of poor whites.[55] Also, declining wealth among the poorest blacks has meant a growing gap in the median wealth of all whites and blacks, despite the gains of better-off black households.[56] To a great extent, the growth of the black underclass and the declining economic position of poor blacks is a consequence of the general economic stagnation and overall increase in inequality described in the previous section.

The economic boom after 1945 fueled a reduction of income inequality between blacks and whites, a reduction accelerated by the civil rights movement. After 1963, the difference between the average income of blacks and that of whites dropped steadily, a convergence consistent with the American dream of progress toward equality. By 1977, this convergence had stopped, locking blacks into a position of permanent income inequality with whites. What seems to have happened is that the loss of good-paying entry-level manufacturing jobs in the economy hit black workers particularly hard. Before the 1960s, racial discrimination denied blacks access to many of these jobs, yet these are the jobs that have traditionally, especially in the post-1945 period, provided most Americans with social mobility. Just as government action to prevent racial discrimination came into force, structural changes in the economy began eliminating these good-paying entry-level jobs. To look at this another way, denied access by racial discrimination to the pre-1973 advantage in life prospects that Levy describes, blacks find that the leveling of the playing field has occurred primarily in a period when the struggle for the American dream has become more difficult for everyone. Behind as a group to begin with, blacks have, not surprisingly, fallen farther behind in the stagnant economy of the past two decades.

Even more alarming for the future of racial equality, black access to educational opportunity is declining just when the value of education to economic success is increasing. The proportion of black students dropping out of school, many from decaying inner-city schools, compared to whites has been increasing. As the difference between the entry-level wages of college graduates compared to high school graduates has increased, the proportion of blacks going to college has decreased. Between 1977 and 1988, while the percentage of whites enrolled in college grew from 27.1 percent to 31.3 percent, the percentage of blacks enrolled declined from 22.6 percent to 21.1 percent. There is a sharp contrast between the experience of the vast majority of black students and that of the small number of very talented, middle-class and poor, black students. While the latter have benefited from affirmative action programs that have attracted them to the country's best universities, affirmative action has not prevented other barriers from rising in the path of most blacks' access to college. To a much greater extent than whites, blacks depend for their early education on deteriorating urban public schools that do not provide adequate college preparation.[57] And state colleges and universities and community colleges have had to raise tuition to cover increasing costs because of funding cutbacks from state legislatures. Like all working-class and poor people, blacks heavily depend on these institutions, and the increasing costs have affected them disproportionately. Finally, levels of student financial aid have declined as well. Given these developments, the decline in black college attendance is understandable, but it will produce greater inequality with whites in access to good jobs in the future.

Growing economic inequality between blacks and whites and the rise of a black underclass have contributed to political polarization on the issue of race. Since the civil rights revolution, public opinion polls show whites to be more tolerant of blacks as individuals than in the past; at the same time, whites, particularly working-class whites, retain very negative perceptions of blacks as a group. Much of this negative perception arises from whites' disgust with underclass behaviors, such as crime, illegitimacy, and drug use, which they associate with blacks. That these behaviors coincide with traditional racist stereotypes of promiscuous, indolent, and violent blacks only reinforces the association. Many whites also perceive blacks as undeserving beneficiaries of government "giveaway" programs, such as welfare, while they perceive themselves as taxpayers required to bear the cost of these programs. Given the increasing economic pressures the working class has faced, resentment of taxes has grown, a resentment many whites associate with the black underclass. White reaction to affirmative action programs has added fuel to this resentment. Implementation of court-ordered affirmative action programs in the 1970s in such working-class occupations as the building trades and police and fire departments put blacks, seeking a toehold on the ladder of social mobility, in direct competition with whites, who felt themselves losing ground.[58] Instead of viewing affirmative action as justified compensation for past discrimination against blacks, whites perceived these programs as providing unfair advantage to blacks at the expense of individual whites — whom they did not consider responsible for past racism. Images of the black underclass, resentment against taxes and government programs, and hostility to affirmative action programs, combined with increasing economic pressure and inequality, have maintained race at the center of the political consciousness of many whites.

As whites have grown more resentful of blacks, the optimism that many blacks felt during the civil rights movement has been shattered by persistent racial inequality. In recent years, more blacks, particularly in poor neighborhoods, have interpreted their lack of economic improvement and the increasing distress of the underclass as a consequence of a white racist conspiracy. Many see the recurrent "wars on drugs" not as efforts to control crime, which they do not seem to affect, but as excuses to kill or imprison blacks. Many even see the presence of drugs as part of a white conspiracy to foment gang violence. One black scholar has claimed that whites will use underclass behaviors "as an excuse to...plunge the country into a race war, and worst of all, be a pretext for genocide."[59] Such an outlook underscores how the growing economic divide between the races and the racially tinged perception of the underclass have polarized the political outlooks of blacks and whites. Black and white Americans differ markedly in their perceptions of race relations. In a careful analysis of public opinion data, Jennifer Hochschild has found that while whites perceive racial discrimination as lessening in American society and the life prospects for blacks as improving, black Americans see worsening conditions. Her analysis focuses specifically on black and white expectations about the American dream described earlier in this chapter. She finds that blacks and whites share equally in the belief in the American dream as a "prescription for their own and other Americans' lives," but blacks believe that discrimination prevents their race from fully achieving it.[60] Hochschild calls the disparity between white and black views the "what's all the fuss about?" paradox. Whites, who assume that discrimination is lessening, cannot understand blacks' continuing preoccupation with the effects of discrimination; therefore, when blacks raise such concerns, whites may believe they are pleading for race-based privileges. Blacks may argue, for example, that affirmative action is essential to counter continuing discrimination — a position unpersuasive to whites who assume that racial discrimination is a thing of the past. Constructive democratic dialogue and deliberation about this and other issues is difficult given such differing race-based perceptions.

Not surprisingly, the polarization of white and black attitudes and perceptions has affected national electoral politics. In the early 1960s, voters saw little difference between the two major parties on race. After all, a Republican president, Dwight Eisenhower, had sent federal troops to integrate Little Rock High School in 1957, and in the early 1960s, resistance to Democratic President John F. Kennedy's civil rights efforts came from southern Democrats in Congress, not from Republicans. The presidential election of 1964 initiated a change in partisan perception of racial issues when the Republican presidential candidate, Barry Goldwater, appealing to southern white Democrats upset over racial integration, opposed President Lyndon Johnson's Civil Rights Act of 1964. Although Goldwater lost the election, he did succeed, for the first time since Reconstruction, in producing Republican victories in several southern states. In 1968 Richard Nixon adopted a more subtle racial strategy to attract the same southern voters, along with urban white Democrats. Instead of explicitly opposing civil rights, Nixon used the theme "law and order" to capitalize on white alarm over urban riots and associate the opposing Democratic Party with the emerging white working-class perception of an irresponsible black underclass. This strategy, in different guises — the "welfare queen" for Reagan in 1980 and Willie Horton for Bush in 1988 — has been the centerpiece of Republican presidential victories for the past twenty years.

At the same time, Democrats, in supporting affirmative action programs and actively seeking the support of black voters, have alienated traditional Democratic whites. Since these voters outnumber blacks, the result was presidential election losses for Democrats beginning in 1968. It has also produced an electorate more sharply divided on race than any other demographic characteristic. In 1988, while 59 percent of white voters supported President Bush, 86 percent of black voters supported the Democratic candidate, Michael Dukakis.[61] Racial polarization persisted even as Clinton has recaptured the White House for the Democrats. In 1996, among voters who chose one of the two major parties, Dole captured 52 percent of the white vote, and Clinton received 88 percent of the black vote.[62] Increasing racial inequality combined with increasing economic inequality has been a potent mixture for partisan polarization.

Along with the polarization of parties along racial lines, the economic and racial divisions in our society are developing a spatial dimension. We are increasingly a geographically divided society in which economically better-off white citizens live in suburban communities apart from and politically independent of poor, mainly black and other minority residents living in central cities. By the 1990s, the gradual suburbanization of American society, a trend that dates to the beginning of the century, had reached the point where a majority of citizens lived in suburbs.[63]

Of course, this characterization of relatively rich, white suburbs in contrast with poor, largely black urban areas is a simplification of a more complex reality. There are some "poor" white suburbs, others are predominately black and rich, others are racially integrated, and some central cities contain substantial numbers of wealthy whites. Nevertheless, the idea of the poor black central city and the white suburb is accurate enough to constitute an important image of how American inequalities are sorting out geographically. This divide is enhancing racial and economic inequalities in a number of ways. First, by living in the suburbs, economically advantaged citizens have been able to avoid the cost of growing social inequality.[64] They are able and willing, according to most studies, to tax themselves for local public services, while they defeat taxes to state and federal governments with jurisdiction over central cities. The consequence for access to quality public services — schools, for example — is that suburban public schools provide well-funded quality programs, while big-city schools deteriorate. The urban poor do not provide an adequate tax base to allow urban governments to support decent schools; at the same time, state and federal governments cannot subsidize cities because the majority of voters living in suburbs resist the taxes needed to do so. Racial imagery promotes this pattern. White suburban voters consider themselves public spirited in supporting their own insular communities and in opposing federal and state taxes to support what they regard as giveaway programs for an undeserving black underclass. This formula can only perpetuate and deepen existing inequalities into future generations — hardly the optimistic vision of the American dream.

Second, suburbanization has walled off the more affluent white majority of Americans from the problems of less fortunate black Americans. At times this takes the form of actual walls: some residential enclaves in suburbia are surrounded by stone walls that can be penetrated only through security gates. Developers promote these areas as places where suburban residents can be secure from the crime and disorder they see on television.[65] Social inequalities of income, job prospects, and educational opportunity come to include as well inequality of security. But this approach to urban problems does nothing to address those problems; it merely insulates privileged citizens from their effects. Again, the suburb/city split becomes a formula for perpetuating inequality.

Finally, growing suburbanization promotes keeping classes and races from contact with one another. Within all-white suburbs, people live their lives with less interaction with flesh-and-blood blacks than was true in the American South at the height of segregation. Their only impression of blacks is derived from media images, and aside from sanitized portrayals of such successful individual blacks as television's Huxtables, the media concentrate on reporting black violence and crime and the assorted disorders of the black underclass. Even whites who have positive encounters with individual blacks at work or school seem to retain an overall negative perception of blacks as a group. Individual "good" blacks are assumed to be exceptions to the rule.[66] For their part, blacks, especially poor blacks, remain equally isolated from white Americans, encountering them only as white police officers, work supervisors, government bureaucrats, and store owners. In the eyes of many blacks, white people are interested in them only to give orders, regulate their behavior, take their money, and imprison them. In the aftermath of the sensational murder trial of O.J. Simpson, media commentators seemed surprised to discover that a majority of blacks believed Simpson to be innocent, the victim of a police conspiracy, while a majority of whites were strongly convinced of his guilt. Given continuing racial segregation and differing experiences of blacks and whites with the criminal justice system, these differences in reactions to Simpson's acquittal should not have been surprising. America remains racially divided today into two societies "separate and unequal."

The combined effect of continuing racial inequality in the United States and worsening economic inequality has been disastrous for the American dream. At the beginning of the twenty-first century, equal access to the fruits of growing prosperity seems farther away than ever. Dr. Martin Luther King's dream remains only a dream — and far from the nightmare of the Los Angeles riots. The growing inequality of the past two decades portends even more inequality and social division in the future. What are the likely effects of this trend on American democracy? Can a society as seemingly unequal and divided as we are becoming survive as a democracy?

INEQUALITY AND DEMOCRACY

Social inequality, particularly income and racial disparities, challenges democracy's survival in at least three ways. First, it undermines a central democratic value: political equality. Second, it becomes a barrier to the sense of community that citizens must have in order to rule themselves. And, finally, social inequality is likely to lead to cycles of rebellion and repression that will engender authoritarian politics.

The first point returns us to the basic insight of the American revolutionaries: social and political inequalities are inevitably linked. The most obvious linkage is in the way social advantages such as wealth are political resources convertible into influence and power. As we saw in earlier chapters, people with high levels of education and income find political participation and representation much less costly than do the poor and less educated. Inequality in having a say in government inevitably follows. Such inequality is tolerable in a democracy if it is not extreme and if inequality on one social dimension, such as race, does not coincide with inequality on others, such as income, educational attainment, and organizational status. Unfortunately for American democracy, social inequalities seem to be moving beyond tolerable levels. Both the increase in income inequality and the way differences in wealth, race, and even geographical location coincide have produced tremendous differences in political power and influence. That the residents of South-Central Los Angeles are not the political equals of those in Simi Valley contradicts the central promise of democracy. Political equality and, therefore, American democracy, cannot exist if divisions between rich and poor, black (and other minorities) and white, and suburbs and cities continue to grow as they have over the past two decades.

The second point also follows from the American revolutionaries' sense of social equality. If we are to have a society in which all citizens have a say in how they are governed, social disparities cannot move beyond the point at which people lose that down-to-earth sense that no one is fundamentally better than anyone else. Such a regard between fellow citizens is needed if they are to accept one another as equal participants in governing the community. Only people who hold one another in mutual regard can begin to understand others' problems and needs and then devise mutually acceptable solutions. More than just failing to understand one another, a lack of mutual acceptance will soon become a barrier to perceiving any common interests. The wide social gulf that exists between the Simi Valleys and the South-Central L.A.s makes it impossible for citizens in either area to perceive that they share goals or are members of one political community.

Without a shared sense of community, not only is democracy impossible, but any sort of common politics is destroyed. Wide social disparities turn politics into a contest between "us" and "them" that can turn violent. Usually, those with less power and fewer resources strike out first. When inequality stands in the way of effective participation and those in power ignore the concerns of the powerless, violence, even senseless destruction, becomes the only way to attract attention. This need to attract the attention of those in power seemed to be on the minds of some of those who took part in the Los Angeles riot. Participants told reporters that they knew that burning buildings in the community and looting stores would make their lives worse, but they were doing it because they knew of no other way to attract society's attention to their plight.[67] Rioting, in such a situation, becomes a desperate attempt at political participation. Rebellion, however, is a dangerous form of political participation, especially when those rebelling are so divided from the rest of society, particularly those in power. In the South-Central Los Angeles riot, the immediate response to the events suggests that Americans are not yet irredeemably divided. After the disorder was brought under control, officials at all governmental levels responded with calls for providing the community with resources and addressing its problems. It remains to be seen how effective these responses will be. If they are not effective, future social explosions are likely and may very well call forth repression rather than attempts at reconciliation. If the inequalities dividing American society get out of hand, a cycle of rebellion and repression could develop. In other countries, when such cycles begin, they usually call forth demands for authoritarian leadership. As R.H. Tawney and others have pointed out, the progression of inequality, societal division, rebellion, repression, and, finally, resort to authoritarian leadership is a classic path to the end of democracy.

DESPITE THE LONG and sustained economic expansion of the 1990s, inequality, both economic and racial, persists as a significant challenge to democracy. Persistent inequality despite a growing economy suggests that specific attention needs to be paid to the differential distribution of economic plenty. Any expectation that we may have had that a strong economy "lifts all boats," as President John F. Kennedy put it many years ago, has been proven wrong by recent experience. Reducing inequality will require specific policies targeted at the problem.

To the degree that inequality is a result, as analysts such as Robert Reich and Frank Levy argue, of differential rewards based on skills and education, sustained attention to improving both the quality of and access to education is crucial.[68] The increasing international economic competition that has had such a devastating impact on the manufacturing heart of our economy results from the ease with which manufacturing can be moved around the globe. The well-paid, but largely unskilled, entry-level "routine production jobs" that provided access to the American dream for so many Americans in the past have been exported abroad because so many foreign workers are available to perform this work for lower wages. Competing for such jobs can only mean a declining standard of living for Americans, more inequality, and stagnant productivity growth. The only way to promote both wage growth and entry-level job opportunities for American workers is to create skilled jobs producing products and services that less-skilled workers abroad cannot produce. This approach requires major public and private investments in education and training.

Such an investment in education would involve addressing directly the inequalities in educational opportunity that have increased in recent years. Educating a skilled, competitive workforce would mean improving basic academic skills in the primary and secondary schools. In order to have an impact on economic growth, attention would have to be paid to improving education in all schools, including those in deteriorated urban areas. Moreover, the skills needed in tomorrow's economy are not the narrow ones associated with traditional vocational education, but higher-order skills in analysis and problem solving associated in the past with "college prep" curricula.[69] Interestingly, this is the sort of education many democratic theorists have said is needed to produce effective democratic citizens. From this perspective, education for a more productive economy is also education for a better democracy.

Democracy and education are linked, as well, in a second approach to improving our economy and reducing inequality. In traditional manufacturing industries of the past, the effective performance of routine production jobs demanded little of individual workers. Their role in the organization of the factory was simply to remain at their posts on an assembly line and carry out simple, repetitive tasks. Effective organization of such workers implied a hierarchical, authoritarian work environment in which supervisors monitored workers to see that they followed orders. Worker involvement in designing work, monitoring quality, or suggesting improvements in efficiency was not necessary, nor were workers trained for this work.

For the workplace of the future, the traditional hierarchical organization of manufacturing is not appropriate. The only way the economy will benefit from more highly skilled workers in the future is if they can participate directly in the design and organization of production. Already, many American firms have found restructuring away from the old hierarchical model to be a successful formula for competitiveness. New facilities, such as GM's Saturn plant, are organized around multiskilled teams of workers who participate collectively in managing all phases of a production process. According to some economists, improving productivity rates will require applying this principle to other aspects of corporate management.[70] Worker democracy in governing the corporation can draw on the collective wisdom of all workers; authoritarian leadership of a small group of elite managers is likely to be inferior to that of the democratically managed corporation. Critical to building a more democratized workplace are stronger labor unions that can shift power back to the average worker in the industrial structure. As in the arguments in favor of political equality in government discussed earlier in this chapter, the assumption that all people (including workers) are equally qualified to rule may be the best formula for governing corporations, as democrats assume it to be for governing polities.[71]

Yet improved education and more democratic workplaces will not be enough to overcome the public policy bias in favor of the rich. Macroeconomic policies aimed at sustaining full employment over a long period of time, as economists such as James K. Galbraith argue, are required if real wages are to rise, especially for the lowest paid workers. Moreover, explicit redistributive policies are needed to improve the standard of living of those at the bottom of the income distribution.

Redistribution is a controversial concept in American politics. Our individualist political culture assumes that people are largely responsible individually for their economic position and ignores how collective forces, such as access to good public schools or the availability of well-paying jobs, affect people's lives. Because of this individualist bias, most Americans support the notion of equal opportunity, equality resulting from both opportunity and individual effort, but are uneasy about equality of condition, particularly if these results involve direct government intervention. Programs perceived as taking from one group and giving to another rarely receive much political support. If recipients of government aid are perceived as "undeserving," many citizens are actively hostile to the redistributive program. Public hostility to "welfare" is tied to this outlook toward redistributive programs and explains the failure of welfare to reduce inequality.[72]

A better model for reducing social inequality in our individualist political culture is the Social Security program. Unlike welfare, Social Security benefits are provided to virtually all American workers on retirement and are perceived as an entitled return on worker payroll-tax contributions. Nevertheless, Social Security is a very successful redistributive program that has substantially reduced inequality among the elderly. The United States needs more programs that, like Social Security, are universal, available as an entitlement to all citizens, but provide special help to the poorest citizens, who need the programs the most. Such programs are common in Europe and have reduced inequality there below American levels. First on the list would have to be universal health insurance. Such a program would eliminate a substantial source of insecurity in the lives of the poor and would receive widespread political support. Second, a universal system of child allowances could replace welfare, eliminate the stigma attached to receiving aid to support children, and provide resources directly to the poorest group of Americans, children. Third, universal child care, in the form of public child-care centers or vouchers for purchasing private care, would ease the anxieties faced by parents in two-earner households and facilitate the integration of poor single mothers into the workforce. Most Americans find these programs consistent with their individualist values, and such programs would ease the chasm between the rich and the poor.

The vast inequalities in wealth ownership could also be addressed directly through programs that would, in the spirit of the nineteenth-century Homestead Act that gave free plots of land to farmers, distribute financial assets directly to individual Americans. In one such proposal, law professors Bruce Ackerman and Anne Alstott propose providing every American who graduates from high school with an $80,000 wealth account that would constitute a "stake" from which each individual could draw for investment in education, starting a business, and/or accumulating savings.[73] The stakes would be financed initially by a 2 percent wealth tax on assets over $80,000, but eventually by a revolving account funded by repayments from stakeholders upon their deaths. Economist Richard Freeman has proposed a similar plan to provide all Americans at birth with an investment fund sufficient to generate a small lifetime income that would be repaid, also, at the end of one's life.[74] Advocates of these asset redistribution plans argue that they would be consistent with the traditional American values of individualism and equal opportunity, but would level the societal playing field significantly.

Investments in education and training, sustained full employment policies, more democratic workplaces and empowered workers, plus redistribution through programs of universal social assistance and "stakeholding" are all paths toward a more equal American society. All deserve more thorough investigation than has been possible in this chapter; students should explore these ideas further in the suggested readings. Mentioning them briefly is intended to show that we do not have to accept as inevitable the trends toward inequality discussed here and the dire consequences they are likely to bring. Although one could argue that a concern for fairness or a spirit of charity should motivate programs to improve the plight of the poor, the point of this chapter has been that attention to reversing increasing inequality in the United States is a *political* necessity. If we are to have democratic government in the future, we must act to promote political equality. To increase political equality, we must reduce social inequality. Failure to reverse the trend toward a more unequal America may spell the end of a democratic America.

THOUGHT QUESTIONS

1. Do you agree that people are basically equal in their capacity to make political judgments, or are some political decisions best left to the experts?

2. If everyone has an equal vote and equal political rights, what does it matter that some people have more money than others? Do you agree that political equality in a democracy depends on a measure of economic and social equality, as this chapter argues?

3. Would you support some redistribution of wealth, such as proposed in the Ackerman/Alstott "stakeholder" plan, for the sake of more equality? What are the arguments for and against such an idea?

4. This chapter emphasizes the dangers that economic and racial inequalities pose for American democracy. What other sorts of inequalities exist in America and what relationship do they have to democracy?

5. According to this chapter, geographic segregation according to race and class exacerbates the impact of inequality in undermining democratic community. What might be some ways to reduce such segregation without interfering with a person's freedom to choose where to live?

SUGGESTIONS FOR FURTHER READING

Ackerman, Bruce A., and Anne Alstott. *The Stakeholder Society.* New Haven: Yale University Press, 1999. A proposal to correct inequality in wealth by providing an $80,000 "stake" to every American high school graduate.

Danziger, Sheldon, and Peter Gottschalk. *America Unequal.* Cambridge: Harvard University Press, 1995. Provides a thorough description of growing income inequality in America and analyzes various explanations for it. Concludes with some specific policy prescriptions to reduce inequality.

Edsall, Thomas Byrne, and Mary D. Edsall. *Chain Reaction: The Impact of Race, Rights, and Taxes on American Politics.* New York: Norton, 1991. Reviews the evolution of American politics since the 1960s and demonstrates how race is at the center of all aspects of our politics.

Galbraith, James K. *Created Unequal: The Crisis in American Pay.* New York: Free Press, 1998. Argues that increasing inequality is a result of slow and unequal wage growth brought on by misguided public policies, not inevitable economic forces.

*Gilder, George. *Wealth and Poverty.* New York: Basic Books, 1980. In contrast to the argument of this chapter, Gilder finds inequality a positive force in American society.

Green, Phillip. *The Pursuit of Inequality.* New York: Pantheon, 1981. A closely argued critique of attempts to justify various forms of social inequality.

Hochschild, Jennifer L. *Facing Up to the American Dream: Race, Class, and the Soul of the Nation.* Princeton: Princeton University Press, 1995. A detailed look at how Americans of different races and classes perceive the American dream.

Levy, Frank. *The New Dollars and Dreams: American Incomes and Economic Change.* New York: Russell Sage Foundation, 1998. Provides a detailed description of the growth of income inequality in the United States since 1973 in contrast with the period prior to 1973.

Reich, Robert. *The Work of Nations.* New York: Vintage, 1992. Provides a systematic analysis of how growing inequality is rooted in structural changes in the world economy and shows what could be done about it.

Walzer, Michael. *Spheres of Justice: A Defense of Pluralism and Equality.* New York: Basic Books, 1983. One of the most distinguished American political philosophers makes a case for creating more equality in democratic societies in a way that also enhances individual freedom.

Wolff, Edward N. *Top Heavy: A Study of the Increasing Inequality of Wealth in America.* New York: The Twentieth Century Fund Press, 1995. An economist provides a clear and readable analysis of the distribution of wealth in America and suggests how policy changes could make its distribution more equal.

*Presents a point of view that disagrees with the arguments presented in this chapter.

SELECTED WEB SITES

http://www.ufenet.org/ United For a Fair Economy, an organization dedicated to remedying economic inequality, provides data on this issue and opportunities to get involved.

http://www.epn.org/ A public policy clearinghouse sponsored by *The American Prospect* magazine; includes links to many organizations interested in economic and racial inequality.

http://www.ssc.wisc.edu/irp/ Provides clear answers and data about the extent of poverty in the United States with links to other key information sources.

http://www.naacp.org/ America's oldest and most prestigious civil rights organization, the NAACP.

CHAPTER 7

The Seventh Challenge: The National Security State

Perhaps it is a universal truth that the loss of liberty at home is to be charged to provisions against danger, real or pretended, from abroad.

—JAMES MADISON

The conjunction of an immense military establishment and a huge arms industry is new in the American experience. The total influence—economic, political, and even spiritual—is felt in every city, every state house, and every office of the federal government.... In the councils of government, we must guard against the acquisition of unwarranted influence, whether sought or unsought, by the military-industrial complex.

—PRESIDENT DWIGHT D. EISENHOWER,
FAREWELL ADDRESS TO THE NATION, 17 JANUARY 1961

THE END OF the Cold War, symbolized by the tearing down of the Berlin Wall in 1989, was a surprise to the whole world. No one, including American intelligence agencies, foresaw the speed with which America's superpower adversary, the Soviet Union—with all its military might—would collapse. For fifty years the American people had feared the USSR and the prospect of the horrendous conflict that would result should Americans and Soviets ever come to direct blows. To avoid this confrontation and to defend against the Soviet threat, they had supported the creation the "national security state"—the conglomerate of agencies, activities, and attitudes put in place since the 1940s to provide for the national defense. This new establishment within the heart of American society had cost trillions of dollars, changed how the United States related to the rest of the world, and profoundly altered the working of our own political institutions. To meet

Opposite: *Infantry soldiers in Vietnam wade through a foreign policy disaster prolonged by distorted information and official deception. (Archive Photos)*

the Soviet challenge, Americans had acquiesced to the creation within their own country of institutional structures that challenged their own democratic ideals. In the midst of the Cold War, many could argue for the necessity for risks to democracy that the national security state posed in light of the external threat to our democratic institutions. The surprising collapse of the Soviet threat opened the possibility that, with the Cold War victory won, Americans could step down from the fifty years of warlike mobilization and dismantle substantial parts of the security machinery that accompanied it. Now, a decade into the post–Cold War era, that demobilization has not occurred. The national security state seems as powerful as it ever was and continues to constitute a challenge to American democracy.

Before World War II, a distinctive feature of the United States was the small size of its military establishment. Although the United States had maintained a standing national army since the ratification of the Constitution in 1789, in times of peace that army had always been extremely small. The basic principle informing America's relation to its military was that the armed forces would consist of a token core of military professionals in peacetime that would be augmented by citizen soldiers mobilized in time of war. As table 7.1 shows, the size of the armed forces increased during times of crisis, but once the crisis ended, the military was substantially reduced. After World War II, this pattern was altered significantly. True, the size of the military was reduced from its massive wartime peak of more than 12 million men and women, but, unlike previous postwar periods, it was not reduced to anything like prewar levels. After 1945, during the period of the Cold War, the United States maintained a peacetime military of about 2 million men and women, a force about ten times the size of the 1930s military. Over the past decade, the end of the Cold War has resulted in a reduction to an active duty force of about 1.5 million supplemented with about 1 million reserve and National Guard forces.[1] If we take into account the increase in population since the 1930s, there are still about five times as many people in the armed forces now as there were in the 1930s.

Another change in the character of the American military, a change instituted only in the past twenty-five years, is the shift to all-volunteer or professional armed forces, as opposed to ones dependent on citizen draftees. Until the early 1970s, the bulk of Americans in military service were drafted to serve for a short period until they returned to civilian life. All American wars up to and including the Vietnam War were fought by citizen soldiers who either volunteered for the duration of a conflict or were drafted for the purpose. Because of the conflicts associated with the draft during the unpopular Vietnam War, Congress, at the urging of the Defense Department, agreed to end the draft and increase military pay and benefits so that the armed forces could attract professional soldiers. By the 1990s, the United States had a peacetime army not only much larger and

Table 7.1 Active-Duty Military Personnel, 1789–1995

Year	Number in Military		Per 10,000 Population
1789	718		1.8
1807	5,323		
1814	46,858	(War of 1812)	
1821	10,587		
1845	20,726		
1848	60,308	(Mexican War)	
1853	20,667		
1860	27,958		
1865	1,062,848	(Civil War)	
1870	50,348		
1896	41,680		
1898	235,785	(Spanish-American War)	
1910	139,344		
1918	2,897,167	(World War I)	
1923	247,011		
1935	251,799		19.0
1945	12,123,455	(World War II)	
1950	1,460,261		96.5
1952	3,635,912	(Korean War)	
1959	2,504,310		140.0
1968	3,547,902	(Vietnam War)	
1975	2,129,000		
1988	2,138,000		94.2
1995	1,518,000		55.6

Source: U.S. Bureau of the Census, *Historical Statistical Abstract of the U.S.* and *U.S. Statistical Abstract* (Washington, D.C.: Government Printing Office, various years).

more powerful than had been the American tradition, but an army made up of professional soldiers.

American citizens of earlier times would have been clearly alarmed at the existence of such a large professional standing army. From the time of the nation's founding, partisans of democracy usually regarded a large standing army as an implicit threat to democratic liberty. The Virginia Declaration of Rights in 1776, for example, pronounced that "standing armies, in time of peace, should be avoided, as dangerous to liberty." Even former generals concurred with this sentiment. General Andrew Jackson promised at his first presidential inaugural in 1829: "Considering standing armies as dangerous to free governments in time of peace, I shall not seek to enlarge our present establishment." Throughout most of our history, Americans viewed a large military as a feature of foreign autocracies that had no place in the democratic new nation they were creating. Threats to national security would be met as they arose, through the temporary mobilization of a democratic citizenry under arms.

The massive mobilization of World War II and that war's outcome dramatically altered this traditional stance. The near-total destruction of other, especially European, powers during the war left the United States as the preeminent world power. In an area that would become known as the "free world," only the United States possessed the economic wealth to support a military force capable of ensuring stability in the world. The United States took over from such prewar colonial powers as France and Great Britain the responsibility for guaranteeing world commerce. After the war, the only power capable of challenging the United States was the Soviet Union — a nation that most Americans regarded as especially threatening. Fear of the spread of Communism, particularly after the establishment of Communist governments in Eastern Europe, China, and North Korea, was the primary factor that legitimized the new, large American military. Americans were convinced that a permanent military establishment was essential to contain expansion of an ideological adversary. The Cold War seemed to require a permanent mobilization to meet an unrelenting threat to freedom.

Two related factors contributed to the new attitude toward a militarized United States. One was the perception that 1930s American isolationism and military weakness had contributed to the growth of German and Japanese power. Americans were told that only constant vigilance would prevent the future rise of comparable threats. An illustration of the staying power of these memories and this argument is the fact that George Bush used it in 1991, almost fifty years after World War II, to justify war against Iraq, as did Bill Clinton in 1999 to justify intervention in Kosovo. A second factor was the increasing complexity of military technology. The military establishment pointed to new, highly sophisticated weapons, most dramatically nuclear weapons, as proof that temporary mobilization of the citizenry would no longer be adequate to forestall military threats. Advances in military technology meant that the nation had to undertake the permanent support of the means to develop and put into operation new weapons. The sophistication of these weapons meant also the maintenance of a large standing army trained in their use.

The institutional foundation for this new international role was provided in the National Security Act of 1947.[2] This legislation created a Department of Defense, consolidating the former departments of War and the Navy. The military services were organized under a Joint Chiefs of Staff, which reported directly to the civilian secretary of defense. Although the act provided for an enhanced political role for the military, civilian control of the Defense Department was supposed to offset concerns about the military's enhanced stature. The act formalized the increased importance of national security issues in the presidency through the establishment of the National Security Council (NSC), composed of the vice-president, the secretaries of the Departments of Defense and State, and other agency heads, to advise the president. In future years, it would be the staff, rather than the council, that would play an important national defense role. The NSC staff would provide presidents with their closest advisers on foreign affairs — advisers who owed allegiance to no other governmental agency. The power of national security advisers such as Henry Kissinger, Richard Nixon's powerful NSC chief, would rival that of Cabinet secretaries.

A very important feature of the National Security Act of 1947 was the section that created the Central Intelligence Agency. The CIA was to have overall responsibility for providing to the president "intelligence estimates" drawn from a variety of sources, including covert agents overseas. Many of the new agency's operatives had formerly worked for the wartime spy agency, the Office of Strategic Services (OSS). Their temporary wartime duty to fight Nazis became a permanent career dueling with Soviet spies of the KGB. Because of pressure from the director of the Federal Bureau of Investigation (FBI), J. Edgar Hoover, Congress explicitly forbade the CIA from any counterintelligence work. This restriction on the CIA was supposed to allay the fears of citizens and elected officials who might have moral qualms about creating an undercover agency. Because they were prohibited from operating within the United States, the chance that the CIA would interfere in domestic democratic politics was supposedly prevented; CIA dirty work would be directed only at foreigners. In later years, this would prove not to be the case.

With the National Security Act, Congress created the core of the national security state, but in the years that followed other institutions emerged to constitute the now-massive segment of government concerned with national security.[3] Intelligence gathering became a concern not only of the CIA but also of expanded military intelligence components in all the military services plus a new agency, the National Security Agency (NSA), which was given responsibility for collecting so-called hard intelligence from electronic intercepts and, eventually, from satellites. Domestically, the FBI expanded its roles in counterintelligence and the surveillance of domestic dissidents. Under J. Edgar Hoover, these roles were the FBI's top priority for thirty years, reflecting Hoover's rather hysterical preoccupation with communist subversion. Even in those areas of government not obviously associated with "national security," the demands of the national security state took priority. The Atomic Energy Commission (AEC) was responsible for developing nuclear warheads for the Defense Department, but with the willing cooperation of the nation's largest business firms, it stimulated as well the development of civilian nuclear reactors. A domestic nuclear industry was considered a national security requirement. Most of the resources of a new government agency to support scientific research, the National Science Foundation (NSF), were directed toward defense-related projects. In the 1950s, Congress justified new initiatives in building roads and in education, the National *Defense* Highway Act and the National *Defense* Education Act, on national security grounds. Supporting all these government activities in the "private" sector were the businesses, universities, and consultants of the "military-industrial complex." Even state and local governments were involved in operating civil defense agencies and military units of the National Guard.

Within a decade after the end of World War II, the national security state had become a massive complex of relationships among much of government with a large sector of domestic society. The agencies connected with the national security state employed millions of civilian bureaucrats and a clear majority of all federal employees, and spent more than half the federal budget. The areas of government concerned with foreign and defense affairs were considerably larger than the foreign policy establishment of the 1930s. At that time, the small Department of State had only a few hundred foreign service officers scattered around the globe, and the military constituted only about 250,000 soldiers and sailors. Simply because of the size of its bureaucracy and budget, the new national security state had to imply changes in the operation of American democracy. In addition to these governmental agencies, a large defense industry, made up of some the largest American corporations, came to depend on contracts for complex and expensive weapons systems for their profits and the wages of their workers. The military-industrial complex, as President Eisenhower called it in his famous farewell speech, intertwined the national security state with both corporate power and the national economy.

Even more than in these institutional dimensions, the rise of the national security state represented a potent shift in the psychology of democratic politics. In his famous "Garrison State" hypothesis formulated in the 1930s, the political scientist Harold Lasswell predicted the consequences of a perpetual crisis mentality brought on by a "continued expectation of violence."[4] In future Garrison States, according to Lasswell, measures sometimes tolerated in democratic societies as temporary, emergency necessities would come to be regarded as permanent and normal. Secrecy, military mobilization, procedural shortcuts, increased power to military professionals, and repressive measures would become constant features of political life and would be readily accepted. Lasswell also wrote that the increasing atmosphere of suspicion fostered in the Garrison State would lead citizens to question one another's loyalty.[5] In the years following the creation of the national security state, the psychology of fear and distrust outlined in Lasswell's Garrison State was frequently a feature of American politics.

Even with the end of the Cold War, the Garrison State mentality remains a feature of the politics of the national security state. The United States has maintained a remarkably high level of military mobilization, even though the collapse of the Soviet Union leaves the United States as the world's only remaining superpower. Spending around $250 billion a year, the American military commands more than seven times the resources of any one of the next largest military powers — Russia, France, Japan, Germany, and Britain — none American adversaries (see figure 7.1, p. 236).[6] In 1999 American military spending alone constituted about one third of the entire world's military spending, and American expenditures combined with those of its closest allies in NATO, Japan, and South Korea equaled two-thirds of all military spending.[7] American spending reductions of the past few years have involved only a reduction from the extremely high levels of the Reagan years. Spending leveled off in the 1990s to average Cold War levels (see figure 7.2, p. 237). As the new century began, the Clinton administration, cheered on by Republicans in Congress, had begun to increase military spending again, and projections were for these expenditures to return soon to levels equal to those at the height of the Cold War. As former Assistant Secretary of Defense Lawrence Korb put it, we will soon have "a Cold War budget without a Cold War."[8] All the institutions of the national security state and the authorizing legislation that created it remain in effect and have changed only marginally since the Cold War's end. The absence of any military threat that comes close to challenging America's colossal military power has not lessened the commitment to maintain a huge, well-oiled national security machine.

As the Berlin Wall came down, many Americans looked to the dismantling of the national security state as a welcome prospect. There was talk of a "peace dividend" that would allow the reallocation of resources, as in the Bible verse, from "swords" into "plowshares." The trillions that would have been needed for weaponry had the Cold War continued could now be spent to educate children, to repair roads, to build better housing, and to bring prosperity to all. Government agencies created to fight the Cold War could be eliminated. In the early 1990s, Senator Daniel Patrick Moynihan argued persuasively that the CIA, which had been created to counter the Soviet KGB, would not be needed in a post–Cold War America. American diplomacy's singular preoccupation with countering the Soviets, which had led to alliances with some disreputable and undemocratic foreign leaders, could now center more firmly on a core American values such as promoting human rights and democratic practices. The new diplomatic and security environment that now confronts the United States would seem to require a complete rethinking of military strategic policy, expenditure requirements, and institutional structure. Unfortunately, the national security state, in the interest of retaining its power and resources, has prevented a reasoned and democratic reexamination of public priorities this new environment demands.

Cold War demobilization was not a welcome prospect for the national security state. During the past decade, the military services, defense contractors, national security bureaucrats in the various security agencies, and their friends

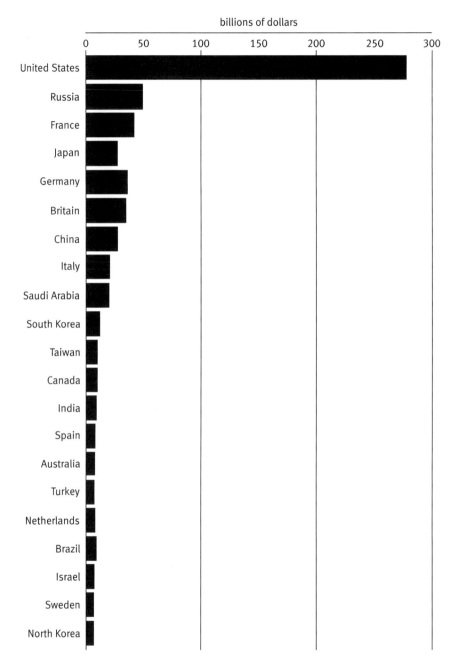

Figure 7.1 U.S. Military Spending vs. the Next Twenty Largest Military Budgets, 1994

Source: Adapted from Randall Forsberg, "Force without Reason," *Boston Review* 20, no. 3 (Summer 1995), 4 (figure 3).

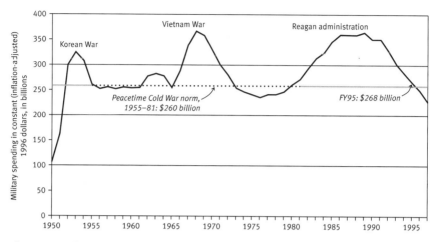

Figure 7.2   The Long-Term Trend in U.S. Military Spending, 1950–97

Source: Adapted from Randall Forsberg, "Force without Reason," *Boston Review* 20, no. 3 (Summer 1995), 3 (figure 1).

in Congress have been largely successful in preserving much of the national security infrastructure from which they derive profits, salaries, careers, and power. The national security state has been somewhat reorganized, much as a corporation reorganizes to face new market challenges, but its basic form remains much intact.

Political and economic interests whose power derives from the existence of the national security state are well positioned to see to its continuance for many years to come. Moreover, although policymakers used the Soviet threat during the Cold War to justify the expansion of the national security state, containing communism was always only part of its rationale. As early as the late 1940s, American leaders saw expanded military power as necessary to establish a U.S.-dominated international economic order. The Soviet threat provided a convenient way to secure domestic political support for policies thought desirable anyway.[9] When President Bush began to speak of a "New World Order" as Soviet might crumbled, he was articulating this alternate rationale that underlay the creation of the national security state from the beginning. American military power is now called upon to maintain the political stability that will allow the smooth flow of investment and commerce in the global economy. The commitment has been made to high levels of military spending and continuation of the national security state without any democratic debate about whether such an American role is in the interest of all Americans.

The creation of the national security state has been justified as necessary to permit the United States to protect itself and its interests in a hostile world.

The specific threats that produced the national security state, the USSR and communism, may be gone, but its continued existence should be worrisome to democrats. The people and institutions that have direct control of the instrumentalities of force and violence pose a special problem for democracies. If the people are to rule, those within the national security state must be willing to acquiesce to the control and direction of the people and the people's representatives. Yet those who wield the weapons and instruments of organized violence clearly have the capacity to resist, defy, and even overturn democratic control. History is replete with popular governments undone when those controlling military power have decided to substitute their own will for that of the people. While democracies, like any other form of government, require military forces and national security states, democratic citizens need to be vigilant that those forces remain subject to democratic control. Unfortunately, America's own recent history provides evidence, some of which will be presented in this chapter, of insufficient citizen vigilance in controlling the national security state. While much of this evidence comes from the period of the Cold War, we should not assume that the Cold War's end has placed the issue of democratic control of the national security state at an end. There seem to be practices and attitudes inherent in the national security state that are problematic in a democracy. As long as the attitudes, practices, and institutions that comprise the national security state exist, democrats need to be aware of the challenge they pose for democracy.

Proponents of democracy identify several dangers in the practices and attitudes associated with the national security state:

1. *Secrecy.* Information relevant to the enactment of public policy is often kept secret from the public and elected officials. The classification of information as secret and censorship are usually justified as necessary to prevent our enemies from using the information against the nation. But keeping crucial information from enemies also prevents citizens from using that same information to hold government officials accountable for their actions and to participate more effectively in the formulation of policy. Also, secrecy is easily abused by public officials who use national security as an excuse to insulate themselves from democratic control.

2. *Centralization.* National security is often a justification for limiting the range of actors involved in making public decisions. Democratic procedures are said to be too cumbersome for the swiftness and decisiveness required for defense and foreign policy decision making. Also, only a small number of officials have access to the secret information and possess the expertise needed for these decisions. In the United States, this has meant concentrating responsibility for these decisions in the president and his close advisers, excluding Congress and the public. Yet decisions of peace and war are among the most important made in any

society. Can a society long remain a democracy if the people are excluded from such important decisions?

3. *Repression.* National security requirements are often used to justify the suspension of civil liberties in order to combat domestic enemies. Fear that fellow citizens may be in traitorous collusion with a foreign enemy leads to campaigns that stifle dissent and interfere with political expression and participation. Police institutions developed to protect national security can become instruments for interfering with legitimate democratic processes.

4. *Distortion.* National security requirements lead to the creation of societal institutions such as a military and defense industry with a vested interest in high levels of mobilization and defense spending. Such institutions also acquire significant power that can be used to influence public policy. Such power can undermine the ability of ordinary citizens to make judgments about the nature and level of security threats. The military-industrial complex exaggerates such threats in order to maintain its power and economic well-being. The existence of a large military concentrates and organizes force in a way that can undermine democracy.

SECRECY

A key value of democracy, common in some degree to all the democratic models discussed in this book, is openness. For democratic societies to operate democratically, citizens must have open and free access to information about public policies and the performance of government officials. Citizens cannot participate effectively in influencing policy unless they know the facts about policy alternatives under discussion. Information that is withheld or available only to certain participants in public debates biases those debates and prevents a democratic outcome. For example, scientific studies about the probability of contamination from nuclear power plants are likely to affect the degree of support for such plants. Unless people have access to such information, they cannot know whether nuclear power is in either their interest or the public interest.

Citizens also need information about the activities of public officials so that they can evaluate official behavior. Democratic accountability is impossible unless citizens know what officials have done and the consequences of those actions. Even the Protective and Pluralist models of democracy, which assume that officials have fairly wide discretion, place a high value on the need for democratic citizens to be able to evaluate the performance of officials. An election cannot function effectively to hold governments accountable if officials can exaggerate their successes and keep their failures secret. The value of openness is intended to facilitate both democratic participation and democratic accountability. This value is in direct conflict with one of the key practices of the national security state: information classification. In 1951 President Truman issued an Executive

Order extending a wartime system of information classification that has become a permanent feature of American government. Under this system, millions of government documents are routinely classified as either confidential, secret, or top secret and are kept from public view. Even after major reform a few years ago intended to reduce the amount of classified information, nearly a billion pages of documents remained classified.[10]

Not only documents are classified. Over the past fifty years, many major foreign policy initiatives of American governments have been in the form of "covert operations" kept secret from the public. Most, although not all, have been carried out by the CIA, and many have had far-reaching consequences for the United States. Among the major covert operations we now know about are the overthrow of democratically elected governments in Iran and Guatemala in the 1950s, the funding of pro-U.S. political parties in Europe, the aborted Bay of Pigs invasion of Cuba in 1961, the "destabilization" of Chile that brought to power the dictator Augusto Pinochet in the 1970s, and the secret *contra* war against Nicaragua in the 1980s. None of these operations were discussed and debated in public, and some, as has been disclosed in congressional investigations, were never revealed to Congress.[11] The budgetary information to support these activities was kept secret as well, despite an explicit constitutional prohibition against such secret accounting.[12]

During the Cold War, secrecy was usually justified by the need for warlike mobilization to counter the threat of communism. Document classification was intended to prevent the Soviets from learning about weapons development and the disposition of American military forces. Covert operations were justified as necessary to counteract the actions of a ruthless enemy. Reagan's National Security Adviser Robert C. McFarlane articulated such a justification for covert actions in his testimony before the Iran-*contra* committee:

> We aren't in competition with a democratic opponent. For the other side, unrestrained covert actions are a way of life, and just as they support Leninist political parties in developing countries, we had better be able to use a range of means to support people who aspire to freedom, or they will perish and our own freedom, as we know it, will be in jeopardy.[13]

For Cold Warriors, American democratic values, such as openness, had to be set aside while the twin menaces of Soviet power and communist ideology were fought.

Even though the end of the Cold War has demolished this rationale, the habits of classifying and keeping secrets remain key features of the national security state. The CIA and other agencies continue to classify millions of documents and resist efforts to declassify—including documents related to long-past operations. Today the CIA is still dragging its feet in declassifying documents from its

1954 coup in Guatemala, the 1953 coup in Iran that installed the Shah, and the 1961 Bay of Pigs invasion, years after any justification for keeping the secrets.[14] This refusal persists despite numerous public promises to declassify historical records. The CIA has succeeded also in keeping even the size of its budget secret, in spite of repeated promises by its own director and by President Clinton that the information would be made public.[15] The long-standing classification of intelligence expenditures is in direct violation of the constitutional requirement that "a regular Statement and Account of the Receipts and Expenditures of all public Money shall be published from time to time." In this, as in many other aspects of the national security state, the U.S. Constitution is deemed not to apply.

Even democracies sometimes need to keep secrets when the success of a government or military action must not be known in advance if it is to succeed. For example, no one would object to government officials keeping secret the time and place of a wartime military attack, such as the invasion of Normandy in 1944 or the date of a planned devaluation of national currency.[16] Unfortunately, very few of the six million new classified documents each year relate to these necessary secrets. More often secrecy is a means for government officials to pursue actions that do not have public and congressional support, to deceive the public about the effectiveness of policies, and to protect themselves from legitimate public scrutiny in order to escape future accountability for their actions. Since the 1940s, government officials have used the instrumentalities of secrecy to deceive the American public as routinely as they have sought to deceive foreign enemies. Even though government classification and covert actions have been justified as needed to combat our enemies, government officials have succumbed frequently to the temptation to use secrecy to combat domestic opponents of their policies.

In a democratic society, disagreement about the wisdom of pursuing a particular policy is supposed to produce discussion and debate about that policy until agreement among, at least, a majority can be reached on a course of action. Pursuing a controversial course of action in secret to avoid this public discussion of public policy constitutes the most serious way secrecy can undermine democracy. A most egregious use of secrecy to conceal a policy without democratic support was the Iran-*contra* affair in the 1980s.

Reagan administration policy in Central America was one of the most controversial foreign policy issues of the era. Continuing policies dating back to the 1950s, Reagan's policy was to support brutal military regimes in the region in the name of fighting communist subversion.[17] Critics of this policy argued that the terror, murder, and war that these American-supported regimes directed at their own people were more of a threat to the emergence of democratic politics there than was "communist subversion." Much of the conflict between the Reagan administration and its critics centered around American policy toward the Sandinista government in Nicaragua that had come to power in 1978 in a popular overthrow of the American-backed military dictator Anastasio Somoza.

The Reagan administration viewed the Sandinista government as a source of communist subversion, and in 1980 CIA Director William Casey began to promote another bloody war in the region through support of a group of anti-Sandinista guerillas called the *contras*. Within a few months, as the *contra* army grew and began mounting terrorist attacks in northern Nicaragua, members of Congress began to question the arms interdiction cover story and to criticize U.S. support for the *contras*. Critics pointed out that the *contras*, a mercenary army led by former officers in Somoza's National Guard, were not likely to gain popular support or bring democracy to Nicaragua. Moreover, in supporting the *contras*, the United States was violating international law: it was interfering in the domestic politics of a country whose government the United States officially recognized as legitimate. Because of these considerations, in October 1984 Congress passed the Boland Amendment, which explicitly prohibited the CIA or "any other agency or entity of the United States involved in intelligence activities" from providing support to the *contras*. In spite of this prohibition, Casey and other Reagan administration officials were determined to find a way to continue getting money to the *contras*.

Casey turned to a member of the staff of the National Security Council (NSC), Marine Lieutenant-Colonel Oliver North, to take charge of finding alternative means of *contra* support. To do so, North resorted to new levels of deception and manipulation. Since the Boland Amendment explicitly forbade the use of U.S. government funds to support the *contras*, North set up a mechanism to raise "private" donations from a variety of sources. The most important sources were contributions from other countries, such as Saudi Arabia and Brunei. North also turned to a private foundation, the National Endowment for the Preservation of Liberty, to raise funds for the *contras* among a handful of wealthy Americans. Later congressional investigations and court testimony revealed that North and other American officials had repeatedly misled and lied to congressional committees about their *contra* funding solicitations.

At the same time he was organizing this covert network to fund the *contras*, North was organizing another secret network for a different purpose. In late 1984 a number of shadowy individuals, Middle Eastern arms dealers and former intelligence agents, contacted NSC staffers claiming that elements in the Iranian government could bring about the release of American hostages, then being held in Lebanon by Iranian-supported groups, if the United States would sell sophisticated American missiles to Iran. The Iranians were at that time in the midst of a bloody eight-year war with Iraq and were known to be anxious to obtain weapons. Proponents of this deal also held out the possibility that the deal would lead to a moderation of Iran's virulent anti-Americanism and improve U.S.-Iranian relations.

Beginning in mid-1985, North organized several shipments of American TOW and Maverick missiles to Iran using a complex network of CIA, Department of Defense (DOD), and Israeli intelligence resources, private arms merchants, and former military and intelligence officers. This network, the "enterprise," would obtain the weapons from the DOD, then sell them to Iran.[18] These profits from this enterprise, deposited in secret Swiss bank accounts, gave Oliver North a "neat idea." Why not use the money from the Iranian arms sales to support the *contras?* This is exactly what happened. Without informing or obtaining authorization from either Congress or (according to Ronald Reagan) the president, North, with the approval of his superior, National Security Adviser John Poindexter (a U.S. Navy admiral), began funneling the Iranian arms sales profits to the *contras.* North and Poindexter, with the encouragement of CIA Director Casey, had established within the government a secret government that used governmental resources to promote their own policy agenda. A handful of men, insulated from any legal or democratic accountability, had obtained resources to pursue a policy that had been prohibited through existing constitutional procedures. Later, both North and Poindexter would justify their actions by claiming that the national security required it. Democrats should question, however, how Poindexter and North arrogated to themselves alone the responsibility for determining what the national security required.

Secrecy not only creates opportunities for deception about what government is doing but also allows deception regarding the effectiveness of public policies. In *The Pentagon Papers,* a secret report on the Vietnam War prepared by the Defense Department in the 1960s, repeated instances of this sort of deception are documented.[19] Throughout the war, various officials in the CIA, the military, and the Defense Department lied and released distorted information to the public, Congress, and even their administrative superiors about the progress of the war. These distortions were intended to maintain support for continuing the war by underestimating the strength of the Vietcong and overestimating the military successes of South Vietnamese and U.S. troops. This manipulation of information contributed to the prolongation of a disastrous policy.[20] Had more Americans, critics and supporters of the war alike, both in and out of government, had less distorted accounts of what was actually happening in Vietnam, the war might have ended much earlier, saving thousands of American and Vietnamese lives.

The national security state has become a convenient way for many officials to avoid criticism for policy failures, even long after the fact. For example, the CIA kept secret for thirty-seven years a detailed 1961 report of the policy mistakes that led to the disastrous Bay of Pigs invasion of Cuba in 1960 merely to escape the critical scrutiny release of the report would have caused.[21] Sometimes secrecy under the guise of national security has allowed officials to avoid public scrutiny of their actions even when those policies have consequences harmful to citizens. Recent revelations about the management of government-owned nuclear power plants that used to produce plutonium and other forms of enriched uranium provide numerous examples of this phenomenon.[22] Over a period of nearly forty years, these plants frequently discharged nuclear contaminants into the air and water supplies of neighboring communities. Because of the security surrounding their activities, this pollution was not monitored by any government agency, including the AEC, which overlooked the health risks of these plants in the interest of maximizing production of nuclear weapons. People who lived in these areas or worked in the plants now suffer from abnormally high rates of cancer and other diseases. Citizens were unable to evaluate the tradeoffs between production of nuclear weapons and the health risks of such production because the potential for these risks was hidden. Even if the public had decided that the need for the weapons merited some measure of risk, those most affected, the plant workers and neighbors, were never allowed to choose the extent to which they were willing to subject themselves to this risk.

Secrecy not only undermines democratic policymaking, but there is some evidence from our experience with the national security state that secrecy can produce very bad policy. Most serious U.S. foreign policy failures have followed from initiatives taken in secret. By making decisions in secret, policymakers have not had their plans critically evaluated by people outside the small circle making the policy. The foolishness of such policy decisions as the Bay of Pigs invasion and the Iran-*contra* arms-for-hostages deal would have been quickly exposed had they not been made in secret. As Senator Daniel Patrick Moynihan has said: "The secrecy system protects intelligence errors, it protects officials from criticism. Even with the best of intentions the lack of public information tends to produce errors; the natural corrective—public debate, academic criticism—are missing."[23] In addition to shielding bad decisions from scrutiny, the deception that often accompanies secret actions can lead to self-deception on the part of policymakers who come to believe the web of lies they weave to cover their actions. The political philosopher Hannah Arendt has written eloquently about how such self-deception led architects of American policy in Vietnam to make bad decisions again and again.[24] Better and wiser government has always been a chief virtue of democracy. It only follows that, by undermining democracy, secrecy fails to achieve wise government.

CENTRALIZATION

All presidents since the rise of the national security state have sought to broaden their control over foreign and military policy. They have tended to interpret their constitutional role in such a way as to exclude all, except for a close circle of advisers, from participation in some of the most important decisions affecting the life of the nation. Although the U.S. Constitution provides that Congress and the presidency shall share responsibilities for foreign affairs and defense, post–World War II presidents have been successful in asserting their constitutional prerogatives and using their control of the apparatus of the national security state to concentrate practical control of national security decisions in their own hands. Treaty making, which requires Senate participation, has often been replaced with executive agreements, which do not. The president's power to be commander-in-chief has frequently been the justification for military action initiated by the president without congressional or public involvement. Throughout this period, public participation in major foreign policy decisions usually has been limited to the public's being informed after the fact of decisions made and actions taken. By the 1990s, presidential autonomy to make major public decisions without consulting anyone has come to be accepted as normal in our government. This is a rather odd state of affairs for a democracy.

Since 1945, numerous military actions, including two major wars, have been presidentially initiated without public or congressional consultation. The first major assertion of presidential war-making power came in 1950 when President Truman sent American troops to fight in Korea under the auspices of the United Nations. Describing the war as a "police action," Truman claimed that action under a UN resolution relieved him of the constitutional requirement to seek a congressional declaration of war. Fifteen years later, Presidents Kennedy and Johnson gradually involved American forces in a major war in Vietnam without significant congressional participation.[25] Throughout that war, Presidents Kennedy, Johnson, and then Nixon made all the crucial decisions about its management mainly with contempt for attempts from Congress or the public to influence those decisions. When a sizable antiwar movement developed to attempt to influence their decisions democratically, both Johnson and Nixon ignored the movement, dismissing it as subversive. In addition to these major wars, numerous smaller military actions have been undertaken throughout the world — in places such as the Dominican Republic, Grenada, and Iran. In addition to these uses of force, presidents have managed individually a variety of "crises," including one — the Cuban missile crisis — that nearly led to a nuclear war, without concern for involving other public officials in a meaningful way.

Until the Vietnam period, most Americans and especially Congress acquiesced to presidential dominance of the national security state. The mobilization against communism and an ideology of "bipartisanship" in foreign affairs made dissent from presidential initiatives difficult. As disaffection with the Vietnam War grew, however, many Americans began to question the wisdom of the growth of presidential war-making and foreign policy powers. Some, such as historian Arthur Schlesinger Jr., worried about the growth of an "imperial presidency" that was at odds with both the Constitution and democratic values.[26] Revelations in *The Pentagon Papers* about presidential deception and manipulation of public opinion during the Vietnam War provided considerable support for these arguments.

In response to these concerns, Congress passed the War Powers Act in 1973, over President Nixon's veto. This legislation was supposed to limit the ability of presidents to involve the nation unilaterally in military conflict without the participation of Congress. The act required the president to consult with Congress before sending troops into hostilities, to inform it in writing within forty-eight hours of the reasons for a military action, and to limit involvement to sixty days unless explicit congressional approval is obtained.

Although the War Powers Act seems to represent a restraint on presidential war power, in practice it has not significantly reduced unilateral presidential control in this area. Every president since the act was passed has claimed that it is unconstitutional, infringing on the president's power as commander-in-chief, despite the absence of any cogent legal justification of such a claim.[27] Each has initiated at least one military action without complying with the requirement that Congress be formally consulted in advance. Although Presidents Ford, Carter, Reagan, and Bush obeyed the requirement to inform Congress within forty-eight hours of the use of military force, all refused to acknowledge the authority of the act in doing so. Nearly three decades after its passage, the War Powers Act has not been effective in restraining presidential war power or broadening democratic control of war-making decisions.

The highly centralized and presidentially dominated process that led to the 1991 Gulf War provides further illustration of the failure of the War Powers Act to democratize decisions of the national security state. From the beginning of the Gulf crisis, when Iraq's President Saddam Hussein invaded Kuwait on 2 August 1990, President Bush and a very small circle of advisers made all the critical decisions about the war.[28] Although Congress eventually passed a resolution supporting the war, there is little evidence that Bush and his advisers ever regarded congressional authorization as needed before initiating hostilities. Their ability to manage the development of the crisis allowed them to control the movement to war, leaving Congress little choice but to acquiesce in their policy.

When Iraq invaded Kuwait in August, Bush immediately dispatched a large force to defend Saudi Arabia without informing Congress or seeking its approval. Unlike his immediate predecessors, who had at least technically complied with the War Powers Act even while denying its constitutionality, Bush refused to send to Congress within forty-eight hours the formal explanation that the act required. Significantly, no real protest arose in Congress. In late October, Bush made a critical decision to double the size of the force in Saudi Arabia so that it would be capable of mounting successful offensive operations, although the decision was not publicly announced until 8 November. When an administration official was asked for an explanation of the delay, he said, "November 8 was a very important date because it was after November 6" (the congressional election).[29] Bush clearly did not want the public to have the opportunity to react democratically to any of his war decisions.

After the buildup to offensive capability, many in Congress began to press for a congressional declaration of war before any hostilities could begin.[30] Initially, the Bush administration opposed any such congressional action. Only when, in January, it seemed likely that a majority of Congress would support the war did the administration stop opposing a vote. Although Bush eventually decided to ask Congress for a resolution authorizing military action, he never acknowledged that he would be bound by a congressional decision.[31] Eventually, a majority in both houses supported a war resolution, and the appearance of congressional authorization for what the president wanted was in place.

Despite the formal congressional authorization of the war, it is unlikely that this incident represents a new assertion of congressional control over the national security state. The president's control of the military allowed him to create a situation that made it very difficult for members of Congress to vote against his policy. Many clearly feared that opposition to the president would be interpreted by voters and used by political opponents as a lack of support for the 500,000 soldiers by that time prepared for battle in Saudi Arabia. These fears were largely confirmed when, after the successful conclusion of the war, some members of the president's party began to label those who had voted against the war resolution "traitors."[32] It seems unlikely that memories of the Gulf War decision process will incline future members of Congress to assert themselves in controlling the president's war power.

President Clinton, like his predecessors, has claimed a unilateral authority to deploy military force. In Haiti, Bosnia, and Kosovo, he claimed no need to seek congressional consent because "the Constitution leaves the President, for good and sufficient reasons, the ultimate decision-making authority."[33] Both the Bush and Clinton presidencies now provide ample evidence that presidential usurpation of the power to make war was no Cold War anomaly. Centralized presidential control over the use of military power is a permanent feature of the national security state.

Some people argue that foreign policy decisions must be highly centralized because democracies are ill equipped to make the kinds of decisions required in a hostile world.[34] This is a point of view with a long history, originating perhaps with Tocqueville in the 1830s, and it underpins much of the centralization of decision making in the national security state. Critics of democratic control of foreign policymaking make three basic points.[35] First, decisions about foreign affairs are said to require expert knowledge unavailable to ordinary citizens. Only elite advisers to the president, with access to secret information, are equipped to know what policy ought to be adopted. Too much influence from outsiders undermines the capacity for competent policymaking.

Second, democracy is often accused of undermining the capacity to be decisive and make clear and unambiguous choices. Supposedly, foreign adversaries are able to take advantage of the policy conflicts that democratic debate over policy usually engenders. Centralized decision processes insulated from democratic controls are thought to allow clear expression of policy choices, preventing one's enemies from exploiting disagreements.

Third, centralized decisions permit continuity and long-range policy planning. This was a key concern of Tocqueville, who feared that a democracy had "little capacity for combining measures in secret and waiting patiently for the result."[36] Democratic pressures on policymakers are supposed to create pressures for immediate satisfactions that often cannot be achieved in foreign policy.

These are familiar accusations, but democrats have strong replies to them. In regard to the need for expertise in foreign policy there can be little quarrel. Problems related to national security and relations with other nations, by their very nature, involve specialized information and benefit from the insights of experts. But is bringing to bear such expertise more or less likely when decisions are highly centralized?

The American experience over the past forty years suggests that highly centralized decisions are more likely than open democratic processes to exclude relevant expertise. As the psychologist Irving Janis has pointed out, decision making by a small policy group is prone to a phenomenon he calls "groupthink," in which independent critical thinking about problems is systematically excluded. In his now-classic study of the phenomenon, he found that a number of crucial American foreign policy failures, including the Bay of Pigs and the escalation of the Vietnam War, were subject to groupthink.[37] Information and expert points of view that could have prevented serious policy mistakes were ignored by decision makers, who formed a tight little group reinforcing a conventional set of views. One antidote to groupthink is democratic participation in decision making that brings a variety of expert opinions to bear on a problem.

Decisiveness may contribute to national security, but it also may be a problem if policymakers are decisive in pursuing foolish policies. In the Iran-*contra* affair, for example, Colonel North and his friends were decisive, certainly, in pursuing trading arms for hostages once they decided on the policy. But this very decisiveness resulted in an extremely unwise policy. Had their plans been exposed to scrutiny and democratic debate, a disastrous policy action would have been decisively prevented. The same could be said about most of the covert actions during the Cold War. Democracy may slow down policy action. But, once decided, policies may be wiser and undoubtedly more supportable by citizens than those made by a handful of policymakers in secret.

Finally, there is little evidence that democratic societies are unable to support long-term policy initiatives. Empirical studies of public opinion and the experience of democratic nations show public opinion in democracies can sustain such initiatives.[38] The American public, for example, has been quite willing to support long-term foreign commitments over extended periods, such as Marshall Plan support for Europe and NATO, when a convincing case for these policies has been made. Sustained support has been more problematic for questionable policies, such as intervention in Central America, where leaders have not been able to make a convincing case. The difference between the Marshall Plan and support for the *contras* was not the degree of "elite autonomy to support long-term policies," but the wisdom of the policies. Leaders in democratic societies do not need to insulate themselves from public control to manage effective foreign policy. Instead, they need to develop policies that a democratic citizenry can support.

REPRESSION

At the heart of American democracy for most Americans are the liberties guaranteed in the Bill of Rights. Freedom to say what you think, organize politically, and associate with whomever you wish are considered key elements of the American way of life. Unfortunately, time and again the national security state has put these fundamental liberties at risk. In the name of protecting society from foreign threats, usually from "communists" or "subversives," government officials have spied on citizens, read their mail, intimidated them, discredited them, forced them from their jobs, and in some cases imprisoned them. The period of the Cold War provides the worst examples of governmental efforts to repress free political activity in American history. Ironically, at a time when the nation was supposedly mobilizing to resist an international threat to its freedom, the national security state was constructing an internal security apparatus that systematically robbed many Americans of their basic freedoms.

The use of foreign threats as an excuse to violate the civil liberties of Americans was not a tactic invented during the Cold War. As early as the 1790s, a few short years after the ratification of the Bill of Rights, the administration of John Adams passed the Alien and Sedition Acts for the ostensible purpose of protecting the new American nation from political ideas and agitation emanating from the French Revolution. Like subsequent experiences, the foreign threat from French revolutionaries was much exaggerated to justify this repressive legislation, and the Adams Federalist government used its provisions more often to harass their political opponents, the Democratic-Republicans, than to ferret out French subversives. During the Cold War, a foreign threat, communist subversion, again was used to justify extraordinary and often secret internal security actions, but as in the 1790s, these actions were often directed simply at those who dissented from mainstream political views or at the political opponents of those in power. By the 1950s and 1960s, the large police bureaucracies of the national security state made these actions more fundamentally threatening to the health of American democracy than had been true in the 1790s, when no such national security bureaucracies existed.

The core of the internal security component of the national security state was the FBI, and its architect was the agency's renowned director, J. Edgar Hoover.[39] Before World War II, the FBI built its reputation on its activities in combating such crimes as kidnapping and bank robbing and in battling gangsters such as John Dillinger. Its image as an apolitical law enforcement institution was a critical part of Hoover's strategy in building support for the bureau in Congress and among the public in the 1920s and 1930s. Hoover emphasized that, unlike domestic intelligence agencies in other countries, the FBI was concerned with fighting crime, in association with local police departments, not monitoring political activity. This stance undercut potential critics, who feared a national police organization would undermine civil liberties and democratic politics.

The bureau's experience in World War II profoundly affected the image of the agency and its director. In 1936, in anticipation of the coming military conflict, President Franklin Roosevelt secretly instructed Hoover to begin a program of systematic surveillance of "subversive" political groups, particularly groups friendly to Nazi Germany.[40] Hoover interpreted his instructions quite broadly and eagerly began collecting information using diverse methods: illegal wiretaps, mail opening, and break-ins. Although Roosevelt was most concerned about the activities of pro-Nazi groups, Hoover, who had a lifelong obsession with communist subversion, made sure equal concern was focused on left-wing groups. Once the war began, the wartime crisis was seen to justify such activities, and Hoover began to publicize the bureau's successes in capturing Nazi spies and foiling Nazi sympathizers. The role of monitoring "subversive" political activity, which in the 1930s might have raised the concerns of civil libertarians, only expanded FBI support in the heat of war. No one worried about FBI surveillance, even with its constitutionally questionable methods, as long as it was directed against foreign enemies. By 1945, the public had come to admire Hoover and his FBI as leaders of the domestic struggle against our wartime enemies.

With the end of the war, Hoover found a new set of foreign enemies to combat: communists. Thereafter, instead of being eliminated, the FBI's internal security apparatus was maintained and expanded as a permanent part of the national security state. Support for its continuation was provided in the atmos-

Fire engulfs the Branch Davidian compound near Waco, Texas, as federal agents seek to drive out cult members suspected of subversive activities. (AP/ Wide World Photos)

phere of anticommunist hysteria that developed in the late 1940s. Through the efforts of ambitious politicians such as Joseph McCarthy and Richard Nixon, concern for foreign communist subversion was shifted subtly to a concern for the "loyalty" of individual Americans. In 1947, under pressure from a Republican Congress and Hoover, the Truman administration established a loyalty and security program that required government boards, with the assistance of the FBI, to review the loyalty of all federal employees.[41] Soon, similar efforts were established in state and local governments and throughout the private sector. Legislation also was passed to provide a legal basis for the political surveillance of Americans. The 1950 Internal Security Act required members of communist and so-called communist-front organizations to register with the attorney general, with imprisonment the penalty for failing to do so.

This law, along with the wartime Smith Act, which made it a crime to advocate the "violent overthrow of the government," gave the FBI and the Justice Department the ability to legitimize political surveillance as a criminal "law enforcement" activity. A wide range of political activity was criminalized in this way. In order to investigate a political activity, the FBI needed only to label it subversive or related to an organization supposedly advocating the overthrow of the government to justify placing it under observation. Since one could discover if organizations or people violated either of these acts only by placing them under surveillance, the FBI used its discretion to monitor any suspicious group, a category that included more groups as the years passed.

In its COMINFIL program to determine the degree of communist subversion in America, the FBI infiltrated thousands of organizations and kept files on thousands of individual Americans. Almost any liberal or left-wing group was considered sufficiently suspect to merit coverage in the COMINFIL program; groups included the American Friends Service Committee, the National Association for the Advancement of Colored People (NAACP), and the American Civil Liberties Union (ACLU). In the 1950s, about one-third of the FBI's entire investigative force (1,600 agents) was involved in such work, with the help of about 5,000 informants.[42] Group surveillance included warrantless mail openings, break-ins, and wiretaps. Secret files were created to maintain records derived from this illegal surveillance.

Not content simply to gather information about supposedly subversive groups, the FBI in its COINTELPRO program involved itself actively in manipulating groups to influence and disrupt their activities. Through COINTELPRO, the FBI became an active force in influencing the political process. One of the most outrageous episodes involved a decade-long effort to undermine Dr. Martin Luther King Jr. and his Southern Christian Leadership Conference (SCLC). Using as an excuse suspicions about the alleged Communist Party ties of one of Dr. King's advisers (although Hoover's lifelong antipathy to civil rights of blacks probably was a prime motivator), COINTELPRO leaked manufactured stories about Dr. King's personal life and financial affairs to the press and political opponents.[43] In the 1960s, similar efforts were mounted against the anti-Vietnam War movement, nearly all civil rights organizations, and critics of Hoover and the FBI. Justified as necessary to protect the country's national security, the FBI's COMINFIL and COINTELPRO programs became general efforts to monitor and disrupt any and all political groups that displeased Hoover and other FBI officials.

The FBI was not the only component of the national security state involved in repressing dissent and interfering in domestic politics. In the mid-1970s, a major congressional investigation led by Senator Frank Church and a separate investigation by the presidentially appointed Rockefeller Commission found that, by the 1960s, political surveillance of domestic politics had become routine in a variety of agencies.[44] In spite of an explicit prohibition against domestic activity, the CIA maintained Operation CHAOS to monitor the supposed foreign ties of domestic political groups, especially the New Left. The military services, under the cover of planning for civil disturbances, monitored a wide range of "left-wing" and "dissident" groups. Paralleling similar programs in the FBI and CIA, the National Security Agency operated its own mail opening and wiretaps of Americans. The Internal Revenue Service, in cooperation with the COINTELPRO program, targeted for audit and special treatment the tax returns of thousands of individuals because of their political activities, including Nobel Prize–winning chemist Linus Pauling and Los Angeles Mayor Tom Bradley. Beyond these federal government agencies, many state and local agencies and police departments maintained political surveillance and disruption activities.

The Church committee investigation of the domestic side of the national security state documented what many frequent targets of these activities had long suspected about the consequences of the preoccupation with foreign subversion. National security had become a blanket excuse to interfere massively in domestic democratic politics. Individuals with dissident or sometimes merely unusual political views were spied on, intimidated, and prevented from exercising the opportunity to try to influence government. During the worst of these abuses, in the 1950s and 1960s, the quality of American democracy was enormously diminished.

After the revelations in the 1970s, all the agencies involved claimed to have reformed their procedures to forestall a repetition of the revealed abuses. Today, those running the FBI and the other implicated agencies claim that the political interference of the past cannot happen again. Also, with the end of the Cold War, the psychological climate that served to justify blatantly unconstitutional and undemocratic practices is gone. Nevertheless, in spite of minor procedural safeguards enacted in the aftermath of the Church committee report, the FBI and other agencies retain the same capacity for abuse that they have had since the inception of the national security state. And even though the Cold War is over, national security bureaucrats easily find new and fearsome enemies, such as "international terrorists" and "the international drug cartel," to support their interfering with political rights. In recent years, new revelations have been made of violations of individual rights and interference in democratic politics in the name of national security. In the early 1980s, the FBI conducted a massive probe of the Committee in Solidarity with the People of El Salvador (CISPES), reminiscent of the COMINFIL and COINTELPRO programs. Again in a style reminiscent of the 1960s, the FBI tried to justify targeting CISPES by reference to supposed "terrorist" activities. But its surveillance actually focused on legitimate political dissent concerning Reagan administration policy in Central America.[45] In spite of assimilating massive amounts of information about CISPES, the FBI was unable to document any instance of the organization's supporting domestic terrorism or any other illegal activity. The probe continued, however, for several years. Abuses of this kind seem very likely to continue as the FBI monitors the political activities of a wide variety of groups. A 1990 report of the General Accounting Office documents nearly 20,000 FBI political investigations between 1982 and 1988 involving monitoring "religious services, political lectures, and street demonstrations attended by people who were not suspected of any criminal activity or membership in any terrorist group."[46] Perhaps less blatant than the political repression of twenty and thirty years ago, the security activities of the FBI and other agencies remain a significant threat to the ability of citizens to involve themselves freely in political activity without fear of harassment or retaliation. Even the end of the Cold War has not ended potential abuse in the name of such new "national security" concerns as terrorism and the war on drugs.

DISTORTION

The creation of the national security state has had a dramatic impact on the distribution of power and influence in American society. The civilian national security bureaucracies, the military services, and the defense industry (usually referred to as the military-industrial complex) have acquired an enormous amount of political power. For the past fifty years, this power has been used to bias public policy in favor of large levels of defense expenditures and an aggressive foreign policy. Even if one accepts the necessity for a substantial defense sector in the contemporary world, the self-interested pressures of the military-industrial complex have served to enlarge that sector beyond what it would otherwise be. Less biased observers have to wonder if most citizens would have chosen the immense defense establishment we now have without the pressures of this special interest. Partisans of democracy should be concerned that the political power of the military-industrial complex distorts in fundamental ways the operation of our democracy.

Since the creation of the national security state, the defense industry has been the nation's largest single industrial sector. A wave of consolidation in the weapons industry in the post–Cold War period, partly subsidized by taxpayers, now means that three gigantic firms, Lockheed Martin, Boeing, and Raytheon, are responsible for most weapons production.[47] In addition, nearly all large U.S. corporations, including such industrial giants as General Electric and General Motors, are involved in some defense contracting. More than 3 million jobs in plants located in nearly every American community are directly linked to defense spending.[48] The post–World War II decision to establish such a large defense sector has had profound consequences for our economy and the structure of our industry. Unlike most of our industrial competitors, who have much smaller defense sectors, the U.S. investment in national defense has precluded making other important societal investments that would make our nation more competitive in the world economy.

Besides being economically important, the defense sector is politically important.[49] Since defense firms depend on governmental decisions for their business, they are very attentive to the need to exert maximum influence over government. They use their profits, earned from government contracts, to support lobbying activities and contribute to the campaigns of elected officials. The defense industry is a major source of campaign contributions, providing $32.2 million to candidates between 1991 and 1997, more money than another industry well-known for its campaign largess, the tobacco industry ($26.9 million).[50] Because many defense firms are major employers in congressional districts, they expect congressmen to be little more than errand boys for their needs. According to a former Defense Department official, referring to the largest employer in Massachusetts, "[Raytheon officials] assume that the Massachusetts delegation will go along with even the most dubious Raytheon defense program because, 'What is good for Raytheon is good for Massachusetts.'"[51] These links to Congress are matched by links to the Pentagon, where defense firms can generally count on a friendly reception. Highly paid positions in the defense industry are usually available for retired military and civilian defense bureaucrats. The cozy links between Congress, the Defense Department, and the defense industry make for one of Washington's strongest iron triangles of influence.

Because of these close relationships and the importance of defense spending for the economy, politicians seeking to expand the defense sector are able to manipulate the political system on behalf of their objectives. In the mid-1980s, Secretary of the Navy John Lehman was interested in obtaining congressional support for a massive expansion of the navy — the 600–ship navy.[52] He developed a program he called "home porting" that involved establishing new port facilities, at the cost of billions of dollars, in numerous cities on the Atlantic, Pacific, and Gulf coasts. The idea was to disperse the large concentrations of ships in existing ports to many smaller ports. Although he claimed the project was for strategic purposes, Lehman did not try to hide the obvious political advantages for the navy of all these home ports in so many states. He realized that increasing the number of home ports would expand the number of members of Congress with a naval presence in their districts, hence providing more support for the 600–ship navy.

The congressional clout of the defense industry has continued in the post–Cold War period as it has campaigned vociferously for policies that expand arms sales. Industry lobbying has been very effective in getting Congress to fund weapons programs, even those the Pentagon does not want. For example, Congress has mandated the purchase of 256 C-130 transport planes since 1978 even though the U.S. Air Force has requested only five![53] Not surprisingly, the C-130 happens to be built at a Lockheed Martin plant in Marietta, Georgia, the district of former House Speaker Newt Gingrich. Other weapons add-ons have included extra Sikorsky Black Hawk helicopters, F-16 fighters, and even a $1.5 million helicopter carrier for the Marines to be built in Senate Majority Leader Trent Lott's home state of Mississippi. Senator John McCain (R-Ariz.) estimates that unrequested congressional add-ons cost $2.5 million in the 1998 Pentagon budget alone.[54] These weapons add-ons create havoc in military budgets because

Congress rarely adds the funds needed to operate and maintain these additional weapons systems. As a consequence, military leaders have to take funds away from other needed programs, such as military pay increases and readiness training, to cover those costs. Paradoxically, excessive spending for military hardware creates shortages in needed programs and the appearance of the need for additional military spending — a situation Pentagon lobbyists have willingly exploited to expand overall spending.

Military sales abroad have been another area of growth for the military-industrial complex, and defense contractors have lobbied hard for foreign policies supporting such sales. For example, only a few weeks after the end of the 1991 Gulf War against Iraq, the Bush administration proposed the revival of a program to subsidize American arms exports to Third World countries. This happened even though the recent war with Iraq was possible only because Iraq's Saddam Hussein was able to buy massive armaments on the world market. Without access to such arms, Iraq, which has only a small arms industry of its own, never would have been a military threat. During the war, the Bush administration had said stopping arms sales to the likes of Saddam had to be a major priority, but at the end of the war it was proposing arms sales to many regions around the world that are as volatile as the Middle East and have dictators as ruthless as Saddam. The reason for the arms export initiative was the extent to which many American firms are dependent on arms exporting, a $16 billion component of the American economy. Even though arms sales might contribute to another war, the defense industry addiction to such sales pressured the Bush administration to recommend a revival of subsidies.[55] The United States, the world's largest weapons supplier, produces half of all weapons sold worldwide. In 1997 the Clinton administration approved Lockheed Martin's sale of F-16 fighter jets to Chile — a decision that some believe will start a South American arms race.[56] Clearly, this shows the extent to which the military-industrial complex distorts democratic politics. Consideration of what is in the best interest of all citizens, preventing future wars, is subordinated to the economic needs of the defense industry.

The economic needs and political pressures of the military-industrial complex demand ever more expensive and complex weapons systems even when there is no credible military rationale to justify them. The Pentagon wish list of high-tech weaponry remains long although collapse of the Soviet Union makes much of it unnecessary. The Center for Defense Information estimates that the United States could save more than $225 billion over the next ten years if advanced weapons systems, originally planned to counter Soviet power but still being promoted, were canceled.[57] One such unneeded but expensive high-tech weapon is the F-22 Stealth fighter currently being designed by Lockheed Martin. Costing $160 million each, this plane was intended to counter two advanced Soviet fight-

The F-22 Stealth fighter heads the Pentagon's wish list of expensive, high-tech weaponry despite the lack of a credible military rationale. (Boeing Media)

ers, neither of which is any longer a threat. Yet the air force wants to go forward with production of 438 of the new planes, although the existing F-16 fighter is capable of outflying any other plane in the world.[58] The United States now has a surplus of F-16s mothballed in the Arizona desert and is selling them to countries around the world. Rather than invest in a whole new fighter, several of our European allies are updating the F-16 with new electronics that provide advanced capabilities. The air force, however, intends to replace our F-16s with the F-22 even without a potential threat to justify the expense. Meanwhile, to justify construction of even more F-22s, air force planners have proposed selling some of them abroad, creating the potential that they could become a threat to our own forces. As one critic responded to this suggestion: "We're in an arms race — with ourselves."[59]

By going forward with design and production of unneeded weapons systems, a tremendous distortion is created in the federal budget. In a time when both Democrats and Republicans support spending restraint to prevent federal budget deficits, continued high levels of defense spending come at the expense of investments in better schools, mass transit systems, renewal of our crumbling highways and bridges, a cleaner environment, and maintenance of the national park system. All of these investments in the domestic economy would contribute to economic growth and greater prosperity for all Americans in the future.

While our economic competitors around the world are making such investments, our inflated defense budgets could undermine America's future economic security. In the name of "national security" against phantom military threats, the military-industrial complex promotes expenditures that may undermine national economic security.

The increasing power of the military-industrial complex has meant an increase in the political power not only of the defense industry but also of the military. As Harold Lasswell predicted when the national security state was young, the role of military officers in American politics has expanded considerably over the past fifty years.[60] In spite of the American tradition of civilian control of the military, more officers such as Lt.-Col. Oliver North have assumed posts in government that are politically sensitive and that, before the rise of the national security state, would certainly have been occupied by civilians. In recent years, close presidential advisers from military backgrounds have been common, whereas they were extremely rare prior to World War II. In the Reagan and Bush administrations, active-duty and retired military officers Brent Scowcroft, Robert McFarlane, Colin Powell, and John Poindexter occupied the post of national security adviser. The modern government has a much more militaristic coloration than has been the American tradition.

This new and enlarged role for military officers in government is a problem in a democracy for two reasons: the undemocratic ethos of military institutions and the military's potential to use its monopoly of force for undemocratic ends. Military organizations are authoritarian. They train their members to follow orders and respect the unified chain of command. The military value of obedience to authority is at odds with the skepticism of authority that is central to the democratic ethos. Training in the military does not prevent soldiers from participating as productive democratic citizens, but, when they do, they must set aside some of the values promoted in their professional training. Not surprisingly, many military officers find this difficult. Since socialization experiences influence the orientations of all people, one should expect the professional socialization of military personnel to be a factor in their orientation to politics. The decidedly authoritarian nature of military socialization poses a potential danger when soldiers are asked to play democratic roles.

The Iran-*contra* affair offers evidence of the dangers of military socialization for democracy. The two principal players in the affair, Oliver North and John Poindexter, were active-duty military officers on leave while they worked in their jobs on the National Security Council staff. In testimony to Congress, both suggested that their military training, particularly their perception of themselves in a unified chain of command under the president, contributed to their blindness to the constitutional and democratic requirement that they were also responsible to Congress and the public. By both, the president was regarded more as the commander-in-chief than a political leader in a democratic system. As North said in his testimony, "And if the commander-in-chief tells this lieutenant colonel to go stand in a corner and sit on his head, I will do so."[61] Such an outlook certainly contributed to North's willingness to carry out the policy of supporting the *contras,* a clear objective of the president, even though the democratic process did not produce the approval of Congress. Democratic procedures were ignored in favor of a good soldier's desire to obey his commander's orders.[62]

The example of North and his colleagues should caution us about the potential danger of the increasing prominence of military officers in what are essentially civilian policymaking positions. So far, the threat of this development in the national security state has contributed to only such minor incidents as the Iran-*contra* affair. Over the long run, however, the large involvement of military officers may undermine the overall sensitivity of government officials to democratic values. At the least, military officers as government officials might be willing to subordinate democratic values to pressing policy concerns, especially in times of crisis.

Crises in democratic systems always raise the specter of the military, in the name of stability and order, intervening directly to overturn democratically determined outcomes. Military coups against democratically elected governments are frequent and a constant threat in many democratic systems around the world. Fortunately, in the United States, the tradition of civilian control of the military and, in spite of the authoritarian character of the training, the broad support for the ideal of democratic politics in the military make this a relatively remote possibility. Yet, although most of us would like to believe that "it can't happen here," prudent democrats ought to think about the potential of some future crisis stimulating military intervention.

Throughout American history, the military's support for civilian control and our democratic system have not been the only factors limiting the likelihood of military coups. Until the rise of the national security state, the small size of the peacetime military establishment meant it had little chance to succeed even if it did attempt to intervene politically. In fact, removing the danger of military intervention was one of the main reasons for the traditional American bias toward small armies. With the increase in the size of the military services since 1945, this traditional constraint on military intervention is gone. Moreover, in recent years, the shift from a primarily conscript military to a professional army represents a further step away from the American tradition of a small peacetime army supplemented with citizen soldiers in time of danger.

Experience in most democratic countries indicates that professional armies are much more threatening to democratic politics in times of crisis than are conscript armies. Soldiers who are draftees, in the armed forces for only a short time, are much less likely to identify with their officers and obey unconstitutional or undemocratic orders than are soldiers who regard the service as a professional career. A conscript army is less likely to cooperate in a military coup than a professional one, as was illustrated in an attempt to overthrow the democratically elected French government in 1961.[63] In that year, a group of army officers revolted against the government, in opposition to President Charles de Gaulle's intention to grant independence to Algeria, where the French army had been fighting a guerrilla insurrection for nearly a decade. The officers' plan was to consolidate control of Algiers and then parachute into Paris and capture de Gaulle. In the first few hours, the plan went smoothly, as hardened professional paratroopers joined their rebellion. Soon, however, they ran into trouble because most of the French draftees, the bulk of the army, refused to go along with the plot. Within hours of its start, the coup collapsed. The outcome would have been much different had the French army in Algeria been an all-volunteer force. French democracy might have come to an abrupt end.

My intention in raising the example of the French experience is not to suggest that our professional army poses a direct threat to democracy. In the French situation, a particular history and the particular dynamics of the Algerian crisis produced the coup attempt. In addition, the willingness of French professional soldiers, as opposed to draftees, to participate in the coup does not mean that American professional soldiers would react in the same way. What the French case suggests, however, is that if we are to have a large, all-professional military, we need to look out for the possibility that such an army will behave undemocratically in a crisis. To prevent that, we need to devise measures to ensure the continued loyalty of our professional soldiers to democratic values. Also, we need to think continually about checks to assure continued civilian control and to prevent military distortion of democratic processes. The armed forces, if they act in a unified way, are the only societal institution capable of eliminating democratic institutions in one blow. Democrats would be foolish to rely solely on the goodwill of soldiers for the survival of democracy.

THE NATIONAL SECURITY STATE remains a challenge to American democracy. The first few post–Cold War years have proven the staying power of national-security-related secrecy, centralization, repression, and distortion. The evaporation of the "Soviet threat" as justification for the national security state has brought to the fore its underlying rationale in the drive to preserve an international capitalist world order. The bipolar U.S.-Soviet confrontation proved an effective context for the growth of the national security state, but now that it is so deeply rooted in the American political system, even the end of the Cold War has not brought about fundamental change.

Without a Soviet threat, Pentagon planners have easily identified new potential threats to justify a massive military establishment. In its 1993 Quadrennial

Defense Review, the DOD identified the need to fight two simultaneous regional conflicts against "rogue states," such as Iraq, North Korea, Libya, or Iran, as justification for $250 billion annual budgets far into the future.[64] Four years later, the Pentagon Quadrennial Defense Review retained rogue states as a key reason for high military expenditures even though none of the potential "rogues" had developed into a credible threat.[65] None have mounted any serious threats to U.S. interests, none seem close to any breakthroughs in nuclear or chemical weapons, and all face major internal challenges that inhibit any serious military threat. North Korea, with the largest military establishment among the "rogue states," was tottering under the effects of a massive famine in 1997. Iraq remained an international outcast and militarily disabled from its loss in the Persian Gulf War. Nearly twenty years after coming to power, the Iranian regime ruled over a stagnant economy that supported military expenditures of about 1 percent of what the United States spends. As the credibility of the rogue-state theory declines, Pentagon planners have begun to speak darkly about a possible future threat of a "peer state," perhaps China or a newly hostile and economically recovered Russia, for whom we must be prepared.[66] Although, given their present economic and military power, it would take many years for either to come close to matching America's military, the far-off future possibility, in the scenarios of Pentagon planners, justifies the national security state's massive budget.

If the threat of a particular nation-state cannot replace the Soviet threat as justification for the national security state, its defenders will turn to the forces of history. This is the approach of national security expert Samuel Huntington in an article in a prestigious foreign policy journal (now expanded into a book).[67] Huntington sees a future "clash of civilizations" as the new threat to American national security. Tensions between Western and non-Western civilizations, especially Islamic countries, will produce future political and military conflict. He reaches a predictable conclusion supportive of the continuation of the national security state: "[The clash of civilizations] will require the West to maintain the economic and military power necessary to protect its interests in relation to these civilizations."[68] The fact that America's first post–Cold War military conflict, the 1991 Gulf War, occurred in the Islamic world gives some credibility to those who would use the "Islamic threat" as the "communist threat" was used in the past. Whether it will be "rogue" or "peer" states or a "clash of civilizations," supporters of the national security state will devise some rationale to convince both themselves and their fellow citizens of its indispensability far into the future. For this reason, democrats must continue to be on their guard to prevent the national security state from challenging our democratic values and practices.

THOUGHT QUESTIONS

1. Is too much secrecy necessarily a problem in a democracy? In what ways might open political debate place democracies at a disadvantage in international politics?

2. In chapter 1, the argument was that the separation of powers allowed too little centralization of policy making in our government, yet this chapter argues that, when it comes to foreign policy, there has been too much centralized presidential control. How can these arguments be reconciled, or can they?

3. Most examples of repression described in this chapter date from the Cold War. To what extent might the abuses during this time have been the consequences of the extreme fear of Soviet power and thus be a diminished problem now? Or might fear of a military threat trigger similar abuses in the future? What sort of national security threat might have this consequence?

4. In the summer of 1999 the House Appropriations Committee eliminated funding for the F-22 Stealth fighter described in this chapter. Lockheed Martin, very much surprised by this event, vowed to have funding restored. Using some of the web sites suggested for this chapter, find out what happened to F-22 funding. Has funding been restored? If so, how? What efforts did Lockheed Martin make to restore funding? What is the likelihood that the F-22 will be built?

5. America's professionalized "volunteer" armed forces are presented in this chapter as a problem for democracy. However, in one respect — racial integration and equality — the U.S. Army is more democratic than the rest of American society. How might the professional and, even, authoritarian character of the army have helped it to promote integration?

SUGGESTIONS FOR FURTHER READING

Clifford, Clark. *Counsel to the President: A Memoir.* New York: Random House, 1991. A thoughtful memoir by one of the architects of the national security state.

Draper, Theodore. *A Very Thin Line: The Iran-Contra Affair.* New York: Hill and Wang, 1991. A dissection of the activities of Oliver North et al. based on tens of thousands of pages of transcripts from congressional hearings and judicial proceedings.

Fisher, Lewis. *Presidential War Power.* Lawrence: University Press of Kansas, 1995. America's leading scholar of presidential-congressional relations details how presidents have come to make war unilaterally. He makes a well-documented argument that they have done so unconstitutionally.

Greider, William. *Fortress America: The American Military and the Consequences of Peace.* New York: Public Affairs, 1998. A collection of articles originally published in *Rolling Stone,* detailing how we retain a Cold War military even without a Cold War.

Halperin, Morton H., Jerry J. Berman, Robert L. Borosage, and Christine M. Marwick. *The Lawless State: The Crimes of the U.S. Intelligence Agencies.* New York: Penguin Books, 1976. A summary of the findings of the various investigations of the national security state, such as the Church committee, conducted in the 1970s.

Hart, Gary. *The Minuteman.* New York: Free Press, 1998. A former United States senator shows how real military reform can restore the concept of a citizen army as the heart of national defense.

*Lord, Carnes. *The Presidency and the Management of National Security.* New York: Free Press, 1988. Lord served on the National Security Council staff during the Reagan years and argues here the need for greater centralization of presidential foreign policy power.

*Revel, Jean-François. *How Democracies Perish*. New York: Harper & Row, 1985. According to this author, democratic regimes are disadvantaged in their ability to conduct effective foreign policy.

Schlesinger, Arthur M., Jr. *The Imperial Presidency*. Boston: Houghton Mifflin, 1973. The classic study of the aggrandizement of presidential power over foreign and defense policy.

Theoharis, Athan G., and John Stuart Cox. *The Boss: J. Edgar Hoover and the Great American Inquisition*. Philadelphia: Temple University Press, 1988. A biography that shows the numerous ways in which the FBI was used to violate the political and civil rights of Americans.

White, John Kenneth. *Still Seeing Red: How the Cold War Shapes the New American Politics*. Boulder, Colo.: Westview Press, 1997. A thoughtful analysis of the Cold War's continuing impact on all aspects of American politics.

Woodward, Bob. *Veil: The Secret Wars of the CIA*. New York: Simon and Schuster, 1987. A history of William Casey's CIA that shows that the Iran-*contra* affair was part of a pattern of surreptitious foreign policy.

*Presents points of view that disagree with the arguments presented in this chapter.

SELECTED WEB SITES

http://www.businessleaders.org/home.htm Business people and retired military officers who advocate lower military spending.

http://www.ned.org/ The National Security Study Group, or Hart-Rudman Commission, is a Pentagon-appointed body charged with studying the security needs of the twenty-first century. Follow closely for signs of new thinking regarding the national security state.

http://www.csis.org/ An influential think tank that provides support to the national security state.

http://www.foreignpolicy-infocus.org/ Detailed reports offering a critical examination of the national security state.

Seven Steps toward Reform

We have frequently printed the word Democracy. Yet I cannot too often repeat that it is a word the real gist of which still sleeps. . . . It is a great word, whose history, I suppose remains unwritten, because that history has yet to be enacted.

— WALT WHITMAN

THIS BOOK HAS argued that American democracy is "in peril." Each of the seven challenges discussed in the previous chapters poses barriers to attaining the central democratic goals of popular sovereignty, liberty, and equality. Because the democratic pathologies defined by each challenge seem to have grown worse in recent years, I think that partisans of democracy are justified in using dramatic words such as *peril* to sound the alarm about undemocratic trends in American politics. To say American democracy is in peril, however, does not mean that it will perish tomorrow. Military coups or dictatorial takeovers are not a feature, thankfully, of our political history and tradition. An abrupt end to democratic practices is not the sort of peril we face. As the discussion in this book should have made clear, the challenges American democracy faces are much more subtle than coups or takeovers by avowed authoritarians. Each challenge produces a gradual erosion of democracy that most Americans are not likely to notice. The very subtlety of the challenge constitutes its danger and justifies the need for words like *peril, alarm, challenge,* and *danger* to describe their collective effects. If American democracy faced a well-organized authoritarian movement, mobilizing citizens to defend democracy would be relatively easy — the statements and actions of the authoritarians themselves would sound the peril to democracy. In the subtle challenges described in this book, showing that each challenge places democracy in peril must be demonstrated. This has been the objective of the book.

Opposite: *Former President Jimmy Carter's Habitat for Humanity advocacy exemplifies the community building effort needed to enhance American democracy. (Corbis)*

For those readers who have become convinced that the challenges described here place democracy in peril, a logical question to ask is, "What is to be done?" Throughout the book, in the discussion of each challenge, some suggestions have been made about how to reduce its harm to democracy. I have suggested reforms relevant to improving democracy as we have gone along. My main focus, however, has been to show how each challenge threatens democracy, rather than to propose concrete solutions. Finding out what needs to be done about the problems is itself a challenge to democracy and must be a product of democratic deliberation. Nevertheless, I would like to propose seven steps toward democratic reform that I think collectively would place us on the road toward counteracting the undemocratic effects of the challenges described in this book.

STEP 1: INSTITUTIONAL REFORM

Popular sovereignty, liberty, and equality can be realized only if democratic politics is conducted through institutions that encourage their realization. Chapter 1 argues that the set of institutional relationships we call the separation of powers impedes, rather than enhances, democracy. The specific reforms discussed in that chapter, such as presidential-congressional team tickets or congressional membership in the Cabinet, are intended to create a more unified governmental structure responsive and accountable to democratic majorities. A movement of constitutional reform to institute such changes would enhance democracy, just as past constitutional amendments made our politics more democratic.

Beyond these reforms in the separation of powers, other institutional changes are needed to address the challenges discussed in this book. The recently enacted "motor-voter" bill, which encourages state governments to register voters as they obtain their driver's licenses, is an institutional change that reduces a major barrier to voter participation. The effectively unregulated financing of recent campaigns, vastly increasing the clout of wealthy contributors, has placed campaign finance reform at the center of any institutional reform agenda. Some form of public financing of campaigns must replace the current financing system if we are to restore the principle of one person, one vote in our elections. These are all examples of institutional changes needed to enhance democracy.

I mention these examples of institutional reform as a reminder that continued attention to the structure of institutions is an imperative part of any serious movement to enhance democracy. The way in which institutions are structured can either enhance or diminish democracy. In all areas of political life, democrats need to think about and debate how governmental institutions might be modified to improve democracy. In addition, whenever any institutional reform comes on the policy agenda, attention must be paid to its potential impact on democratic values, even if the relevance of the contemplated reform to democracy is not immediately obvious.

STEP 2: BUILDING A COMMUNITARIAN MOVEMENT

Chapter 2 presents the case for Americans to adopt a communitarian outlook to counteract the antidemocratic effects of radical individualism. Thoughtful readers may have noted the relationship between this challenge to democracy and some of the other challenges. Radical individualism exacerbates the challenges that inequality, low participation, and the "privileged position" of business, to name but three examples, pose for democracy. Individualists, looking out for themselves, may have a difficult time even noticing inequality and the concerns of less fortunate Americans; understanding the implications of inequality for democracy is impossible for radical individualists. Disinterest in the public good is not likely to lead to the levels of participation needed for democracy. Business people lacking a communitarian outlook are not going to worry about how the exercise of their privileged position might harm a community. The concept of democracy is so intertwined with communitarian values that excessive individualism is part of all the challenges.

Promoting communitarian values within our political culture could ameliorate all the challenges discussed here; hence the imperative to build a communitarian movement. Fortunately, in recent years, a number of Americans have begun to build such a movement. Communitarians, such as the movement's leader, sociologist Amitai Etzioni, seek to renew communities and the sense of individual civic obligation in ways that enhance democracy. A communitarian perspective, in the words of "The Responsive Community Platform," "recognizes both individual human dignity and the social dimension of human existence... [and] that the preservation of individual liberty depends on the active maintenance of the institutions of civil society."[1] The communitarian movement promotes such an outlook through its journal, *The Responsive Community,* and numerous books and articles. In the few years since the issuance of their platform in 1991, communitarians have received much attention and have begun to have an impact on both public policy and national politics. They have been a force in the passage of community-supporting legislation such as the Family Leave Act and President Clinton's National Service Program. Communitarian themes in the speeches of the president and First Lady Hillary Clinton reflected the presence on the White House staff, in the first term, of political scientist and communitarian leader William Galston. Etzioni hopes the communitarian movement will have a reform impact in moderating excessive individualism and promoting community-regarding policies equivalent to the widespread policy impact of the Progressive movement.[2]

Inspiring young people to acquire an understanding of the importance of community through the performance of public service, as in the National Service Program, is a key part of the communitarian agenda. Besides Clinton's national program, a number of colleges and universities around the country have begun to include requirements for public service as part of their curriculums. At Providence College, for example, the Feinstein Institute for Public Service offers an academic major in public and community service studies that integrates student community service with specific courses on citizenship and the nature of political community. Similar programs have sprung up or are under consideration elsewhere. All reflect a sense that radical individualism in the United States has gone too far and that learning the value of community needs to be part of a liberal education.[3] These developments, and the communitarian movement generally, are a hopeful sign that this key challenge to democracy is being addressed.

STEP 3: BUILDING GRASSROOTS MOVEMENTS

Chapter 3 describes the emergence of grassroots citizen organizations in several cities, such as the COPS program in San Antonio and BUILD in Baltimore. These organizations are based on a premise familiar to such political theorists as Tocqueville and John Stuart Mill: People learn to be democratic citizens through involvement in solving local problems together. This "backyard" revolution of local citizen groups is one of the most heartening developments in contemporary American politics. The success of these localized efforts suggests that the democratic vision of the widespread participation of ordinary people in governing themselves remains alive despite the perils to democracy described in this book. Central to defeating these perils is the spread of grassroots democratic participation throughout the United States.

In his book *Strong Democracy,* the political theorist Benjamin Barber advocates institutionalization of grassroots movements through the creation of a system of neighborhood assemblies.[4] These assemblies would serve neighborhoods from 1,000 to 5,000 people and would be both arenas for collective action on local problems and places for deliberation about local *and* national political issues. No longer dependent on petitioning sometimes remote representatives, every citizen, according to Barber's vision, could go directly to his or her neighborhood assembly to voice concern on issues and to work with neighbors to lobby legislatures or city councils for neighborhood needs. Although Barber envisions these assemblies to be initially arenas for discussion, deliberation, and lobbying of existing representative bodies, he foresees that they could evolve into institutions with decision-making authority of their own on neighborhood matters. Like the New England town meeting or the Athenian Assembly, neighborhood assemblies would be places where direct democracy would be integrated as a component of representative democracy.

While the idea of a comprehensive system of neighborhood assemblies is far from a reality throughout the United States, similar systems are germinating in many cities. In cities as diverse as Birmingham, Portland, Dayton, and St. Paul, structures of neighborhood organizations linked to city governing bodies have taken on a powerful role in affecting municipal decisions and promoting citizen participation.[5] None of these experiments fits precisely Barber's model of citizen neighborhood assemblies, but all involve mechanisms that empower neighborhood residents and increase citizen efficacy. In Portland, for example, autonomous neighborhood associations encompassing the entire city are linked by seven District Coalition Boards.[6] Each board has its own budget and staff and works with the neighborhood groups to address neighborhood needs, organize crime-prevention teams, undertake neighborhood-based planning, and organize discussion of citywide issues. A major study of structures of neighborhood democracy in five cities, including Portland, found them to be successful in empowering citizens, increasing their sense of efficacy, and affecting municipal decision making.[7] Just as the Developmental and Participatory models predict, citizen participation in governance itself has created, in these cities, a more democratically capable and less apathetic citizenry. The spread of such urban experiments to other cities would be an important step toward reducing American democracy's peril.

STEP 4: PROMOTING DEMOCRATIC DELIBERATION

Finding ways to deliberate about public problems is difficult in a representative democracy. With responsibility for decision making centered in representative assemblies, it is easy for most citizens to become detached from thinking through problems themselves and to expect deliberation to be the exclusive concern of their representatives. Without direct involvement in democratic deliberation, citizens come to regard their role as solely one of pressuring on behalf of their special interests without regard for how their individual interests affect the interests of others or the broader public interest. Eventually, under self-interested constituency pressures, the ability of representatives to deliberate about public problems in a meaningful way is also diminished. In several chapters we saw the absence of democratic deliberation in American politics to be one of our perils. Chapter 4, in particular, documents the decline of meaningful deliberation in American elections. Another step toward reducing democracy's peril must be to create opportunities for meaningful citizen deliberation on public issues. Electronic technology offers some promise for creating opportunities for public deliberation. Televised town meetings, interactive cable systems, electronic mail, and CD-ROM access to public information are some of the ways advocates of better deliberation have proposed to involve citizens directly in the discussion of public issues. Advocates of these technologies claim they can link individual citizens into one giant electronic assembly for discussing, debating, and perhaps voting on public issues. Critics point out the danger of these same technologies becoming vehicles for demagogic manipulation for whoever controls the agenda of the electronic network. Unfortunately, some recent examples of "electronic democracy," such as Ross Perot's televised town meetings, have seemed to support the critics' fears. Unless electronic networks are organized carefully to provide for meaningful deliberation, they are more likely to imperil democracy than to promote it.

Utilization of electronic technology can be a component of promoting deliberation if organized properly, as in James Fishkin's proposal for "deliberative opinion polls," described in chapter 4. Yet, for all the potential for deliberation via electronic connections, we should not overlook the possibilities of structuring low-tech means of citizen deliberation. Sometimes, involving citizens in meaningful deliberation involves no more than getting people together in one room to talk. This is the basic premise behind an interesting experiment in public deliberation sponsored by the Kettering Foundation.[8] The Kettering National Issues Forums link about 3,000 civic and educational groups in the discussion of important public issues. Each local group is provided with well-prepared issue booklets providing background information and alternative "solutions" to a given public policy problem. After studying the issue booklets, group members get together to discuss what solution to adopt. An interesting feature of this process are pre- and postforum ballots on the issue under discussion that gauge how deliberation forms and alters a group's outlook on the issue. Results of the forums are collated by the foundation and distributed to public officials. So far, Kettering has organized National Issues Forums on nearly twenty issues, among them health-care reform, abortion, and the federal budget deficit. Such forums are an example of how citizens can be brought into democratic deliberation. Structuring similar opportunities for more citizens and integrating them into our formal governmental institutions would be a major step toward reducing democracy's peril.

STEP 5: REBUILDING POLITICAL PARTIES AND LABOR UNIONS

A theme of this book has been a concern for the hardening of categories of privilege in American society. Whether it is the privileged position of business or the privileges that generally follow from wealth, the economic advantages of some have created different classes of citizenship. The advantages of some for gaining access to government on behalf of their interests contrast with the growing powerlessness of ordinary citizens. In part, this situation derives from the class structure of a capitalist society that will always place those with access to wealth and capital, as argued in chapter 5, in a privileged position. But even within the constraints of a capitalist economy, ordinary workers and citizens can contain these privileges with the help of organizations that represent their interests. The experience of most capitalist democracies shows that the crucial institutions needed to advance the interests of most ordinary people are strong political parties responsive to their interests (in Europe these are usually labor or social democratic parties) and strong labor unions. The hardening of categories of privilege in contemporary America is a reflection of the weakness of these organizations. Rebuilding them has to be part of an agenda to revitalize democracy.

Neither political parties nor labor unions are particularly popular in the United States today. The history of party bossism combined with the Progressive reforms that undermined political parties, as described in chapter 5, have obscured in the minds of most Americans the connections between strong political parties and effective democracy. Labor unions, which represented nearly 40 percent of the workforce in the mid-1950s, represent only about 16 percent today and may represent only about 5 percent in the twenty-first century.[9] Nevertheless, political parties and labor unions are crucial to the representation of the interests of ordinary people. As argued in chapter 5, political parties reduce the bias of electoral representation because they need and organize the one political resource every ordinary citizen possesses: the vote. Labor unions not only represent the interests of workers in the workplace but also have been in the forefront of lobbying for public policies that help workers, such as minimum-wage laws, worker health and safety regulations, unemployment compensation, and national health insurance. The growing weakness of labor is part of the explanation for the reduction in social protections in the Reagan-Bush years and the difficulties Clinton faced in trying to restore some of them. The effort of the new AFL-CIO President John Sweeney to reverse the decline of labor through stepped-up union organizing should be supported for democratic reasons. Renewed labor unions will not only bring better wages and working conditions to average Americans, they will also increase their power as democratic citizens.

What labor unions and political parties have in common is that their strength depends on their ability to organize masses of people, not on their access to capital or wealth. Even political parties, which often seek financial support from the wealthy, depend ultimately not on their ability to attract contributions but on their ability to organize votes. As pointed out in chapter 5, the wealthy do not need to contribute to parties to gain influence; they can contribute directly to individual candidates. In the long run, catering to the wishes of the wealthy will be fatal to parties as they become increasingly irrelevant in candidate-centered elections. Political parties need the support of ordinary people to prosper; so, in a system with strong parties, ordinary citizens are empowered. Despite their current unpopularity, revitalization of political parties and labor unions is needed to counteract the power of privilege.

STEP 6: REVITALIZING AMERICA'S WELFARE STATE

Empowering a democratic citizenry requires more than appropriate and democratic political structures. Attention to the public weal cannot occur when people are preoccupied with obtaining the necessities of subsistence. Extreme economic inequality means that the poorest citizens will be unable to carry out their public responsibilities. Moreover, extremes of wealth and poverty divide citizens from one another and destroy their understanding of themselves as fellow citizens. For the good of democracy, then, government policies to reduce inequality and moderate economic want are essential not just on grounds of fairness, justice, and charity, but also in order to provide for common citizenship. As argued in chapter 6, the attack on the American welfare state over the past decade was also an attack on the quality of our democracy.

Revitalizing the welfare state means not only restoring some of the benefits lost in the past decade but reforming and expanding it. Part of the reason for the success of recent attacks on the welfare state stems from real flaws in the way many social programs have been organized. The universal condemnation of the former Aid to Families with Dependent Children (AFDC), or "welfare," is the prime example. Although welfare is only a small part of the entire welfare state, it has received the most attention among critics of programs that help the poor. AFDC was an easy target because it had few supporters, even among recipients. The welfare "reform" passed in 1996 that replaced AFDC with the new Temporary Assistance to Needy Families (TANF) moves the country in the wrong direction democratically. It abolished the sixty-year federal government commitment to provide a safety net of last resort for the neediest children and their mothers. Under the new law, states receive a fixed amount of funds each year to support welfare families, no matter what the extent of need. If the need exceeds available funds, states have the choice to meet the need from state revenues or to deny assistance. In the past few years, much attention has been given to the reduction in the numbers of welfare recipients since TANF passed, yet no one knows whether these reductions are a result of former recipients finding jobs in the prosperous economy of the late 1990s or whether they have been forced from the rolls by state administrative red tape. Certainly TANF has done nothing to reduce the continuing rise in the numbers of children living in poverty. Nothing in the new welfare "reform" requires states to develop the education, training, and jobs programs that the poor need to improve their lives.

A more constructive approach to welfare reform would be to replace it with universal entitlements modeled on the Social Security program. While welfare is universally unpopular, Social Security is universally popular and successful. No other program raises as many people out of poverty as Social Security. Building on the success and popularity of this program is the best strategy for expanding the welfare state to reduce economic inequality. New programs such as universal national health insurance and expanded child care would contribute to the capacity of ordinary people to be more effective democratic citizens. Reforms to enhance the incomes of the working poor, such as a higher minimum wage and an expanded Earned Income Tax Credit, work with universal entitlement programs to improve the standard of living of the poor. Whatever particular reforms are adopted, democrats need to understand that social programs contribute to a strong democracy. Attention to creating a stronger welfare state reduces American democracy's peril while making American society more just.

STEP 7: DISMANTLE THE WAR ECONOMY AND RETURN TO A CITIZEN ARMY

Since World War II, the defense industry has been central to the U.S. economy. Millions of Americans depend on defense spending for their jobs and standard of living. As argued in chapter 7, this contributes to the political power of advocates of the national security state and the challenge it poses to democracy. Reducing democracy's peril, then, requires reducing the economy's dependence on the production of armaments. Fortunately, the end of the Cold War offers an opportunity to dismantle much of the defense industry.

Dismantling the war economy, however, must be done carefully. Because so many depend on defense jobs, careful attention must be given to conversion of defense industries to civilian production. Unfortunately, despite Clinton administration rhetoric about defense conversion, little seems to be happening to provide for such conversion. Instead, cutbacks in military orders have created massive layoffs of defense workers without sufficient provision for retraining or investment in alternative industries. As suggested in chapter 7, without effective conversion plans, former defense workers will create political pressures to maintain the national security state and a massive defense industry. The post–World War II alliance of defense industrialists, their workers, the military, security services, and defense intellectuals will conjure up a new international threat to replace the threat of communism. Such a development might be prevented if the defense industry is converted quickly into building nonmilitary products. To do so will require a systematic industrial policy encouraging the development of such new products as high-speed rail systems to replace defense production. The rapid dismantling of our war economy would not only reduce democracy's peril but would have positive effects on the economy and standard of living of most Americans. Workers freed from building tanks, planes, and bombs so that they can rebuild our economic infrastructure would make the United States more prosperous *and* more democratic.

Without the Cold War, we have an opportunity to make citizen soldiers the backbone of our armed forces. Former Senator Gary Hart has proposed just such a reform.[10] He believes that we now have an opportunity to return to the vision of John McAuley Palmer, West Point graduate and World War I commander, who drafted the National Defense Act of 1920, which established the modern National Guard and reserve system. Palmer understood the threat posed by a large standing professional army in a democracy yet realized the need for highly trained and sophisticated forces in the modern era. His solution was an armed forces structure built around a small core of professional soldiers that could be expanded quickly in times of national emergency with trained and equipped part-time citizen-soldiers. Our current military has turned Palmer's vision upside down. Current armed forces consist of 1.5 million regular soldiers, constantly ready and responsible for facing all emergencies, with about

1 million National Guard and reserve forces available to supplement the professional army. The regular military has tended to neglect the "citizen-soldiers" and has not integrated them into regular units or defense planning as well as they could.[11]

Hart advocates reversing the present ratio of three-fourths regular professional forces and one-fourth National Guard and reserve forces to an armed forces structure of one-third regular forces and two-thirds National Guard and reserve. The "citizen-soldiers" of the National Guard and reserve would be the backbone of the military, highly trained and kept in a state of readiness. The National Guard and reserve would be more highly integrated with regular forces than is presently the case and would train regularly with those forces, yet they would remain part-time soldiers — fulfilling their duty to defend the nation while remaining full-time members of their communities. The core professional army, reduced to about 600,000, would be organized in elite, rapid-deployment forces for use around the world for small-scale conflicts such as those in Bosnia and Kosovo. Regular forces would be responsible, also, for training and organizing the larger force of citizen-soldiers so that they could be quickly mobilized to fight in a large scale conflict. Such an armed forces structure takes into account the need for highly trained forces capable of using today's technologically sophisticated weaponry. It also permits a response to the kind of conflict most likely to involve U.S. forces today, peacekeeping missions such as the Kosovo conflict, while maintaining an expandable force for a large regional war, such as the Gulf War of 1990. Hart's proposal is realistic given the strategic challenges of the current era, and it is much more compatible with the ideals of democracy than is our current large standing army.

THESE SUGGESTIONS FOR reform do not provide a comprehensive or complete program for reform of our democracy. They are one college professor's modest suggestions of some ameliorative steps. The true task of democratic reform can be accomplished only if ordinary citizens are mobilized to insist on change. This is the lesson of transforming democratic struggles, such as the civil rights movement. Only if people accept the necessity of taking action on behalf of democracy will democracy be gained. In this struggle, people will devise the reforms needed to bring about a more democratic society. This chapter only suggests an outline of what needs to be considered to advance democracy.

Implementing these seven reform steps would relieve, not eliminate, the contemporary peril of American democracy. Even a more far-reaching prodemocracy movement modeled on the civil rights movement would never eliminate democracy's peril. The challenges described in this book, along with others not mentioned, must always be of concern to democracy's partisans. Because it is such a complex form of government, democracy will always be in peril. The past two hundred years' struggle for democracy in the modern world is just a beginning.

Many more years of struggle with these and other challenges will be required to bring Americans and all of humankind the promise of self-government.

Meanwhile, the struggle for democracy must continue. For this struggle to be fruitful, democratic citizens need to understand the perils democracy faces. The aim of this book has been to engage its readers in reflecting on how contemporary democracy falls short of attaining democratic values. If the reader is now more attentive to the ways democracy is at stake in resolving contemporary political issues, the peril of American democracy is already less.

SELECTED WEB SITES

http://www.cpn.org/index.html A listing of organizations promoting more democratic participation.

http://www.livingdemocracy.org/ Source for practical suggestions for improving democratic participation.

http://www.ned.org/ The National Endowment for Democracy is a government agency responsible for promoting democracy around the world.

http://www.democracyonline.org/ The Democracy Online project, sponsored by the Pew Charitable Trusts, examines whether democratic participation on the internet can enhance democracy.

Notes

INTRODUCTION: MODELS OF DEMOCRACY

1. The models are based on those presented in C.B. Macpherson, *The Life and Times of Liberal Democracy* (Oxford, England: Oxford University Press, 1977). The names of some of the models and the descriptions of them differ from Macpherson in several respects. Readers interested in Macpherson's more complete analysis are encouraged to read his book. Similar models are employed in David Held, *Models of Democracy* (Stanford, Calif.: Stanford University Press, 1987). Held draws as well on Macpherson, but he identifies a total of *nine* distinct models in democratic theory.
2. Ted C. Lewellen, *Political Anthropology: An Introduction* (South Hadley, Mass.: Bergin and Garvey, 1983), 18–29.
3. John V.A. Fine, *The Ancient Greeks: A Critical History* (Cambridge: Harvard University Press, 1983), 383–441.
4. Held, *Models of Democracy,* 20–23.
5. Plato discusses democracy as part of his typology of governments in the *Republic* (London: Penguin, 1974). Aristotle's discussion of democracy can be found in *Politics* (London: Penguin, 1969), 115–16, 154–55. For a summary of the basic values of Greek democracy, Pericles's famous Funeral Oration is the classic source. It is reported in Thucydides' *The Peloponnesian War* (London: Penguin, 1972).
6. Held, *Models of Democracy,* 23.
7. Ibid.
8. Ibid., 14.
9. Montesquieu, *The Spirit of the Laws,* ed. David Wallace Carrithers (Berkeley: University of California Press, 1977), 176–77.
10. Jean-Jacques Rousseau, *The Social Contract* (London: Penguin, 1968).
11. The concept of representation itself antedated the American and French revolutions. Many polities utilized representative assemblies prior to the late eighteenth century, but these earlier bodies, like the Roman Senate or the English Parliament, provided representation to only an elite portion of citizens. The representative assemblies instituted in the new French and American polities were different in that they were intended to represent the entire democratic citizenry. For a brief discussion of the history of representation, see Robert Dahl, *On Democracy* (New Haven, Conn.: Yale University Press, 1998), 22–25, 104–5.
12. *The Federalist,* ed. Jacob E. Cooke (Cleveland, Ohio: Meridian, 1967), 56–65.
13. The views of John Locke discussed here can be found in his *Second Treatise on Government* (Indianapolis: Bobbs-Merrill, 1953); Hobbes's famous political work is *Leviathan.*
14. Plato's *Republic* is an example of an earlier political theory that posits the "good" as the goal of political society.
15. Locke, *Second Treatise on Government,* 71.
16. Michael Margolis, *Viable Democracy* (London: Penguin, 1979), 32.
17. J. Samuel Valenzuela and Arturo Valenzuela, *Military Rule in Chile* (Baltimore: Johns Hopkins University Press, 1986).
18. C.B. Macpherson, *The Political Theory of Possessive Individualism* (Oxford, England: Oxford University Press, 1962), 248.
19. These models are based on those found in C.B. Macpherson, *Life and Times of Liberal Democracy.* I have called Macpherson's "Equilibrium Democracy" Pluralist Democracy.
20. Ibid., 34.
21. Ibid., 36.
22. *The Federalist,* 57.
23. Macpherson, *Life and Times of Liberal Democracy,* 48.
24. John Dewey, "Democracy as a Way of Life," in *Frontiers of Democratic Theory,* ed. Henry S. Kariel (New York: Random House, 1970), 14–15.
25. Ibid., 13–14. See also Ernest Barker, "Democracy as Activity," in ibid., 7.

26. John Stuart Mill, *Considerations on Representative Government* (Indianapolis: Bobbs-Merrill, 1958), 55.
27. Alexis de Tocqueville, *Democracy in America* (Garden City, N.Y.: Doubleday, 1969), 60.
28. The essential works by the authors presenting this argument are Roberto Michels, *Political Parties: A Sociological Study of the Oligarchical Tendencies of Modern Democracy* (New York: Dover, 1959); Gaetano Mosca, *The Ruling Class* (New York: McGraw-Hill, 1939); and Vilfredo Pareto, *The Rise and Fall of Elites* (Totowa, N.J.: Bedminster Press, 1968).
29. Bernard Berelson, Paul Lazarsfeld, and William McPhee, *Voting* (Chicago: University of Chicago Press, 1954).
30. Ibid, 314.
31. Joseph Schumpeter, *Capitalism, Socialism, and Democracy,* 3d ed. (New York: Harper & Bros., 1950), 269.
32. The best exposition of the democratic function of interest groups remains David Truman, *The Governmental Process* (New York: Knopf, 1952).
33. Robert Dahl, *Dilemmas of Pluralist Democracy* (New Haven: Yale University Press, 1982).
34. For a thorough analysis of the events surrounding the writing of the Port Huron Statement and a thoughtful analysis of it, see James E. Miller, *Democracy Is in the Streets* (New York: Simon and Schuster, 1987). The complete text of the Port Huron Statement is included as an appendix.
35. There are a number of edited collections of the relevant articles. One of the best collections is Kariel, *Frontiers of Democratic Theory.* Kariel includes important articles by the leading participants in the exposition of more Participatory alternatives to Pluralist democracy, such as Jack L. Walker, Steven Lukes, Peter Bachrach, Morton Baratz, and Christian Bay.
36. An example of such impatience was the Iran-*contra* affair during Ronald Reagan's administration. Several National Security Council officials, such as Admiral John Poindexter and Colonel Oliver North, preferred to find illegal means to fund the *contras,* a group of Nicaraguans fighting the Nicaraguan Sandinista government, rather than concentrate on convincing Congress of the need for such funding. See chapter 7 for more details.

CHAPTER 1   THE FIRST CHALLENGE: SEPARATION OF POWERS

1. For a history of Americans' reverential regard for the Constitution, see Michael Kammen, *A Machine That Would Go of Itself* (New York: Knopf, 1986).
2. Gordon Wood, "Democracy and the Constitution," in *How Democratic Is the Constitution?* ed. Robert Goldwin and William Schambra (Washington, D.C.: American Enterprise Institute, 1980), 12. For a detailed discussion of these state legislatures, see Wood's *The Creation of the American Republic, 1776–1787* (Chapel Hill: University of North Carolina Press, 1969).
3. James L. Sundquist, *Constitutional Reform and Effective Government* (Washington, D.C.: Brookings Institution, 1986), 19.
4. Max Farrand, ed., *The Records of the Federal Convention of 1787* (New Haven: Yale University Press, 1966), 1: 26–27.
5. The classic attack on the elitist character of the founding is Charles Beard, *An Economic Interpretation of the Constitution* (New York: Macmillan, 1913). The now-classic critiques of Beard's view are Robert E. Brown, *Charles Beard and the Constitution* (Princeton: Princeton University Press, 1956); and Forrest McDonald, *We the People* (Chicago: University of Chicago Press, 1958).
6. Alexander Hamilton, John Jay, and James Madison, *The Federalist,* ed. Jacob E. Cooke (Cleveland: Meridian, 1961), 349.
7. James MacGregor Burns, *The Deadlock of Democracy* (Englewood Cliffs, N.J.: Prentice Hall, 1963), 36.
8. James L. Sundquist, "Needed: A Political Theory for the New Era of Coalition Government in the United States," *Political Science Quarterly* 103 (Winter 1988–89): 613–36.
9. A thorough review of the political science literature seeking to explain divided government can be found in Morris Fiorina, *Divided Government* (New York: Macmillan, 1991).

10. Walter De Vries and V. Lance Tarrance, *The Ticket-Splitter: A New Force in American Politics* (Grand Rapids, Mich.: William B. Eerdmans, 1972).

11. Sundquist, "Needed," 631. For a discussion of the Republican lock on the Electoral College, see Nelson Polsby and Aaron Wildavsky, *Presidential Elections*, 10th ed. (New York: Chatham House, 2000), 189. For the power of congressional incumbents, see Morris Fiorina, *Congress: Keystone of the Washington Establishment* (New Haven: Yale University Press, 1989).

12. Gary C. Jacobson, *The Electoral Origins of Divided Government* (Boulder, Colo.: Westview Press, 1990), 105–36.

13. This logic applied to the creation of a bicameral legislature as well as the separation of powers. James L. Sundquist describes the famous breakfast meeting at which George Washington explained this logic to Thomas Jefferson: "When Jefferson asked why a second legislative chamber had been created, Washington asked, 'Why did you pour your coffee into your saucer?' 'To cool it,' Jefferson answered. 'Even so,' said Washington, 'we pour legislation into the senatorial saucer to cool it.' " Sundquist, *Constitutional Reform*, 22.

14. Ann Stuart Diamond, "Decent, Even Though Democratic," in Goldwin and Schambra, *How Democratic Is the Constitution?* 37.

15. Americans are less satisfied with their health-care system than are citizens of most other industrial nations. Erik Eckholm, "Rescuing Health Care," *New York Times,* 2 May 1991, B12.

16. Theodore R. Marmor, *The Politics of Medicare* (Chicago: Aldine, 1973).

17. Clarke E. Cochran, Lawrence C. Mayer, T.R. Carr, and N. Joseph Cayer, *American Public Policy: An Introduction* (New York: Worth Publishers, 1999), 266; Tom Pugh, "A Million More Going without Health Policies," *Newark Star-Ledger,* 4 October 1999, 1.

18. Two accounts of the failure of the Clinton health-care reform plan detail how the separation-of-powers system helped the plan's opponents: Haynes Johnson and David S. Broder, *The System: The American Way of Politics at the Breaking Point* (Boston: Little Brown, 1996); and Theda Skocpol, *Boomerang: Clinton's Health Security Effort and the Turn against Government in U.S. Politics* (New York: Norton, 1996).

19. Barbara Sinclair, "The President as Legislative Leader," in *The Clinton Legacy,* ed. Colin Campbell and Bert A. Rockman (New York: Chatham House, 2000), 78.

20. Adam Clymer, "Democrats Surrender on Jobs Bill," *Providence Journal-Bulletin,* 22 April 1993, 1.

21. Throughout the spring and summer of 1993, the press provided numerous accounts of the resistance Clinton faced from his own party. For a few examples of such articles, see Adam Clymer, "Single-minded President," *New York Times,* 3 April 1993, 1; David E. Rosenbaum, "Clinton and Allies Twist Arms in Bid for Budget Votes," *New York Times,* 27 May 1993, 1; idem, "Clinton Facing Threat of Revolt on Budget Plan," *New York Times,* 28 July 1993, 1; and Michael Wines, "The Joy of Being Undecided: Senators Bask in the Lights," *New York Times,* 7 August 1993, 1.

22. Sinclair, "Trying to Govern," 105–8.

23. Skocpol, *Boomerang,* 1–6.

24. Two similar accounts of Cooper's role in the health-care reform debate can be found in ibid., 104–5; and Johnson and Broder, *The System,* 309–37.

25. Johnson and Broder, *The System,* 337.

26. Adam Clymer, "President Vetoes Credit Extension: Shutdown Looms," *New York Times,* 14 November 1995, A1.

27. The propensity of separation-of-powers systems to create such breakdowns is one reason many political scientists consider them dangerously unstable. While the United States has been spared such a result, institutional deadlock has been a prime cause of military coups in Latin American regions with separation-of-powers systems. See Juan Linz, "Presidential or Parliamentary Democracy: Does It Make a Difference?" in *The Failure of Presidential Democracy,* ed. Juan Linz and Arturo Valenzuela, vol. 1 (Baltimore: Johns Hopkins University Press, 1994), 7.

28. Richard E. Cohen, "Campaigning for Congress: The Echo of '94," in *Toward the Millennium: The Elections of 1996,* ed. Larry J. Sabato (Boston: Allyn and Bacon, 1997), 169–70.

29. Ibid., 169.

30. Robert Pear, "Bush Campaigning Fiercely against Democratic Phantom," *New York Times,* 21 September 1991, A1.

31. In doing so, they were behaving no differently than they had in the previous decade, as argued in Morris Fiorina, "The Decline of Collective Responsibility in American Politics," *Daedalus,* Summer 1980, 25–45.

32. Even the remarkable Republican capture, for the first time in forty years, of majorities in both the House and the Senate did not alter the power of incumbency. The new Republican majorities came about through the capture of "open" seats where no incumbent was running; incumbents, in fact, did quite well in 1994, winning reelection 91 percent of the time in the House and 92 percent in the Senate. Thomas Patterson, *We the People,* updated ed. (New York: McGraw-Hill, 1996), 344.

33. Cohen, "Campaigning for Congress," 177–88. See also Nicol C. Rae, *Conservative Reformers: The Republican Freshmen and the Lessons of the 104th Congress* (Armonk, N.Y.: M.E. Sharpe, 1998), 207–8.

34. Kathleen Sullivan, "Madison Got It Backward," *New York Times,* 16 February 1999, A19.

35. The account of the S&L scandal follows that found in L.J. Davis, "Chronicle of a Debacle Foretold: How Deregulation Begat the S&L Scandal," *Atlantic,* September 1990, 50–66.

36. Ibid., 66.

37. G. Calvin MacKenzie and Saranna Thornton, *Bucking the Deficit* (Boulder, Colo.: Westview Press, 1996), 148–51.

38. Richard E. Cohen and David Bauman, "No Done Deal on the Hill," *National Journal,* 1 and 9 January 1999, 24–26.

39. Amy Goldstein and John F. Harris, "Medicare Panel Fails to Agree on Recommendations," *Washington Post,* 17 March 1999, A2.

40. The European system that comes closest is France. Its Fifth Republic constitution provides for both a president and a prime minister, with the president possessing independent powers over foreign affairs. Since 1958, however, when the constitution took effect, the same party has controlled both branches of government except for three brief periods (1986–88; 1993–95; and beginning in 1997). In each of these periods, in what the French call "cohabitation," the government headed by the prime minister has had, save for some consultation with the president, complete control of domestic policy and has enacted his party's program into law. This was the case when Gaullist Prime Minister Jacques Chirac served in conjunction with Socialist President François Mitterrand in 1986–88, and it proved to be the case once again when a Socialist, Prime Minister Lionel Jospin, was elected in 1997 to serve in cohabitation with President Chirac. In practice, the French system has operated more like a parliamentary system than a separation-of-powers system, even in periods of cohabitation. For more detail, see Vincent Wright, *The Government and Politics of France* (New York: Holmes and Meier, 1989), 76–98; see also Mark Kesselman et al., *European Politics in Transition,* 3d ed. (Boston: Houghton Mifflin, 1997), 180–88.

41. This possibility is intriguingly explored in Joy E. Esberey, "What If There Were a Parliamentary System?" in *What If the American Political System Were Different?* ed. Herbert M. Levine (Armonk, N.Y.: M.E. Sharpe, 1992), 95–148.

42. Alan Cowell, "Impeachment: What a Royal Pain," *New York Times,* 7 February 1999, Week in Review Section, 5.

43. Guilt or innocence would, of course, come into play as a factor in determining the political viability of a prime minister suspected of criminal behavior. Under a parliamentary system, however, the legislature is not forced to perform the awkward quasi-judicial role that Congress must under impeachment procedures: making, itself, a determination of guilt or innocence. In a parliamentary system, strong evidence of criminal conduct would most likely lead to resignation or removal of the suspected minister (otherwise the party might suffer at the next election), but the truth of a criminal accusation would be, more appropriately, determined in court. Furthermore, depending on the circumstances, nothing would prevent a minister exonerated in a court trial from returning to active government service.

44. Two political scientists come to this same conclusion after a comprehensive empirical survey of presidential (separation-of-powers) and parliamentary systems worldwide. See Alfred Stepan and Cindy Skach, "Constitutional Frameworks and Democratic Consolidation: Parliamentarism versus Presidentialism," *World Politics* 46 (October 1993): 1–22.

45. Leon D. Epstein, "Organizing the Government: Political Parties," in *Mr. Madison's Constitution and the Twenty-First Century: A Report from the Project '87 Conference, Williamsburg, Virginia, October 1987* (Washington, D.C.: American Political Science Association, 1988), 20.

46. Some of the greatest names in political science have been advocates of strong parties, including one of America's first political scientists, Woodrow Wilson. Some major works advocating strong parties are Austin Ranney, *The Doctrine of Responsible Party Government* (Champaign: University of Illinois Press, 1962); E.E. Schattschneider, *Party Government* (New York: Farrar & Rinehart, 1942); idem, *The Semi-Sovereign People* (New York: Holt, Rinehart and Winston, 1960); V.O. Key, *Politics, Parties, and Pressure Groups* (New York: Crowell, 1958). For critical reviews of the issue of responsible parties, see Evron M. Kirkpatrick, "Toward a More Responsible Two-Party System: Political Science, Policy Science, or Pseudo-Science?" *American Political Science Review,* December 1971, 965–90; Gerald Pomper, "Toward a More Responsible Two-Party System? What, Again?" *Journal of Politics,* November 1971, 916–40.

47. Committee on Political Parties of the American Political Science Association, *Toward a More Responsible Two-Party System* (New York: Rinehart, 1950).

48. An eloquent appeal for this point of view can be found in Sundquist, *Constitutional Reform.* In 1982, for example, a group of distinguished citizens formed the Committee on the Constitutional System to recommend changes in the Constitution. Cochaired by Lloyd Cutler, former counsel to President Jimmy Carter; C. Douglas Dillon, former treasury secretary under John F. Kennedy; and Republican Senator Nancy Kassebaum, the committee produced a number of specific proposals to overcome the separation of powers. This can be found in Donald L. Robinson, ed., *Reforming American Government: The Bicentennial Papers of the Committee on the Constitutional System* (Boulder, Colo.: Westview Press, 1985).

49. Sundquist, *Constitutional Reform,* 84–93.

50. Sundquist has little hope that either of these proposals would necessarily be effective in preventing divided government. See ibid., 93–98.

51. These proposals can be found in Robinson, *Reforming American Government.*

52. Robert Dahl, *Democracy and Its Critics* (New Haven: Yale University Press, 1990), 155.

53. Ibid., 156.

54. Burns, *Deadlock of Democracy,* 40–41.

55. James Q. Wilson, "Does the Separation of Powers Still Work?" *Public Interest,* Winter 1987, 50.

CHAPTER 2   THE SECOND CHALLENGE: RADICAL INDIVIDUALISM

1. Kay Lehman Schlozman and Sidney Verba, *Injury to Insult: Unemployment, Class, and Political Response* (Cambridge: Harvard University Press, 1979), 191.

2. Samuel P. Huntington, *American Politics: The Promise of Disharmony* (Cambridge: Harvard University Press, 1981), 23–30; see also Seymour Martin Lipset, *The First New Nation* (New York: Basic Books, 1963).

3. Gordon Wood, *The Radicalism of the American Revolution* (New York: Knopf, 1991).

4. Alexis de Tocqueville, *Democracy in America,* ed. J.P. Mayer (New York: Doubleday, 1969), 506–8.

5. Cited in Herbert McClosky and John Zaller, *The American Ethos: Public Attitudes toward Capitalism and Democracy* (Cambridge: Harvard University Press, 1984), 112–13.

6. Herbert Gans, *Middle American Individualism: Popular Participation and Liberal Democracy* (New York: Oxford University Press, 1988), 2.

7. Mary Ann Glendon, *Rights Talk: The Impoverishment of Political Discourse* (New York: Free Press, 1991), 9.

8. Tocqueville, *Democracy in America,* 506.

9. Ibid., 692.

10. Ibid., 511.

11. Ibid., 287.
12. Robert N. Bellah, Richard Madsen, William M. Sullivan, Ann Swidler, and Steven M. Tipton, *Habits of the Heart: Individualism and Commitment in American Life* (Berkeley: University of California Press, 1985).
13. Ibid., 6.
14. Ibid.
15. Ibid., 6–7.
16. Ibid., 198.
17. Ibid., 206. Bellah also identifies a third conception of politics — "the politics of the nation," related to "high affairs of national life" such as war and peace.
18. Ibid., 200.
19. Ibid., 201.
20. Gans, *Middle American Individualism,* 1–22.
21. Ibid., 71–72.
22. Ibid., 15.
23. Frances Fitzgerald, *Cities on a Hill: A Journey through Contemporary American Cultures* (New York: Simon and Schuster, 1986).
24. Gerald Marzorati, "From Tocqueville to Perotville," *New York Times,* 28 June 1992, E17.
25. Jane Gross, "In Simi Valley, Defense of a Shared Way of Life," *New York Times,* 4 May 1992, B7.
26. Ibid. Both quotes are from Simi Valley residents.
27. For a thoughtful exposition of the libertarian view, see David Boaz, *Libertarianism: A Primer* (New York: Free Press, 1997).
28. The Libertarian Party platform offers a précis of extreme radical individualism: "We, the members of the Libertarian Party, challenge the cult of the omnipotent state and defend the rights of the individual. We hold that all individuals have the right to exercise sole dominion over their own lives, and have the right to live in whatever manner they choose, so long as they do not forcibly interfere with the equal right of others to live in whatever manner they choose." Quoted in Lyman Tower Sargent, *Contemporary Political Ideologies: A Comparative Analysis* (Belmont, Calif.: Wadsworth, 1993), 188–89; for a comprehensive philosophical defense of libertarianism, see Boaz, *Libertarianism.*
29. Paul Brace, *State Government and Economic Performance* (Baltimore: Johns Hopkins University Press, 1993), 9–13.
30. Douglas Preston, *Cities of Gold: A Journey across the American Southwest in Pursuit of Coronado* (New York: Simon and Schuster, 1992). This fascinating book is only incidentally about cattle ranching. While retracing the route that the Spanish explorer Coronado took in his search for the seven cities of gold, Preston befriends several Arizona ranchers who educate him on the problems related to the use of public grazing land in the West today.
31. It is also possible, sometimes, to solve the problem of the tragedy of the commons by changing a common pool resource into a private one. It is conceivable that the ranchers in this example might choose this solution by fencing off pieces of the common grazing land for each family. The ranchers would then graze their own cattle on only their own private land and would derive full benefit from wise management of it. Although changing common pool resources into private property can be a solution, it is not always possible or economically desirable. Some common pool resources simply cannot be privatized. Clean air and water are the best examples; they cannot be "fenced." In some cases, even though you might be able to privatize a common pool resource, it would be more desirable not to. This seems to be true with ranching in parts of the American West today. One needs to own vast amounts of land to support cattle on open grazing land. The cost to purchase and manage (buying and repairing all that fencing!) so much land is high. For many ranchers, the investment needed to ranch is much lower if common (public) grazing land can be used. Many readily accept collective regulation of their herd sizes rather than bear the expense of owning private land. In addition, to return to the imaginary case of families on a common grazing land, even if they opt to solve their problem through privatization, this is also a *collective* solution. They will have to agree

collectively on how to divide the land and formulate a set of laws of private property to govern its ownership. As the republics of the former Soviet Union are now discovering, creating a system of private property where there is none is a daunting collective endeavor.

32. Isaiah Berlin, *Four Essays On Liberty* (Oxford: Oxford University Press, 1969), 118–72.

33. Robert Putnam, "The Prosperous Community: Social Capital and Public Life," *American Prospect,* Spring 1993, 35–42.

34. Putnam, "The Prosperous Community," 36.

35. Ibid.

36. Robert Putnam, "Bowling Alone: America's Declining Social Capital," *Journal of Democracy* 9 (1995): 65–78; see also "The Strange Disappearance of Civic America," *American Prospect* 24 (Winter 1996): 34–48.

37. *The American Prospect* ran a series of articles critical of Putnam's thesis under the rubric "the Tocqueville Files" in issues 25 (March–April 1996) and 26 (May–June 1996). These can be found at the EPN Civil Society web site. Reverend Andrew Greeley's web site also contains a detailed critique of Putnam. For a measured review and critique, plus additional data and analysis, see the excellent article by W. Lance Bennett, "The UnCivic Culture: Communication, Identity, and the Rise of Lifestyle Politics," *PS: Political Science and Politics* 31 (December 1998): 741–61.

38. National Commission on Civic Renewal, *A Nation of Spectators: How Civic Disengagement Weakens America and What We Can Do about It,* Final Report (College Park, Md.: NCCR, 1998). The report can be found at the Commission web site (see list).

39. Wendy M. Rahn and John E. Transue, "Social Trust and Value Change: The Decline of Social Capital in American Youth, 1976–1995" *Political Psychology* 19, no. 3 (1998): 545–63.

40. Robert Pear, "Privacy Concerns Threaten a 'Backlash,' Census Director Fears," *New York Times,* 2 April 2000, A-15.

41. Bellah et al., *Habits of the Heart,* 84.

42. Thomas A. Spragens Jr., "The Limitations of Libertarianism, Part II," *Responsive Community,* Spring 1992, 45–47.

43. Glendon, *Rights Talk,* passim.

44. Ibid., 9.

45. Robert Dahl, *On Democracy* (New Haven, Conn.: Yale University Press: 1998), 48–50.

46. Glendon, *Rights Talk,* 12. This contrasts sharply with Canadian naturalization ceremonies, which emphasize "getting along with one's neighbors."

47. Benjamin R. Barber, "The Reconstruction of Rights," *American Prospect,* Spring 1991, 44.

48. Ibid.

49. Glendon, *Rights Talk,* passim. See also Amitai Etzioni, *The Spirit of Community: Rights, Responsibilities, and the Communitarian Agenda* (New York: Crown, 1993).

50. Etzioni, *Spirit of Community,* 9.

51. Ibid., 3.

52. *College Students Talk Politics.* Prepared for the Kettering Foundation by the Harwood Group (Dayton, Ohio: Kettering Foundation, 1993), 42.

53. Glendon, *Rights Talk,* 47–75.

54. Etzioni, *Spirit of Community,* 3.

55. Glendon, *Rights Talk,* 64–66.

56. This is happening in Missouri and Wisconsin, where pro-life and pro-choice groups are working together to help women with unwanted pregnancies. See Tamar Lewin, "On Common Ground: Pro-Life and Pro-Choice," *Responsive Community,* Summer 1992, 48–53.

57. I do not intend to argue that the judiciary should never play a policymaking role. The line between adjudication and policymaking is too fuzzy for that to be possible. In addition, in their democratic role of protecting political rights and assuring the democratic integrity of legislative processes, courts and judges will have an impact on major public policy issues. The American judiciary has expanded and protected democracy in this way many times. The most important was, surely, the *Brown* v. *Board of Education* desegregation decision, which pushed American policy in the direction of recognition of the political rights of black Americans.

When policy issues should be of concern to the judiciary is an extremely important question for democracies, one I cannot address in this chapter. Nevertheless, in a democratic society, whatever guidelines are agreed on to define the judiciary's policy role would have to limit that role to a considerable degree, otherwise the central democratic presumption that rule by the people is best would be violated.

58. David Price, "Our Political Condition," *PS: Political Science and Politics,* December 1992, 682.
59. Quoted in ibid.
60. Jeffrey Goldfarb, *The Cynical Society* (Chicago: University of Chicago Press, 1991), 4–6.
61. A call for a new communitarianism is found in Etzioni, *Spirit of Community,* passim.
62. Juan Williams, "Japan: A Case of Too Many Responsibilities, Too Few Rights," *Responsive Community,* Spring 1992, 36–42. In Japan, schoolchildren have been bullied by classmates and even killed for being too individualistic and not conforming to group norms. David E. Sanger, "Student's Killing Displays Dark Side of Japan Schools," *New York Times,* 3 April 1993, A1.

CHAPTER 3   THE THIRD CHALLENGE: CITIZEN PARTICIPATION

1. Sidney Verba and Norman Nie, *Participation in America: Political Democracy and Social Equality* (New York: Harper & Row, 1972), 4–5.
2. Quoted in ibid., 5.
3. Alexis de Tocqueville, *Democracy in America* (Garden City, N.Y.: Doubleday Anchor, 1969), 68–70, 158–63.
4. Jacob E. Cooke, ed., *The Federalist* (Cleveland: Meridian Books, 1961), 62.
5. Seymour Martin Lipset, *Political Man* (Baltimore: Johns Hopkins University Press, 1981), 87–126.
6. In this chapter, *eligible* is used to refer to the *age*-eligible proportion of the population, a group that also includes some people over age 18 who are not legally eligible to vote, such as convicted felons or noncitizen residents (it also excludes Americans voting abroad). The Census Bureau measures turnout in relation to the total age-eligible part of the population because it has found it too difficult to develop an accurate count of all legally eligible voters, given diversity in state laws regarding the eligibility of felons and the mentally incompetent and difficulty in estimating the precise number of noncitizens in the population. The best estimates suggest that turnout would increase by about 3 percent (rising to about 52 percent in 1996) if measured in terms of only the legally eligible population. See Committee for the Study of the American Electorate, *Final Post Election Report,* 9 February 1999, http://tap.epn.org/csae/cgans5.html, 1–2.
7. Ibid., 6.
8. The discussion of voter turnout is based, primarily, on two sources: Ruy A. Teixeira, *Why Americans Don't Vote: Turnout Decline in the United States, 1960–1984* (New York: Greenwood Press, 1987), 3–36; and Frances Fox Piven and Richard Cloward, *Why Americans Don't Vote* (New York: Pantheon, 1989), 3–25.
9. Teixeira, *Why Americans Don't Vote,* 15–21.
10. Sidney Verba, Kay Lehman Schlozman, and Henry E. Brady, *Voice and Equality: Civic Voluntarism in American Politics* (Cambridge: Harvard University Press, 1995), 416–60.
11. Piven and Cloward, *Why Americans Don't Vote,* 19.
12. Steffen W. Schmidt et al., *American Government and Politics Today, 1997–1998* (Belmont, Calif.: West, 1997), 338.
13. Teixeira, *Why Americans Don't Vote,* 7–8.
14. Piven and Cloward, *Why Americans Don't Vote,* 17.
15. Peter Baker, "Motor Voter Apparently Did Not Drive Up Turnout," *Washington Post,* 6 November 1996, B7.
16. Verba and Nie, *Participation in America,* 339–40.
17. Piven and Cloward, *Why Americans Don't Vote,* 54.
18. Progressives introduced other reforms, such as the Australian ballot, which also made participation more difficult for less educated voters.
19. Some scholars attribute the moderate rise in voter turnout that began in the 1930s and

continued to 1960 to a renewal of political party organizations that occurred during the New Deal period. This renewal ran its course by the early 1960s, and a new wave of party reform further undermined political party organizations. Turnout, once again, began to decline. See Piven and Cloward, *Why Americans Don't Vote*, 122–80.

20. Teixeira, *Why Americans Don't Vote*, 78.

21. Michael Nelson, "The Election: Turbulence and Tranquillity in Contemporary American Politics," in *The Election of 1996*, ed. Michael Nelson (Washington, D.C.: CQ Press, 1997), 72–73.

22. M. Margaret Conway, *Political Participation in the United States*, 2d ed. (Washington, D.C.: CQ Press, 1991), 8.

23. Joseph N. Cappella and Kathleen Hall Jamieson, *Spiral of Cynicism: The Press and the Public Good* (New York: Oxford University Press: 1997).

24. Russell J. Dalton, *Citizen Politics: Public Opinion and Political Parties in Advanced Industrial Democracies* (Chatham, N.J.: Chatham House, 1996), 47–51.

25. Verba, Schlozman, and Brady, *Voice and Equality*, 509.

26. Thomas Cronin, *Direct Democracy: The Politics of Initiative, Referendum, and Recall* (Cambridge: Harvard University Press, 1989), 47.

27. Ibid., 197.

28. Harry C. Boyte, *The Backyard Revolution: Understanding the New Citizen Movement* (Philadelphia: Temple University Press, 1980).

29. Ibid., 64. For a more up-to-date account of the activities of COPS, see William Greider, *Who Will Tell the People? The Betrayal of American Democracy* (New York: Simon and Schuster, 1992), 222–41.

30. Harry C. Boyte, *Commonwealth* (New York: Free Press, 1989), 90–91.

31. Boyte, *Backyard Revolution*, 3–4.

32. Greider, *Who Will Tell the People?* 224.

33. David O. Sears and Jack Citrin, *Tax Revolt: Something for Nothing in California* (Cambridge: Harvard University Press, 1982).

34. Craig Rimmerman, *The New Citizenship: Unconventional Politics, Activism, and Service* (Boulder, Colo.: Westview Press, 1997), 63–71.

35. Kay Lehman Schlozman and John T. Tierney, *Organized Interests and American Democracy* (New York: Harper & Row, 1986), 45–47.

36. Verba, Schlozman, and Brady, *Voice and Equality*, 49–96.

37. Schlozman and Tierney, *Organized Interests and American Democracy*, 60.

38. Dalton, *Citizen Politics*, 82.

39. Hedrick Smith, *People and the Power Game*, prod. and dir. Hedrick Smith, 4 hours, Hedrick Smith Productions, 1996, videocassette.

40. Darrell M. West and Burdett A. Loomis, *The Sound of Money: How Political Interests Get What They Want* (New York: W.W. Norton, 1999), 60–64.

41. The possibility that new forms of participation compensate for decline in traditional group memberships is argued in both of the following works: Robert Wuthnow, *Loose Connections: Joining Together in America's Fragmented Communities* (Cambridge: Harvard University Press, 1999) and Everett Carll Ladd, *The Ladd Report* (New York: Free Press, 1999).

42. Michel Crozier, Samuel Huntington, and Joji Watanuki, *The Crisis of Democracy* (New York: New York University Press, 1975), 59–118.

43. Samuel Huntington, *American Politics: The Promise of Disharmony* (Cambridge: Harvard University Press, 1981), 102–6.

44. Ibid., 113.

45. Ibid.

46. Peter Peterson and Neil Howe, *On Borrowed Time* (San Francisco: ICS Press, 1988).

47. This is the general theme of the memoir of Reagan's OMB director, David Stockman. See *The Triumph of Politics: Why the Reagan Revolution Failed* (New York: Harper & Row, 1986).

48. One best-selling American government textbook makes this argument its central theme.

See Thomas Dye and Harmon Zeigler, *The Irony of Democracy,* 9th ed. (Belmont, Calif.: Wadsworth, 1993).

49. Thomas Byrne Edsall, *The New Politics of Inequality* (New York: Norton, 1984). These developments are discussed in more detail in chapters 5 and 6, "The Fifth Challenge: The Privileged Position of Business" and "The Sixth Challenge: Inequality."

50. William Greider, *The Education of David Stockman and Other Americans* (New York: New American Library, 1986), documents the class bias of Reagan policies. David Stockman found it easy to impose spending cuts on programs for the poor, but was prevented from interfering with probusiness programs and those benefiting the affluent, such as the Export-Import Bank and subsidies for private airplane manufacturers.

51. Piven and Cloward, *Why Americans Don't Vote,* 12–13.

52. John R. Petrocik, "Voter Turnout and Electoral Preference: The Anomalous Reagan Elections," in *Elections in America,* ed. Kay Schlozman (London: Allen and Unwin, 1987).

53. Verba, Schlozman, and Brady, *Voice and Equality,* 468–503.

54. Piven and Cloward, *Why Americans Don't Vote,* 26–95.

55. For data on public support for more generous social welfare programs, see Benjamin Page and Robert Shapiro, *The Rational Public: Fifty Years of Trends in Americans' Policy Preferences* (Chicago: University of Chicago Press, 1992), 117–71.

56. This argument follows W. Lance Bennett, *The Governing Crisis: Media, Money, and Marketing in American Elections* (New York: St. Martin's Press, 1992).

57. Ibid., 16.

58. Daniel Yankelovich, "A Missing Concept," *Kettering Review,* Fall 1991, 54–66.

59. Ibid., 59.

60. Richard C. Harwood, *Citizens and Politics: A View from Main Street America* (Dayton, Ohio: Kettering Foundation, 1991).

61. Ibid., 23.

62. Ibid., 17.

63. Thomas Ferguson and Joel Rogers, *Right Turn* (New York: Hill and Wang, 1986).

64. See chapter 6 of this book, "The Sixth Challenge: Inequality," for documentation.

65. James Fishkin, *Democracy and Deliberation* (New Haven: Yale University Press, 1991).

66. Greider, *Who Will Tell the People?* 222–41.

CHAPTER 4   THE FOURTH CHALLENGE: TRIVIALIZED ELECTIONS

1. A recent study of new democracies throughout the world by a prominent social scientist uses the presence or absence of competitive elections as the sole indicator of democratic politics. See Samuel P. Huntington, *The Third Wave: Democratization in the Late Twentieth Century* (Norman: University of Oklahoma Press, 1991), 5–13.

2. R.K. Sinclair, *Democracy and Participation in Athens* (Cambridge: Cambridge University Press, 1988), 17.

3. Aristotle, *The Politics,* trans. T.A. Sinclair (Harmondsworth, England: Penguin, 1962), 241. See also M.I. Finley, *Democracy: Ancient and Modern,* rev. ed. (New Brunswick, N.J.: Rutgers University Press, 1985), 19.

4. Finley, *Democracy,* 22.

5. Benjamin Ginsberg and Alan Stone, *Do Elections Matter?* 2d ed. (Armonk, N.Y.: M.E. Sharpe, 1991), 3.

6. E.E. Schattschneider, *Party Government* (New York: Rinehart, 1942), 208.

7. Lewis Lipsitz and David M. Speak, *American Democracy,* 3d ed. (New York: St. Martin's Press, 1993), 326–27.

8. Remarks made to the 1990 meeting of the Northeast Political Science Association; the process is fully described in Alan Ehrenhalt, *The United States of Ambition: Politicians, Power, and the Pursuit of Office* (New York: Times Books, 1992). Former Senator Bill Bradley said he made both his decision *not* to run for president in 1988 and his decision to run in 1998 by literally looking in a mirror. See Richard L. Berke, "Bradley Takes Early Party Prize: He Goes One-on-One with Gore," *New York Times,* 20 April 1999, A1.

9. For a description of recruitment of party leaders in Britain, see Alex N. Dragnich, Jorgen S. Rasmussen, and Joel C. Moses, *Major European Governments,* 5th ed. (Pacific Grove, Calif.: Brooks/Cole, 1991), 156. For a summary of Margaret Thatcher's background, see Dennis Kavanagh, *Thatcherism and British Politics: The End of Consensus,* 2d ed. (Oxford: Oxford University Press, 1990), 198–99. Kavanagh says that Thatcher's fifteen-year service in Parliament made her a relative "newcomer" when she challenged for the leadership in 1974 compared to the even longer apprenticeships of her predecessors.

10. For a comprehensive and up-to-date analysis of current campaign laws, see Herbert E. Alexander, *Financing Politics: Money, Elections, and Political Reform,* 4th ed. (Washington, D.C.: CQ Press, 1992). For a detailed look at the role of PACs, see Larry Sabato, *PAC Power: Inside the World of Political Action Committees* (New York: Norton, 1985).

11. Anthony Corrado, "Financing the 1996 Elections," in *The Election of 1996,* ed. Gerald M. Pomper (Chatham, N.J.: Chatham House, 1997), 137.

12. W. Lance Bennett, *The Governing Crisis: Media, Money, and Marketing in American Elections* (New York: St. Martin's Press, 1992), 53.

13. Stephen Engleberg and Katharine Q. Seelye, "Gingrich: Man in Spotlight and Organization in Shadow," *New York Times,* 18 December 1994, A1.

14. Corrado, "Financing the 1996 Elections," 161–62.

15. "PAC Supplements Are Growing, Study Shows," *New York Times,* 19 July 1992, 19.

16. Center for Responsive Politics, "Bigger Bundles in Third-Quarter Presidential Filings Show Rising Importance of $1,000 Donors to Front-Runnners," press release, 4 November 1999, http://www.opensecrets.org.

17. Thomas Ferguson and Joel Rogers have developed the notion of the hidden election most fully. See their *Right Turn: The Decline of the Democrats and the Future of American Politics* (New York: Hill and Wang, 1986).

18. Ryan J. Barilleaux and Randall E. Adkins, "The Nomination: Process and Patterns," in *The Elections of 1992,* ed. Michael Nelson (Washington, D.C.: CQ Press, 1993), 30.

19. Ibid., 38.

20. Corrado, "Financing the 1996 Elections," 142.

21. Berke, "Bradley Takes Early Party Prize," A1.

22. Don Van Natta Jr., "Aura of Invincibility Is Drying Up the Money Pool for Bush's Rivals," *New York Times,* 10 June 1999, A1. See also David Firestone, "Alexander Cuts Staff and Travel," *New York Times,* 3 June 1999, A19.

23. Public Campaign, "White Gold: The Zip Codes That Matter Most to the Presidential Candidates," press release, 14 December 1999, http://www.publiccampaign.org/gl-whitegold.html.

24. Larry J. Sabato, *The Rise of Political Consultants: New Ways of Winning Elections* (New York: Basic Books, 1981), 13.

25. Doris Graber, *Mass Media and American Politics,* 4th ed. (Washington, D.C.: CQ Press, 1993), 251.

26. Ibid., 250–53.

27. Veteran politicians also employ campaign consultants whose past political experience and affiliation may be at odds with their own party. In 1996 President Clinton called on the services of Dick Morris, a professional consultant with a reputation for doing business with politicians regardless of party affiliation or political ideology. In recent years, he had worked most often for prominent Republicans, such as the conservative Mississippi Republican Senator Trent Lott. Concerns about Morris's commitment to the political values of the Democratic Party created tension among Clinton's campaign advisers. See George Stephanopoulos, *All Too Human: A Political Education* (Boston: Little Brown, 1999), 328–41.

28. Graber, *Mass Media,* 251.

29. David Mayhew, *Congress: The Electoral Connection* (New Haven: Yale University Press, 1974).

30. The following analysis is based on data from Common Cause. See Common Cause, "Incumbents Dominate '98 Fundraising: The Latest House and Senate Campaign Finance Stats," 8 April 1999, http://www.commoncause.org/publications/april99/congelect_hanaly.htm.

31. Paul Starr, "Democracy v. Dollar," *American Prospect,* March–April 1997, 6.

32. Alexander, *Financing Politics,* 83.
33. Corrado, "Financing the 1996 Elections," 135. The Center's report on the 1996 election can be found at its web site: http://www.opensecrets.org/pubs/bigpicture/overview/bpoverview.htm.
34. Bennett, *Governing Crisis,* 32.
35. Corrado, "Financing the 1996 Elections," 152.
36. Brooks Jackson, "Financing the 1996 Campaign: The Law of the Jungle," in *Toward the Millennium: The Election of 1996,* ed. Larry J. Sabato (Boston: Allyn and Bacon, 1997), 245. Contribution amounts are rounded off.
37. Common Cause, "National Parties Raise $193 Million in Soft Money during 1997–1998 Election Cycle," http://www.commoncause.org/publications/020399.htm.
38. Don Van Natta Jr., "Campaign Fund-Raising Is at Record Pace," *New York Times,* 10 October 1999, 1.
39. Jackson, "Financing the 1996 Campaign," 61.
40. Dan Clawson, Alan Neustadtl, and Mark Weller, *Dollars and Votes: How Business Campaign Contributions Subvert Democracy* (Philadelphia: Temple University Press, 1998), 111–12.
41. Finley, *Democracy,* 22.
42. Graber, *Mass Media,* 261.
43. Ibid., 260. For a table documenting decreasing news coverage of presidential campaigns, see Marion Just, "Candidate Strategies and the Media Campaign," in Pomper, *Election of 1996,* 85.
44. James Fishkin, "Talk of the Tube," *American Prospect,* Fall 1992, 47. See also Just, "Campaign Strategies."
45. Thomas E. Patterson, "The Press and Its Missed Assignment," in Nelson, *Elections of 1988,* 98.
46. Thomas E. Patterson, *Out of Order* (New York: Vintage Books, 1994), 69.
47. Ibid., 59–60.
48. Graber, *Mass Media,* 270.
49. Ibid, 147–8
50. Neil Postman, *Amusing Ourselves to Death* (New York: Penguin, 1986), 89.
51. Kathleen Hall Jamieson, *Eloquence in an Electronic Age: The Transformation of American Political Speechmaking* (New York: Oxford University Press, 1988).
52. Jay Rosen, "Playing the Primary Chords," *Harper's Magazine,* March 1992, 22–25.
53. For two accounts of the Willie Horton story and the Bush campaign, see Jack W. Germond and Jules Witcover, *Whose Broad Stripes and Bright Stars? The Trivial Pursuit of the Presidency, 1988* (New York: Warner Books, 1989), 10–15; and Sidney Blumenthal, *Pledging Allegiance* (New York: HarperCollins, 1990), 264–65.
54. Nicol C. Rae, *Conservative Reformers: The Republican Freshmen and the Lessons of the 104th Congress* (Armonk, N.Y.: M.E. Sharpe, 1998), 40.
55. Rosen, "Playing the Primary Chords," 24.
56. Stephanopoulos, *All Too Human,* 328–75.
57. Just, "Candidate Strategies," 90.
58. Kathleen Hall Jamieson, quoted in James Carlson, "Can American Democracy Survive Television?" *Ms.,* 1992, 11.
59. Jack W. Germond and Jules Witcover, *Mad as Hell: Revolt at the Ballot Box 1992* (New York: Warner Books, 1993), 494–95.
60. This analysis of the 1992 campaign follows the argument of Paul Quirk and Jon K. Dalager, "The Election: A 'New Democrat' and a New Kind of Presidential Campaign," in Nelson, *Elections of 1992,* 57–88.
61. Diana Owen, "The Press' Performance," in Sabato, *Toward the Millennium,* 205.
62. Matthew Robert Kerbel, "The Media: Viewing the Campaign through a Strategic Haze," in Nelson, *Elections of 1996,* 93.
63. Ibid., 82.
64. Ibid., 97.
65. Bennett, *Governing Crisis,* 30.
66. Ibid., 7.
67. Sinclair, *Democracy,* 17.

68. Ginsberg and Stone, *Do Elections Matter?*

69. Ibid., 4.

70. Steve Coll, *The Deal of the Century: The Breakup of AT&T* (New York: Simon and Schuster, 1986).

71. Benjamin Ginsberg and Martin Shefter, *Politics by Other Means: The Declining Importance of Elections in America* (New York: Basic Books, 1991), 26–31.

72. Stephen Labaton, "Ex-Arkansas State Employee Files Suit Accusing Clinton of a Sexual Advance," *New York Times,* 7 May 1994, A9.

73. Ginsberg and Stone, *Do Elections Matter?* 3.

74. Donald L. Barlett and James B. Steele, *America: What Went Wrong?* (Kansas City: Andrews and McMeel, 1992), 180–82.

75. Bennett, *Governing Crisis,* 206–11.

76. Larry Sabato, *The Party's Just Begun* (Glenview, Ill.: Scott, Foresman, 1988), 176–241. Sabato provides a detailed program for party renewal; several of the ideas in this chapter are drawn from his account.

77. Even minor adjustments to the campaign laws do not come easily. The 1993 campaign reform act was the first major revision of federal campaign financing since 1974, yet it left in place provisions for PAC contributions and provided for only voluntary limits on campaign spending. Opposition to even these minor adjustments was intense. See Drew, "Watch 'Em Squirm"; and Adam Clymer, "Stirrings of Self-Restraint on Campaign Spending," *New York Times,* 20 June 1993, Sec. 4, 3.

78. James S. Fishkin, *Democracy and Deliberation: New Directions for Democratic Reform* (New Haven: Yale University Press, 1991), 1–3; see also his "The Case for a National Caucus: Taking Democracy Seriously," *Atlantic,* August 1988, 16–18. Fishkin tried out his idea for a deliberative opinion poll in Britain in April 1994. With the support of the Granada television network and the British newspaper *The Independent,* he gathered a random sample of British citizens together in Manchester to deliberate on the issue of crime. Portions of the debate were televised throughout the U.K. Polls taken before and after the deliberation process showed that participant opinion about crime changed significantly after the opportunity to deliberate about the issue. *The Independent,* 9 March 1994, 8.

CHAPTER 5   THE FIFTH CHALLENGE: THE "PRIVILEGED POSITION" OF BUSINESS

1. Charles E. Lindblom first elaborated the "privileged position" of business in his now-classic *Politics and Markets: The World's Political-Economic Systems* (New York: Basic Books, 1977). This chapter draws liberally on Lindblom's arguments.

2. David Truman, *The Governmental Process* (New York: Knopf, 1951).

3. Besides Truman's work, another key case study from the period is Earl Latham, *The Group Basis of Politics: A Study in Basing-Point Legislation* (Ithaca, N.Y.: Cornell University Press, 1952).

4. Truman, *Governmental Process,* 449, 486.

5. Ibid., 114.

6. For a good review of various critiques of Pluralism, see David Ricci, *Community Power and Democratic Theory: The Logic of Political Analysis* (New York: Random House, 1971). Ricci provides a bibliography of the major critical works.

7. Along with Lindblom, see G. William Domhoff, *Who Rules America Now?* (Englewood Cliffs, N.J.: Prentice Hall, 1983); Thomas Dye, *Who's Running America? The Reagan Years* (Englewood Cliffs, N.J.: Prentice Hall, 1984); Thomas Edsall, *The New Politics of Inequality* (New York: Norton, 1984); Thomas Ferguson and Joel Rogers, *Right Turn* (New York: Hill and Wang, 1986); James W. Lamare, *What Rules America?* (St. Paul, Minn.: West, 1988); Grant McConnell, *Private Power and American Democracy* (New York: Knopf, 1966); Kim McQuaid, *Big Business and Presidential Power from FDR to Reagan* (New York: Morrow, 1982); Beth Mintz and Michael Schwartz, *The Power Structure of American Business* (Chicago: University of Chicago Press, 1985).

8. One major study of interest-group activity in Washington classifies the various groups involved in lobbying as follows: peak business associations, trade associations, unions, professional associations, farm groups, citizens' groups, and civil rights and social welfare groups. Kay Lehman Schlozman and John T. Tierney, *Organized Interests and American Democracy* (New York: Harper & Row, 1986), 40.

9. Edsall, *New Politics of Inequality,* 124–25.

10. Rajiv Chandrasekaran and John Mintz, "Microsoft's Window of Influence," *Washington Post,* 7 May 1999, A1.

11. Schlozman and Tierney, *Organized Interests,* 67.

12. Ibid., 82.

13. Ibid., 117.

14. Ibid., 293.

15. Darrell M. West and Burdett A. Loomis, *The Sound of Money: How Political Interests Get What They Want* (New York: Norton, 1999), 63; for patching techniques see ibid., 61–62.

16. Schlozman and Tierney, *Organized Interests,* 317.

17. The 1974 FECA amendments limited contributions of individuals to any one campaign to $1,000. This altered significantly how business contributors supported campaigns and transformed campaign financing tremendously. For a review of the impact of these reforms, see Herbert E. Alexander, *Financing Politics: Money, Elections, and Political Reform,* 4th ed. (Washington, D.C.: CQ Press, 1992).

18. Federal Election Committee Report, January 1999, http://www.fec.gov/press/pacchart.htm.

19. Federal Election Committee, http://www.fec.gov.press/pacsum98.htm.

20. Sorauf, *Money in American Elections,* 311–12.

21. Quoted in ibid., 313.

22. Quoted in Lamare, *What Rules America?* 110.

23. Ibid., 109.

24. Ellen S. Miller and Micah L. Sifry, "Money Is Everything on Capitol Hill," Public Campaign, http://www.publiccampaign.org/articles/em12_14_99.html.

25. Edsall, *New Politics of Inequality,* 116–17.

26. West and Loomis, *Sound of Money,* 58–59.

27. Ibid., 39.

28. Elizabeth Kolbert, "Special Interests' Special Weapon," *New York Times,* 26 March 1995, A20.

29. Chandrasekaran and Mintz, "Microsoft's Window of Influence," A1.

30. Edsall, *New Politics of Inequality,* 117–20.

31. Lance Bennett, *The Governing Crisis: Media, Money, and Marketing in American Elections* (New York: St. Martin's Press, 1991), 84.

32. Douglas Kellner, *Television and the Crisis of Democracy* (Boulder, Colo.: Westview Press, 1991), 82–85.

33. The argument in this section follows Lindblom's summary of his position in "Democracy and the Economy," in C.E. Lindblom, *Democracy and the Market System* (Oxford: Oxford University Press, 1988), 115–38. This article, written in 1983, provides a concise statement of the position he originally developed in *Politics and Markets* but also elaborates on certain elements in response to critics of his earlier work.

34. J. Allen Whitt, *Urban Elites and Mass Transportation: The Dialectics of Power* (Princeton: Princeton University Press, 1982), 45–47. Details of the involvement of such automobile interests as General Motors and Firestone Tire and Rubber in the destruction of America's trolley system were reported in a congressional investigation in 1974. See Bradford C. Snell, *American Ground Transport,* Report presented to the Subcommittee on Antitrust and Monopoly of the Committee on the Judiciary, U.S. Senate, 26 February 1974 (Washington, D.C.: Government Printing Office).

35. Lindblom, *Democracy and the Market System,* 120.

36. Doron P. Levin, "G.M. Picks 12 Plants to Be Shut As It Reports a Record U.S. Loss," *New York Times,* 25 February 1992, A1.

37. Such threats are commonplace and are enormously effective. For example, in October 1992,

the CEO of one of Rhode Island's largest manufacturers made a speech announcing that the corporation was considering closing down all Rhode Island operations unless certain policy reforms, especially reduction of workers' compensation costs, were not enacted. "Hasbro Warns It May End Manufacturing in RI," *Providence Journal,* 29 October 1991. The next spring, the state legislature passed a major workers' compensation reform bill.

38. Levin, "G.M. Picks 12 Plants," D6.
39. Malaysia's encounter with the global economy is recounted in detail in William Greider's *One World, Ready or Not* (New York: Simon and Schuster, 1997), 81–102.
40. Ibid., 89
41. Lindblom, *Politics and Markets,* 202. See also Benjamin Ginsberg, *The Captive Public* (New York: Basic Books, 1986).
42. Lindblom, *Politics and Markets,* 203–6.
43. *The Nation,* 30 March 1992, 427.
44. Hanna Fenichel Pitkin and Sara M. Shumer, "On Participation," in *Higher Education and the Practice of Democratic Politics,* ed. Bernard Murchland (Dayton, Ohio: Kettering Foundation, 1991), 107.
45. See Carole Pateman, *Participation and Democratic Theory* (Cambridge: Cambridge University Press, 1970), 22–44, for a discussion of these issues. The argument presented here is developed, in particular, in her discussion of the theory of G.D.H. Cole.
46. A number of recent works advocate the need to democratize business organizations if we are fully to achieve democracy in the United States. For a short, cogent presentation of this thesis, see Robert Dahl, *A Preface to Economic Democracy* (Berkeley: University of California Press, 1985).
47. Bennett Harrison and Barry Bluestone, *The Great U-Turn* (New York: Basic Books, 1988), 38.
48. Robert Reich, *The Work of Nations* (New York: Knopf, 1991), 46.
49. Ibid., 48.
50. Paul Krugman, *The Age of Diminished Expectations* (Cambridge: MIT Press, 1992), 11.
51. Benjamin Friedman, *Day of Reckoning* (New York: Vintage Books, 1989), 188.
52. Harrison and Bluestone, *Great U-Turn,* 9.
53. Ibid., 8.
54. Ibid., 21–75.
55. Reich, *Work of Nations,* 8.
56. For two alternatives based on public investment, see Reich, *Work of Nations,* 243–315; Harrison and Bluestone, *Great U-Turn,* 169–96.
57. Journalist William Greider labels these policies aimed at protecting the value of financial assets the "rentier regime." For a detailed analysis of the logic of this regime, see his *One World, Ready or Not,* 285–315.
58. Lawrence Mishel, Jared Bernstein, and John Schmitt, *The State of Working America: 1998–99* (Ithaca, N.Y.: Cornell University Press, 1999).
59. Ron Scherer, "Wall Street Braces for a Fed Rate Hike," *Christian Science Monitor,* 15 June 1999, 2.
60. Robert Hessen, ed., *Does Big Business Rule America?* (Washington, D.C.: Ethics and Public Policy Center, 1981) is a collection of essays, several of which argue this point of view. See especially the essay by James Q. Wilson.
61. David Vogel, *Fluctuating Fortunes: The Political Power of Business in America* (New York: Basic Books, 1989).
62. Ibid., 13.
63. Ibid., 7.
64. Ibid., 68–69; G. William Domhoff, *The Power Elite and the State* (New York: Walter de Gruyter, 1990), 273.
65. There is a massive literature on the politics of the capture of regulatory agencies by those they are supposed to regulate. A classic history and analysis is Marver Bernstein, *Regulation by Independent Commission* (Princeton: Princeton University Press, 1955). The economist George Stigler earned a Nobel Prize based largely on his analysis of the economic logic of

regulatory capture. See his "The Theory of Economic Regulation," *Bell Journal of Economics and Management Science* 2 (Spring 1971): 3–21.

66. Many political scientists have studied the advantages accruing to business interests when legislation delegates power to the bureaucracy. One of the best remains Grant McConnell, *Private Power and American Democracy* (New York: Vintage Books, 1966); see also Theodore Lowi, *The End of Liberalism,* 2d ed. (New York: Norton, 1979).

67. A classic example of business's capacity to delay implementation of policy enactments is the twenty-year battle over the installation of airbags in automobiles. In 1969 the National Highway Traffic Safety Administration issued a regulation under the National Traffic and Motor Safety Act to require passive restraints, including airbags, in all cars. The auto industry maneuvered successfully to delay for many years the implementation of the regulation. One of the leaders of this effort was Ford president and then Chrysler CEO Lee Iacocca. One of the interesting sidelights of the Watergate affair was the discovery of a tape on President Nixon's White House taping system of a secret meeting Iacocca held with the president to ask for Nixon's help to delay NHTSA action on airbags. The president complied. In spite of this record, which has undoubtedly contributed to the deaths of thousands who would have been saved by airbags, Iacocca in 1991 made a commercial for the Chrysler Minivan touting the lifesaving properties of its airbag. Even though the industry began installing airbags in some of its most expensive models in the early 1990s, it was successful in delaying implementation of the passive-restraint regulation for all models for more than two decades. A thorough account of this history can be found in Larry N. Gerston, Cynthia Fraleigh, and Robert Schwab, *The Deregulated Society* (Pacific Grove, Calif.: Brooks/Cole, 1988), 142–66.

68. For analysis of the defeat of Humphrey-Hawkins, see Kay Lehman Schlozman and Sidney Verba, *Injury to Insult: Unemployment, Class, and Political Response* (Cambridge: Harvard University Press, 1979), 336–46. For labor law reform, see Vogel, *Fluctuating Fortunes,* 150–59. For a general discussion of business power over labor issues during this period, see Domhoff, *Who Rules America Now?* 276–82.

69. Vogel, *Fluctuating Fortunes,* 296–97.

70. Ibid., 298–300.

71. John B. Judis, "The Pressure Elite: Inside the Narrow World of Advocacy Group Politics," *American Prospect,* Spring 1992, 22.

72. This account follows West and Loomis, *Sound of Money,* 141–66.

73. Ibid., 143.

74. Ibid., 165.

75. Michael Walzer, *Spheres of Justice* (New York: Basic Books, 1983), 295–302.

76. Quoted in ibid., 297.

77. Quoted in ibid., 298.

78. Ibid.

CHAPTER 6   THE SIXTH CHALLENGE: INEQUALITY

1. Tim Rutten, "A New Kind of Riot," *New York Review of Books,* 11 June 1992, 52.

2. Jane Gross, "In Simi Valley, Defense of a Shared Way of Life," *New York Times,* 4 May 1992, B7.

3. Five years after the uprising, South-Central Los Angeles remained an economically depressed area. Unemployment and poverty persisted, despite the general economic recovery in California and nearly $400 million in corporate and $900 million in government investment in the area. Per capita income in South-Central L.A. was about one-half the average for all of Los Angeles County. Early promises from large corporations to open new factories to employ area residents have not been fulfilled. The South-Central L.A./Simi Valley contrast is as strong as ever. James Sterngold, "5 Years after Los Angeles Riots, Inner City Still Cries Out for Jobs," *New York Times,* 28 April 1997, A1.

4. Economic Policy Institute, *Quarterly Wage and Employment Series* 1999:1, www.epinet.org.

5. Timothy M. Smeeding, Michael O'Higgens, and Lee Rainwater, *Poverty, Inequality and Income Distribution in Comparative Perspective* (Washington, D.C.: Urban Institute Press, 1990).

6. Michael Walzer, *Spheres of Justice: A Defense of Pluralism and Equality* (New York: Basic Books, 1983), 285.

7. F.M. Cornford, *The Republic of Plato* (New York: Oxford University Press, 1945), 195–96.

8. Walzer, *Spheres of Justice,* 285.

9. Of course, one of the judgments democrats often must make is which decisions should be turned over to experts because they require special technical competence. Like decisions about political ends, there are no clear technical criteria for making such judgments, hence democrats would say all people are equally capable of participating in deciding when to call on the experts. For an excellent discussion of the role of technical competence in democratic decision making, see Robert Dahl, *After the Revolution* (New Haven: Yale University Press, 1990), 21–30.

10. Robert Dahl calls this proposition in democratic theory the "presumption of personal autonomy." See his *Democracy and Its Critics* (New Haven: Yale University Press, 1989), 100–101.

11. Gordon Wood, *The Radicalism of the American Revolution* (New York: Knopf, 1992), 229–43.

12. Ibid., 232.

13. Ibid., 234.

14. Ibid.

15. Ibid., 239–40.

16. Ibid., 234.

17. Alexis de Tocqueville, *Democracy in America,* ed. J.P. Mayer (New York: Harper & Row, 1969), 50–58.

18. For comparative analyses of various social revolutions, see Barrington Moore, *Social Origins of Dictatorship and Democracy: Lord and Peasant in the Making of the Modern World* (Boston: Beacon Press, 1966); or Theda Skocpol, *States and Social Revolutions: A Comparative Analysis of France, Russia, and China* (Cambridge: Cambridge University Press, 1979). For analysis of more recent transitions to democracy in Europe and Latin America, see Guillermo O'Donnell and Philippe Schmitter, *Transitions from Authoritarian Rule: Tentative Conclusions about Uncertain Democracies* (Baltimore: Johns Hopkins University Press, 1986).

19. Walzer, *Spheres of Justice,* xiii.

20. Paul Krugman, *The Age of Diminished Expectations* (Cambridge: MIT Press, 1992), 3.

21. Bennett Harrison and Barry Bluestone, *The Great U-Turn: Corporate Restructuring and the Polarizing of America* (New York: Basic Books, 1988), 134.

22. All figures cited in the paragraph are calculated from table 10 of U.S. Census Bureau, *Current Population Reports: Consumer Income,* Series P-60, No. 151 (Washington, D.C.: Government Printing Office, April 1986), 29.

23. U.S. Census Bureau, *Current Population Reports, Consumer Income,* Series P-60, No. 184 (Washington, D.C.: Government Printing Office, September 1993).

24. Robert Reich, *The Work of Nations* (New York: Vintage, 1992), 197.

25. Gary Burtless, "Growing American Inequality," *Brookings Review,* Winter 1999, 32–33.

26. Silvia Nasar, "The 1980's: A Very Good Time for the Very Rich," *New York Times,* 5 March 1992, A1.

27. "Executive Pay at New Highs," *New York Times,* 11 May 1992, D5.

28. David Leonhardt, "Ideas and Trends: Why Is This Man Smiling? Executive Pay Drops Off the Political Radar," *New York Times,* 16 April 2000, sec. 4, 5.

29. Chuck Collins, Betsy Leondar-Wright, and Holly Sklar, *Shifting Fortunes: The Perils of the Growing American Wealth Gap* (Boston: United for a Fair Economy, 1999).

30. Sylvia Nasar, "Fed Gives New Evidence of 80's Gains by Richest," *New York Times,* 21 April 1992, A1; Keith Bradsher, "Gap in Wealth in U.S. Called Widest in West," *New York Times,* 17 April 1995, A1.

31. Edward N. Wolff, "How the Pie Is Sliced: America's Growing Concentration of Wealth," in *Ticking Time Bombs,* ed. Robert Kuttner (New York: Norton, 1996), 75–76. The 1992 U.S. calculation is based on Collins et al., *Shifting Fortunes;* see figure 6.2 (p. 208).

32. Nasar, "Fed Gives New Evidence"; Bradsher, "Gap in Wealth."

33. U.S. Census Bureau, *Historical Poverty Tables—People,* Table 2: Poverty Status of People, by Family Relationship, Race, and Hispanic Origin, 1959 to 1997, http://www.census.gov/hhes/poverty/histpov/hstpov2.html.

34. David M. Cutler and Lawrence F. Katz, "Untouched by the Rising Tide: Why the 1980s Economic Expansion Left the Poor Behind," *Brookings Review,* Winter 1992, 41–45.

35. Harrison and Bluestone, *Great U-Turn,* 132–35.

36. Ibid., 133.

37. Frank Levy, *The New Dollars and Dreams: American Incomes and Economic Change* (New York: Russell Sage Foundation, 1998), 189.

38. Frank Levy, *Dollars and Dreams: The Changing American Income Distribution* (New York: Norton, 1988), 63. The annual rate of productivity growth averaged less than .5 percent between 1973 and 1988, the worst performance in the twentieth century. See Krugman, *Age of Diminished Expectations,* 11–12. Why did productivity drop? According to Krugman, economists do not know; they can offer a "set of explanations...that are little more than sophisticated cocktail party chatter" (p. 14). Levy has updated his analysis in *New Dollars and Dreams.* The analysis in this section is drawn from both works.

39. Levy, *Dollars and Dreams,* 5–7.

40. Ibid., 7.

41. Andrew Hacker, *Money: Who Has How Much and Why* (New York: Scribner, 1997), 182.

42. Reich, *Work of Nations,* 209.

43. Harrison and Bluestone, *Great U-Turn,* 117.

44. Reich, *Work of Nations,* 216.

45. Ibid., 205–6.

46. Ted Halstead, "A Politics for Generation X," *Atlantic Monthly,* August 1999, 36.

47. James K. Galbraith, *Created Unequal: The Crisis in American Pay* (New York: Free Press, 1998), 9–10, 213–31.

48. Ibid., 242

49. The Swedish scholar Gunnar Myrdal first labeled the conflict between American ideals and the place of blacks in American society "the American dilemma" in his classic *An American Dilemma,* published in the 1940s.

50. Thomas Byrne Edsall and Mary D. Edsall, "Race," *Atlantic Monthly,* May 1991, 54–55.

51. Ibid., 55.

52. Ibid., 85.

53. Edward N. Wolff, *Top Heavy: A Study of the Increasing Inequality of Wealth in America* (New York: The Twentieth Century Fund, 1995), 17.

54. William Julius Wilson, *The Truly Disadvantaged: The Inner City, The Underclass, and Public Policy* (Chicago: University of Chicago Press, 1987).

55. Edsall and Edsall, "Race," 85.

56. Wolff, *Top Heavy,* 17.

57. Edsall and Edsall, "Race." For the deterioration of public schools and the growing inequality of schools, see Jonathan Kozol, *Savage Inequalities* (New York: Crown, 1991).

58. Edsall and Edsall, "Race," 69.

59. Quoted in Thomas Byrne Edsall and Mary D. Edsall, *Chain Reaction: The Impact of Race, Rights, and Taxes on American Politics* (New York: Norton, 1991), 237.

60. Jennifer L. Hochschild, *Facing Up to the American Dream: Race, Class, and the Soul of the Nation* (Princeton: Princeton University Press, 1995), 55.

61. Harold Stanley and Richard Niemi, *Vital Statistics on American Politics,* 2d ed. (Washington, D.C.: CQ Press, 1990), 100.

62. Gerald M. Pomper, "The Presidential Election," in *The Election of 1996,* ed. Gerald M. Pomper (Chatham, N.J.: Chatham House, 1997), 180.

63. William Schneider, "The Dawn of the Suburban Era in American Politics," *Atlantic,* July 1992, 33–57.

64. Edsall and Edsall, "Race," 84–85.

65. Schneider, "Dawn of the Suburban Era," 34.

66. Isabel Wilkerson, "The Tallest Fence: Feelings on Race in a White Neighborhood," *New York Times,* 21 June 1992, sec. 1, 18.

67. Don Terry, "Decades of Rage Created Crucible of Violence," *New York Times,* 3 May 1992, A1.

68. The following argument echoes those found in Reich, *Work of Nations,* and Harrison and Bluestone, *Great U-Turn.*

69. Reich, *Work of Nations,* 225–40.

70. See Bowles, Gordon, and Weisskopf, *After the Wasteland.*

71. Robert Dahl, *A Preface to Economic Democracy* (Berkeley: University of California Press, 1985).

72. See Theda Skocpol, "Fighting Poverty without Poverty Programs," *American Prospect,* Summer 1990, 58–70.

73. Bruce Ackerman and Anne Alstott, *The Stakeholder Society* (New Haven: Yale University Press, 1999).

74. Richard B. Freeman, *The New Inequality: Creating Solutions for Poor America* (Boston: Beacon Press, 1999).

CHAPTER 7   THE SEVENTH CHALLENGE: THE NATIONAL SECURITY STATE

1. Gary Hart, *The Minuteman: Restoring an Army of the People* (New York: Free Press, 1998), 6.

2. For a detailed account of the rise of the national security state, see Daniel Yergin, *Shattered Peace: The Origins of the Cold War and the National Security State* (Boston: Houghton Mifflin, 1977).

3. One little-discussed agency established by the National Security Act of 1947 was the National Security Resources Board, which is responsible for coordinating defense production.

4. Harold D. Lasswell, "The Garrison-State Hypothesis Today," in *National Security and American Society,* ed. Philip S. Kronenberg and Frank Trager (Lawrence: University of Kansas Press, 1973), 434. In this remarkable essay written in 1962, Lasswell evaluates the extent to which his 1935 prediction had come to pass. For the original essay, see "The Garrison State and Specialists on Violence," *American Journal of Sociology,* January 1941, 455–68.

5. Harold D. Lasswell, *National Security and Individual Freedom* (New York: McGraw-Hill, 1950), 32.

6. Randall Forsberg, "Force without Reason," *Boston Review* 20, no. 3 (Summer 1995): 3.

7. William D. Hartung, "Military-Industrial Complex Revisited: How Weapons Makers Are Shaping U.S. Foreign and Military Policies," www.foreignpolicy-infocus.org/papers/micr/fig_2.html.

8. Lawrence Korb, "Why a Cold War Budget without a Cold War?" www.businessleaders.org/Korb-report.htm.

9. Benjamin Schwarz, "Why America Thinks It Has to Run the World," *Atlantic Monthly,* June 1996, 94.

10. Thomas Powers, "The Black Arts," *New York Review of Books,* 4 January 1999, 23.

11. U.S. Senate, *Final Report of the Select Committee to Study Governmental Operations with Respect to Intelligence Activities,* 94th Cong., 2d sess., bks. I–III (Washington, D.C.: Government Printing Office, 1976) [Church Committee Report]; see also Morton H. Halperin et al., *The Lawless State: The Crimes of the U.S. Intelligence Agencies* (New York: Penguin Books, 1977), 13–58.

12. Woods, *Ending the Cold War,* 5.

13. "Iran-*Contra* Hearings: McFarlane Testifies: Praises North and Covert Operations," *New York Times,* 15 July 1987, 14.

14. Tim Weiner, "C.I.A.'s Openness Derided as a 'Snow Job,' " *New York Times,* 20 May 1997, A16. A recent *New York Times* article examined American involvement in the coup in Iran, but that exposé was based on a leaked copy of the official report, still unreleased by the CIA. James Risen, "Secrets of History: The C.I.A. in Iran—A Special Report," *New York Times,* 16 April 2000.

15. Tim Weiner, "Research Group Is Suing C.I.A. to Reveal Size of Spy Budget," *New York Times,* 20 May 1997.

16. Powers, "Black Arts," 20.

17. This account of the Iran-*contra* affair is based on a series of articles by Theodore Draper in the *New York Review of Books:* "The Rise of an American Junta," 8 October 1987; "The Fall of an American Junta," 22 October 1987; "An Autopsy," 17 December 1987. It is also based on Bob Woodward's account of William Casey's CIA, *Veil* (New York: Simon and Schuster, 1987). For further background on Central America and U.S. policy, see Morris J. Blachman and Kenneth Sharpe, "De-democratizing American Foreign Policy: Dismantling the Post-Vietnam Formula," *Third World Quarterly,* October 1986, 1271–1308; and Robert H. Trudeau, *Guatemalan Politics: The Popular Struggle for Democracy* (Boulder, Colo.: Lynne Rienner, 1993).

18. The arms-for-hostages exchange turned out in the end to be an enormous fiasco. On several trips to Iran, North and others discovered that the supposed "moderate" elements in the Iranian leadership had neither the power nor the desire to help obtain the release of the hostages. Even though their contacts had assured them that all American hostages would be released if arms were provided, North and his friends were able to obtain the release of only two hostages, and the hostage takers replaced these individuals in short order with additional kidnappings. It turned out that the Iranians with whom North dealt exaggerated their power in Iran as much as North himself lied about his access to President Reagan. North was famous for inventing tales about his frequent meetings with the president, including weekends at the presidential retreat at Camp David, which never happened. Reagan later testified that he barely knew who North was and never had a private meeting with him.

19. Neil Sheehan et al., *The Pentagon Papers* (New York: Bantam Books, 1971).

20. Clark Clifford, "Memoirs—The Vietnam Years II," *New Yorker,* 13 May 1991, 45–83.

21. Peter Kornbluh, "The CIA Secret Kept for 37 Years," *Washington Post,* 15 March 1998, C1.

22. Joseph A. Davis, "Nuclear Weapons Woes Await Congress," *Congressional Quarterly Weekly Report,* 24 December 1988, 3556–59; for an account of a similar situation regarding nuclear weapons testing, see Phillip A. Fradkin, *Fallout: An American Nuclear Tragedy* (Tucson: University of Arizona Press, 1989).

23. Daniel P. Moynihan, "The Peace Dividend," *New York Review of Books,* 28 June 1990, 4.

24. Hannah Arendt, *Crises of the Republic* (New York: Harcourt Brace Jovanovich, 1972), 34.

25. Sheehan et al., *Pentagon Papers,* 234–306.

26. Arthur M. Schlesinger Jr., *The Imperial Presidency* (Boston: Houghton Mifflin, 1973).

27. Louis Henkin, *Constitutionalism, Democracy, and Foreign Affairs* (New York: Columbia University Press, 1990), 30–31.

28. For details about the Gulf War decision process, see Michael Massing, "The Way to War," *New York Review of Books,* 28 March 1991; and Thomas L. Friedman and Patrick E. Tyler, "From the First, U.S. Resolve to Fight," *New York Times,* 3 March 1991.

29. Friedman and Tyler, "From the First," 18.

30. In November 1990, fifty members of Congress filed suit in federal court to prohibit going to war without congressional approval. In spite of a favorable district court ruling, the Bush administration refused to be bound by the decision. See Woods, *Ending the Cold War,* 24.

31. In fact, in a speech several months after the war, Bush argued explicitly that he was *not* required to seek congressional approval. For a discussion and critique of Bush's argument, see Theodore Draper, "Presidential Wars," *New York Review of Books,* 6 September 1991, 64–74.

32. Anthony Lake, "Republicans vs. Democracy," *New York Times,* 24 March 1991.

33. Theodore Draper, "Capturing the Constitution," *New York Review of Books,* 7 May 1995, 40.

34. See Jean-François Revel, *How Democracies Perish* (New York: Harper & Row, 1985), for an example of this sort of argument.

35. These points are made succinctly in Michael Ledeen, "The Future of Foreign Policy," *American Spectator,* June 1987.

36. Quoted in Leon Wieseltier, "Democracy and Colonel North," *New Republic,* 26 January 1987, 24.

37. Irving L. Janis, *Groupthink,* 2d ed. (Boston: Houghton Mifflin, 1982).

38. Bruce Russett, *Controlling the Sword: The Democratic Governance of National Security* (Cambridge: Harvard University Press, 1990), 52–86.

39. There are many good biographies of this fascinating individual. One that documents well Hoover's disregard for democracy and civil liberties is Athan Theoharis and John Stuart Cox, *The Boss: J. Edgar Hoover and the Great American Inquisition* (Philadelphia: Temple University Press, 1988).

40. Halperin et al., *Lawless State,* 95–96.

41. For a fascinating account of the political pressures that led to the federal security program, see the memoirs of a key Truman aide who set up the program. Clark Clifford, "Annals of Government (The Truman Years—Part II)," *New Yorker,* 1 April 1991, 56–58.

42. Halperin et al., *Lawless State,* 107.

43. Ibid., 61–89. For evidence of Hoover's hostility toward blacks, see Theoharis and Cox, *The Boss,* 10. See also David Garrow, *The FBI and Martin Luther King* (New York: Norton, 1981).

44. Documentation for all these activities can be found in Halperin et al., *Lawless State;* and Athan Theoharis, *Spying on Americans* (Philadelphia: Temple University Press, 1978). Both books rely primarily on the Church committee and Rockefeller reports in documenting these abuses. Theoharis was a consultant to the Church committee.

45. Gary M. Stern, *The FBI's Misguided Probe of CISPES,* Report No. 111 (Washington, D.C.: Center for National Security Studies, June 1988).

46. Woods, *Ending the Cold War,* 18.

47. William Greider, *Fortress America: The American Military and the Consequences of Peace* (New York: Public Affairs, 1998), 79.

48. Daniel Hellinger and Dennis R. Judd, *The Democratic Façade* (Belmont, Calif.: Wadsworth, 1991), 209.

49. Hedrick Smith, *The Power Game* (New York: Random House, 1988).

50. William D. Hartung, "Military-Industrial Complex Revisited," www.foreignpolicy-infocus.org/papers/micr/companies.html.

51. Lawrence J. Korb, "Defense, Industry, and Procurement," in *Business in the Contemporary World,* ed. Herbert L. Sawyer (Lanham, Md.: University Press of America, 1988), 40.

52. Smith, *Power Game,* 191–92.

53. Hartung, "Military-Industrial Complex Revisited."

54. Ibid.

55. Clyde H. Farnsworth, "White House Seeks to Revive Credits for Arms Exports," *New York Times,* 18 March 1991, A1.

56. John M. Brodeur, "In Washington, It's Never Farewell to Arms," *New York Times,* 11 May 1997, E16.

57. Greg Spector, *In Search of Security* (Northampton, Mass.: National Priorities Project, 1994), 6–7.

58. Mark Thompson, "The Sky's the Limit," *Time,* 24 March 1997, 52.

59. Ibid. And the F-22 is not the only advanced high-tech fighter on the drawing boards. Plans are well under way to spend billions on the "Joint Strike Fighter" to be ready early in the twenty-first century.

60. Lasswell, *National Security,* 40. See also C. Wright Mills, *The Power Elite* (Oxford: Oxford University Press, 1956), 198–224.

61. Theodore Draper, "An Autopsy," *New York Review of Books,* 17 December 1987, 69.

62. An interesting feature of the Iran-*contra* affair is the number of former military officers involved in North's secret network. Other key actors were General John Singlaub, Major General Richard V. Secord, Air Force Colonel Robert Dutton, Air Force Lieutenant Colonel Richard Gadd, and, of course, Poindexter's predecessor as national security adviser, Colonel Robert McFarlane. The balance of participants were mostly former CIA agents. See ibid., 67.

63. Benjamin Barber and Patrick Watson, *The Struggle for Democracy* (Boston: Little Brown, 1988), 226–30; see also John Steward Ambler, *The French Army in Politics* (Columbus: Ohio State University Press, 1966), 259–61.

64. Michael T. Klare, "Beyond the Rogues' Gallery," *The Nation,* 26 May 1997, 22–26.

65. Philip Shenon, "Pentagon Urges Trims in Military and New Round of Base Closings," *New York Times,* 20 May 1997, A1.

66. Klare, "Beyond the Rogues' Gallery," 25.

67. Samuel P. Huntington, "The Clash of Civilizations?" *Foreign Affairs,* Summer 1993, 22–49.

68. Ibid., 49.

CONCLUSION: SEVEN STEPS TOWARD REFORM

1. Amitai Etzioni, *The Spirit of Community: Rights, Responsibilities, and the Communitarian Agenda* (New York: Crown, 1993), 253.

2. Ibid., 231–33.

3. Benjamin Barber, *An Aristocracy of Everyone: The Politics of Education and the Future of America* (New York: Ballantine, 1992), 230–61.

4. Benjamin Barber, *Strong Democracy: Participatory Politics for a New Age* (Berkeley: University of California Press, 1984), 267–73.

5. Jeffrey M. Berry, Kent E. Portney, and Ken Thomson, *The Rebirth of Urban Democracy* (Washington, D.C.: Brookings Institution, 1993), 12–15.

6. Ibid., 13.

7. Ibid., 232–99.

8. The Kettering Foundation has published a number of booklets in connection with its National Issues Forums. See, for example, *The Health Care Crisis: Containing Costs, Expanding Coverage,* ed. Keith Melville (Dayton, Ohio: National Issues Forum, 1992). For information on the forums, contact National Issues Forum, 100 Commons Road, Dayton, Ohio 45459-2777. Phone 1-800-433-7834.

9. Richard Rothstein, "New Bargain or No Bargain," *American Prospect,* Summer 1993, 33.

10. Gary Hart, *The Minuteman* (New York: Free Press, 1998), 147–71.

11. Ibid., 148.

Index